European Yearbook of Constitutional Law

Volume 1

The *European Yearbook of Constitutional Law* (EYCL) is an annual publication devoted to the study of constitutional law. The yearbook provides a forum for in-depth analysis and discussion of new developments in constitutional law in Europe and beyond. Each issue is dedicated to a specific theme. Papers are subject to editorial and double-blind peer review. The yearbook is published by T.M.C. ASSER PRESS in cooperation with Springer Publishers.

Contact

To get in touch, please send an e-mail to eycl@tilburguniversity.edu

More information about this series at http://www.springer.com/series/16431

Ernst Hirsch Ballin · Gerhard van der Schyff ·
Maarten Stremler
Editors

European Yearbook of Constitutional Law 2019

Judicial Power: Safeguards and Limits in a Democratic Society

ASSER PRESS

Springer

Editors
Ernst Hirsch Ballin
Tilburg University
Tilburg, The Netherlands

and

University of Amsterdam
Amsterdam, The Netherlands

Gerhard van der Schyff
Tilburg University
Tilburg, The Netherlands

Maarten Stremler
Tilburg University
Tilburg, The Netherlands

ISSN 2405-6111 ISSN 2405-612X (electronic)
European Yearbook of Constitutional Law
ISBN 978-94-6265-358-0 ISBN 978-94-6265-359-7 (eBook)
https://doi.org/10.1007/978-94-6265-359-7

Published by T.M.C. ASSER PRESS, The Hague, The Netherlands www.asserpress.nl
Produced and distributed for T.M.C. ASSER PRESS by Springer-Verlag Berlin Heidelberg

This T.M.C. ASSER PRESS imprint is published by the registered company Springer-Verlag GmbH, DE part of Springer Nature.
The registered company address is: Heidelberger Platz 3, 14197 Berlin, Germany

Preface

This is the inaugural issue of the *European Yearbook of Constitutional Law* (EYCL), an annual publication that will be devoted to the study of constitutional law. It aims to provide a forum for in-depth analysis and discussion of new developments in the field, both in Europe and beyond. Each issue will be dedicated to a specific theme.

While a number of journals cover the topic of constitutional law, there has until now been no *yearbook* dedicated to the study of the discipline. The benefit of a yearbook is that it can be devoted to specific themes, with a different aspect of the field being covered each year. Although this is also possible in journals, some journals avoid 'special issues', whereas others allow such issues, but remain focused on publishing series of mostly unrelated articles.

The theme of the present volume is 'Judicial Power: Safeguards and Limits in a Democratic Society', while the next volume will concentrate on 'The City in Constitutional Law'. We are grateful to T.M.C. Asser Press and Springer for their support in publishing this yearbook, to Tilburg Law School for its commitment to bringing this project to fruition, and to the authors and anonymous reviewers of this year's volume.

Tilburg, The Netherlands

Ernst Hirsch Ballin
Gerhard van der Schyff
Maarten Stremler

Contents

Editors and Contributors

About the Editors

Ernst Hirsch Ballin is Distinguished University Professor at Tilburg University and Professor of Human Rights Law at the University of Amsterdam. He is the president of the Asser Institute for International and European Law and a Member of the Royal Netherlands Academy of Sciences. Previously, he has served as deputy justice in the Appellate Court for the Public Service and Social Security Law, as judge and President of the Judicial Division of the Council of State and as the Minister of Justice of the Kingdom of the Netherlands. His current research focusses on Dutch and transnational constitutional law, migration and citizenship, and legal research methods.

Gerhard van der Schyff is Associate Professor in the Department of Public Law and Governance at Tilburg University in the Netherlands. He lectures and conducts research on constitutional law and fundamental rights in comparative and European perspective. In 2015, he held a Humboldt Fellowship for Experienced Researchers at the Chair of Christian Calliess at the Free University in Berlin, dealing with the topic of constitutional identity.

Maarten Stremler is Researcher and Lecturer in Constitutional Law in the Department of Public Law and Governance at Tilburg Law School and a guest staff member in the Department of Constitutional and Administrative Law at Leiden Law School. His primary research interests are constitutional law and constitutional theory. He is writing a Ph.D. thesis on constitutional oversight by the European Union. He is co-author of *Constitutional Preambles: A Comparative Analysis* (Edward Elgar, 2016).

Contributors[*]

Geerten Boogaard Leiden University, Leiden, The Netherlands

Marc Bossuyt University of Antwerp, Antwerp, Belgium

Petra Bárd Eötvös Loránd University, Budapest, Hungary;
Legal Studies Department, Central European University, Budapest, Hungary

Alfonso Celotto 'Roma Tre' University, Rome, Italy

Marios Costa City, University of London, London, UK

Paul Daly University of Cambridge, Cambridge, UK

Ernst Hirsch Ballin Tilburg University, Tilburg, The Netherlands;
University of Amsterdam, Amsterdam, The Netherlands

Eirik Holmøyvik University of Bergen, Bergen, Norway

Dimitry Kochenov University of Groningen, Groningen, The Netherlands

Jörg Luther University of Eastern Piedmont Amedeo Avogadro, Alessandria, Italy

Evelyne Maes Saint-Louis University, Brussels, Belgium

Egbert Myjer Leiden, The Netherlands

Anne Sanders University of Bielefeld, Bielefeld, Germany

Anja Seibert-Fohr University of Heidelberg, Heidelberg, Germany

Eivind Smith University of Oslo, Oslo, Norway

Maarten Stremler Tilburg University, Tilburg, The Netherlands

Gerhard van der Schyff Tilburg University, Tilburg, The Netherlands

Francois Venter North-West University, Potchefstroom, South Africa

[*]The full information on each contributor is included at the end of the chapter they contributed to.

Part I

Chapter 1
Introduction: Safeguards and Limits of Judicial Power

Ernst Hirsch Ballin, Gerhard van der Schyff and Maarten Stremler

Contents

1.1 Judicial Power and Judicial Independence

This first volume of the *European Yearbook of Constitutional Law* is devoted to the theme of judicial power. Countless treatises on the judiciary have preceded the publication of this yearbook. Although the various authors of this volume have naturally relied on these preceding publications, they have also chosen on this occasion to focus on a specific angle, in which the *power* of judges has been problematized. By taking binding decisions, judges exercise far-reaching powers. While their decisions can protect, they can also seriously limit the freedom of citizens or otherwise determine how this freedom is used. Modern courts can also influence and even drive processes of national transformation such as in

E. Hirsch Ballin (✉) · G. van der Schyff · M. Stremler
Tilburg University, Tilburg, The Netherlands
e-mail: ballin@tilburguniversity.edu

G. van der Schyff
e-mail: g.vdrschyff@tilburguniversity.edu

M. Stremler
e-mail: m.stremler@tilburguniversity.edu

E. Hirsch Ballin
University of Amsterdam, Amsterdam, The Netherlands

Hirsch Ballin, Van der Schyff & Stremler (eds.), *European Yearbook of Constitutional Law 2019*, European Yearbook of Constitutional Law 1,
https://doi.org/10.1007/978-94-6265-359-7_1

post-conflict societies, or processes of integration and constitutionalization such as that of the European project.[1] Judicial power needs, as a consequence of such potential, to be subject to constraints. The common phrase of 'judicial independence' suggests the absence of restraint. In the context of a constitutional democracy, however, no power can be absolute and without some element of restraint or confinement. Hence the demand for *safeguards and limits* on judicial power. The authors of this yearbook analyse and discuss these safeguards in a variety of constitutional systems, both at a national and supranational level in Europe and beyond.

According to the classical doctrine of 'judicial independence', independence indicates the absence of opportunities for politics and governance to influence the judiciary.[2] The judicial independence recognized in human rights treaties and many constitutions – whether credible or otherwise – is designed to ensure that the judiciary is impartial and not subject to instructions from other state powers. While the *separation* of state powers is intended to serve as a blueprint for this, judicial independence does not exist in a separate or parallel universe. Instead, the judiciary is part of the constitutional system and operates within a legal order that connects the citizens and powers of that state to each other. Looking at judicial independence from this broader perspective, the traditional *trias politica* would appear no longer to adequately represent the diversity and complexity of constitutional systems and their democratic legitimacy in today's world.[3]

Tim Koopmans, for example, has characterized modern constitutionalism as 'bipolar'.[4] By this he means that political institutions, understood as the executive and the legislature, are nowadays held to account not only through elections and political checks and balances, but also through review by national and supranational courts. This development, which amounts to a reconfiguration of the *trias politica*, highlights the need for a new assessment of judicial power in the contemporary constitutional context. Similarly, the political theorist Pierre Rosanvallon speaks of the 'judicialisation of politics', by which he means the tendency of citizens to use the judicial process in order to achieve what they fail to accomplish via the ballot box.[5] This he views as an example of 'counter-democracy', understood to mean an expression of democratic distrust that actually serves to buttress and complement electoral democracy instead of fundamentally opposing it.

Also illustrating the limits of the *trias politica* as a definitive frame of analysis, Mark Tushnet points not only to the emergence of the administrative state as a

---

[1] For analyses of the transformative function with a focus on the Constitutional Court of South Africa, see Robertson 2010, pp 255–270 and Chap. 8 by Venter in this volume. See Stone Sweet 2004, pp 64–96 for an account of the constitutional impact of the European Court of Justice (and its dialogue with national courts), and compare Claes 2006, who develops a 'bottom-up' view in this regard centred on the perspective of national courts in the European Union.

[2] Consider Bell 2006, pp 26–29. See also Venter 2010, pp 67–70.

[3] Ackerman 2017, p 40.

[4] Koopmans 2003, pp 248–251.

[5] Rosanvallon 2008, pp 8; 227–247.

fourth branch of governance, but also to a possible fifth branch.[6] The latter branch would address the need in modern systems of governance to prevent constitutional corruption and decay and address conflict-of-interests problems that do not easily fit the separation of powers. This branch he distinguishes from the judiciary, while noting that institutions within the new branch might take some inspiration from the courts in wanting to combine independence and accountability – but probably in a different configuration to that found in courts.[7] Tushnet also explores what he describes as going beyond the fifth branch. This pertains to a discussion of Roberto Mangabeira Unger's proposal to create a 'destabilization branch' with which to interrupt routines and prevent ossification in social institutions, to which government bureaucracies and agents also belong.[8] This is definitely appealing as a way to conceptualize judicial power today, given that courts can and do destabilize bureaucracies in the service of constitutional rights in this manner.[9] There is also no denying that acting in this way courts generate political controversy, which leads to questions about the proper role of the judicial function.[10]

Observations and discussions like these reinforce, once more, the need to look afresh at judicial power in its present-day context.

Many treatises on judicial independence focus on the need to ensure an absence of risks emanating from politics and governance. There are good reasons for this. But while the importance of insulating the judiciary from improper political pressure exerted by members of the executive or legislature can hardly be over-emphasized, this yearbook investigates the idea of judicial independence somewhat differently: not in an – untenable – conceptual separation, such as the traditional notion of separation of powers would seem to involve, but instead as an institutionalizing of relationships that legitimize the power of the courts. No institution in a constitutional democracy can have its legitimacy in isolation; legitimacy is acquired within the wider context of the constitutional system as a whole. The judiciary is part of the state system and operates in a legal order that connects the citizens and institutions of that state – increasingly in a multi-level environment. The notions of 'safeguards' and 'limits' indicate the reciprocally enabling and protecting nature of these relationships.

In recognition of this, the contributions to this volume analyse these safeguards and limits as relations existing within a complex constitutional architecture. The authors, coming from a variety of legal cultures, mainly European, demonstrate the diversity of these relations. Despite the simplicity of the *trias politica* model, a constitutional order is characterized by complexity. However, this must not lead to

---

[6] Tushnet 2018, pp 107–123.

[7] *Ibid.*, p 119.

[8] *Ibid.*, pp 123–124.

[9] *Ibid.*, p 125.

[10] *Ibid.*

instability with regard to fundamental characteristics, such as judicial independence. This architecture is not a fixed system; it can only work and retain its legitimacy if it is able to absorb internal and external system turbulences appropriately, while also continuing to uphold its constitutional principles.

1.2 Judges in a Democratic Society

A constitutional democracy is the organizational framework for opinion-forming and decision-making for a democratic society. The phrase 'democratic society' plays a central role in the European Convention on Human Rights and Fundamental Freedoms.[11] It functions like a chorus, as the only situation in which legislators may impose restrictions on fundamental rights such as the freedom of expression and the freedom of religion is when these restrictions are 'necessary in a democratic society'. When it comes, however, to the fundamental rights of fair trial and an effective remedy (Articles 6 and 13), such restrictions seem out of place because access to justice serves and guarantees the democratic society in which fundamental rights are to be effected.

Here, however, we encounter an antinomy[12] that is currently contributing to serious tensions around judicial independence, and specifically the question of how to prevent a situation in which judges exercising their independence become detached from the democratic society that they are required to protect. In a number of European countries, populist parties, which all came to power on the basis of free elections, have recently attempted to thwart the independence of the judiciary.[13]

In many countries, the judiciary is the frontline where questions of legitimacy and populist criticism of supposed elitism manifest themselves. This is made particularly clear in the contribution to this volume by Dimitry Kochenov and Petra Bárd. Discussing developments in Hungary and Poland in Chap. 11, they describe how autocratic regimes, operating in the name of 'democracy' and under the pretext of 'reform', have curbed the powers of the courts and effectively captured the judiciary. They also note that while the political institutions of the European Union seem to lack the political will to take concrete measures in the face of what the authors call 'rule of law backsliding' in the Member States, the Court of Justice is developing new case law contributing to the formation of supranational standards of judicial independence.

---

[11] Van der Schyff 2005, pp 198–211.

[12] The notion of antinomies between fundamental constitutional decisions was coined by Norbert Achterberg. See Achterberg 1969.

[13] See the contributions by Gábor Attila Tóth, Dimitry Kochenov and Kim Lane Scheppele in Adams et al. 2017. See also AIV 2017.

The discussions about how the European Court of Human Rights (ECtHR) perceives its responsibilities are another manifestation of the aforementioned tension. This becomes clear from the debate in this volume between Marc Bossuyt, the former President of the Constitutional Court of Belgium, and Egbert Myjer, former judge on the bench in Strasbourg. While Bossuyt in Chap. 13 contends that the Strasbourg Court has been expanding its mandate by attributing positive obligations to civil rights and by its close scrutiny of asylum cases in the absence of an express right to asylum in the Convention, Myjer in Chap. 14 counters that the High Contracting Parties have never criticized the Court for interpreting the Convention 'without borders'. Myjer recalls that the Court interprets the Convention as a living instrument in the light of present-day conditions and mentions the duty of the Court to protect the rights and freedoms of those residing within its jurisdiction.

1.3 Varieties of Safeguards and Limits

Constitutional jurisdiction, whether as a separate discipline or otherwise, occupies a distinguished place in this yearbook. The contributions relate mainly to continental European, codification-based legal systems, with contributions from countries representative of various parts of the continent. But Brexit or not, the question of how to prevent a situation in which judges exercising their independence become detached from the democratic society that they are required to protect also arises in the world of common law. That is why this yearbook also gives a place to judicial independence in the legal system of England and Wales, as well as to the legal system of South Africa, where civil and common law traditions meet in a constitutional framework that a quarter of a century ago, after the abolition of Apartheid, was just starting out on the path towards building a democratic society.

While all the countries discussed in this yearbook can be regarded as constitutional democracies, the individual chapters demonstrate that the safeguards and limits to judicial power vary considerably. As Geerten Boogaard explains in Chap. 5 on the Netherlands, this diversity is the result of historical developments, which are different for each state. The principle that judges are independent of the legislature and executive can safely be said to be a common point of departure in most constitutional systems. But while in some countries the financial and organizational position of the judiciary is also included in the constitutional set-up, this dimension is lacking in others.

The method of appointing judges is a characteristic of their independence, or lack of it. In the Netherlands, appointments of judges are traditionally for life and made by Royal Decree on the proposal of the Minister of Justice. In the case of appointments to the Supreme Court (i.e. the Court of Cassation), the House of Representatives (the Chamber of Deputies) nominates three people, while other judges are appointed on a recommendation from the Council for the Judiciary. The role of the Minister of Justice has gradually been reduced to a procedural one, without any amendments to the Constitution in this respect. From this we can see that independence depends not only on explicit constitutional standards, but also on conventions and other behavioural patterns that have developed over time in the relationship between the highest state institutions.

Like Boogaard does for the Dutch judiciary, Alfonso Celotto in Chap. 4 situates the position of the Italian Constitutional Court in a bipolar schema of constitutional relationships. Judges in Italy rule on constitutional questions, but not as the sole actors. Although the Italian Constitution firmly and clearly enshrines the Constitutional Court in its legal system, Celotto observes a greater measure of restraint in the Court's relationship with the country's political institutions than in its relationship with other courts.

Paul Daly in Chap. 7 outlines the highly contrasting position of the British judiciary, with a particular focus on the legal system of England and Wales. The whole constitutional development of the United Kingdom is one of principled pragmatism rather than system design. For instance, the Supreme Court in that country has no normative basis to place its judgement on the constitutionality of laws above that of Parliament. Judicial pay and pensions are vulnerable to changes in the political climate. What is even more remarkable is the way in which the other highest state organs relate to the judiciary. Based on recent examples, these arrangements would appear to be insufficiently characterized by an awareness of the constitutional value of courts' independent jurisdiction.

In contrast to the principled pragmatism of British constitutionalism, the South African system can rightly be regarded as an example of constitutional design, and even grand design. Francois Venter explains in Chap. 8 how the judiciary in that country, and in particular the Constitutional Court, has established itself as the most important instrument in developing and protecting constitutionalism. In this system, Koopmans' above-mentioned notion of bipolar constitutionalism is plain to see. Venter's analysis also shows the tensions generated by seeking to protect constitutional supremacy through the judicial function in such a fundamental manner.

A reliance on the judicial branch to safeguard the country's Constitution is also apparent in German constitutionalism. In Chap. 3 on Germany, Anja Seibert-Fohr explains that the constitutional role of judges is key in balancing the tension between democracy and the rule of law in a system where the courts have a duty to protect the Constitution. She stresses the interplay of democratic legitimation and the qualification of professional judges in making judicial appointments. But there is more: in her view, constitutional jurisprudence itself also plays an important role in striking a balance in the same bipolar zone of conflict. The methodology of interpretation and the judges' practice of restraint concerning political decisions concretize their relationship to democratically legitimated majority decisions.

As Evelyne Maes illustrates in Chap. 2 on the Belgian Constitutional Court, the independence of an institution is determined not only by the constitutional entrenchment of its existence, competences and composition and by its normative, organizational and financial autonomy, but also by the independence and impartiality of each of its members. Although she concludes that the Belgian Constitutional Court is a strong and independent institution, she is critical of cuts in the Court's funding, as well as of the procedure for nominating new judges. This procedure does not always involve a parliamentary hearing, at least not necessarily one of a serious nature, while, in her view, Parliament's involvement in the appointments procedure is crucial if constitutional judges are to have true democratic legitimacy.

The appointment of judges is also a matter of discussion in Norway, as the contribution by Eivind Smith shows. Unlike many other countries, Norway has not assigned the task of judging the constitutionality of formal legislation and other acts of parliament to a constitutional court, but instead to courts of general jurisdiction. In such a system, where judges may be involved in the task of authoritative norm-setting, it could be argued that it is far from obvious that judicial independence requires judges to be selected in complete isolation from the political branches of government. In Chap. 6 Smith contends that elements of open political appointments may even be necessary to ensure a sufficient level of legitimacy, regardless of the high level of social trust present in that country.

Whereas most contributions to this volume focus on the independence of the judiciary in states, Chap. 10 by Marios Costa examines the role played by the Court of Justice of the European Union with regard to accountability in the EU. In analysing the EU access to documents regime from a perspective of accountability, Costa argues that the case law of the Court creates a substantial accountability gap because of restricting the right to access documents.

In addition to the European Union, the Council of Europe offers a constitutional meta-level on a pan-European scale. This applies particularly in the case law of the ECtHR, but also in the Council's efforts as an institution, fuelled by the 'Venice Commission'. With regard to the Council of Europe, Jörg Luther in Chap. 9 examines the general principles of judicial independence and legal accountability as they relate to the ECtHR and calls for the further development of the Court's institutional independence. Meanwhile, in Chap. 12 Eirik Holmøyvik and Anne Sanders outline the elements of a stress test for judicial independence, concluding with the pertinent question of whether it is the constitutional arrangement or rather the constitutional culture that ensures the independence of the judiciary.

1.4 Deliberative Constitutionalism

The most important source of legitimacy for judicial decisions is the legality of the law in force, which always needs to be explained when being applied. In the past, the law in force was viewed as a single legal order, but today's reality of a multi-layered order and multi-level governance makes this much more complicated.

Judges have to identify the sources of their legitimacy in this complex legal structure. We are no longer talking here of a single legitimating legal source (usually a certain piece of legislation), but rather of a plurality of anchor points in a complex network. Within the confines of a single legal order, it could be assumed that the law is something that can be found 'out there'. In a pluralist, layered legal order, however, judges are themselves co-actors in a dynamic process, such as that of European legal development.[14] The legitimacy of a judicial decision is not implied by the democratic content of the sources of law on which it is based, but instead requires further deliberation and argumentation. This is especially true for international judges, whose constitutional embeddedness is quite rudimentary,[15] and for constitutional judges, whose work begins where the highest legislative bodies have left ambiguity.[16]

In all these situations – in one more so than the other – judges themselves become actors in the deliberative constitutionalism characterizing a democratic society: 'Judicial decision can trigger dialogue.'[17] It is a role that judges cannot evade in a democratic society, and they have to fulfil it in an acceptable, procedurally legitimating way. Like other actors in this process, judicial institutions have to define their own constitutional position in interaction with the other institutions and the citizens of the state. The more effectively the safeguards that anchor judges in the constitutional system function, the more judges will be able to avoid rigidity in respect of the limits set on their role.

In the meantime, changes in political culture mean these political state institutions are themselves involved in a fundamental transformation of what they understand their function to entail, particularly as a result of the vehement desire for direct control that, through the ballot box, is challenging the moderating effect of guarantees of fundamental rights and the rule of law. The judiciary cannot maintain these guarantees if political support is weakening. Several contributions to this volume provide examples of political criticism and pressure on the judiciary, against which the usual guarantees are unable to provide protection. The pressure on judges in many states shows that the risk of the rule of law being eroded is not limited to the EU Member States Poland and Hungary, which are being criticized in various EU circles, as evidence of the fragility of constitutional arrangements in times when power questions dominate is visible in other countries as well.

When judicial power comes into direct confrontation with political power, the very foundations of a constitutional system are put to the test. The rejection, especially by populist movements, of judicial rulings that protect the weak is a phenomenon perceptible in many Western democracies today. If their rigorous

[14] Hirsch Ballin 2004.

[15] Von Bogdandy and Venzke 2014, p 215.

[16] Möllers 2011.

[17] Young 2018, p 133.

rejection of migrants, for example, is not compatible with judicial review, such movements boast of voicing the 'will of the people'. A constitutionalist-minded response requires careful argumentation and should focus specifically on confirming what all state institutions need: a legitimacy that ultimately lies in the principle of protecting every human being and everyone's life situation, including in a political and economic sense.

Complex systems, to which democratic constitutional orders under the rule of law unquestionably belong, encompass a multitude of stabilizing and destabilizing features. Going back to the idea of merely 'separating' powers is desperately inadequate. This is why a convincing and effective response to threats to the judiciary's independence requires a detailed and precise analysis of the judiciary's constitutional safeguards and limits.

References

Achterberg N (1969) Antinomien verfassunggestaltender Grundentscheidungen. Der Staat 8:159–180

Ackerman B (2017) Good-bye, Montesquieu. In: Ackerman S R et al (eds) Comparative Administrative Law. Edward Elgar, Cheltenham, pp 38–43

Adams L H J et al (eds) (2017) Constitutionalism and the Rule of Law: Bridging Idealism and Realism. Cambridge University Press, Cambridge

AIV (2017) The will of the people? The erosion of democracy under the rule of law in Europe. Adviesraad voor Internationale Vraagstukken, The Hague

Bell J (2006) Judiciaries within Europe: A Comparative Review. Cambridge University Press, Cambridge

Claes M (2006) The National Courts' Mandate in the European Constitution. Hart Publishing, Oxford/Portland

Hirsch Ballin E M H (2004) Reflections on co-actorship. In: Hirsch Ballin E M H, Senden L (eds) Co-actorship in the Development of European Law-Making: The Quality of European Legislation and its Implementation and Application in the National Legal Order. T.M.C. Asser Press, The Hague, pp 3–23

Koopmans T (2003) Courts and Political Institutions: A Comparative View. Cambridge University Press, Cambridge

Möllers Ch (2011) Legalität, Legitimität und Legitimation des Bundesverfassungsgerichts. In: Jestaedt M et al (eds) Das entgrenzte Gericht: Eine kritische Bilanz nach sechzig Jahren Bundesverfassungsgericht. Suhrkamp, Berlin, pp 281–405

Robertson D (2010) The Judge as Political Theorist: Contemporary Constitutional Review. Princeton University Press, Princeton/Oxford

Rosanvallon P (2008) Counter-Democracy: Politics in an Age of Distrust. Cambridge University Press, Cambridge

Stone Sweet A (2004) The Judicial Construction of Europe. Oxford University Press, Oxford

Tushnet M (2018) Advanced Introduction to Comparative Constitutional Law. Edward Elgar, Cheltenham/Northampton MA

Van der Schyff G (2005) Limitation of Rights: A Study of the European Convention and the South African Bill of Rights. Wolf Legal Publishers, Nijmegen

Venter F (2010) Global Features of Constitutional Law. Wolf Legal Publishers, Nijmegen

Von Bogdandy A, Venzke I (2014) In wessen Namen? Internationale Gerichte in Zeiten globalen Regierens. Suhrkamp, Berlin

Young A L (2018) Dialogue, Deliberation and Human Rights. In: Levy R et al (eds) The Cambridge Handbook of Deliberative Constitutionalism. Cambridge University Press, Cambridge, pp 125–138

Ernst Hirsch Ballin is Distinguished University Professor at Tilburg University and Professor of Human Rights Law at the University of Amsterdam. He is the president of the Asser Institute for International and European Law and a Member of the Royal Netherlands Academy of Sciences. Previously, he has served as deputy justice in the Appellate Court for the Public Service and Social Security Law, as judge and President of the Judicial Division of the Council of State and as the Minister of Justice of the Kingdom of the Netherlands. His current research focusses on Dutch and transnational constitutional law, migration and citizenship, and legal research methods.

Gerhard van der Schyff is Associate Professor in the Department of Public Law and Governance at Tilburg University in the Netherlands. He lectures and conducts research on constitutional law and fundamental rights in comparative and European perspective. In 2015, he held a Humboldt Fellowship for Experienced Researchers at the Chair of Christian Calliess at the Free University in Berlin, dealing with the topic of constitutional identity.

Maarten Stremler is Researcher and Lecturer in Constitutional Law in the Department of Public Law and Governance at Tilburg University and a guest staff member in the Department of Constitutional and Administrative Law at Leiden Law School. His primary research interests are constitutional law and constitutional theory. He is writing a PhD thesis on constitutional oversight by the European Union. He is co-author of *Constitutional Preambles: A Comparative Analysis* (Edward Elgar, 2016).

Chapter 2
The Independence of the Belgian Constitutional Court

Evelyne Maes

Contents

Abstract The independence of a constitutional court depends on the independence of the institution itself and of its members. This chapter argues that the Belgian Constitutional Court is a strong, independent institution. Its existence, competences and composition are entrenched in strong legislation: the Belgian Constitution and the Special Act on the Constitutional Court. The Belgian Constitutional Court also enjoys normative and operational autonomy. The financial autonomy of the Constitutional Court is however not fully guaranteed in practice, for two reasons. Firstly, the government forces the Constitutional Court to cut down on its expen-

E. Maes (✉)
Saint-Louis University, Brussels, Belgium
e-mail: evelyne.maes@lozie.com

Hirsch Ballin, Van der Schyff & Stremler (eds.), *European Yearbook of Constitutional Law 2019*, European Yearbook of Constitutional Law 1,
https://doi.org/10.1007/978-94-6265-359-7_2

ditures, regardless of the consequences on its functioning. Secondly, the House of Representatives wants to have more control on the budget and the expenditures of the Constitutional Court than the Special Act on the Constitutional Court allows for at the moment. It is argued that more control by the House of Representatives would endanger the independence of the Constitutional Court and the principle of the separation of powers. It is furthermore argued that the independence of the constitutional judges is also quite well safeguarded. Nevertheless, the appointment procedure could be ameliorated by the obligation for Parliament to organize a public hearing before confirming the nomination of a candidate-judge. This would contribute to the legitimacy and thus independence of the Constitutional Court. Finally, it is argued that the accountability of the Constitutional Court could be reinforced if the Constitutional Court would use a more deliberative argumentation style and would allow separate opinions.

Keywords appointment procedure · budget and expenditures control · Constitutional Court of Belgium · deliberative argumentation style · entrenched legislation · financial autonomy · judicial independence · public hearing · separate opinions

2.1 Introduction

In a *Rechtsstaat* (*état de droit*, a democracy governed by the rule of law), the independence of the judiciary is crucial to safeguard the balance of power between the legislator, the executive and the judiciary. As constitutional courts are competent to annul legislation, they have an even more important role in this balance of power. The independence of such a constitutional court is therefore paramount.

History has however shown us that the independence of constitutional courts has not always been safeguarded. Therefore international courts are (and should be) the watchdog to oblige states to safeguard the independence of their (constitutional) judges. In this chapter, I investigate whether the Belgian constitutional court, as an institution, is truly independent. First, I look at the factors that guarantee the independence of the institution. Those factors are the entrenchment in strong legislation of the existence, competences and composition of the constitutional court and its autonomy. An institution is however just as (in)dependent as its members are. Therefore, I look at the factors that determine the independence of the constitutional judges. The appointment procedure is an important factor to assess the independence of a judge, as a constitutional judge should also enjoy democratic legitimacy. I investigate whether the demands of democratic legitimacy can be reconciled with the demands of independence. Further, I look at the duration of the mandate and the rules on removal from office to assess whether the Belgian constitutional judges are truly independent. Finally, I have a quick regard to the way the Belgian constitutional judges are accountable for the role they take in balancing powers in the Belgian (federal) state.

Having in mind the threats to its independence a constitutional court can suffer, I will argue that the Belgian Constitutional Court is a strong, independent institution. Its existence, competences and composition are entrenched in strong legislation (the Constitution and the Special Act on the Constitutional Court). The Belgian Constitutional Court also enjoys normative and operational autonomy. The financial autonomy of the Constitutional Court is however not fully guaranteed in practice. I will argue that the independence of the constitutional judges is also quite well safeguarded. Nevertheless, the appointment procedure could be ameliorated by the obligation to Parliament to organize a public hearing, before confirming the nomination of a candidate-judge. Finally, I argue that the accountability of the Constitutional Court could be reinforced, if the Constitutional Court would use a more deliberative argumentation style and would allow separate opinions.

2.2 The Independence of a Constitutional Court and the Rule of Law

2.2.1 Threatening the Independence of Constitutional Courts

Constitutional history has showed us that even the most independent constitutional courts have been subject to attempts, by the legislator and/or the executive, to weaken the independence of constitutional courts. Legislators and executives have tried to influence the case law of constitutional courts by changing its composition or competences or have flatly ignored judgements of constitutional courts.

One of the most famous examples of a threat to the independence of a constitutional court is the so-called 'court packing plan' of President Roosevelt of the United States of America in response to the case law of the US Supreme Court regarding the New Deal legislation.[1] With the New Deal legislation President Roosevelt tried to combat the financial and economic crisis of 1929. The US Supreme Court considered this legislation however unconstitutional as it violated the limited competence of the federal state in interstate commerce. In 1936, President Roosevelt was re-elected as President with a great majority of votes. He considered this electoral victory as a confirmation of his New Deal policy. To tackle the Supreme Court, he introduced a Bill to change the composition of the US Supreme Court (the 'court packing plan'): according to the Bill the President would be able to nominate an additional Justice, with a maximum of six, for every Justice

[1] The US Supreme Court is not a constitutional court in the European sense of a constitutional court. It is a Supreme Court, which reviews the judgements of lower cases. In practice, the US Supreme Court considers its jurisdiction over constitutional issues as its main mission and scrutinises mainly legal norms and their implementation to the US Constitution. Bishop et al. 2006, p 26 and Shapiro 2013, p 64.

that would not retire at the age of 70. The Supreme Court would then count fifteen Justices instead of nine. Less than two months after the introduction of the Bill, the Supreme Court changed its case law on the interstate commerce clause in the case *West Coast Hotel Co. v. Parrish.* Important New Deal legislation was found constitutional. This case is called the 'switch in time that saved nine'. The Bill to pack the US Court was later rejected by Congress.

The US legislator has also tried to influence the case law of the US Supreme Court by changing the competence of the Supreme Court. To avoid a declaration of unconstitutionality, Congress legislated in 1869 that the Supreme Court, while a case was pending, no longer had the competence to scrutinize a habeas action.[2] The court session had already taken place, the Court Opinion however was not yet delivered. Due to the constitutional competence of Congress to decide on the competence of the Supreme Court regarding its appellate jurisdiction, the Supreme Court accepted that it had lost its competence to decide the case. The Supreme Court rejected the appeal.[3]

Unfortunately, there are also more recent examples. At the elections of 2010 and 2014, the party Fidesz got a two third majority in the Hungarian Parliament. This large majority enabled this party to change the constitution and to establish a new constitution. This party has used this competence to change the case law of the Hungarian Constitutional Court and to limit its competences.

The Hungarian legislator limited firstly the competence of the Constitutional Court after the Constitutional Court had decided that a taxation of 98% on very high termination fees for public servants was unconstitutional. The Constitution was amended and the Constitutional Court was no longer competent to decide on financial and budgetary legislation.[4] This constitutional amendment was contested before the Hungarian Constitutional Court. In the absence of substantial limitations to the power to amend the constitution, the Hungarian Constitutional Court denied itself the authority to perform a review on the substance of the amendment. In a later decision, the Hungarian Constitutional Court indicated that it might be competent to review constitutional amendments from the perspective of substantive constitutionality.[5]

The Council of Europe disapproved the constitutional changes in Hungary. According to the Venice Commission, the constitutional amendments in order to

---

[2] The Congress has this competence on the ground of Article III, Section 2, para 2, *fine* US Constitution: 'In all the other Cases before mentioned, the supreme Court shall have appellate Jurisdiction, both as to Law and Fact, with such Exceptions, and under such Regulations as the Congress shall make.'

[3] SC 12 April 1869, *Ex parte McCardle*, 74 U.S. 506 (1869). The Supreme Court had the possibility to decide the case before the entering into force of the new Act. The majority of the Supreme Court Justices did not want to do that. Choper 1974, p 852 and Hall 1999, p 180.

[4] The Hungarian Constitutional Court is now only competent to scrutinise legislation for violations of the right to life and human dignity, the protection of privacy, the freedom of thought, of conscience and religion and the rights regarding Hungarian citizenship.

[5] Kovács 2013, pp 3–4.

change the case law and competences of the Constitutional Court were a threat for constitutional justice and for the supremacy of the basic principles contained in the Constitution of Hungary. The limitation of the role of the Constitutional Court leads to a risk that it may negatively affect all three pillars of the Council of Europe: the separation of powers as an essential tenet of democracy, the protection of human rights and the rule of law.[6]

The European Commission also raised questions about the conformity of the Hungarian constitutional changes with the rule of law but awaited the report of the Venice Commission.[7] Constitutional lawyers called up the European Commission to start an infringement procedure against Hungary.[8] The European Commission has not done that for the constitutional amendments regarding the competence of the Constitutional Court.

The European Commission however has started an infringement procedure against Poland for violating the principle of independence of the Constitutional Tribunal.[9] The European Commission asks Poland to restore the independence and legitimacy of the Constitutional Tribunal as guarantor of the Polish Constitution. Its independence and legitimacy are violated because the current composition of the Constitutional Tribunal is illegal. The European Commission demands that Poland ensures that the judges, the President and the Vice- President of the Constitutional Tribunal are lawfully elected and appointed. Therefore, Poland should implement the judgments of the Constitutional Tribunal of 3 and 9 December 2015 which require that the three judges that were lawfully nominated in October 2015 by the previous legislature can take up their function of judge in the Constitutional Tribunal. Secondly, the three judges nominated by the new legislature without a valid legal basis should no longer adjudicate without being validly elected. The European Commission also asks to publish and implement fully the judgments of the Constitutional Tribunal of 9 March 2016, 11 August 2016 and 7 November 2016.

2.2.2 *The Rule of Law and the Independence of (Constitutional) Judges*

The abovementioned examples show that the independence of a constitutional court can be threatened by several means: changing the law on the competence and the

[6] Venice Commission Opinion 720/2013, p 20.

[7] European Commission, 'Hungary and the Rule of Law - Statement of the European Commission in the Plenary Debate of the European Parliament', http://europa.eu/rapid/press-release_SPEECH-13-324_en.htm Accessed 8 March 2019.

[8] https://verfassungsblog.de/evade-constitution-case-hungarian-constitutional-courts-decision-judicial-retirement-age-part-ii/ Accessed 8 March 2019.

[9] European Commission 20 December 2017, COM(2017) 835 final, 2017/0360 (APP).

composition of a constitutional court, illegally appointing new constitutional judges, no implementation of the judgements, etc. The independence of the judiciary is a cornerstone of the principle of separation of powers and of the right to a fair trial.[10] This principle and right have always been and are fundamental to the rule of law.[11] In a democracy under the rule of law, a constitutional court should enjoy the same degree of independence as the judiciary, in order to safeguard the separation of powers.

Rightly, the European Court of Justice (ECJ) and the European Court of Human Rights (ECtHR) try to protect the (constitutional) courts against threats to their independence by the legislator or executive of a member state. The ECtHR has judged that in a state governed by the rule of law a court that falls under the scope of Article 6 of the European Convention on Human Rights (ECHR) should be established by law and the law should guarantee the competences of the courts.[12] The right to access to a judge and the principle of legal certainty demand that judgements have binding force and are implemented.[13]

The ECJ considers the independence of national courts in particular essential to the proper working of the judicial cooperation system embodied by the preliminary ruling mechanism under Article 267 TFEU. Only a body responsible for applying EU law which satisfies the criterion of independence,[14] can ask a preliminary ruling from the ECJ.[15] According to the ECJ, the concept of independence presupposes that the court exercises its judicial functions wholly autonomously, and that it is protected against external interventions or pressure liable to impair the independent judgment of its members and to influence their decisions. Secondly, like the protection against removal from office of the members of the body concerned, the receipt by those members of a level of remuneration commensurate with the importance of the functions they carry out constitutes a guarantee essential to judicial independence.[16]

The jurisprudence of the ECJ and the ECtHR on the independence of constitutional courts is, by its nature, casuistical and does not give an all-round legal

---

[10] Jacquelot 2009, p 5 and Zähle 2011, pp 174–175.

[11] Cf. Coke, 12 Co. Rep. 64–65 or 77 Eng. Rep. 1342–1343 (*Prohibitions del Roy*). See also Cartier 2011, p 34.

[12] ECtHR, *DMD Group v. Slovakia*, 5 October 2010, application no. 19334/03, ECLI:CE:ECHR:2010:1005JUD001933403, para 58; ECtHR, *Jorgic v. Germany*, 12 July 2007, application no. 74613/01, ECLI:CE:ECHR:2007:0712JUD007461301, para 64; ECtHR, *Lavents v. Latvia*, 28 November 2002, application no. 58442/00, ECLI:CE:ECHR:2002:1128JUD005844200, para 81.

[13] See for example ECtHR, *Süzer and Eksen Holding v. Turkey*, 23 January 2013, application no. 6334/05, ECLI:CE:ECHR:2012:1023JUD000633405, para 75 and ECtHR, *Brumarescu v. Romania*, 28 October 1999, application no. 28342/95, ECLI:CE:ECHR:1999:1028JUD002834295, para 61.

[14] ECJ, *Wilson*, 19 September 2006, case C-506/04, EU:C:2006:587, para 51, and, ECJ, *Margarit Panicello*, 16 February 2017, case C-503/15, EU:C:2017:126, para 37.

[15] ECJ, *Associação Sindical dos Juízes Portugueses v Tribunal de Contas*, 27 February 2018, case C-64/16, EU:C:2018:117, para 43.

[16] *Ibid.*, paras 44–45.

framework to guarantee the independence of constitutional courts. Therefore, in this chapter, the independence of the Belgian Constitutional Court will be scrutinized, using the jurisprudence of the ECJ and ECtHR, but also the opinions of the Venice Commission and the doctrine.

2.3 The Institutional Independence of the Belgian Constitutional Court

Having in mind the possible threats to the independence of a constitutional court, I will investigate in this section whether the Belgian constitutional court is an independent court. I take into account the abovementioned factors:

- Is the court established by law and does the law guarantee its competences and composition?
- Does the constitutional court enjoy autonomy?
- How are the constitutional judges elected?
- What is the duration of the mandate and are there incompatibilities?
- Are the constitutional judges protected against removal from office?

Before investigating the degree of independence that the Belgian Constitutional Court enjoys, we should emphasize that the Belgian Constitutional Court is an autonomous institution. It enjoys a separate place in the Belgian constitutional order. It has a separate place in the Constitution (Chapter V of Title III 'on the Constitutional Court, on the prevention and resolution of conflicts'). The Constitutional Court therefore does not belong to one of the three state powers and is independent from them.[17] Some authors suggest that the Constitutional Court belongs to the 'constitutional power', together with the constitutioner.[18]

The independence of the Belgian Constitutional Court depends on several safeguards. We should firstly distinguish the conditions safeguarding the independence of the *institution* and the conditions safeguarding the independence of the *judges*. The first mentioned conditions are the entrenchment of the existence, competence and composition of the Constitutional Court in legislation and the normative, operational and financial autonomy of the Constitutional Court (Sect. 2.3). The conditions safeguarding the independence of the judges are the appointment procedure, the duration of the mandate and its incompatibilities and the rules on discipline and removal from the office (Sect. 2.4).

---

[17] Alen and Muylle 2011, p 486.

[18] Delpérée and Rasson-Roland 1990, pp 21–23; Delva 1991, p 78 and Velaers 1990, p 97.

2.3.1 The Conditions for Independence of the Institution

2.3.1.1 The Legal Foundations of the Belgian Constitutional Court

Having in mind the abovementioned examples of threats to the independence of constitutional courts, we need to examine whether the existence, competences and composition of the Belgian Constitutional Court is safeguarded by, so-called, entrenched or strong legislation. For the independence of a constitutional court is defined by the rigidity of the law that establishes the constitutional court and that regulates its competences and organization. Does the constitution or another strong legislative act protect the Constitutional Court against threats by the legislator or executive?

The Belgian Constitutional Court indeed enjoys strong foundations in the Belgian Constitution. In Article 142 of the Constitution, three essential elements of the Constitutional Court are entrenched. First of all, the Constitution entrenches the existence of the Belgian Constitutional Court. Secondly, in Article 142 of the Constitution it is determined that the Constitutional Court reviews all (federal and federalized) legislation upon its compatibility with the competence-dividing rules of the federal state and with some provisions of the Constitution.[19] Those provisions of the Constitution are enumerated in Article 142 of the Constitution or in the *Bijzondere Wet* of 6 January 1989 on the Constitutional Court (hereafter 'the Special Act on the Constitutional Court'[20]). Thirdly, Article 142 of the Constitution determines the *locus standi* rules: it establishes the right of every person, entitled by law or having interest, to bring a case before the court and the right of every court to request an answer through the prejudicial question procedure.

Those three elements regarding the Constitution Court can only be changed through a rigid procedure of revision of the Constitution. This rigid procedure entails two phases: firstly, the current Parliament decides which Articles of the Constitution should be amended. Following this decision, the Parliament is dissolved and new elections are held within forty days. The then newly elected Parliament can amend the Constitution when two third of the members of Parliament are present and two third of the present members approve of the amendment.[21]

The Constitutional Court is not only the guardian of the Constitution, but also of the Belgian federal state structure. This is shown by the fact that Article 142 of the Constitution demands that the competence, functioning and composition of the Constitutional Court is (further) stipulated in a Special Act. Every modification of this Special Act requires the support of a special parliamentary majority, with a special quorum. The federal Parliament counts two language groups: the Dutch and

---

19 The competence of the Constitutional Court can be enlarged by a Special Act.

20 In footnote this Act will be abbreviated by Special Act CC.

21 Article 195 of the Constitution.

the French speaking language group.[22] To enact a Special Act, a majority of every language group needs to be present (quorum) and a majority of every language group should vote in favour of the Act.[23] The decrees executing the Specific Law on the Constitutional Court are adopted by the Council of Ministers. No delegation to a Minister is possible.[24]

The constitutional entrenchment of the existence, competence and the *locus standi*-rules and the obligation to regulate the competence, functioning and composition by a Special Act guarantee the independence of the Belgian Constitutional Court. Compared to other constitutional courts, the Belgian Constitutional Court stands on firmer foundations.[25] In Belgium, a normal legislature/government can only influence the composition of the Constitutional Court by changing the retirement age.[26] If the competence or composition of the Constitutional Court needs to be changed, the Specific Act on the Constitutional Court or the Constitution should be changed. For the abolishment of the Constitutional Court, the Constitution needs to be amended.

2.3.1.2 The Autonomy of the Belgian Constitutional Court

Next to entrenched legislation that safeguards the independence of the constitutional court, a constitutional court needs to be autonomous. To fulfil its duties, the Belgian Constitutional Court needs a place, competent staff and a good library. It is crucial for the independence of a constitutional court that it enjoys the autonomy to decide for itself on those subjects: if the recruitment and payment of staff or investments in the building or in the library is dependent on the permission of another authority, this authority would be able to influence the functioning of the constitutional court and as such the independence would no longer be guaranteed.[27] There are three sorts of autonomy: normative autonomy, operational autonomy and financial autonomy.

Normative autonomy is twofold. First, it means the power of a constitutional court to participate in the enactment of legislation that is applicable to the constitutional court.[28] Secondly, the court must be able to enact its own regulations on the functioning of the court. For Favoreu, this autonomy is essential for 'constitutional justice'.[29]

[22] Article 43 of the Constitution.

[23] Article 4, 3rd paragraph of the Constitution.

[24] Artikel 123, para 2 Special Act CC.

[25] See *supra*, the examples of the US Supreme Court (court packing plan and changing the competence of the US Supreme Court).

[26] At this moment, the age for retirement is 70 years. Article 4 of the Act 6th January 1989 'betreffende de wedden en pensioenen van de rechters, de referendarissen en de griffiers van het Grondwettelijk Hof'.

[27] See also Thomas 2010, p 88.

[28] Thomas 2010, p 97.

[29] Thomas 2010, p 97.

The Belgian Constitutional Court enjoys a certain normative autonomy. Although not prescribed by law, the Belgian Constitutional Court, represented by its two Presidents, is generally involved in the enactment of legislation that is applicable to the Constitutional Court.[30] The Court is also competent to review the legislation that is applicable to the Constitutional Court. It is competent to review the Special Act on the Constitutional Court upon its compatibility with the competence-dividing rules and the constitutional provisions.[31] The Constitutional Court also enacts its own code of order, which must be publicized in the *Belgisch Staatsblad*.[32]

Secondly, to enjoy full independence, an institution should have operational autonomy. It should be able to decide on its staff: how many employees are necessary for which jobs, their salary, their evaluation, hiring and firing, etc.[33]

The Constitutional Court enjoys this functional autonomy.[34] It hires and fires the staff it needs and decides on its tasks, its replacement, its absences, holidays, etc.[35] The Special Act on the Constitutional Court lays down the maximum number of law clerks (*referendarissen*), but the Constitutional Court decides how many law clerks are necessary.[36] One of the most important decisions on the functioning of the Constitutional Court is that the Court decides how the Presidents of the Court are elected.

For a constitutional court to be independent, it is thirdly crucial that it enjoys financial autonomy. This enables a court to execute its operational autonomy and to guarantee the proper functioning of the court.[37] A constitutional court should be able to decide on its budget. It should receive the necessary means and should be able to spend the money freely.[38]

According to Article 123, § 1 of the Specific Act on the Constitutional Court, the Constitutional Court receives a fund (*dotatie*). A fund is an allocation on the federal expenditure budget that can be freely disposed of by the institution that receives the fund.[39] As a result of an agreement between the Chamber of Representatives and the Constitutional Court, the Constitutional Court draws up an estimate. This

[30] See for example *Parl. doc* Senate 2002–03, n° 2–897/6, 169ff. See also Debry 2010, p 65 (footnote 100).

[31] CC 28 March 2002, n° 62/2002; 19 January 2000, n° 1/2000 and 26 May 1999, n° 55/99 (three preliminary rulings on the constitutionality of Article 26 Special Act CC).

[32] Article 122 Special Act CC.

[33] Favoreu et al. 2012, p 258; Thomas 2010, p 94 and Zurn 2007, p 278.

[34] Article 42 Special Act CC. Bossuyt et al. 2011, p 6.

[35] Arcticles 42 and 43 Special Act CC.

[36] See *Parl.doc* Senate 2002–03, n° 2–897/6, 175.

[37] Alen and Muylle 2011, p 487; Henneuse and Rosoux 2006, p 10 and Zurn 2007, p 277.

[38] Di Manno 1994, pp 53 and 60; Thomas 2010, p 89 and 'Rapport national français - Séparation des pouvoirs et indépendance des cours constitutionnelles et instances équivalentes', available at https://www.venice.coe.int/WCCJ/Rio/Papers/FRA_Conseil_constitutionnel_f.pdf Accessed 8 March 2019, at 4.

[39] Alen and Muylle 2011, p 487.

estimate is the basis for the fund that is communicated to the president of the Chamber of Representatives and to the minister of Budget. Each year the Constitutional Court, represented by its Presidents or its registrars, is invited to discuss about the fund in the parliamentary Audit Commission.[40] After the budgetary year, the Constitutional Court approves its accounts, after advice by the Court of Audit.[41]

Since 2000, Representatives of the Chamber try to limit the financial autonomy of the Constitutional Court. They try to put the Constitutional Court under a more stringent financial supervision. They want to supervise the budget, the execution of the budget and the accounts. The first attempt to limit the financial autonomy was a decision by the parliamentary Commission for accountability,[42] then in June 2002 a protocol between the Chamber and the presidents of the Constitutional Court,[43] and the third attempt were legislative initiatives.[44] The Chamber and the Senate however disagreed on the scope of financial supervision by Parliament. '[To protect the Court] against any possible revenge by the Chamber of Representatives because of the annulment of legislation by the Court',[45] the Senate only wanted to limit the financial supervision by the Chamber to the verification and approval of the accounts.[46] The Chamber assumed it should be competent to supervise the budget estimates, to approve the budget, to verify the execution of the budget and the accounts and to approve the accounts.[47] As the government was brought down in 2010, the bill was not enacted; presumably not to the regret of the Constitutional Court that, on the occasion of the decision of the parliamentary Audit Commission, already had stated:

> In the state the [Constitutional Court] is instituted to resolve disputes between the several legislators of the federal Belgium and to act as a supervisor of their legislative acts. It is probably incompatible with the constitutional order that the [Constitutional Court] would be subject to a stringent supervision by (only) one of the legislators or an organ that is the emanation of it.[48]

---

[40] See also Debry 2010, p 66.

[41] On 24 March 2000 the parliamentary Commission for accountability decided that the Court of Audit will control the execution of the budget and the accounts and will report to the Commission. *Parl.doc Chamber* 1999–2000, n° 50–693/1, 5. The Belgian Constitutional Court agreed to this in a Protocol of 20 June 2002, signed by the Constitutional Court and the Chamber of Representatives. See Debry 2010, p 57.

[42] *Parl.doc Chamber* 1999–2000, 'Arbitragehof – begroting van het begrotingsjaar 2000 – aanpassing van de dotatie van het begrotingsjaar 2000', n° 50–693/1, 4–5.

[43] *Parl.doc Chamber* 2003–04, n° 51–552/1, 15.

[44] *Parl.doc Chamber* 2000–2001, n° 50–987/1, and *Parl.doc Chamber* 2008–2009, n° 52–1937/1.

[45] *Parl.doc Chamber* 2008–2009, n° 50–1936/2, 3.

[46] *Parl.doc Chamber* 2008–2009, n° 52–1937/1.

[47] *Parl.doc Chamber* 2008–2009, n° 52–1937/4 and n° 52–1937/5.

[48] *Parl. doc Chamber* 1999–2000, n° 50–693/1, 10.

Analyses of the estimates and the accounts of the last ten years show that the estimate of the Constitutional Court is always very cautious. Each year the Constitutional Courts spends less than it has estimated. In the last decade, only rarely a budget item was exceeded. The fund that the Constitutional Court demands increases every year, because the wages of the staff are the largest expenditure item (85%): the wages of the members of the Constitutional Court, of the law clerks and of the personnel.

To see whether the Constitutional Court enjoys real financial autonomy, it is important to check whether the Chamber of Representatives actually grants to the Constitutional Court the fund it asks. In the beginning, it did, and the Court also sometimes was granted an extra fund for specific reasons.[49] Since more than ten years, however, the Chamber no longer grants the fund that the Constitutional Courts asks. Each year, the estimated fund for the next budgetary year is decreased with the boni of the previous year and with the reserve that the Constitutional Court has built up before 2000. In other cases, the estimated fund is only granted thanks to surpluses of the fund of other institutions (such as the Court of Audit).

Sometimes the Constitutional Court receives even a lower fund than the year before. This enforces the Constitutional Court to cut down on its expenditures. This happened for the first time in 2009: the federal government suggested that a lower fund should be granted than the Court had received in 2008. In 2009 it was decided that the Constitutional Court had to spend less in 2010 than it had spent in 2008. For the budget of 2013, the Audit Commission decided to take into account the full reserve of the Constitutional Court (2,008,000 euro – plus the estimated interest) and the boni of the year before, to determine the fund. The reserve that the Constitutional Court had built up before 2000, thus had to be used completely to finance the functioning of the Constitutional Court.[50] Finally, since 2014 the Constitutional Courts has had to cut down 2% every year (as has every other government institution).[51]

Each time when significant savings were imposed, the Presidents of the Constitutional Court had to explain / defend the requested funding in the *Commissie voor de Comptabiliteit* (a parliamentary Audit Commission). Notwithstanding the fact that the Presidents do recognize that each institution should make an effort in budgetary difficult times, they still had strong objections against significant saving rounds.

---

[49] In 2003, the Constitutional Court received an extra fund because of the enlargement of its competences. In 2000, it received an extra of 7,800,000 frank (cc. 194,352 euro) to finance the XIIth Conference of European constitutional courts in Brussels in May 2002. *Parl.doc Chamber* 1999–2000, n° 50–693/1, 3.

[50] *Parl.doc Chamber* 2012–2013, n° 53–2521/8, 5 and *Parl.doc Chamber* 2012–2013, n° 53–2578/1, 14. To safeguard its autonomy the Constitutional Court prefers to have a reserve that allows the proper functioning for six months. This reserve should be five million euro. *Parl.doc Chamber* 2012–2013, n° 53–2578/1, 13. Henneuse and Rosoux 2006, p 11.

[51] *Parl.doc Chamber* 2014–2015, n° 54–68/1, 10.

In 2009, the President explained that the requested raise in funding was required to cover the higher staffing costs caused by three index jumps in 2008, a possible index jump in 2009, salary alignments and an increase in travel costs; all costs that are outside the reach of control of the Court. Furthermore and rightfully so, the President objected to the fact that no prior consultation had been initiated by either the Prime Minister or the Minister of Budget. Finally, he emphasized the fact that a reduction in funding would deteriorate the functioning of the Court and that it was crucial for the autonomy and well-functioning of the Court that the reserve should be maintained and protected as it serves to pay invoices before any funding is available and to ensure renewal and refurbishing works.[52] Because of these objections, the parliamentary Audit Commission did an extra effort to propose higher funding than the government had done.

In 2014, the President emphasized that the basis for the linear saving of 2% should be done on the (adjusted) budget and not on the funding. Furthermore, he explained the budgetary consequences of some of the specific aspects of the organization and functioning of the Constitutional Court. First of all, the Constitutional Court has little say in the staffing costs: the number of law clerks is determined by a specific law and has decreased since 2010. Because of the increasing workload since the 6th Reform of the State further savings on staffing are impossible. On top of that, there are numerous operating expenses because of legal obligations. The Constitutional Court has proposed to reduce the latter by intervention of the legislation. An additional element is the cost of the building which has been in use since over 20 years. And finally the President emphasized that the Constitutional Court is only able to meet its responsibilities as custodian of the fundamental rights and liberties and of the division of powers, if it disposes of sufficient means to do so.[53] These arguments were repeated in 2015.[54]

A constitutional court needs to have financial autonomy, yet it cannot be unlimited. The principles of democracy require that a (federal) institution should approve the budget. This serves as a control on the constitutional court: a means to political accountability of the constitutional court. In Belgium, for instance, the parliamentary Audit Commission is by far not a formality and often does not approve the requested funding. On top of that, the mandated institutions can supervise the spending of the expenses.

However, the way in which the Chamber of Representatives exercises the supervision of the budget and the accounts of the Constitutional Court and grants the fund can be seriously criticized: the exclusive mandate of the Chamber of Representatives to approve the budget and its custom to check the accounts raise principal objections. Furthermore, its actual method raises practical objections. I elaborate further on those objections.

52 *Parl.doc Chamber* 2008–2009, n° 52–1636/1, 18–19.

53 *Parl.doc Chamber* 2014–2015, n° 54–68/1, 11–12.

54 *Parl.doc Chamber* 2015–2016, n° 54–1497/1, 8–11.

The power of the Chamber of Representatives to approve the funding of the Constitutional Court first of all raises a principal question in the light of the separation of the powers and the Belgian federal state structure. Based on the constitutional separation of duties between the Chamber of Representatives and the Senate, the approval of the budget of a federal institution belongs to the competence of the Chamber of Representatives. However, due to the specificity of the Constitutional Court, one should reconsider whether the Chamber of Representatives is indeed the most appropriate organ to – on its own – approve the funding of the Constitutional Court. Indeed, the Court actually checks the constitutionality of legislation enacted by the federal parliament but also legislation enacted by the parliaments of the communities and regions. In the light of the separation of powers and the Belgian federal state structure, it seems improper that the Chamber solely approves the funding; preferably, it should happen in concertation with the Senate (as in Germany). Indeed, in the Senate, all communities and regions are represented and as such the funding would be approved – whether directly or indirectly – by all legal institutions subject to the legal supervision of the Constitutional Court.

The second principal objection relates to the non-compliance of the principles of a fund by the Chamber of Representatives. The Special Act on the Constitutional Court stipulates clearly that the Constitutional Court is entitled to a fund (*dotatie*). What is typical about a fund is that it is a credit which is included in the federal budget, but the spending of which is determined autonomously and freely by the entitled institution. Obviously, it is recommendable that – in the light of transparency and the good spending of government finances – the Constitutional Court makes a detailed budget and publicizes the parliamentary reports of the accounts. This requirement for transparency however does not mean that the Chamber of Representatives is entitled to check whether the Constitutional Court has exceeded certain budget items, provided the fund in total has not been exceeded. However, this is exactly what the Chamber of Representatives does.

Thirdly, the proceedings of the Chamber of Representatives also reveal practical objections. In the case that a lower funding than requested has been approved by the Chamber of Representatives, no checks are done on the consequences of this decision on the functioning of the Court. The parliamentary reports show that the members of parliament do not try to seek information on the consequences of their austerity measures. However, in this matter, the Court as well has to take its own responsibility. In the past, the Court is represented by a registrar in the parliamentary Audit Commission. In the period 2002–2013, only at two occasions the Court was represented by its two Presidents. Each time they explained in large why a smaller funding would cause functional problems at the Court. In 2009, in response to this explanation, the parliamentary Audit Commission did the utmost to approve a larger funding than the government had proposed. As is the case in other constitutional courts, it is the duty of both Presidents of the Constitutional Court to discuss in the Audit Commission the budget and requested funding and to explain which consequences a possible saving would have. Moreover, this would increase the mutual respect for the institutions and the openness to dialogue.

Finally, a serious change of the financial autonomy is only possible by amending the Special Act on the Constitutional Court. Only changing this Special Act will allow an extension of the supervision of the budget proposals and the Court's accounts. The Constitutional Court is competent to judge whether these amendments are constitutional: for instance by scrutinizing whether those changes violate the legal principles of the independence of a judge and of the balance of powers. Obviously, it is not the intention that Parliament and the Constitutional Court should confront each other in such a collision course. However, should Parliament restrict the financial autonomy of the Constitutional Court in a significant way, it is not to be excluded that the Constitutional Court will feel compelled to preserve the independent functioning of this institution.

2.4 The Independence of the Judges

The independence of an institution is not only determined by the entrenchment of its existence, competences and composition in sharing legislation and by its normative, organizational and financial autonomy, but also – and essentially so – by the independence and impartiality of each of its members. Hereafter I assess the factors that safeguard the independence of the judges: the appointment procedure, the mandate and the rules on removal from office. Finally, I will argue that allowing dissenting opinions at the Constitutional Court would enhance the independence of the judges.

2.4.1 The Appointment Procedure

The appointment procedure of a constitutional judge is a very important factor to guarantee the independence of a constitutional court. The appointment procedure however also has to realize other demands: it should give the constitutional judges democratic legitimacy. The procedure should also contribute to the dignity[55] of the institution and of the judges and, in a federal state structure, it should include the cooperation of the federations.[56]

In the majority of the member states of the Council of Europe the appointment of the constitutional judges is a 'teamwork of the juridical and politics': politicians nominate the constitutional judges.[57] In a study on the nomination procedures in 40

---

[55] The dignity of the appointment procedure of the US Supreme Court Justices is threatened by the high media attention and the private questions during the auditions. Davis 2005, p 23.

[56] Venice Commission, Report on the composition of constitutional courts, CDL-JU (97) 34 rev2, 6.

[57] Szymczak 2006, p 426.

countries, the Venice Committee has distinguished three kinds of nominations:[58] the direct nomination, the nomination by election and finally a hybrid system that has two types of examples: a parliamentary confirmation of the candidate that is proposed by the Head of State (as in the United States) and a choice by the Head of State of a candidate proposed by the parliament (as in Belgium).

In Belgium, it is the King – read the Council of Ministers – who takes the decision, who nominates the judges for the constitutional court from a list of two candidates, proposed in turns by the Chamber or the Senate.[59] The Representatives and Senators express a vote based on the curriculum vitae of the candidates, who have to achieve a two third majority.[60] The King, who in theory has the choice between the two candidates, always nominates the first candidate on the list.[61]

As in Germany, it is common practice in Belgium that the posts of the constitutional judges are spread amongst the political parties: (in principle) according to the D'hondt system, it is decided which political party, with exception of non-democratic parties,[62] is entitled to the available post.[63] In principle, the other political parties consent to the candidates as proposed by the entitled party. This means that, without the support of the (president[64] of the) political party,[65] a candidate has no chance whatsoever to be nominated.[66]

The Chamber or the Senate approves of the candidate by a two third majority. Being confirmed by such a large majority gives a constitutional judge democratic legitimacy. Especially for a constitutional judge it is crucial to enjoy democratic legitimacy. Constitutional courts struggle with legitimacy-issue, so that a

---

[58] Venice Commission, Report on the composition of constitutional courts, CDL-JU (97) 34 rev2, 4–6. See also Rousseau 1998, p 49.

[59] Until 1993, only the Senate nominated candidate judges. The language groups in the Senate reflected the communities in Belgium. That way the balance between the communities was safeguarded. See old Article 32 Special Act CC and *Parl. Doc Senate* 1981–82, n° 246/2, 140. This was changed by the Special Act of 16 July 1993, without having regard to the involvement of the communities. See *Parl.doc Senate* 1992–93, n° 558/1, 62–63. See Courtoy 2000, p 539; Delpérée and Rasson-Roland 1990, 29 and Delpérée 1988, p 104.

[60] Article 32 Special Act CC. See also Rasson-Roland 2004, p 26.

[61] Verdussen 2013, 69 and Rasson-Roland 2004, p 26.

[62] Courtoy 2000, p 25. The so-called anti-democratic party Vlaams Blok was not entitled to nominate a judge.

[63] Rasson-Roland 2004, p 25 and Courtoy 2000, p 540.

[64] Verdussen 2012, p 150.

[65] There is one example where the Parliament did not merely vote for the two candidate-judges that were nominated by the entitled party. In 2007, a candidate-judge, Mia De Schamphelaere, did not receive the two-third majority. This was remarkable, as the other candidate-judge, Trees Merckx-Van Goey, received firstly the two-third majority. Therefore, the King would appoint Merckx-Van Goey as constitutional judge. According to the media, the other political parties wanted to give a sign that a candidate-judge renowned for having conservative ideas on the legislation regarding abortion and euthanasia, would never be appointed as a constitutional judge. See *Hand.* Senate 2007–08, 9 October 2007, 18 and '"Majeur politiek incident" in Senaat', *De Standaard*, 11 October 2007 and 'Cinema II', *De Morgen*, 11 October 2007.

[66] Rasson-Roland 2004, 25.

-onfirmation of its judges by Parliament is a crucial element in the balance of power between the legislator and a constitutional court. Unless directly elected by the people, it is difficult to conceive of a nomination procedure in which a candidate judge obtains democratic legitimacy without political parties or politicians playing a role in it.

The confirmation by two third of the members of the Chamber or the Senate should not be problematic in the light of the independence of a constitutional judge. The ECtHR states that, even though a constitutional judge should be independent from the legislator and from the executive, a political nomination by the legislator is – in essence – not a reason to doubt the independence of these judges.[67] The ECtHR confirms this in the decision *Ruiz-Mateos*.[68] The ECtHR is especially attentive to the oath that the magistrates take at their inauguration. This oath emphasizes the independence of the judicial function.[69] Other elements that safeguard the independence, according to the ECtHR, are the duration of the mandate the incompatibilities as defined by law and the constitution.[70]

The ECtHR has not yet decided on the independence and impartiality of constitutional judges nominated by the government. There is no reason to assume that the ECtHR would be stricter for nominations of constitutional judges than for those of other judges.[71] This allows that lessons can be learned from the case law on the appointment of judges of the judiciary. In this case law the ECtHR decided that a nomination by the government and the fact that also political preferences play a role in the nomination process, is – as such – not a cause to doubt the independence of the judges.[72]

---

67 ECtHR, *Crociani v. Italy*, 18 December 1980, application no. 8603/79 etc., ECLI:CE:ECHR:1980:1218DEC000860379.

68 ECtHR, *Ruiz-Mateos v. Spain*, 6 November 1990, application no. 12952/87, ECLI:CE:ECHR:1993:0623JUD001295287.

69 ECtHR, *Salaman v. United Kingdom*, 15 June 2000, application no. 43505/98, ECLI:CE:ECHR:2000:0615DEC004350598.

70 For election by parliament of extra judges in the Italian Constitutional Court, see ECtHR, *Crociani v. Italy*, 18 December 1980, application no. 8603/79 etc., ECLI:CE:ECHR:1980:1218DEC000860379. For other judges, see ECtHR, *Ninn-Hansen v. Denmark*, 18 May 1999, application no. 28972/95, ECLI:CE:ECHR:1999:0518DEC002897295; ECtHR, *Filippini v. San-Marino*, 26 August 2003, application no. 10526/02, ECLI:CE:ECHR:2003:0826DEC001052602 (appointment by the legislator) and ECtHR, *Zolotas v. Greece*, 2 June 2005, application no. 38240/02, ECLI:CE:ECHR:2005:0602JUD003824002, para 24 and 26 and ECtHR, *Campbell and Fell v. United Kingdom*, 28 June 1984, application no. 7819/77, ECLI:CE:ECHR:1984:0628JUD000781977, para 79 (appointment by the government). See also Szymczak 2006, p 428.

71 Szymczak 2006, p 427.

72 ECtHR, *Zolotas v. Greece*, 2 June 2005, application no. 38240/02, ECLI:CE:ECHR:2005:0602JUD003824002, para 24 and 26 and ECtHR, *Campbell and Fell v. United Kingdom*, 28 June 1984, application no. 7819/77, ECLI:CE:ECHR:1984:0628JUD000781977, para 79.

It certainly should be recommended that the parliament (and not the government) should have its say in the nomination procedure of the constitutional judges.[73] In Austria, for instance, in 1929 the nomination procedure was changed so that constitutional judges no longer were nominated by the parliament but by the government. By consequence, the government only nominated judges that were allies to the government. For Kelsen, this meant the beginning of a political evolution that inevitably led to fascism and that was responsible for the fact that the annexation of Austria by the Nazi's did not encounter much resistance.[74]

Especially in the light of the principle of balance of power, it is recommended that the parliament should be involved in the nomination of constitutional judges. The checks on constitutionality which these judges will need to perform, form indeed a supervision of these parliaments (or of the legislator).

In Germany and Belgium, the political nomination procedure, as practiced, ensures a proportional representation of all political parties in the constitutional court. This practice increases the independence of the constitutional court. For a court should not be the instrument of the parliament nor of the government. The proportional representation encourages the legitimacy of the constitutional court and as such the authority of its rulings. A disadvantage however is that this practice entails that good candidate-judges who are politically neutral, shall not be appointed as a constitutional judge.[75]

The Committee of Ministers of the Council of Europe nevertheless advises in its recommendation about the independence, efficiency and accountability of the judges – which is also valid for the judges of a constitutional court[76] – that:

> [...] where the constitutional or other legal provisions prescribe that the head of state, the government or the legislative power take decisions concerning the selection and career of judges, an independent and competent authority drawn in substantial part from the judiciary (without prejudice to the rules applicable to councils for the judiciary contained in Chapter IV) should be authorised to make recommendations or express opinions which the relevant appointing authority follows in practice.[77]

Taking this recommendation into consideration, in Belgium, it is possible to ask the High Council of Justice (or other stakeholders) to give a recommendation or advise about the candidate constitutional judges.[78] It is up to the members of parliament whether they will take this advice into account or not. For the moment, the High Council of Justice does not play a role in the nomination of the judges of

---

[73] See also *Parl.doc. Senate* 1981–82, n° 246/2, 155. *Pro*, Verdussen 2004, p 53. *Contra*, Robert and Rousseau 1998, 1.

[74] Kelsen 1942, p 188.

[75] Benda et al. 2012, 70 (para 5, n° 139).

[76] Recommendation CM/Rec(2010)12 of the Committee of Ministers to member states on judges: independence, efficiency and responsibilities, Article 1.

[77] *Ibid.*, Article 47.

[78] *Ibid.*, Article 47.

the Constitutional Court. An even more far-reaching option would be that the High Council of Justice receives the mandate to – with respect for the proportional representation – draw up a list of candidates from which the Chamber or the Senate can propose two candidate-judges.[79]

The Belgian practice, whereby the entitled party (president) determines the candidate-judge, leads to the consequence that obtaining a two third majority in the Chamber or in the Senate is a mere formality. The members of the parliament do not get a free choice. They are supposed to vote for the candidate judges that are proposed by the entitled party. Nevertheless this step should be maintained in the appointment procedure as only a parliament can give enough democratic legitimacy to an appointment procedure and to the nominated judge. Furthermore, the requirement to find a two third majority for a nomination obliges the nominating instance to only propose valid candidates.

This obligation should be strengthened by subjecting the candidate-judges to a parliamentary hearing. In Belgium, there is no legal obligation for the members of parliament to organize hearings for the nomination of constitutional judges. Before 1996, it never happened. On October 24th 1996, a few days after the 'Witte Mars',[80] the Senate thought that it would not be opportune to nominate at that moment two candidate judges for the constitutional court and enforced upon themselves a reflection period. Next, they decided to organize hearings for these nominations, to allow the candidates to introduce themselves to the *Commissie voor de Institutionele Aangelegenheden* (Commission for Institutional Affairs). The modalities for these hearings were defined *ad hoc*. They were not public.[81] The proposition to ask for the advice of a Council of Wise Men was discarded.[82]

This example became a precedent without legal basis and with very limited impact.[83] Only when the Senate needs to propose two candidate judges as judges-lawyers,[84] the committee organizes – in principle – non-public hearings.[85]

---

[79] As happens in South-Africa. The President of South-Africa appoints the judges on advice of the Judicial Service Commission: the JSC nominates one candidate-judge for the judiciary, so the President does not enjoy a discretionary power. For the appointment of constitutional judges, the JSC nominates several candidates, so the President can choose one candidate. Murray 1999, p 865.

[80] A March held to contest the political and juridical situation in Belgium after the Dutroux affair. One of the criticisms was that the appointment of judges of the judiciary was too political and therefore did not guarantee quality and independence. The government promised to reform the judiciary to make it more independent and politically neutral.

[81] *Hand.* Senate 1996–97, 20 December 1996, 2186.

[82] *Parl. doc Senate* 1996–97, n° 1–491/1, 20.

[83] The 'Reglement' of the Senate does not regulate these hearings. See *Parl.doc Senate* 1996–97, n° 1–491/1, 9.

[84] The Constitutional Courts is composed of twelve judges: six of them are so-called 'judges-lawyers': professors, judges or law clerks at the highest Courts (Cour de Cassation, Conseil d'Etat or Constitutional Court). Six of them are the so-called 'judges-politicians': they are appointed thanks to their political expertise (a parliamentary mandate of minimum five years).

[85] *Hand.* Senate 2017–2018, 13 July 2018, *Hand.* Senate 2013–14, 19 December 2013, 29; *Hand.* Senate 2000–01, 7 December 2000, 23 and *Hand.* Senate 1996–97, 20 December 1996, 2186. In

No hearings are organized if the Senate proposes members of parliament as judges (for the so-called 'judges-politicians') or if the Chamber of Representatives proposes candidate judges.[86] It happened a second time in November 2000. Because of the lack of a serious number of candidates, of the presence of members of the committee, of a formal framework for the hearing and of objective evaluation criteria, the use of the hearing was put in question. Or as Verdussen puts it: '[...] c'était pour une visite de courtoisie qui ressemblait plus à un *five o'clock* dans un salon de thé qu'à une audition digne de ce nom.'[87]

In 2010 however, the Senate did not organize a hearing when a candidate judge-jurist was proposed.[88] None of the senators requested a hearing: did their memory not reach far enough or was there a reason why they felt they did not need a hearing? We do not know. The senators voted on the basis of the curriculum vitae of the candidates. In 2013 however, the Senate again organized a hearing for the proposal of a candidate-judge-jurist: most probably the parties of the majority wanted a hearing because the candidate was proposed by a non-majority party (the N-VA). In 2018, the Senate also organized a hearing.

Because there was no hearing in 2010 and yet a hearing in 2013, the precedent of 1996 is not only a precedent without legal basis and with limited impact, but also with a random application. The fact that the nomination procedure for a judge of a constitutional court is subject to such inequity, does not improve the trust in the institutions nor the respect for a judge of the Constitutional Court. As such this random procedure can harm the independence of this office.

A constitutional judge needs to have a true democratic legitimacy and needs to represent the diversity of ideas and ideologies in our society. Therefore, the involvement of the parliament in the appointment procedure should be more than a mere voting for proposed candidates. The members of parliament should execute their task properly and transparently:[89] independently and with the required knowledge whether a candidate-judge would be a proper constitutional judge. This entails that the members of parliament should have a greater ambition than simply abide to the practice of the political nomination: with respect for the practice or rule of law that it is up to a certain party or person to propose candidate judges, they should ensure themselves about the capability of the candidate judge.

I therefore argue in favour of the obligation to organize a public hearing in the nomination process of a constitutional judges. In Germany, some constitutional authors warn for the risk of such hearings. Fearing such a hearing, potentially good constitutional judges would not present their candidacy; good candidates would not

---

this hearing, candidate-judges would be tested on their knowledge of the other official languages and their neutrality regarding the Belgian language questions. Courtoy 2000, p 540.

[86] See *Hand.* Senate 2007–08, 9 October 2007, 18; *Hand.* Chamber, 2009–2010, 11 March 2010, 34ff; *Hand.* Chamber 2003–04, 4 March 2004; *Hand.* Chamber 2000–2001, 15 February 2001, 34 and 40 and *Hand.* Chamber 1999–2000, 10 November 1999, 14.

[87] Verdussen 2012, p 150 and Rasson-Roland 2004, pp 26–27.

[88] François Daout (and Pierre Vandernoot). *Hand.* Senate 2010–2011, 9 December 2010, 20.

[89] Kischel 2013, pp 972–973.

shine in the hearing and thus not be elected; parties would not withdraw from asking awkward questions and questions could be asked about subjects that should be judged by the constitutional court.[90] They argue that confidentiality is more important than the wish for transparency.[91]

These risks assume that the hearings would evolve into American practices. However, qualitative hearings and debates should oblige the political parties to only propose appropriate and valid candidates. A competent candidate-judge for a constitutional court will not be deterred by a hearing.[92] A parliamentary committee can ask the candidate about his views about the role of the constitutional court, about the interpretation of the constitutional law, about the relation between international and national law and about certain themes (freedom of education, freedom of speech, etc.) without however wanting to learn how a judge would decide in certain cases.[93] These hearings should be public so that not only the members of parliament, but also experts, the media and interest groups can form an opinion about the quality of the candidate.[94] A hearing should expose the professional qualities of the candidate, not his personal life. Through their questions, the members of the committee should guarantee that the dignity of the nomination procedures is not attacked.

Opponents of hearings often state that there is a link between a request for hearings and the qualification given to the constitutional court. Those who prefer hearings, consider the constitutional court as a political organ; the others as a proper court.[95] This theorem is not supported. On the contrary, there is strong pleading for public hearings as an instrument to force the members of parliament to exercise their duty in an independent and informed manner: to give a two-third majority to the election of a judge. This is only possible if the members of parliament ensure themselves of the competence and ideology of the candidate-judge and not when they merely vote as marionettes of the party in charge. Only then will the judges of the constitutional court truly enjoy democratic legitimacy.

Finally, through these hearings, the media would also pay more attention to the nomination of a new constitutional judge: this would add to a better knowledge of the public of the role of the constitutional court and of the constitutional judges.[96] This further adds to the democratic legitimacy of the judge, as he or she is then also supported by society.

---

[90] Benda et al. 2012, p 68 (para 5, n° 134) and Kischel 2013, pp 974–975.

[91] Benda et al. 2012, 68 (para 5, n° 134).

[92] Carcassonne 2008, p 5. See for the United Kingdom, Clark 2010, pp 466 and 477.

[93] For guidelines to candidate-justices how to answer questions, see Alleman and Mazzone 2010, pp 1378–1381. For the kind of questions that should or should not be asked, see Kischel 2013, p 973.

[94] Verdussen 2012, p 150.

[95] Kischel 2013, pp 977–978.

[96] Clark 2010, p 467.

2.4.2 The Mandate and its Incompatibilities

The duration of the mandate of constitutional judge, the possible renewal of it and its incompatibilities are three important factors that determine how independent a constitutional judge is.

The duration of the mandate and whether the mandate is renewable is essential for the functioning of a constitutional court: both factors influence the (political) shifts in a court, the independence of the judges and the stability of the institution.[97] A *conditio sine qua non* for the independence of the institution is that the mandate is not renewable.[98] In Germany and France the mandate is limited in time: 12 years for the *Bundesverfassungsgericht* (or till the end of the month when the judge turns 68)[99] and 9 years for the appointed members of the *Conseil constitutionnel.*[100] The judges of the Belgian Constitutional Court are appointed 'for life', but retire at the age of 70.[101] The legislator did not want that the mandate only lasted 15 years.[102] If however the mandate only lasts for 9 or 12 years, what can the judge do after his mandate? The independence of a constitutional court forbids of course that he or she would take up a political office. Therefore, for the independence of a constitutional court, it is preferred that judges should be nominated for life.

The average duration of the mandate of the Belgian constitutional judges is about 10.5 years (shortest: 2 years and 1 one month, longest: 19 years and 4 months). Lately, the mandates last much longer than the average: more than 15 and several even more than 20 years. Long mandates have however the disadvantage that a few constitutional judges have the longest expertise and dominate the court.[103]

For the independence of a constitutional court it is crucial that a constitutional judge holds no other office than his mandate as a judge. Belgian constitutional judges are only allowed to teach at university while they are judge.

---

[97] Venice Commission, Report on the composition of constitutional courts, CDL-JU (97) 34 rev2, p 14.

[98] *Ibid.*, pp 14–15. See also Benda et al. 2012, p 62 (para 5, n° 119); Robert and Rousseau 1998, p 1753; Rousseau 1998, p 58 and Umbach et al. 2005, p 198 (para 4, n° 8).

[99] Article 4, para 1 *BVerfGG*. See *BVerfG* 3 December 1975, *BVerfGE* 40, 356. See Benda et al. 2012, pp 62–63 (para 5, n° 120).

[100] Article 56 French Constitution and Article 12 Organic act *Conseil constitutionnel*. This is criticized by Fromont 2007; p 52. Nine years is not too short, according to former judge Robert in Robert and Rousseau 1998, p 1753 and is ideal according to Drago 2003, p 76.

[101] Article 4 of the Act of 6 January 1989 'betreffende de wedden en pensioenen van de rechters, de referendarissen en de griffiers van het Grondwettelijk Hof', *BS* 7 January 1989, *err. BS* 1 February 1989.

[102] The proposal to limit the mandate to fifteen years and non-renewable was rejected by a large majority of votes. See *Parl.doc* Senate 1981–82, n° 246/2, 156–157, such as a proposal to have a renewable mandate of six years, see *Parl. doc* Senate 1981–82, n° 246/2. See also Courtoy 2000, p 539.

[103] See also Benda et al. 2012, p 63 (para 5, n° 121) and de Visser 2014, p 219.

2.4.3 Discipline and Dismissal

The ECtHR has many times stated that the impossibility for the executive power to dismiss a judge is a corollary of the independence of a judge.[104] For the independence of a constitutional court, it is mandatory that the court can decide itself whether a constitutional judge, in his functioning, meets the requirements of a constitutional judge.

The Belgian Constitutional Court indeed has the power to decide itself to dismiss a candidate. The Constitutional Court defines the disciplinary regime that applies to the judges and decides via a ruling, decided in plenary meeting, about the dismissal. So far, no constitutional judge has ever been dismissed.

2.5 No Dissenting Opinions by Constitutional Judges

A constitutional court can only be accountable through its case law: it should proof that it uses a high quality of decision-making. One of the possible proofs thereto is the presence of separate opinions. Separate opinions show that the court has debated the case thoroughly, that not the opinion of one judge has dominated[105] and that the decision is based on valid – legal or non-legal – arguments.[106] This is a means for constitutional judges to be accountable. Because of the composition of a constitutional court and the political nature of its decisions, there is more need for such accountability, and thus for separate opinions.[107] In the doctrine, it is argued that dissenting opinions also enhance the independence of constitutional judges.[108]

The judges of the Belgian Constitutional Court cannot publish their separate opinions. The deliberations of the court are secret (Article 108 Special Act on the Constitutional Court). In Belgium this principle entails that judges are not allowed to state their private opinion on the case.[109]

From time to time, members of parliament argue that constitutional judges should be allowed to publish their separate opinion.[110] They think it would increase the seriousness and credibility of the Court; it would enforce the objectivity of the

---

[104] See for example ECtHR, *Campbell and Fell v. United Kingdom*, 28 June 1984, application no. 7819/77, ECLI:CE:ECHR:1984:0628JUD000781977, para 80.

[105] Fuld 1962, p 927; Moorhead 1952, p 822 and Voss 1992, p 653.

[106] Feyen 2012, p 274.

[107] Sohier 1986, p 767 and Zweigert 1968, D. 28.

[108] Prignon 2011, p 115; Douglas 1948, pp 105–106; Mastor 2001, p 230; Zweigert 1968, D. 30 and D. 37.

[109] Cass. 13 March 2012, P.11.1750.N/8. See Martens 2013, pp 806–807.

[110] *Parl.doc Chamber* 2008–09, n° 52–1912/1; *Parl.St.* Senate 1981–82, n° 246/2, 195 and 202; *Parl St.* Chamber 1980–81, 704/1, 53; *Parl.doc Chamber* 1982–83, n° 647/5, 15. See also Velaers 1990, pp 521–522.

judgements, as the judgements would have to answer to the arguments that are raised in the case;[111] it would oblige the judges to take up responsibility and be accountable;[112] it would exclude the presumption that a judgement is based on communitarian reasons;[113] it would allow to define the authority of a decision;[114] it would serve legal scholarship;[115] and it would be necessary because the Court has no advocate-general, who normally presents the issues of a case and argues on the possible solutions.[116]

The competent minister and the majority of the parliament have never accepted those arguments. They see the disadvantages: they think separate opinions are dangerous because of the special communitarian situation in Belgium, the equal composition of the Court and the delicate federal cases that the Court has to decide;[117] Belgium does not have this tradition;[118] the objectivity of the debate should be safeguarded;[119] and there would be the risk that judges would give priority to their own reputation rather than to the reputation of the Court.[120]

The Belgian Constitutional Court is, together with the European Court of Justice,[121] one of the few constitutional courts that does not use separate opinions.[122] The majority of Belgian constitutional scholars and judges of the Constitutional Court are not in favour of separate opinions, because of the communitarian situation in Belgium.[123] I however think that it is not the communitarian situation that prohibits separate opinions for the constitutional judges, but the (French) legal tradition, which uses the Cartesian argumentation style. By using a more deliberative argumentation style in its decisions, the Constitutional Court would contribute to a constitutional dialogue, to its accountability and to its independence.[124] This deliberative argumentation style entails that the Constitutional

111 *Hand.* Senate 1982–83, 5 May 1983, n° 57, 1917.

112 *Parl.St.* Senate 1981–82, n° 246/2, 196 and 202; *Hand.* Chamber 1982–83, 2 June 1983, n° 81–82, 2416; *Hand.* Senate 1982–83, 27 April 1983, n° 52, 1802.

113 *Hand.* Chamber 1982–83, 2 June 1983, n° 81–82, 2416.

114 *Hand.* Senate 1982–83, 27 April 1983, n° 52, 1802.

115 *Hand.* Chamber 1982–83, 2 June 1983, n° 81–82, 2416; *Hand.* Senate 1982–83, 27 April 1983, n° 52, 1802.

116 *Hand.* Senate 1982–83, 27 April 1983, n° 52, 1802.

117 *Parl.St.* Senate 1981–82, n° 246/2, 195 and 202.

118 *Parl.St.* Senate 1981–82, n° 246/2, 202.

119 *Parl.St.* Senate 1981–82, n° 246/2, 197.

120 *Parl.St.* Senate 1981–82, n° 246/2, 196ff, 202ff and 223; *Hand.* Senate 1982–83, 5 May 1983, n° 57, 1917 and 26 April 1983, 1782.

121 Edward 1995, p 539–558; Weiler 2001, pp 8–9; Wouters 2001, p 346 and Korah 1997, pp 98–103.

122 Passaglia 2007, p 881.

123 Verdussen 2004, p 67.

124 Verdussen 2004, pp 66–67.

Court explains that the legal question can have various right solutions, but that, for such and such (legal and non-legal) arguments, the Constitutional Court has chosen for one solution. Because of the Cartesian argumentation style, together with the absence of separate opinions, makes the case law of the Belgian Constitutional Court somewhat opaque. It is difficult to know the real arguments that have led the constitutional judges to decide a case. This leads to questions about the accountability and the independence of the Belgian Constitutional Court.

2.6 Conclusion

Having in mind the threats to its independence a constitutional court can suffer, we conclude that the Belgian Constitutional Court is a strong, independent institution. Its existence, competences and composition are entrenched in strong legislation (the Constitution and the Special Act on the Constitutional Court). The Belgian Constitutional Court also enjoys normative and operational autonomy. The financial autonomy of the Constitutional Court is however not fully guaranteed in practice. Cuts in the dotation and a more extensive review on the finances of the Constitutional Court by the Chamber of Representatives limit the financial autonomy, more than the Special Act on the Constitutional Court allows. A great limitation on the financial autonomy threatens the independence of a constitutional court. The doctrine should therefore be vigilant towards the review and acts of the Chamber of Representatives.

The independence of the constitutional judges is also safeguarded by an appropriate appointment procedure, a non-renewable mandate for life and a strong protection against the removal from office. The appointment procedure gives a role to the Parliament and political parties, which as such does not limit the independence of the constitutional judge. Nevertheless, the appointment procedure could be ameliorated by the obligation to Parliament to organize a public hearing, before confirming the nomination of a candidate-judge. In this hearing, the members of Parliament could judge for themselves on the qualities of the candidate-judge. A public hearing would also give more media attention to the appointment procedure. This would enforce the constitutional dialogue. The democratic legitimacy and the independence of the constitutional judge would be strengthened.

Finally, I argue that allowing dissenting opinions at the Constitutional Court would enhance the independence of its judges and the accountability of the court. Its accountability could be reinforced, if the Constitutional Court would use a more deliberative argumentation style and would allow separate opinions. The nowadays used Cartesian argumentation style and the prohibition on separate opinions makes it sometimes difficult to know the real arguments that decided a case. The independence and legitimacy of a constitutional court demand however that there should be no secrecy on the real arguments of a judgement.

Acknowledgement I would specifically like to thank Mia Lozie for the great help regarding the translation of my contribution.

References

Alen A, Muylle K (2011) Handboek van het Belgisch Staatsrecht. Kluwer, Mechelen
Alleman R, Mazzone J (2010) The Case for Returning Politicians to the Supreme Court. Hastings L.J. 2010:1353–1406
Benda E et al (2012) Verfassungsprozessrecht: ein Lehr- und Handbuch. C.F. Müller, Heidelberg
Bishop TS et al (2006) Tips on Petitioning for and Opposing Certiorari in the U.S. Supreme Court. Litigation 34:26–3126
Bossuyt M, Leysen R, Renauld B (2011) Séparation des pouvoirs et indépendance des cours constitutionnelles et instances équivalentes - Rapport de la Cour constitutionnelle de Belgique. Conférence on Séparation des pouvoirs et indépendance des cours constitutionnelles et instances équivalentes, Rio de Janeiro, 16–18 January 2011
Carcassonne G (2008) Les membres du Conseil constitutionnel: 1958–2008. Colloque du Cinquantenaire du Conseil constitutionnel, Paris, 3 November 2008
Cartier E (2011) La récusation et le déport devant le Conseil constitutionnel: cote mal taillée ou réelle avancée. Petites Affiches 2011, (22) 34
Choper JH (1974) The Supreme Court and the Political Branches. Univ. Penns. L.R. 122:810–858
Clark ML (2010) Introducing a parliamentary confirmation process for new Supreme Court justices: its pros and cons, and lessons learned from the US experience. Public Law 2010:464–481
Courtoy C (2000) La formation et le renouvellement de la Cour d'Arbitrage de Belgique. CDPK 2000:538–542
Davis R (2005) Electing Justice, Fixing the Supreme Court Nomination Process. Oxford University Press, New York.
Debry JT (2010) La désignation et les attributions des présidents de la Cour constitutionnelle. In: Martens P (ed) Liège, Strasbourg, Bruxelles: parcours des droits de l'homme. Liber Amicorum Michel Melchior. Anthemis, Brussels, pp 49–71
Delpérée F (1988) Les juges constitutionnels. In: Belgique in X (ed) Annuaire international de justice constitutionnelle. Economica, Paris, pp 101–115
Delpérée F, Rasson-Roland A (1990) Recueil d'études sur la Cour d'Arbitrage 1980–1990. Bruylant, Brussels
Delva J (1991) Staatsrechtelijk profiel van het Belgisch Arbitragehof. TBP 1991, 69–90
Di Manno T (1994) Le Conseil constitutionnel et les moyens et conclusions soulevés d'office. Economica, Paris
Douglas W (1948) Dissent: A Safeguard of Democracy. J.AM. Judicature Society 32, 104–107
Edward D (1995) How the Court of Justice Works. E.L.Rev. 1995:539–558
Favoreu L, Gaïa P, Ghevontian R et al (2012) Droit constitutionnel 2012. Dalloz, Paris
Feyen S (2012) Afwijkende meningsuitingen in het Belgische Grondwettelijk Hof: mensenrechtelijk beschermd, wenselijk of gevaarlijk? In: Alen A, Theunis K (eds) Leuvense Staatsrechtelijke Standpunten. die Keure, Bruges, pp 227–288
Fuld SH (1962) The Voices of Dissent. Colum.L.Rev. 62:923–929
Hall KA (1999) The Oxford Guide to United States Supreme Court Decisions. Oxford University Press, New York

Henneuse R, Rosoux G (2006) L'indépendance des juges constitutionnels en Belgique: aspects institutionnels, aspects individuels. Séminaire international sur les 'garanties pour l'indépendance des juges constitutionnels', Bucharest, 23–24 November 2006
Jacquelot F (2009) L'organisation et le fonctionnement du Conseil constitutionnel par la loi organique et les règlements d''auto-organisation': de la dualité au dualisme. Les Petites Affiches 2009: 5–7
Kelsen H (1942) Judicial Review of Legislation. A Comparative Study of the Austrian and the American Constitution. JOP 1942:183–200
Kischel K (2013) Party, Pope, and Politics? The Election of German Constitutional Court Justices in Comparative Perspective. Int. J. Const. L. 11:962–980
Korah V (1997) Tetra Pak II - Lack of Reasoning in Court's Judgement. ECLR 1997:98–103
Kovács K (2013) Keeping the guardian under control: the case of Hungary. 'Conference on the theoretical and practical aspects of reviewing the constitutionality of the constitutional norms', Batumi, Georgia, 29–30 June 2013
Martens P (2013) Solitude du juge et cohérence du droit. JT 2013:805–810
Mastor W (2001) Les opinions séparées des juges constitutionnels
Moorhead R (1952) The 1952 Ross Prize Essay: Concurring and Dissenting Opinions. A.B.A. J. 1952:821–824
Murray Ch (1999) Who Chooses Constitutional Court Judges? S. African L.J. 1999:865–868
Passaglia P (2007) Présidentialisme versus collégialité? À la recherche des modèles d'organisation des cours constitutionnels" In: Renouveau du droit constitutionnel. Mélanges en l'honneur de Louis Favoreu. Dalloz, Paris, pp 875–885
Prignon B (2011) Le secret du délibéré. Ius & Actores 109–116
Rasson-Roland A (2004) Le renouvellement des juges de la Cour d'Arbitrage. In: Rasson-Roland A et al (eds) La Cour d'Arbitrage vingt ans après. Bruylant, Brussels, pp 21–35
Robert J, Rousseau D (1998) Neuf années au Conseil constitutionnel. RDP 1998:1748–1770
Rousseau D (1998) La justice constitutionnelle en Europe. Montchrestien, Paris
Shapiro SM et al (2013) Supreme Court Practice, 10th edn. Bloomberg BNA, Arlington
Sohier J (1986) 'Vote secret' ou 'vote dissident'. In: Mélanges offert à Raymond Vander Elst, Nemesis, Brussels, pp 755–768
Szymczak D (2006) La Convention européenne des droits de l'homme et le juge constitutionnel national. Bruylant, Brussels
Thomas J (2010) L'indépendance du Conseil constitutionnel. Fondation Varenne, Paris
Umbach D et al (2005) Bundesverfassungsgerichtsgesetz. C.F. Müller, Heidelberg
Velaers J (1990) Van Arbitragehof tot Grondwettelijk Hof. Maklu, Antwerp
Verdussen M (2004) Les douze juges. Éditions Labor, Brussels
Verdussen M (2012) Justice constitutionnelle. Larcier, Brussels
Verdussen M (2013) Le mode de composition de la Cour constitutionnelle est-il légitime? RBDC 2013:67–86
Voss E (1992) Dissent: Sign of a Healthy Court. Ariz. St.L.J. 24:643–686
Weiler J (2001) Europe 2000 - The constitutional agenda. An outline. In: Kellerman AE et al (eds) The Constitutional Impact of Enlargement. Kluwer Law international, The Hague, pp 3–14
Wouters J (2001) Institutional and Constitutional Challenges for the European Union: Reflections in the Light of the Treaty of Nice. E.L.Rev. 2001:342–356
Zähle K (2011) Die Ausschließung und Ablehnung eines Richters nach §§ 18, 19 BVerfGG in der Rechtsprechung des Bundesverfassungsgerichts. AöR 2011:174–204
Zurn C (2007) Deliberative Democracy and the Institutions of Judicial Review. Cambridge University Press, Cambridge

Zweigert K (1968) Empfielht es sich, die Bekanntgabe der abweichende Meinungen des überstimmten Richters (Dissenting Opinion). In: Verhandlungen des siebenundvierzigsten deutschen Juristentages. C.H. Beck Verlagsbuchhandlung, Munich, pp D1–D59

Evelyne Maes is attorney and professor in constitutional law. In her doctoral research, she combined her interests in constitutional law and legal theory by researching what the rule of law demands regarding the competences and composition of and the procedure before constitutional courts. She teaches non-discrimination law at the University of Liège and a seminar in legal theory at Université Saint-Louis. Her main research topics are federalism and the principles of legality and separation of powers.

Chapter 3
Judicial Independence and Democratic Accountability: The Function and Legitimacy of the German Federal Constitutional Court

Anja Seibert-Fohr

Contents

Abstract This chapter examines the legitimation of the German Federal Constitutional Court. It shows that the Court's function and its legitimation are intimately bound up with one another. Balancing democracy and the rule of law in the appointment of the judges depends crucially on the Court's special tasks. In this respect, one must take into account that a court's function is by no means static but

A. Seibert-Fohr (✉)
University of Heidelberg, Heidelberg, Germany
e-mail: sekretariat.seibert-fohr@jurs.uni-heidelberg.de

Hirsch Ballin, Van der Schyff & Stremler (eds.), *European Yearbook of Constitutional Law 2019*, European Yearbook of Constitutional Law 1,
https://doi.org/10.1007/978-94-6265-359-7_3

rather is subject to development. Such changes are reflected accordingly in the judges' appointment and their legitimation.

Keywords appointment procedure · democratic legitimation · functional legitimation · German Federal Constitutional Court · judicial independence · judicial selection · legal development

3.1 Introduction

Since *Marbury v. Madison*, constitutional jurisdiction has oscillated in the constant tension between democracy and the rule of law.[1] On the one hand, it is in the interest of a constitutional system to submit the legislator's acts to a constitutional review. On the other hand, this form of review fundamentally calls into question the legislator's will as a democratically legitimized power.[2] This poses weighty questions of legitimacy for constitutional jurisprudence. For when courts oversee the compliance with the constitutional order, the question arises in turn: *quis custodiet ipsos custodes?*[3] To whom must the constitutional judges answer as the supervisors of liberal democracy? And even more importantly: from what source do the judges derive their legitimation? After all, they too must be appointed to their office in some way.[4]

If one emphasizes the principle of judicial independence in this context, then a lot speaks for an appointment dissociated from the other powers at first. But if one highlights the need for democratic legitimation, then the appointment of judges necessitates a tie to the democratically legitimized state bodies. None of these demands is convincing in its absoluteness. If one left the judicial appointment up to the third branch of government alone, then a democratic legitimation equal to the power of the court would be lacking. If one prioritized solely the democratic

[1] US Supreme Court, *Marbury v. Madison*, 5 U.S. 1 Cranch 137 (1803). For the tension between judicial autonomy and accountability, see Kommers 2001, p 151; Guarnieri and Pederzoli 2002, p 150. For the counter-majoritan difficulty, see Bickel 1962. But see Dahl 1957; Friedman 2009; Ginsburg 2003; Hirschl 2004. According to Cassese, the stereotype that opposes justice to democracy is simplistic and should be reconsidered in the light of a more careful research that takes into account that judicial review is subject to intrinsic limitations, such as the missing control over its caseload, the case or controversy requirement, and the adversarial procedure. Cassese 2011, pp 16, 24. Habermas argues that judicial review should protect the integrity of the democratic process. Habermas 1992, pp 292–348.

[2] For the ambivalence of judicial review as a safeguard for and constraint on democracy, see Lübbe-Wolff 2016, p 19.

[3] Juvenal ± 115, Satire VI, lines 347–348.

[4] For a comprehensive comparative account of the legitimation of constitutional court judges, see Seibert-Fohr forthcoming 2019.

legitimation, however, then the independence of constitutional jurisprudence would be called into question because of the periodic reelection of the judges. Judges would have to fear for their reelection during their term, which would entail the risk of influencing their jurisprudence.

This demonstrates that the appointment of constitutional judges vacillates between the same poles as constitutional jurisdiction as such, namely in the zone of conflict between democracy and the rule of law. In world-wide comparison, there are thus hardly any examples of the extremes delineated here.[5] Rather, as a rule, one tries to find the middle ground that makes possible a democratic legitimation without calling the judges' independence into question *per se*. The various constitutional systems answer the question of how to balance this tension differently, however. In fact, the different modes of appointment display significant differences. While in Great Britain, for instance, where the British Supreme Court among other things also exercises constitutional powers, the independence of judges has priority,[6] in the United States, democratic legitimation is particularly emphasized in appointing the US Supreme Court judges.[7] The nomination by the President and the Senate's confirmation transmits this legitimation.

Of course, these examples involve systems of integrated constitutional jurisdiction. In contrast, the Federal Republic of Germany offers an example of a system of specialized constitutional jurisdiction with the Federal Constitutional Court.[8] This too is based on its own model of legitimation, which seeks to balance the tension between democracy and the rule of law in its very own way.[9] In the essay that follows, I will therefore examine the legitimation of the Federal German constitutional judges, in order to demonstrate how the German constitutional system deals with the tension between democracy and the rule of law.[10] In the process, I will show that the Court's function and its legitimation are intimately bound up with one another. For in each case, balancing the conflict of the stated principles in the appointment of the judges depends crucially on the special tasks of a constitutional court. In this respect, one must take into account that a court's function is by no means static but rather is subject to development. Such changes are reflected accordingly in the judges' appointment and their legitimation.

---

5 Brewer-Carías 2006, pp 153, 178–180.

6 Malleson and Moules 2010, p 206; Oliver 2003, p 331; Kentridge 2003, p 62; Stevens 2002, p 143.

7 Resnik 2005, pp 593–594; McGinnis and Rappaport 2010, p 42; Marshall 2005, pp 536–537.

8 Kommers and Miller 2012; Vanberg 2004.

9 According to Esward Blankenburg, the German judiciary constitutes an institution that emphasized autonomy from politics at the expense of democratic legitimation. Blankenburg 1996, p 249. But see Kommers 2001, p 131.

10 For the historical development of constitutional review in Germany, see Möllers 2014, pp 4–5.

3.2 The Function of the Federal Constitutional Court Over the Course of Time

Vested with the power of abstract and concrete judicial review of the formal and substantive compatibility of federal law or *Länder* law with the Basic Law and of the compatibility of *Länder* law with other federal law, the Federal Constitutional Court has a special status in Germany.[11] Its jurisdiction extends essentially from constitutional complaints to abstract and concrete judicial review to federal disputes and *Organstreitverfahren*. According to Section 1 Federal Constitutional Court Act, the Constitutional Court is not only an independent federal court but also a federal constitutional organ. Thus, it has a dual function within the constitutional structure.[12]

The Federal Constitutional Court is independent of all other courts. Although jurisdiction concerning the constitution does not lie exclusively in its hands, it is the only organ empowered to declare a law unconstitutional. Even though as a result, the Federal Constitutional Court has the power to review the judgments of other courts with authority, insofar as they deal with questions of the compatibility of laws with the constitution, it does not act as a general court of appeal.[13]

In its role as the supreme judicial body in constitutional matters, the Constitutional Court specializes in applying and interpreting the Basic Law. Due to the general terms of the Basic Law, the Constitutional Court is called upon to interpret and specify its meaning. Because it performs adjudicatory functions, the Constitutional Court is part of the third branch, like other federal courts. Yet since its jurisdiction is limited to constitutional matters, it differs from the other courts of the German judiciary. At the same time, the Constitutional Court has competences that exceed its general judicial function. As a constitutional organ, the Court maintains for itself the role of the supreme guardian of the constitution. Its mandate is to ensure that all other bodies comply with the Basic Law. All other institutions are bound by its decisions, which can even have the force of law. The court is not a political constitutional organ, but, as it gives meaning to the existing constitutional law, its decisions have a strong impact on German politics.[14]

The Constitutional Court's power of judicial review illustrates its prominent position in the area of constitutional adjudication. Anchored in the Basic Law, the power of the Federal Constitutional Court to decide on the conformity of statutes with the Basic Law set an important course for the Court's relationship with the legislative branch, already at the time when the constitution took effect.[15] This

[11] For an overview, see Grimm 2017.

[12] For a critique, see Möllers 2014, p 20.

[13] For the relationship between the Federal Constitutional Court and other courts, see Möllers 2014, pp 8–9, 20.

[14] Möllers gives three examples for the Court's influence on the political branches. Möllers 2014, pp 10–13.

[15] For the relationship, see Kirchhof 1998, p 5.

mapped out possible divergences from the beginning and established the tension between majoritarian democracy and constitutionalism.[16]

Yet although this course was set, the function of the Federal Constitutional Court in the federal German constitutional system cannot be determined statically.[17] Instead, its role demonstrates a dynamic development in the history of the Federal Republic.[18] Its function was in no way comprehensively pre-determined with the adoption of the Basic Law. During the drafting of the Basic Law in the Parliamentary Council, there was already a widespread consciousness of the fact that the Court would not only take on exclusively judicial functions. But the relationship to politics remained contested, with the consequence that the regulations of the Basic Law represented a compromise that was deliberately kept open to development. With the Basic Law's entry into force, the scope of the Federal Constitutional Court's tasks was thus only sketched out and was subsequently left to legislation and the Court itself.

The Court's function was essentially determined by its own initiative and by the reaction of the other powers.[19] The openness of the Federal Constitutional Court Act made it possible for the Court to position itself early on as a state body of equal stature. Thus, already in early judgments, the Court claimed its independence and the power to make the final decision in constitutional questions. For instance, it stipulated in 1952 that judicial review must prioritize 'the task of the Federal Constitutional Court as guardian of the constitution'.[20] The role of the Court as the instance of final decision in constitutional questions was deduced from the primacy of the constitution stipulated in Article 1 para 3 Basic Law and from the obligation of government powers to follow the Basic Law according to Article 20 para 3 Basic Law. Consequently, since then, the Court claims supremacy of its jurisprudence.[21] Interacting with the other state bodies, the Court obtained a central position in the Federal German power structure in the course of its jurisprudential activity and lastingly shaped the state and the legal system of the Federal Republic.[22]

---

16 Lübbe-Wolff 2016.

17 For the special role of the Federal Constitutional Court, see Jestaedt et al. 2011. For the historical development of constitutional review in Germany, see Möllers 2014.

18 For a detailed account of its jurisprudence, see Kommers and Miller 2012.

19 Möllers 2014, pp 6–7.

20 BVerfGE 1, 184, 195–196.

21 Lepsius 2011, p 163.

22 BVerfGE 1, 208; 2, 1; 6, 32; 6, 309; 7, 198; 123, 267 (for an English version of this decision, see http://www.bverfg.de/e/es20090630_2bve000208en.html. Accessed 19 July 2018).

3.2.1 *Transformation of the Legal System on the Basis of Fundamental Rights*

One of the Court's central functions lay and still lies today in maintaining fundamental rights.[23] The constitutional complaint adopted in the Federal Constitutional Court Act in 1951 soon developed into the most frequent kind of action.[24] It enabled the Court to illuminate the diverse aspects of the legal system from the perspective of constitutional law. The groundbreaking significance of the fundamental rights jurisprudence for the entire legal system already emerged in the *Elfes* judgment, which the Federal Constitutional Court made in 1957.[25] At the time, the plaintiff was refused the extension of his passport, and so his departure from Germany had been made impossible. In its review of his constitutional complaint, the Federal Constitutional Court interpreted the right of personality in Article 2 para 1 Basic Law broadly, so that this also protected the general freedom of action and the plaintiff's freedom to depart.

With the derivation of this general freedom of action, the Court instituted a complete protection of fundamental rights, for there is hardly a state action imaginable that would not touch upon the individual's freedom to act.[26] This jurisprudence, which made Article 2 Basic Law into an umbrella right, was maintained later despite critical voices.[27] The jurisprudence on the general freedom of action opened a broad scope of application for the Federal Constitutional Court for its own decisions. The Court thus gained the power of comprehensively reviewing legality, without the particular infringement as such having to show a special relation to the plaintiff.[28] For since an intervention in the general freedom of action may only take place on the basis of a constitutionally issued statute, an unlawful intervention in the general freedom of action can itself result from violations of formal provisions establishing legislative power or procedure.[29] Interpreted in this way, the Basic Law's regulatory breadth enables the Court to have a comprehensive power of review. This provides it with the basis for an extensive review of legality of legislation, administration, and courts.

Beyond this, the *Lüth* case of 1958 set the course in a fundamental way.[30] The proclamation of fundamental rights as an objective value system (*objektive Wertordnung*), which applies to all areas of law including private law, and its radiating effect on all legal relations including procedural law penetrated every area

---

23 See Papier 2009, p 1007.

24 For statistical data, see http://www.bundesverfassungsgericht.de/DE/Verfahren/Jahresstatistiken/jahresstatistiken_node.html. Accessed 19 July 2018; see also Limbach 1999, p 8.

25 BVerfGE 6, 32, 36.

26 Kahl 2000; Kröger 1998, p 94.

27 BVerfGE 64, 208; 80, 137, 154; 91, 176, 177; 92, 191, 196.

28 Möllers 2014, p 11.

29 BVerfGE 44, 308, 313; 13, 237, 239; 68, 193, 216–217.

30 For a summary of this case, see Limbach 1999, p 11.

of life.[31] With the Court's help, the German constitutional system thus quickly unfolded into a value system with substantive stipulations for the entire legal and societal order.[32] The Court held an important if not exclusive function in developing the free liberal state. In this respect, it acted not only in the capacity of review but also of development on the basis of constitutional law. Essentially, this capacity resulted from the value orientation of the constitutional system founded on the Basic Law, in combination with the Court's corresponding authority of interpretation. Since then, the Court participates in the authority and normativity of the constitution, whose effectiveness and intensity it determines itself.[33] Due to the Basic Law's comprehensive guarantee of the rule of law, in combination with the broadly conceived jurisdiction of the Court, there will hardly be a case that could not be presented to the Court for a decision.[34] The significance of the judgments thus exceeds the individual dispute resolution.[35]

This can be explained historically first and foremost, for the Basic Law was the beginning of a fresh start, which necessitated a transformation of the entire state.[36] With the central participation of the Federal Constitutional Court in building a free democratic basic order and the expansion of the Basic Law's scope of application in the *Elfes*[37] and *Lüth*[38] judgments as well as the adoption of positive fundamental rights dimensions, the Court exercised a historical function of transformation, in contrast for instance to the British Supreme Court.[39] This function was sustained by the wish to help fundamental rights achieve comprehensive effectiveness. In this way, fundamental rights aided the Court in transforming the entire legal system.[40]

After the Court had positioned itself in this way in the structure of state powers, it fully exhausted the frequently invoked function as 'guardian of the constitution', so that subsequently, the question was posed again and again – and arises to the current day – whether the Court has not by now become the master of the constitution.[41] At any rate, the entire legal and societal system was lastingly shaped by its jurisprudence.[42]

---

[31] BVerfGE 7, 198.

[32] Limbach 1999, p 13.

[33] See, e.g., BVerfGE 123, 267, 434.

[34] Heidebach 2014, p 153.

[35] Limbach 1999, p 10.

[36] The Federal Constitutional Court was the answer to the failure of democratic self-government after the experience of National Socialism. See Möllers 2014, p 5.

[37] BVerfGE 6, 32, 36.

[38] BVerfGE 7, 198.

[39] Wahl 2004, p 756, mn 14.

[40] Würtenberger 1998, p 60.

[41] Lepsius 2011, p 180.

[42] Limbach 1999, pp 14–19; see, e.g., BVerfGE 4, 7; 39, 1; 121, 317; 125, 175 (http://www.bverfg.de/e/ls20100209_1bvl000109en.html. Accessed 19 July 2018); 128, 326 (http://www.bverfg.de/e/rs20110504_2bvr236509en.html. Accessed 26 July 2018); 133, 377.

3.2.2 *Legal Development on the Basis of State Duties*

Constitutional jurisprudence advanced increasingly into the domain of legal development by adopting positive dimensions promoting fundamental rights and positive state duties. With the acknowledgment of positive fundamental rights dimensions, which imposes positive duties of protection and participation on the state,[43] and the interpretation of the principle of the social state, following the guarantee of human dignity, the Federal Constitutional Court has contributed to state duties no longer being limited to the protection of order and safety but also having an effect in numerous ways on the economic, social, and cultural life of society.[44]

While in principle, the Federal Constitutional Court grants the legislator freedom of design in social legislation,[45] the latter is nevertheless restricted due to constitutional stipulations.[46] This restriction of legislative discretion is amplified, because fundamental rights are taken into account as a measure of review. The fundamental right that guarantees a subsistence minimum compatible with human dignity, deduced from Article 1 para 1 in conjunction with Article 20 para 1 Basic Law, justifies the relevant judicial review.[47] Thus, the recourse to human dignity extends the principle of the social state with a subjective-legal component. The result is the adoption of an individual, directly constitutional entitlement to a subsistence minimum compatible with human dignity.[48]

In this way, the mandate of Article 20 para 1 Basic Law for the legislature to secure a subsistence minimum worthy of human dignity for everyone is actionable for any concerned party. The implementation of the social-state principle, which, according to the Federal Constitutional Court, requires the legislator to concretize and continuously update provisions in order to adapt the necessary benefits to the changing level of development of the public and the living conditions,[49] is subject to judicial review. To this extent, the Court asserts itself as guarantor of a social order worthy of human dignity following its own definition. Möllers even speaks of an 'agenda-setting role, in which the Court not only reacts to legislative decisions in its review, but also initiates them.'[50] Here lies an essential difference for instance from British understanding, where the constitution, in so far as it is recognized as an instrument of law, is at most viewed as a normative framework for political processes.[51] The US Constitution does

[43] For the Abortion Cases as an example, see Möllers 2014, pp 10–11.

[44] Limbach 1999, pp 13–14.

[45] BVerfGE 125, 175, 222; 123, 267, 362–363; 100, 271, 284.

[46] BVerfGE 45, 376, 387.

[47] BVerfGE 125, 175, 222.

[48] *Ibid.*

[49] *Ibid.*

[50] Möllers 2014, p 11; Möllers 2013, p 138.

[51] Loughlin 2007, p 244, mn 55; see Feldman 2005.

not provide any state goals here either and is limited substantively to fundamental liberal rights.[52]

3.2.3 The Federal Constitutional Court and the Division of Powers

The Federal Constitutional Court has shaped the order of the Federal Republic of Germany not only in substantive but also in institutional terms.[53] The Court has contributed to forming both the legal division of powers and the political order.[54] This applies particularly to the federal system. In Article 93 para 1 no. 3 Basic Law, the Basic Law assigns the Federal Constitutional Court a comprehensive competence to decide all differences in opinion about rights and duties of the federation and the states. With the argument that it is its duty to clarify what is lawful,[55] the Federal Constitutional Court claimed a central function for itself in the constellation of the federal bodies that clarify legal disputes between the federation and the states. So while the substantive development function of the Federal Constitutional Court manifests itself in the domain of fundamental rights protection and state duties, the Court performs the function of a state court (*Staatsgerichtshof*) in relation to the federal-state order. To a greater degree than in fundamental rights protection, this function resembles that of a referee.

On the whole, the Court occupies a central position in the Federal German structure of the division of powers. Due to the already portrayed development of jurisprudence in the areas of fundamental rights and of the determination of state goals, the Federal Constitutional Court's role in relation to the political powers has repeatedly been perceived and criticized as a force advancing into the areas of competence of the legislative and executive branches.[56] Often, the Federal

---

[52] Epstein and Walker 2016, p 7; Jackson and Tushnet 2006, p 1651.

[53] BVerfGE 62, 1. According to Möllers, the court second-guessed the political attitudes of the members of parliament, see Möllers 2014, pp 11–12.

[54] Lübbe-Wolff 2016, pp 27–28; see BVerfGE 2, 1; 5, 85; 144, 20 (http://www.bverfg.de/e/bs20170117_2bvb000113en.html. 16 August 2018); 36, 1; 73, 339; 82, 316, 320; 82, 322; 89, 38; 89, 155; 108, 34 (http://www.bverfg.de/e/qs20030325_2bvq001803.html. Accessed 9 August 2018); 123, 267; 130, 318 (http://www.bverfg.de/e/es20120228_2bve000811en.html. Accessed 9 August 2018); 131, 152 (http://www.bverfg.de/e/es20120619_2bve000411en.html. Accessed 16 August 2018); 134, 366 (http://www.bverfg.de/e/rs20140114_2bvr272813en.html, Accessed 2 August 2018); 135, 317 (http://www.bverfg.de/e/rs20140318_2bvr139012en.html. Accessed 26 July 2018); 142, 123 (http://www.bverfg.de/e/rs20160621_2bvr272813en.html. Accessed 26 July 2018); BVerfG, order for reference of the Second Senate of 18 July 2017 – 2 BvR 859/15, 2 BvR 1651/15, 2 BvR 2006/15, 2 BvR 980/16.

[55] BVerfGE 6, 309, 325.

[56] Würtenberger 1998, p 69; Lepsius 2008, p 112.

Constitutional Court provides the legislative branch with detailed specifications for the constitutional development of statutes.[57] Sometimes, when a statute is declared invalid because of unconstitutionality, it provides interim regulations itself until a new statute is passed.[58]

This also crucially distinguishes it from the US Supreme Court. In the United States, the Supreme Court participates in the system of mutual checks and balances and functions as a counterbalance to the other powers without standing in a relation of superiority to them. Instead of the conflict between the public powers, which shapes American constitutional life, in the Federal Republic, there is the constitutional jurisprudence – relevant in many domains – of the Federal Constitutional Court as the ultimate deciding authority.[59] Political dispute, as it is carried out above all in the Parliament in the United Kingdom, is supplanted in Germany by the substantive stipulations of the Basic Law in the interpretation of the Federal Constitutional Court.

3.2.4 *The Role of the Federal Constitutional Court in Relation to the European Union*

In the European integration process, the Federal Constitutional Court has not taken on the role of mediator between the levels but rather asserts itself over the European Union.[60] In this context, the Court has also been described as guardian of integration and its limits.[61] Concerning the question what role the Federal Constitutional Court plays with regard to European integration, the Court reserved the guarantee of fundamental rights protection vis-à-vis European acts of public authority early on.[62] After the *Solange II* decision, it only makes use of this for general problems, however, when the European fundamental rights protection falls short of the fundamental rights standard provided by the Basic Law.[63] Added to this is the legal figure of the *ultra vires* act (*ausbrechender Rechtsakt*), developed in the

---

57 BVerfGE 93, 181; Möllers 2014, pp 10–11.

58 See BVerfGE 24, 300; 50, 290, 335; 56, 54, 78; 72, 330, 333; 88, 203, 209–211, 270–272; 93, 386, 402–403; 100, 104, 106.

59 Lepsius 2011, p 246.

60 According to Möllers, the Court's approach to the European integration process is 'quite activist and relatively unusual'. Möllers 2014, p 12. He refers *inter alia* to a case concerning the European rescue mechanism in which the Court strengthened parliamentary participation and effectively blocked the installation of European bonds. He concludes that the Court 'substantiates the political procedure to allow the Court to intervene in decisions that have a degree of political legitimacy of their own.' *Ibid*., p 13.

61 Gusy and Kutscher 2011, p 136.

62 BVerfGE 73, 339.

63 BVerfGE 37, 271.

Maastricht judgment, which allows the Federal Constitutional Court to perform an *ultra vires* review concerning the European Union.[64]

With the *Lisbon* judgment, the review function of the Federal Constitutional Court regarding the European integration process has been extended by another aspect: the identity review.[65] On this basis, the Court evaluates whether Union legal acts violate the values of the Basic Law that establish identity pursuant to Article 79 para 3 Basic Law, meaning in particular the untouchable core content of fundamental rights (Article 1 para 1 Basic Law) and the constitutional principles of Article 20 Basic Law (*inter alia* democracy and the rule of law). Since in transferring competences to the Union, the German legislator may not restrict these constitutional guarantees in favor of the Union, the Union's acts of public authority and measures based upon them may not infringe these guarantees either, according to the Court.

As guardian of this constitutional identity, the Court so also positions itself in relation to the other bodies of constituted power. It opposes a development which increasingly questioned the importance of the German Constitution due to the superimposition of European on German law. The *Lisbon* judgment restituted the significance of the Basic Law, which produced an effect not only in the German but also in the entire European context. The Federal Constitutional Court is accorded the power of final decision in questions of the unalterable constitutional base, over which it claims the sovereignty of definition. Despite the openness to European law, the Court claims a final decision reserve, which is not restricted to a narrowly defined function of review alone but also shows features of legislative creation, due to the Court's sovereignty of definition in relation to constitutional identity.

3.2.5 The Mediating Function of the Federal Constitutional Court

As the previous remarks demonstrate, one would not do justice either to the original conception of the Parliamentary Council or to the actual performance of duties and the role of the Court within the federal German state and governmental system if one reduced the portrayal of the Federal Constitutional Court's jurisprudence exclusively to the application of law.[66] Its *sui generis* role is indisputable.[67] It emerges in the intimate connection between legal review and legal development in the Court's jurisprudence.

---

[64] BVerfGE 89, 155.

[65] BVerfGE 123, 267, 353–354.

[66] See also Möllers 2011, p 350.

[67] Leibholz 1957, pp 120–121.

The overlap of the review and the development functions emerges not only in the domain of fundamental rights protection, but also in other areas of duties that the Court performs, starting with the guarantee of the social order, to defending constitutional identity, whose meaning it increasingly develops, to the function of democratic securing,[68] in which the Court became a catalyst for the development of the democratic system.[69] For legislation, the Federal Constitutional Court's jurisprudence has taken over the function of catalyst or supervisor in other domains of regulation as well.[70]

With this basic conception, which does not only apply the law, one can explain why the Court ultimately performs a balancing function aimed at equilibrium and moderation in considering the positions relevant to the dispute, in particular in politically contested cases.[71] The idea of this substantive equilibrium[72] manifests itself in different ways, be it in applying the principle of proportionality, which aims to balance colliding interests, or in producing a practical concordance in the ambit of fundamental rights,[73] in applying the social-state principle or deriving federal loyalty, which demands mutual consideration and assigns the Federal Constitutional Court a mediating role. Procedurally, the idea of balance appears for instance in the Court's decision to grant transitional periods and refrain from declaring a statute unconstitutional.[74] Here, the Court seeks not only to create a procedural balance in the sense of an equilibrium of the various actors; rather, substantive balance is the ultimate goal. This balance is an essential reason for the legitimacy of the Federal Constitutional Court. For it founds its acceptance, and so its authority, on the ability to move substantially in the framework of a presumed social fundamental consensus and so to grant the constitutional system stability.[75]

The idea of balance ultimately also describes the Federal Constitutional Court's relationship to the European courts. Where the European Court of Human Rights and the European Court are concerned, the Court tries to achieve this balance by referring to the constitutional commitment to international and to European law.[76] In this way, it is able to take up a mediating position despite the reserved competence of final decision. This mediating stance only threatens confrontation, but in

---

[68] BVerfGE 2, 1; 40, 296; 80, 188; 84, 304; 6, 84; 95, 335; 99, 1.

[69] Bryde 2006, pp 324–326.

[70] BVerfGE 10, 59; 12, 205; 25, 167; 33, 303; 65, 1; 98, 218; 120, 274 (http://www.bverfg.de/e/rs20080227_1bvr037007en.html. Accessed 19 July 2018); 133, 59 (http://www.bverfg.de/e/ls20130219_1bvl000111en.html. Accessed 19 July 2018).

[71] Schneider 1987, p 312.

[72] Würtenberger 1998, p 58.

[73] BVerfGE 93, 1, 21.

[74] Schneider 1987, pp 308–309, 310–311.

[75] Gusy and Kutscher 2011, p 133.

[76] BVerfGE 126, 286 (http://www.bverfg.de/e/rs20100706_2bvr266106en.html. Accessed 26 July 2018).

the application of set rules acts more considerately than it may initially appear.[77] Ultimately, this corresponds to a practice that shapes the Federal Constitutional Court's jurisprudence as a whole. While the development of standards often seems categorical and excessive,[78] this is not true to the same degree of their concrete legal application, which is exercised more moderately. While the Court continues to claim the competence of the final decision, in practice it confronts the political powers more rarely than one might think after reading the part on standards, especially in the politically sensitive areas of state organization.[79]

3.3 Personal, Substantive, and Institutional Legitimation

If one compares the central function of the Federal Constitutional Court with its personal, special, and institutional legitimation,[80] it is scarcely surprising that the personal legitimation of the judges plays a central role. The legitimation conveyed in the figure of the judge (personal legitimation) supplements the institutional and substantive legitimation transmitted by the Basic Law. Due to the broad scope of interpretation the Basic Law alone would scarcely legitimate the Court's jurisprudence. The function of development claimed by the Federal Constitutional Court requires a further basis for legitimation, which is essentially transmitted by democratically legitimated bodies.[81]

In contrast, the Constitutional Court enjoys a great deal of independence, once the judges have been appointed. As a constitutional organ, the Federal Constitutional Court is structurally largely independent of the other branches and organs.[82] It is equal to and independent of other constitutional organs such as the *Bundestag* (Federal Parliament), *Bundesrat* (Federal Council), *Bundespräsident* (Federal President) and the *Bundesregierung* (Federal Government). The Federal Constitutional Court is not subordinate to any ministry, either, because its organization is based on self-administration. Nevertheless, the Federal Constitutional Court is interrelated with other branches of government and state organs that focus on justice-related issues.

---

[77] BVerfGE 126, 286; 111, 307 (http://www.bverfg.de/e/rs20041014_2bvr148104en.html. Accessed 12 July 2018).

[78] Lepsius 2011, p 158.

[79] See, e.g., BVerfGE 62, 1; 114, 107; 114, 121 (http://www.bverfg.de/e/es20050825_2bve000405en.html. Accessed 28 August 2018).

[80] For the Court's institutional legitimacy, see Möllers 2014, pp 22, 24.

[81] See also Heidebach 2014, p 153.

[82] See Möllers 2014, p 7.

3.3.1 The Personal Legitimation of the Constitutional Judges

During the deliberations in the Parliamentary Council, the problem arose in shaping personal legitimation how to guarantee judicial independence with simultaneous democratic accountability.[83] In this process, the particularity of constitutional jurisdiction was recognized from the start and taken into account in shaping the parameters of legitimation.

3.3.1.1 Election of the Judges

Although the necessary independence of the constitutional judges was recognized, in view of the Court's meaningful role in the constitutional life of the Federal Republic, it was decided overall that the bodies of the *Bundestag* and the *Bundesrat* would transmit legitimation, hence opting for a distinctly democratic legitimation. The *Bundestag* and the *Bundesrat* have the power to elect the constitutional judges. They thus decide on the personal composition of the Court, which is of utmost importance for the performance of its interpretative function. Accordingly, it is not only the judges' qualifications in judicial specialization that is considered when selecting the Federal Constitutional Court's judges. Rather, their legitimation has always been shaped by the political process of the election of the judges. The constitutional judges' special function explains the difference from the legitimation of the judges in other courts.[84]

Whereas Article 94 para 1 sent 2 of the Basic Law prescribes that an equal number of judges be elected by the *Bundestag* and *Bundesrat*, it does not indicate how the election procedure is structured nor does it specify the relevant qualification criteria for the candidates. Article 94 para 2 of the Basic Law delegates this task to the legislator instead.[85] The *Bundestag* fulfilled this mandate by adopting the Federal Constitutional Court Act (FCCA) in 1951. Sections 2 to 7a FCCA contain the key provisions for the appointment of judges.[86]

The election of judges is a political process, which has been criticized because of its lack of transparency.[87] Section 6 para 1 FCCA sets forth that judges must be elected by secret ballot by the plenary of the *Bundestag* upon proposal by the selection committee. After the committee has made its proposal, the plenary of the *Bundestag* elects a candidate with a two-thirds majority in accordance with

[83] Niclauß 2015, p 193.

[84] Voßkuhle 2018, Article 94 mn 8.

[85] For the selection of Federal Constitutional Court's judges, see, e.g., Kommers 2001, pp 148–150; Maunz 2018, Article 94 mn 14, 18.

[86] For a general description of the selection process to the Federal Constitutional Court, see Clark 1988, pp 1826–1829.

[87] Heidebach 2014, p 158.

Section 6 para 1 sent 2 FCCA. With respect to the *Bundesrat*, Section 7 FCCA also provides that the justices are elected by this chamber with a two-thirds majority. The judges are thus legitimated partly on the basis of the principle of parliamentary democracy and partly on the basis of federal democracy. According to Section 9 Federal Constitutional Court Act, the President and Vice-President of the Constitutional Court are elected alternately by the *Bundestag* and the *Bundesrat* in a political process too. This is a distinctive feature of the German system, as in many other systems the court president is elected by her or his fellow judges.

Already in drafting the Federal Constitutional Court Act, it was clear that due to the crucial role of the political bodies in the judicial election, the selection of judges would be influenced by other considerations in addition to the criteria of specialized qualifications. Accordingly, the Act stipulates that the Court is composed of professional judges and judges with other work experiences. In this way, the appointment of judges has reflected from the start that the Federal Constitutional Court is not merely a court. Since three judges of each panel (*Senat*) must be elected from among the judges of the Supreme Federal Courts, it is still guaranteed that the judicial experience plays a central role in finding justice.[88] What is more, all judges must prove that they are qualified for judicial office. Thus, it is a court composed only of lawyers. This emphasizes the normativity of the Basic Law and its interpretation, which is guided by legal methodology.[89]

Because of the central role of the *Bundesrat* and *Bundestag* in the judicial appointment, political considerations, guided by the party affiliation or the party proximity of the candidates, determine their selection, in addition to their legal qualification. It was acknowledged early on that the politically shaped appointment ensured that the judges would show an understanding for the political powers.[90] Yet already in developing the Federal Constitutional Court Act in 1950, it was largely agreed that judicial appointment would be designed so that the Federal Constitutional Court would not become the mirror of the political majority in question.[91] The requirement of the qualified majority in elections in the *Bundestag* or *Bundesrat* ensures that this is so. This hurdle has a consensus-forming effect, unlike in the American judicial appointment, which depends on the relevant political majorities. Overall, this brings about a balance within the Federal Constitutional Court when it is composed, because the parties take turns.[92] Informal arrangements between the parties as well as practices shaped by party-political interests contribute to achieving the qualified majority.[93] So if in the judicial

[88] Section 2 para 3 FCCA secures judicial expertise for both *Senates*. It provides that in each *Senate* three judges must have previously served at one of the federal supreme courts for at least three years.

[89] Voßkuhle 2018, Article 94 mn 6.

[90] Leibholz 1957, p 122.

[91] Protokoll vom 21.3.1950, ParlA I 115 A, pp 136, 151.

[92] Kommers 2001, p 149.

[93] For the informal procedure, see Kommers 2001, p 149; Heidebach 2014, p 155.

appointment, what is at stake is preserving the ideological balance in the Court as a whole, then this form of legitimation correlates with the Court's mediating function described in the first part of this essay. In other words, the Court's efforts at achieving a balance between opposing positions can be traced back to the mode of judicial appointment.

3.3.1.2 Term of Office and Exclusion of Reelection

While democratic legitimation is foregrounded in the appointment of the judges, after they are appointed, their democratic accountability diminishes in the interest of judicial independence, as is customary.[94] Other parameters of legitimation take their place. An essential element in securing legitimation is therefore the regulation of the term of office and the exclusion of reelection.

Originally, the Federal Constitutional Court Act still provided for the possibility of reelecting the constitutional judges. But in the interest of judicial independence, this was later abolished,[95] for, as the federal government puts it when stating the grounds of the bill, 'the reputation of the judges' independence is enhanced by the fact that the members of the Federal Constitutional Court, appointed for a defined period of time, are not reelected by electoral bodies whose constitutional actions they review.'[96] Previously, a third of the members of the Federal Constitutional Court were reelected every four years, with the exception of the professional judges. By changing the Federal Constitutional Court Act in 1970, the term of office was standardized to 12 years and at the longest until the judges' age limit of 68 years.[97]

Upon closer inspection, the intimate connection between this regulation and the changing function of the judges emerges. For the elimination of the renewal possibility was temporally connected to the introduction of dissenting opinions. At the time, it was feared that the renewal could be abused as a sanction against the legal views expressed in the judges' dissenting opinions.[98] To prevent this and to secure judicial independence, the legislator therefore decided on a longer term of office, but without the possibility of renewal.

In this way, the term of office of the Federal Constitutional Court's judges functions as a complementary parameter of legitimation, which supplements the procedure of judicial appointment legitimatorily, in the interest of democracy *and*

---

94 Cassese 2011, p 14: 'A genetic link connects them [political bodies and constitutional courts], although the relationship of accountability between the appointer and its appointee is broken: constitutional judges are of political derivation, although they are not required to answer to politics.'

95 Kommers 2001, p 149.

96 BT-Drucks. VI/388, p 6.

97 Section 4 para 1 FCCA.

98 Laufer 1968, p 216.

judicial independence, even reconciling the two to a certain extent.[99] With the exclusion of renewal, firstly, the judges' independence is secured for their entire term as soon as they are appointed, since there is no need for political considerations in the interest of re-election. Secondly, the new filling of the seats enables a periodic renewal of the democratic legitimation.

As with the appointment procedure, the regulation of the term of office is also shaped by the idea of balance. The twelve-year duration of this term takes the desire to renew the democratic legitimation into account, but the long term in office nevertheless uncouples this legitimation from the political majorities.[100] Although seats are newly filled more frequently in comparison to repeated reelection of the same judges, the twelve-year term in office (as well as the requirement of a qualified majority) entails that the respective elected judges are independent of political fluctuations, for the term in the Federal Constitutional Court exceeds the legislative period threefold. This underscores once more the independence of political majorities, while at the same time acknowledging the necessity of a renewal of democratic legitimation. Simultaneously, the regulation of the term in office brings about a compromise between the requirement of democratic legitimation and the continued fulfilment of judicial duties.[101]

3.3.2 Legitimation During the Term in Office

Not only reappointment is excluded in the interest of judicial independence. The administration of the judges is also secured against other external threats. As will be seen in what follows, essential elements here are the protection of personal independence during the tenure – a protection that is only restricted in the case of grievous official misconduct in the interest of the rule of law and judicial accountability – as well as the regulations of incompatibility and bias.

3.3.2.1 Personal Independence Through the Protection Against Removal or Transfer

In addition to the guarantee of substantive independence, due to their judicial function, the judges' personal independence is comprehensively protected during their term in office in the form of a fundamental impossibility of removal or transfer. Apart from securing their judicial salary and the performance of their official duties, they are largely protected against disciplinary measures. The removal of a judge of the Federal Constitutional Court requires an authorization from the

---

[99] Kommers 2001, p 149.

[100] See also Cassese 2011, p 14.

[101] Schefold 1988, p 293.

Federal President through a decision of the Court's plenary assembly, made with a majority of two-thirds of the Court's members.[102] Neither the *Bundestag* nor the *Bundesrat* have a say in this. The threshold of intervention is high because of the procedural prerequisites arising from the principle of the Court's collective accountability. It is additionally secured by the substantive prerequisites for removal. A judge's lasting invalidity is the prerequisite for mandatory retirement. In the case of a removal, the precondition is a 'dishonorable act', a final conviction to imprisonment of more than six months, or such a gross breach of duty that it precludes the judge from remaining in office.[103] That this is a high threshold of intervention is proven by the fact that the pertinent requirements have not become relevant in the history of the Federal Constitutional Court, which has existed for over six decades by now.

3.3.2.2 Incompatibility and the Safeguarding of Personal Independence

The safeguarding of personal independence is flanked by the regulations on incompatibility. These aim to guarantee the internal independence of the judges by protecting the independent and unbiased administration of office. Therefore, these rules are in the interest of both the rule of law and democratic legitimation, which would otherwise be interrupted in case of an extraneous influence on jurisprudence. In order to do justice to their judicial review function vis-à-vis the other powers and to the principle of the division of powers, the judges of the Federal Constitutional Court may not belong either to the *Bundestag* or the *Bundesrat* or the federal government during their term in office, according to Article 94 para 1 sent 3 Basic Law.

In order to avoid collisions of duties, which would be detrimental to judicial independence, the civil-service rights and duties are suspended for the duration of their term in office also for those civil servants appointed as judges of the Federal Constitutional Court.[104] Furthermore, with the exception of university professor, secondary employment is excluded, in order to guarantee the Court's ability to work.[105]

---

[102] Section 105 paras 1, 2 and 4 FCCA.

[103] Section 105 para 1 FCCA.

[104] Section 101 para 1 sent 2 FCCA.

[105] Section 3 para 4 FCCA.

3.3.2.3 Impartiality in Light of the Constitutional Court's *Sui Generis* Nature

The rules on impartiality and bias in the Federal Constitutional Court Act also serve to secure judicial impartiality and its external perception and so take the judicial function of the Federal Constitutional Court into account in the interest of due process. At the same time, they are based on the concern to ensure the functioning of the Court.

In this context, it is interesting how bias is defined. In recusal proceedings, the Federal Constitutional Court elaborated: 'The natural, even desired, basis of the provisions concerning the election of judges of the Federal Constitutional Court (Article 94 para 1, Section 3.3 ff FCCA) is that also those persons who have exercised political functions as party representatives in the parliaments or have held other political offices in the governments can be elected and appointed as members of the Federal Constitutional Court, in order to mobilize their political experiences for the constitutional jurisdiction. This is accompanied by the expectation of the constituent power and legislature that they will perform their new role as judges independently of earlier party-political disputes.'[106]

Despite the interest in securing judicial independence, which might initially speak for a personal distance from the legislative bodies, this takes into account the special nature of the Federal Constitutional Court. If the previous participation in the legislative branch as such is not in principle viewed as impairing independence, then this shows that the understanding of judicial independence expressed by the judges' legitimation must not be confused with neutrality but aims to protect against judicial bias or partisanship and to ensure the Court's general openness to different constitutional positions. As Section 18 para 2 FCCA underscores, the purpose is not to exclude different ideological positions. Rather, it is acknowledged that the judges are shaped by their ideological positions and their personal circumstances, such as background, family status, and profession. As long as they maintain their openness to diverging arguments and do not judge on the basis of their political affiliation, the impartiality of the Court is not called into question according to this fundamental understanding. The law only draws the line where there is the threat of bias and the danger that the balance within the Court no longer works due to external interference.

Except in cases of disqualification because of partiality, a judge can also be recused from the rest of the proceedings by resolution of the Court, without participation of the recused – on application of a party to the proceedings or at his or her own request (self-recusal) – because of the concern of bias pursuant to Section 19 FCCA. The jurisprudence of the Federal Constitutional Court establishes stringent requirements for the recusal of a judge. These exceed the standards for other jurisdictions and therefore frequently lead to the rejection of a petition for

[106] BVerfGE 99, 51, 56–57.

recusal.[107] The judges point out that in principle one must assume that the judges are impartial and objective, due to the qualified majority required for the judicial election.[108] Moreover, the Court justifies the particularly exacting standard with the possible consequences for jurisprudence that the change of majorities in the Court entails.[109]

The statement of grounds shows that the answer to the question of bias is again based on the *sui generis* nature of the Federal Constitutional Court and more particularly considers the special features of the judicial election. In this way, the Court shows that it intends to prevent motions to dismiss from being instrumentalized in a way that endangers judicial independence. If the Court is largely concerned with preserving the composition of the Court and thus the weighting of votes in the particular *Senat*, then what is expressed is that the idea of balance within the Court essentially shapes its legitimation. This influences the legitimation of the individual judges in as much as a recusal can dissolve the balance within the body. The Court recognizes its plural composition, which preferably should not be disturbed. In other words, in general, the democratic legitimation of the Court as a college shall not be compromised by the recusal of a judge.

As a result, the rules concerning both exclusion and recusal reflect the conception that underlies judicial appointment in the first place: The proximity to a political party or party affiliation alone is not grounds for bias. Judges are considered legitimated to take part in the decision as long as they are willing to weigh factors and do not take a side beyond the basic conviction that is accepted and even desired in judicial appointment.

3.3.2.4 Deliberative Legitimation

As we have seen so far, the judges' democratic accountability is restricted by the limitations on their dismissal during their tenure in the interest of judicial independence. The initial legitimation effected by the appointment thus requires an accompanying continuous legitimation during the term in office. In this phase, alternative mechanisms of accountability are important, which are the Court's own responsibility. Soft control mechanisms, such as the principle that reasons must be given, as articulated in Section 30 para 1 FCCA, entail that the accountability necessary for democratic legitimation can be upheld without judicial independence being at issue. Thus, legitimation is produced by the contentious proceedings, which guarantee a fair hearing and the hearing of different interests, as well as by the publicity of proceedings or the explanatory work of the Court vis-à-vis the parties and the wider public, for they guarantee a comprehensive deliberation not

---

107 Geck 1998, pp 723–724, mn 39–40; see also BVerfGE 35, 246, 251; 73, 330.

108 BVerfGE 35, 171, 173.

109 BVerfGE 35, 171, 172–173.

only within the Court but also in relation to those who are legally concerned.[110] The exchange of opinions serves to allow for opposing positions, the self-review of the Court, and so a balanced decision-making process. Beyond this, these deliberative elements make it possible to reconnect to public opinion. As a whole, these parameters bring about a balance between the demands of democratic legitimation and the guarantee of judicial independence.

3.3.3 Complementarity of the Parameters

In summary, at this junction one can retain the following: in addition to the election of judges, the regulations on term of office, incompatibility and impartiality belong to the parameters of legitimation that play a role in personal legitimation. The individual parameters have a complementary function and are crucially shaped by the guarantee of democracy, the rule of law, federalism, and the division of powers. At times, these fundamental principles are in conflict and must be balanced when developing the individual parameters.[111] While the election of the judges ensures *democratic legitimation*, which is vital according to the jurisprudence of the Federal Constitutional Court,[112] the requirement of the qualified majority vote prevents a biased influence from the particular governing party.[113] The legal qualification is meant to secure the *independence of the judges* and their competence for jurisprudential activity despite the political appointment. Due to the participation of the *Bundestag* and *Bundesrat*, the principle of equal appointment applies,[114] which expresses the *federal structural principle*.[115] It can be explained with the Federal Constitutional Court's responsibility for federal disputes, which requires the balanced participation of both chambers, so that the Court can fulfil its arbitrational function in disputes between the federation and the states. At the same time, judicial election effects an *interweaving of powers*, which takes the fact into account that the Federal Constitutional Court is appointed to review the other state bodies.

On the whole, the design of judicial legitimation is essentially based on the fundamental idea of complementarity. The Court unites different qualifications and ideological perspectives, in order so to achieve a certain balance institutionally. This is demonstrated not only by the different substantial basic convictions of the judges, but also by the Court's composition of professional judges and members who are not professional judges. The plural composition is intended to bring in different expertise, which the Court needs to fulfil its tasks. In this way, the judges

---

110 See also Cassese 2011, p 20.

111 Laufer 1968, p 207.

112 BVerfGE 40, 356, 366.

113 Heidebach 2014, p 159.

114 BVerfGE 65, 152, 155.

115 Heidebach 2014, p 153.

complement one another and accommodate the special nature of constitutional jurisdiction. At the same time, the regulation of the term of office brings about a certain adaptability of the Court over time. The twelve-year term of the judges without the possibility of re-election stands for a balance of preservation and efficiency on the one hand and the dynamism of constitutional jurisprudence on the other hand. If the judicial appointments have hardly encountered essential criticism in society so far,[116] this proves that substantially legitimation in the Federal Republic is commensurate with output legitimation. Accordingly, the public's acceptance of the jurisprudence endows the Court with a high degree of legitimacy.[117]

3.4 Legitimacy and Function as Mirror Images

As indicated above, if one compares the function and legitimacy of the Federal Constitutional Court, then one notices that the legitimation of the judges clearly reflects the special role of the Court in the Federal German constitutional system. This synchronization of function and legitimation became apparent especially in those times when parameters of legitimation were adapted to the Court's changing function. Some reforms of the Federal Constitutional Court Act were justified with its special tasks. Thus, for instance, the elimination of the possibility of reelection took the change of function brought about by the introduction of dissenting opinions into consideration.

Conversely, the legitimation of the judges, as it is designed in the Federal Republic of Germany, is also reflected in the Federal Constitutional Court's concrete performance of its duties. The Court, which is composed by means of a political process, performs a dual function that cannot be reduced to a mere judicial review function but also displays characteristics of legal development. Hence, the Court's concrete performance of its duties reflects the interplay of democratic legitimation and the qualification of professional judges in the judicial appointment. The thesis of the function guided by legitimation, developed at the beginning of this essay, is thus confirmed.

3.5 Significance for Other Constitutional Systems

The theory of functional legitimation is important for other democratic constitutional systems as well. Concretely, it can be of use whenever the matter at stake in judicial appointment is determining the relationship between democracy and the

[116] For an academic critique, see Heidebach 2014, pp 158–159.

[117] Möllers 2014, pp 14, 21.

rule of law. For as mentioned in the beginning, in the legitimation of judges who perform constitutional functions, the concern of democratic legitimation and the safeguarding of judicial independence do not always coincide. Both principles can strengthen one another: for instance, provisions concerning impartiality and incompatibility – much like requirements for the judges' legal qualification – serve the concern of democratic legitimation as well as the securing of due process. Yet at the same time, both principles can also stand in tension. If the principle of democracy for example generally demands a periodic review and renewal of legitimation beyond the act of appointment, such a regular renewal of legitimation in the shape of re-election challenges the guarantee of personal independence.

With the introduction of constitutional jurisdiction, this tension was by no means decided unilaterally, with constitutionality taking precedence over democracy. Conversely, invoking the principle of democracy is also not suitable as a unilateral influence on the composition of the Court. Rather, a continuous balancing of both principles is required.[118] Accordingly, the plural composition of the Federal Constitutional Court imparts the equilibrium needed for the constitutional jurisdiction, despite the crucial role of the political bodies in the election of judges. So the underlying understanding of democracy cannot be reduced to a simple majority principle. Rather, for constitutional jurisdiction, democratic legitimation means a balanced reconnection to the people as a whole. After all, constitutional jurisdiction would be unnecessary if it were only a reflection of the particular political majorities and therefore could not perform its review function.

How the tension between democracy and the rule of law is balanced concretely in essence depends on what function the judges have or should have according to the constitutional lawmaker. This is influenced for one by the catalogue of competences of the court in question, but for another also by how the nature of constitutional jurisprudence as the subject of legitimation is defined. Here lie the fundamental decisions of constitutional theory, which shape the concrete design of judicial legitimation in a crucial way. In addition to judicial appointment, constitutional jurisprudence itself also plays an important role in striking a balance in the zone of conflict. The relevant methodology of interpretation and the judges' practice of restraint concerning political decisions concretize the relationship to democratically legitimated majority decisions. This is a dynamic process that requires all constitutional bodies to engage in continuous reflection.

118 According to Lübbe-Wolff there is no 'one and only' proper solution to the democracy dilemma implicit in the question of constitutional review. Lübbe-Wolff 2016, p 19.

References

Bickel A (1962) The Least Dangerous Branch. Bobbs-Merrill, Indianapolis/New York

Blankenburg E (1996) Changes in Political Regimes and Continuity of the Rule of Law in Germany. In: Jacob H, Blankenburg E, Kritzer H M, Provine D M, Sanders J (eds) Courts, Law and Politics in Comparative Perspective. Yale University Press, New Haven, pp 249–274

Brewer-Carías A R (2006) The Question of Legitimacy: How to Choose the Judges of the Supreme Court? The European Doctrine and the Latin-American Contrast. In: Pernice I, Kokott J, Saunders C (eds) The Future of the European Judicial System in a Comparative Perspective, pp 153–183. Nomos, Baden-Baden

Bryde B O (2006) Der Beitrag des Bundesverfassungsgerichts zur Demokratisierung der Bundesrepublik. In: Van Ooyen R C, Möllers M H W (eds) Das Bundesverfassungsgericht im politischen System. VS Verlag für Sozialwissenschaften, Wiesbaden, pp 321–333

Bundestag-Drucksache VI/388. http://dipbt.bundestag.de/doc/btd/06/003/0600388.pdf. Accessed 19 July 2018

Cassese S (2011) In the Name of the People or in the Name of the Constitution? Constitutional Courts, Democracy and Justice. https://www.irpa.eu/wp-content/uploads/2011/10/Firenze-4-novembre-In-the-name-of-the-people-Constitutional-Courts-Democracy-and-Justice-trad_1.5-2.pdf. Accessed 26 July 2018

Clark D S (1988) The Selection and Accountability of Judges in West Germany: Implementation of a Rechtsstaat. Southern California Law Review 61:1795–1847

Dahl R A (1957) Decision-making in a Democracy: The Supreme Court as a National Policy-Maker. Journal of Public Law 6:279–295

Epstein L J, Walker T G (2016) Constitutional Law for a Changing America: Institutional Powers and Constraints, 9th edn. CQ Press, Washington

Feldman D (2005) None, One or Several? Perspectives on the UK's Constitution(s). The Cambridge Law Journal 64:329–351

Friedman B (2009) The Will of the People: How Public Opinion Has Influenced the Supreme Court and Shaped the Meaning of the Constitution. Farrar Strauss and Giroux, New York

Geck W K (1998) Wahl und Status der Bundesverfassungsrichter, 2nd edn. In: Isensee J, Kirchhof P (eds) Handbuch des Staatsrechts der Bundesrepublik Deutschland, Volume 2. C F Müller, Heidelberg, pp 697–737

Ginsburg T (2003) Judicial Review in New Democracies. Cambridge University Press, Cambridge

Grimm D (2017) Federal Constitutional Court of Germany (Bundesverfassungsgericht). In: Wolfrum R, Grote R, Lachenmann F (eds) Max Planck Encyclopedia of Comparative Constitutional Law. http://oxcon.ouplaw.com/view/10.1093/law-mpeccol/law-mpeccol-e528. Accessed 15 May 2018

Guarnieri C, Pederzoli P (2002) The Power of Judges: A Comparative Study of Courts and Democracy. Oxford University Press, Oxford

Gusy C, Kutscher H H (2011) 60 Jahre Bundesverfassungsgericht. Recht und Politik 47:129–139

Habermas J (1992) Faktizität und Geltung: Beiträge zur Diskurstheorie des Rechts und des demokratischen Rechtsstaats. Suhrkamp, Berlin

Heidebach M (2014) The election of the German Federal Constitutional Court's judges: A lack of democracy? Ritsumeikan Law Review 31:153–160

Hirschl R (2004) Towards Juristocracy: The Origins and Consequences of the New Constitutionalism. Harvard University Press, Cambridge MA

Jackson V C, Tushnet M (2006) Comparative Constitutional Law, 2nd edn. New York, Foundation Press

Jestaedt M, Lepsius O, Möllers C, Schönberger C (eds) (2011) Das entgrenzte Gericht. Suhrkamp, Berlin, pp 159–281

Juvenal D I (±115) Satire VI (unknown)

Kahl W (2000) Die Schutzergänzungsfunktion von Art. 2 Abs. 1 GG: Zugleich ein Beitrag zur Lehre der Grundrechtskonkurrenzen. Mohr Siebeck, Tübingen

Kentridge S (2003) The Highest Court: Selecting the Judges. Cambridge Law Journal 62:55–71
Kirchhof P (1998) Verfassungsgerichtsbarkeit und Gesetzgebung. In: Badura P, Scholz R (eds) Verfassungsgerichtsbarkeit und Gesetzgebung: Symposion aus Anlaß des 70. Geburtstages von Peter Lerche. C H Beck, Munich, pp 5–22
Kommers D P (2001) Autonomy versus Accountability: The German Judiciary. In: Russell P H, O'Brien D M (eds) Judicial Independence in the Age of Democracy: Critical Perspectives from around the World. University of Virginia Press, Charlottesville, pp 131–154
Kommers D P, Miller R A (2012) The Constitutional Jurisprudence of the Federal Republic of Germany, 3rd edn. Duke University Press, Durham/London
Kröger K (1998) Grundrechtsentwicklung in Deutschland: Von ihren Anfängen bis zur Gegenwart. Mohr Siebeck, Tübingen
Laufer H (1968) Verfassungsgerichtsbarkeit und politischer Prozeß: Studien zum Bundesverfassungsgericht der Bundesrepublik Deutschland. Mohr, Tübingen
Leibholz G (1957) Der Status des Bundesverfassungsgerichts: Bericht des Berichterstatters des Bundesverfassungsgerichts an das Plenum des Bundesverfassungsgerichts zur „Status"-Frage vom 21.3.1952. Jahrbuch des öffentlichen Rechts der Gegenwart 6:109–221
Lepsius O (2008) Zur Bindungswirkung von Bundesverfassungsgerichtsentscheidungen. In: Scholz R, Lorenz D, Pestalozza C (eds) Realitätsprägung durch Verfassungsrecht. [publisher?], pp 103–119
Lepsius O (2011) Die maßstabsetzende Gewalt. In: Jestaedt M, Lepsius O, Möllers C, Schönberger C (eds) Das entgrenzte Gericht. Suhrkamp, Berlin, pp 159–281
Limbach J (1999) The Effects of the Jurisdiction of the German Federal Constitutional Court. In: Limbach J, Bingham T H (eds) EUI Working Paper LAW No. 99/5. European University Institute, Florence, pp 6–22. http://cadmus.eui.eu/bitstream/handle/1814/150/law99_5.pdf?sequence=1&isAllowed=y. Accessed 12 April 2018
Loughlin M (2007) Grundlagen und Grundzüge staatlichen Verfassungsrechts: Großbritannien. In: von Bogdandy A, Cruz Villalón P, Huber P M (eds) Handbuch Ius Publicum Europaeum: Volume 1 Grundlagen und Grundzüge des Verfassungsrechts. C F Müller, Heidelberg, pp 217–273
Lübbe-Wolff G (2016) Constitutional Courts and Democracy: Facets of an Ambivalent Relationship. In: Meßerschmidt K, Oliver-Lalana A D (eds) Rational Lawmaking under Review: Legisprudence According to the German Federal Constitutional Court, pp 19–32
Malleson K, Moules R (2010) The Legal System, 4th edn. Oxford University Press, Oxford
Marshall W P (2005) Constitutional Law as Political Spoils. Cardozo Law Review 26:525–541
Maunz T (2018) Artikel 94 Grundgesetz. In: Maunz T, Dürig G (eds) Grundgesetz-Kommentar, Volume 6. C H Beck, Munich
McGinnis J O, Rappaport M B (2010) In Praise of Supreme Court Filibusters. Harvard Journal of Law & Public Policy 33:39–47
Möllers C (2011), Legalität, Legitimität und Legitimation des Bundesverfassungsgerichts. In: Jestaedt M, Lepsius O, Möllers C, Schönberger C (eds) Das entgrenzte Gericht. Suhrkamp, Berlin, pp 281–423
Möllers C (2013) The Three Branches: A Comparative Model of Separation of Powers. Oxford University Press, Oxford
Möllers C (2014) Scope and Legitimacy of Judicial Review: The Court versus the Political Process. In: Pünder H, Waldhoff C (eds) Debates in German public law. Hart Publishing, Oxford, pp 3–27
Niclauß K (2015) Der Parlamentarische Rat und das Bundesverfassungsgericht, 2nd edn. In: Van Ooyen R C, Möllers M H W (eds) Das Bundesverfassungsgericht im politischen System. Springer VS, Wiesbaden, pp 191–205
Oliver D (2003) Constitutional Reform in the United Kingdom. Oxford University Press, Oxford

Papier H J (2009) Das Bundesverfassungsgericht als Hüter der Grundrechte. In: Merten D, Papier H J (eds) Handbuch der Grundrechte in Deutschland und Europa: Volume 3 Grundrechte in Deutschland. C F Müller, Heidelberg, pp 1007–1033
Protokoll über die 23. Sitzung des Ausschusses für Rechtswesen und Verfassungsrecht des Deutschen Bundestages vom 21.3.1950, ParlA I 115 A, Volume 1. In: Schiffers R (ed) Grundlegung der Verfassungsgerichtsbarkeit: Das Gesetz über das Bundesverfassungsgericht vom 12. März 1951. Droste, Dusseldorf
Resnik J (2005) Judicial Selection and Democratic Theory: Demand, Supply, and Life Tenure. Cardozo Law Review 26:579–658
Schefold D (1988) Zur Problematik der beschränkten Amtszeit von Verfassungsrichtern. Juristenzeitung 43:291–296
Schneider H P (1987) Richter oder Schlichter? Das Bundesverfassungsgericht als Integrationsfaktor. In: Fürst W, Herzog R, Umbach D C (eds) Festschrift für Wolfgang Zeidler, Volume 1. De Gruyter, Berlin, pp 293–315
Seibert-Fohr A (forthcoming 2019) Verfassungsrichter: Ihre Funktion und Legitimation in der rechtsstaatlichen Demokratie. Mohr Siebeck, Tübingen
Stevens R (2002) The English Judges: Their Role in the Changing Constitution. Hart Publishing, Oxford
Vanberg G (2004) The politics of constitutional review in Germany. Cambridge University Press, Cambridge
Voßkuhle A (2018) Artikel 94 Grundgesetz, 7th edn. In: von Mangoldt H V, Klein F, Starck C (eds) Kommentar zum Grundgesetz, Volume 3. C H Beck, Munich, pp 861–887
Wahl R (2004) Die objektiv-rechtliche Dimension der Grundrechte im internationalen Vergleich. In: Merten D, Papier H J (eds) Handbuch der Grundrechte in Deutschland und Europa: Volume 1 Entwicklung und Grundlagen. C F Müller, Heidelberg, pp 745–783
Würtenberger T (1998) Zur Legitimität des Verfassungsrichterrechts. In: Guggenberger B, Würtenberger T (eds) Hüter der Verfassung oder Lenker der Politik? Das Bundesverfassungsgericht im Widerstreit. Nomos, Baden-Baden, pp 57–81

Anja Seibert-Fohr holds the Hengstberger Chair in Public Law, International Law and Human Rights Law at Heidelberg University and is Director of the Institute for Constitutional Law, Constitutional Theory and Philosophy of Law. Until 2018, she served as a member and Vice-Chair of the UN Human Rights Committee. Her research focuses on the rule of law, comparative constitutional law and international human rights. She has published a large number of works, including *Judicial Independence in Transition* (Springer, 2012).

Chapter 4
Italy and Its Constitutional Court

Alfonso Celotto

Contents

A. Celotto (✉)
'Roma Tre' University, Rome, Italy
e-mail: alfonso.celotto@uniroma3.it

Hirsch Ballin, Van der Schyff & Stremler (eds.), *European Yearbook of Constitutional Law 2019*, European Yearbook of Constitutional Law 1,
https://doi.org/10.1007/978-94-6265-359-7_4

Abstract This contribution analyses the constitutional and legislative rules aimed at ensuring the independence of the Italian Constitutional Court and its accountability, both as a whole and in relation to the single judges. The effectiveness and the impact of such rules are then assessed in practice, also in light of bipolar constitutionalism. The author concludes that the Italian Constitution seems to be strongly inclined towards a solid independence of the Court, with a rather low degree of accountability. It is also concluded that such rules work properly in practice, making the Court an independent institution, and allowing it to effectively protect the Constitution from possible manipulations by the dominant groups. It is then argued that the Court is able to serve as an intermediary between law and politics, 'jurisdictionalising' politics into the legal procedures and, at the same time, 'politicizing' its judicial role through the political nature of the matters examined and the political effects of its decisions.

Keywords bipolar constitutionalism · Constitutional Court of Italy · judicial accountability · judicial independence · jurisdictionalisation · politicisation

4.1 Introduction: Judicial Independence and Accountability in the Italian Legal Order

The independence of the judiciary represents one of the fundamental principles of the Italian constitutional order, as of many other democratic legal systems. Article 104 of the Constitution states that '[t]he Judiciary is a branch that is autonomous and independent of all other powers', and Article 101 states that '[j]ustice is administered in the name of the people' and that '[j]udges are subject only to the law'.[1]

This principle of independence applies also to the Constitutional Court, whose main role is to protect the citizens from certain types of unconstitutional conduct of the powers of the State, such as the passing of unconstitutional laws or breach of the constitutional rules on the allocation of power.[2]

---

[1] In this contribution, the English translation of the articles of the Constitution is from the text published by the Parliamentary Information, Archives and Publications Office of the Senate Service for Official Reports and Communication, available on the website of the Senate: https://www.senato.it/documenti/repository/istituzione/costituzione_inglese.pdf. Accessed 1 March 2019.

[2] Article 134 of the Constitution.

According to a widely accepted definition, an institution could be considered to be independent when the decisions it adopts are not meant to favour the interests of the members of that institution (or of subjects with similar interests) or of subjects who can in the future 'reward' the members of that institution.[3] Therefore, a court can be considered to be independent when its judges do not adopt their decisions to gain a personal advantage or to allow other subjects to gain any advantage in exchange for money or any other form of compensation. This, applied to a constitutional court could mean that this court is independent 'insofar as it is not the agent of either the executive or the legislative branch, or of both'.[4] However, as correctly pointed out, independence should be considered as a 'matter of degree' and it is probably 'never complete and never totally lacking'.[5]

Judicial independence is considered as an essential element of liberal democracy[6] but at the same time it is considered crucial that this is balanced with judicial accountability. In other words, although it is generally agreed that judges (including in particular judges exercising constitutional functions) are independent from other powers (in particular, the legislative and the executive powers), it is also felt necessary in democratic legal orders that they are held accountable to the institutions and the public.[7]

Both the principle of independence and the principle of accountability serve the purpose of allowing the constitutional courts to have the legitimacy to exercise the delicate and sensitive powers they have been attributed. However, the application of the same principles could expose the courts to the risk of being excessively detached from the political context and to the opposite risk of being excessively politicized.[8]

This chapter is structured as follows: first of all, it provides an overview of the powers and of the role of the Constitutional Court in the Italian legal system; it then provides a description of the main rules (mainly contained in the Constitution itself or in constitutional laws[9]) aimed at ensuring the independence of the Court; the following section includes an analysis of the application and effect of those rules in

---

[3] Breton and Fraschini 2003, p 320.

[4] Fiorino et al. 2007, p 688.

[5] Breton and Fraschini 2003, p 320.

[6] Russell 2001, p 1, where the author notes that, however, there is 'little agreement on just what this condition of judicial independence is, or on what kind or how much judicial independence is required for a liberal democratic regime, or on the societal conditions on which judicial independence depends'.

[7] Peri 2012, p 2, where it is argued that more and more countries in the world are now finding themselves in what has been defined (by A Paterson) as a 'conundrum of the apparently insoluble tension between judicial independence and judicial accountability'. As noted by the author, judicial accountability shall be considered separate from judicial responsibility because 'the last one generally arises from the violation of norms', while accountability 'affects in some way ethics and governance (for this reason it is often called "ultimate responsibility"' (Peri 2012, p 3).

[8] *Ibid.*, p 4.

[9] These are laws with the same strength as the Constitution and that are adopted following the special procedure provided by Article 138 of the Constitution.

practice and in light of the principles of bipolar constitutionalism; finally, conclusive remarks are offered in relation to the role of the Court within the Italian legal order and in relation to its degree of independence.

4.2 The Italian Constitutional Court

4.2.1 The Establishment of an Ad Hoc Court Entrusted with Centralized Constitutional Review

The Italian 1948 Constitution, adopted by the Constituent Assembly after the fall of the Italian Fascist regime and the end of the Second World War, introduced for the first time a Constitutional Court in the country. This Court was entrusted with the protection of the new 'rigid' Constitution, i.e. a Constitution which could be amended only through a complex process, different from the one for the passing of ordinary laws.[10]

The establishment of the Court, in other words, mainly aimed at addressing the need for a judicial constitutional review of the legislation in the newly established 'constitutional democracy',[11] where the people has the sovereignty but where it (and its representatives) must act in compliance with the provisions of the Constitution itself.[12] The members of the Constituent Assembly opted for a form of centralized, rather than de-centralized,[13] constitutional review and decided to establish a dedicated Court.[14]

---

[10] Under Article 138 of the Constitution '[l]aws amending the Constitution and other constitutional laws shall be adopted by each House after two successive debates at intervals of not less than three months, and shall be approved by an absolute majority of the members of each House in the second voting. Said laws are submitted to a popular referendum when, within three months of their publication, such request is made by one-fifth of the members of a House or five hundred thousand voters or five Regional Councils. The law submitted to referendum shall not be promulgated if not approved by a majority of valid votes. A referendum shall not be held if the law has been approved in the second voting by each of the Houses by a majority of two-thirds of the members'.

[11] Zagrebelsky and Marcenò 2018, p 63. The previous Constitution, i.e. the 1848 'Statuto Albertino', was a flexible constitution as it could be amended through an ordinary legislative procedure and therefore created no need for a judicial review of the legislation.

[12] Article 1, para 2 of the Constitution, states that 'Sovereignty belongs to the people and is exercised by the people in the forms and within the limits of the Constitution'.

[13] However, it has been argued that 'the experience of more than 50 years of judicial review in Italy (…) has seen an evolution towards a much more decentralized system, (…) a system in which the ordinary judges also play an important role in constitutional review' (Groppi 2008, p 101).

[14] Actually, the idea of establishing a court with the role of ensuring and protecting the rigidity of the Constitution emerged even before the start of the works of the Constituent Assembly. However, in the first phases of the debate, no real discussion took place in relation to the composition of such a court or in relation to its independence.

As soon as the subjects and the political parties involved in the debate started discussing the features of the new Court, it became immediately clear that the objective shared by the majority of them was to shape the Court as a body with a mixed nature, i.e. a body which was neither purely political nor purely legal.[15]

4.2.2 The Powers of the Constitutional Court

The Italian Constitutional Court can be called to pass a judgment in the following cases:[16] (i) controversies on the constitutional legitimacy of laws and enactments having force of law issued by the State and Regions;[17] (ii) conflicts arising from allocation of powers of the State and those powers allocated to State and Regions, and between Regions; (iii) charges brought against the President of the Republic, according to the provisions of the Constitution, in cases where he is accused of high treason and attempt to overthrow the Constitution;[18] and (iv) to adjudicate on the admissibility of requests for referenda directed at the repealing of laws.[19]

Hence, the powers of the Italian Constitutional Court appear to be more limited than those of the constitutional courts in other jurisdictions.[20] First of all, it cannot exercise control relating to more political aspects, such as for example in relation to electoral issues, or the supervision of political parties or to ascertain the incapacity of the President of the Republic. Secondly, the main power of the Court, i.e. the power to adjudicate on disputes relating to the constitutionality of laws, is strictly limited from many points of view. In particular, the access to the Court is indirect and is decided by ordinary judges, and the constitutionality review takes place *ex post*. The question of constitutionality of a law can be raised within ordinary judicial proceedings (where the

---

[15] According to one of the proposals discussed by the Constituent Assembly, the nature of the Court should have been at the same time political, legal and technical 'because these are the elements of any norm'. As a result, it was proposed that the Court should have been composed of members elected by the Parliament, members elected by the judicature or coming from the legal profession, together with deans of the faculties of engineering, of medicine, or natural sciences.

[16] As noted in Groppi 2008, p 102, these powers are typical of constitutional tribunals.

[17] The analysis of the decisional practice of the Court shows that this is the power that has been exercised the most over the years, in particular as regards the 'incidental' review of certified questions.

[18] Article 134 of the Constitution.

[19] Article 2 of Constitutional Law no. 1/1953. Pursuant to article 75 of the Constitution, the referendum to repeal laws can be promoted by 500,000 voters, or five regional councils.

[20] See Groppi 2008, pp 102–104.

contested law should be applied), either upon request of one of the private parties or on its own motion by the court.[21]

In addition, the powers of the Court are rather limited both in terms of acts that can be submitted to its review (only laws and enactments having force of law, and not delegated or administrative legislation) and in terms of the scope of the review itself, which is restricted to the question submitted and to the limit of the challenge brought forward.[22] Furthermore, the Court may in principle only choose among a limited number of categories of decisions to conclude its proceedings, whose effects are also made very clear by the applicable rules. If it does not issue an interlocutory judgment or rejects the question on the basis of procedural grounds, the Court may in theory only opt either for a decision upholding the question on the constitutionality of the law (*sentenze di accoglimento*)[23] or a decision rejecting such question (*sentenze di rigetto*),[24] but has in practice developed a rich variety of judgments.[25]

4.3 The Rules Aimed at Ensuring the Independence of the Constitutional Court and Its Accountability

The Italian Constitution and other constitutional and ordinary laws provide for several rules aimed at ensuring the independence of the Constitutional Court.

---

[21] A form of direct review is however possible when the national government or a regional government challenge, respectively, a regional or a national statute (Article 127 of the Constitution). Individual citizens, parliamentary groups or local governments do not have direct access to the Court. It is to be noted that this form of review is very relevant in quantitative terms: more than 35% of the decisions of the Court in 2017 were in direct review cases.

[22] Under Article 27 of Law no. 87/1953, 'The Constitutional Court, when it accepts an application or petition involving a question of constitutionality of a law or act having force of law, shall declare, within the limit of the challenge, which of the legislative provisions are illegitimate', although in any case the Court may also decide to state 'which are the other legislative provisions whose illegitimacy arises as a consequence of the decision adopted'.

[23] Such judgments are universally binding and produce retroactive effects, with the exception of the principle of *res iudicata* (except for criminal cases).

[24] Such decisions do not state the constitutionality of the law but they simply reject a specific challenge which was submitted against that law, and only in the form in which it was submitted to its review. In addition, they do not have an *erga omnes* effect.

[25] As noted in Groppi 2008, pp 105–106, the Court was able - due to the wide discretion it enjoys in interpreting its procedure and practice - to develop such a variety of judgments, with the aim of addressing the necessity to respond to specific practical needs.

4.3.1 The Independence of the Constitutional Court as a Whole: The Composition and the Process for the Appointment of Judges[26]

It is widely recognized that the procedures and the rules on the selection of the members of a court have a considerable impact on its status and on its role within the legal order.[27] The rules on the composition of the Italian Constitutional Court and the values underlying such rules determined and still determine the way the Court functions and the way it interacts with the other components of the constitutional system (and, *in primis*, the other powers of the State).[28]

In fact, it does not come as a surprise that the *Leitmotiv* of the discussion within the Constituent Assembly was that the issue of the composition of the Court was directly and closely connected with its legitimation and with its functions; for this reason, the new Court needed to be at the same time highly political (because it was called to exercise its review on the content of the legislation) and highly prestigious (both in terms of the selection of the members and in terms of the *status* recognized to those members). However, several different positions emerged on how this mixed nature of the Court should have been achieved in practice.[29]

---

[26] The systematization applied here is only one of the many possible systematizations that have been proposed by the doctrine in relation to the different rules aimed at ensuring the independence of the Court.

[27] In other words, 'judicial selection process is not a neutral procedure: norms which refer to judicial selection, like all the positive norms in the system, convey a value'. This is because 'the method to select the judiciary is so rooted in a broader context which involves various individuals, groups and political institutions which can influence judicial independence' (Peri 2012, pp 2–3).

[28] Just as in many other constitutional legal orders, the rules on the composition of the Italian Constitutional Court are contained either in the Constitution or in constitutional laws. This is considered to be a way not only to emphasize the special status of the Court but also to give it the necessary legitimation to exercise its role in terms of review of the legislation and for the institutional compromises. However, it can be noted that Italy belongs to the jurisdictions where the written procedural rules on the appointment of the constitutional judges are not excessively detailed and this lack of detailed rules is not compensated by a considerable transparency and involvement of the public in the process of appointment (as it is for example in the United States, where the procedure is very informal but involves several institutional and non-institutional players) (Peri 2012, pp 6–7).

[29] The tension between these two features influenced the debate between the political parties sitting in the Constituent Assembly. In the same context, it was stressed that the Court should also have a strong judicial character, in order to ensure its impartiality and its independence from the legislative power (which it was called to control) and from the government. On the other hand, it was proposed to establish a link between the election of the judges of the Court and the political elections: according to this proposal, the Parliament would have elected the judges at the beginning of each legislature and the term of both the Parliament and the Court would have had the same duration. However, this proposal was rejected, together with several other alternatives, in order to ensure the independence of the Court from the political parties sitting in the Parliament and in order to avoid establishing an excessively close connection between the Court and the political power. The original wording of the relevant provision regulating the procedure for the renewal of

The solution which prevailed in the Constituent Assembly was that the Court should be composed - in its ordinary configuration - of fifteen judges[30] to be appointed by the Parliament (the Chamber of Deputies and the Senate in joint sitting), by the three highest Courts (three judges are elected by the Supreme Court of Cassation, one by the Council of State, one from the Court of Audit)[31] and by the President of the Republic (one third, i.e. 5 judges, each).[32]

However, despite the diversified appointment procedure, it is underlined that all the three components of the Court are homogeneous and united by the fact of being all independent from the institutions that have elected them, and act as a single body.[33] Such independence and separation from the electing body is achieved through different means, depending on the single component.

As regards in particular the judges elected by the legislature, a majority of the two thirds of the members of the Parliament is required in the first two ballots to elect the constitutional judges, while a majority of the three fifth is required for the following ballots. Such thresholds have been raised in 1967,[34] in order to reduce the political nature of such election and avoid that the judges be identified with any political

---

the composition of the Court foresaw a partial renewal, designed in order to ensure the maximum level of independence of the Court from the political parties who had elected its members. However, such mechanism proved to be so difficult to be applied in practice that it was necessary to amend it rather soon; at the same time, the whole provision of the Constitution concerning the composition of the Court was substantially amended, leading to its current language.

[30] The high number of judges is coherent with the role and the nature of the Italian Constitutional Court, which is called to ensure the balance in the constitutional system and exercise a role of guardian of respect for the Constitution. It is in fact observed that bigger courts are in general conceived to increase the 'judiciousness' of their decisions, thus making them fitter for such a guaranty role (Peri 2012, p 7).

[31] It has been noted that the judges elected by the highest Courts come from the same single Courts electing them, but this is not considered to be an issue for the independence of the Court, which is considered to be sufficiently ensured by the whole system for the election of the judges. See Breton and Fraschini 2003, p 322.

[32] The mixed composition of the Court recalls the traditional separation of powers described by Montesquieu (Celotto 2006, p 34) but it is also considered to be a consequence of the mixed nature of the body, which is neither representative nor bureaucratic, and which needs to be able to play a role which is at the same time technical and political in nature (Conti 2006). As explained by Zagrebelsky 1992, the meaning of the composition of the Court is linked to the balancing between legal needs (consistent with the fundamentally judicial nature of the Italian constitutional review) and the institutional-political needs (consistent with the nature of the role attributed to the Court). In addition, it has also been noted that the three components of the Court represent a way of merging in an independent body three different elements: the representatives of the people (the Parliament), the national unity (the President of the Republic) and the primacy of the law (the judicature) (D'Orazio 1966, p 160). This mixed composition is aimed at ensuring that the Court has the technical knowledge and the political sensibility needed to carry out its functions and, at the same time, the strong legitimation, the credibility and the authority towards the subjects who are called to implement its decisions (i.e. the judges, the Parliament and the rest of the country) (Conti 2006).

[33] D'Orazio 1966, p 165.

[34] Article 3 of Constitutional Law no. 2/1967, amending Article 3 of Law no. 87/1953, which required the majority of the three fifth of the members of the Parliament for the first three ballots and the majority of the three fifth of the members of the Parliament present at the voting.

orientation or affiliation. In other words, the fact that a wide majority is required to elect the judges to the Court forces the political parties to find an agreement and a compromise on a list of names, because each one of the (main) political groups enjoys a sort of veto power on the names proposed by the other political groups.[35]

In relation to the judges appointed by the President of the Republic, it has been noted that this component could be considered as a way of re-balancing the composition of the Court, depending on the selection made by the Parliament and by the judiciary. In other words, the President would be called to adjust his selection in order to reinforce the technical or the political component, depending on which one is under-represented from time to time. In practice, it has been observed that the President has in some cases consulted the Court itself, before taking his choice, thus leading someone to conclude that the appointment of the five 'presidential' judges represents a sort of co-optation of the new judges by the Court, further reinforcing its independence.[36]

In conclusion, it should be noted that the importance of the appointment process of the judges of the Court (in relation to its independence) is further underlined by the rules on the composition of the Panel of Justice (*Collegio dei Giudici*), which is appointed by the President of the Court for each case and decides by simple majority on the draft decisions prepared by the rapporteur. The minimum number of judges in the Panel is eleven, in order to avoid the situation in which a group of five judges from the same extraction (i.e. having been appointed by the Parliament, judiciary or the President) can reach the majority in a case, and this has been considered a further sign of the fact that the composition of the Court is 'expected to

---

[35] For several years (between the end of World War Two and the beginning of the Nineties), the consolidated practice in the election of the members of the Court by the Parliament was that the main political parties would share the judges as follows: two judges to the Christian Democrats, one to the Socialist Party, one to the Communist Party and one to the smaller parties (liberal and republican parties).

Now that the Italian political scenario is more complicated and less stable this practice does not always apply with the same degree of certainty. Bin 2009, p 4026, argues that only an 'institutional slovenliness' can explain why there is not a practice requesting that the justices are heard and examined by the Parliament in joint session before their appointment, as it happens for example in the United States.

[36] The doctrine has in fact clarified that the President is autonomous in his decision for the appointment of the five presidential judges. Contrary to what happens for the ordinary decrees of the President of the Republic (the DPRs), which are proposed by the Government or by the Ministers and signed by the President, the decree for the appointment of the judges of the Constitutional Court is proposed and signed by the President, although it is also counter-signed by the President of the Council of Ministers. There are however opposite views on this aspect, of those who claim that, in practice, because the President is elected by the two chambers by absolute majority, he can be considered as an agent of the Parliament, also in the act of appointing the judges of the Constitutional Court and that this theory is further supported by the fact that the appointment of the five presidential justices is preceded by informal consultations with the political parties and the Government (Fiorino et al. 2007, p 689).

influence the sort of jurisprudence and the degree of independence of the Court'.[37] As a result of the mechanism described above, the structural independence of the Court cannot be considered to be a constant, in the sense that it changes for every decision, depending on the composition of each Panel. This is argued to the extent that even absences may affect the independence as they change the effective composition of the Panel compared to that originally conceived by the President; even a bigger impact is created by vacancies, as judges to be appointed by the Parliament are usually not immediately replaced when they terminate their tenure.[38]

4.3.2 *The Independence of the Individual Judges of the Court: The Status of the Judges*

The concept of the *status* of the judges of the Constitutional Court has been thoroughly investigated by the Italian doctrine over the years. Several definitions of such concept have been proposed by many different scholars and it is considered to be connected with the idea of independence of the Court and of its members.

4.3.2.1 The Qualifications of the Candidates to Become Members of the Court

The first element that defines the status of the judges of the Court is connected with the fact that they need to belong to one of the following categories: (i) judges of the highest ordinary or administrative courts; (ii) professors of law; and (iii) lawyers

---

[37] Fiorino et al. 2007, p 690.

[38] Fiorino et al. 2007, p 690, where it is noted that the Court already operated with less than fifteen judges in several occasions (sometimes also for long time) and this impacted its structural independence. Several legislative proposals have been tabled, over the years, aiming at changing the rules on the composition of the Court. In particular, in 2004 a proposal was discussed by the Italian Parliament, which would have changed the rules for the selection of the judges, by reducing the number of the judges appointed by the President of the Republic and by the judiciary (from five to four each) and by increasing the number of judges appointed by the Parliament. In addition, the parliamentary nominees would have been appointed by a Federal Senate, and not by the two chambers of the Parliament in joint sitting. The reform failed to be adopted and the content of the new rules was criticized by several commentators, in particular because it was considered as increasing the weight of the political component of the Court (by reducing the number of judges which were not appointed according to political criteria). Furthermore, it was argued that the proposed changes would have introduced a sort of 'federalist factor' to the Constitutional Court, thus changing the nature and the position of the body, especially in relation to the conflicts between the State and the Regions (Peri 2012, p 18).

after twenty years of practice.[39] This 'mixed' composition of the Court serves the purpose of ensuring that different points of view are applied when the Court examines and assesses the cases brought before it: the impartiality of the judge, the scientific approach of the professor and the attention to the individual rights and interests of the lawyer.[40]

The fact in itself that the members of the Court may apply such a diversified and rich approach to the law could be in itself considered an element of independence. Comparative studies on the professional requirements and the professional background required to be eligible for the appointment in Supreme and Constitutional Courts show that the higher these requirements, the higher the degree of independence of the court. In fact, strict and high requirements substantially reduce the degree of discretion in the selection of the judges and therefore reduce the political influence on such process. Therefore, the fact that the Parliament, the Government and the President of the Republic select the members of the Court on the basis of objective criteria (and not on the basis of ideological criteria) limits the risk of politically driven nominations. In addition, it has been observed that a Court made of jurists will be more inclined to act, think and proceed according to legal categories and considerations, rather than on the basis of political or in general external factors, and this is expected to further increase the independence of the institution.[41]

Moreover, another element that makes this provision a demonstration of the independence of the Court is the fact that it is for the Court itself (by an absolute majority vote) to verify that the subjective and individual requirements are met by each judge.[42] Traditionally, the Court has exercised such function in full autonomy and independence, also in cases where an intense debate arose in connection with the election of specific judges: in those cases, the Court confirmed the election of the judges, even if criticisms and doubts had been raised in relation to the proposed candidates.[43]

---

39 Article 135, second paragraph, of the Constitution.

40 Conti 2006.

41 Peri 2012, p 8. This observation seems to be confirmed by the fact that the judges of the Italian Constitutional Court typically come from the judiciary or academia, with no or very limited involvement in politics. This is the current composition of the Court: five members are former members of the judiciary, while nine members are former professors of law.

42 Article 2 of Constitutional Law no. 2/1967.

43 Debated cases relating to the Court's responsibility to verify that its members meet the criteria set out above are the confirmation of judge Bucciarelli Ducci in 1977, of judge Contri in 1996 and of judge Napolitano in 2006. In particular, in the first case the Court argued that the fact that the candidate had served as the President of the Chamber of Deputies would correspond to the exercise of the functions of judge of the supreme courts, because it was a proof of the same level of independence and impartiality.

4.3.2.2 Rules on Incompatibility

Another prominent component of the independence of the Court is traditionally identified with the rules relating to the incompatibility of the function as a judge of the Court with other roles and responsibilities. In particular, justices are subject to an absolute prohibition to hold any other post or function, to exercise any professional, commercial and industrial activity, or to serve as directors of companies. As a result, professors and ordinary or administrative judges are temporally suspended from their functions when they become members of the Court (with the right of re-assuming their original post at the end of their tenure) and the judges of the Court cannot be members of the selection boards in competitions or being candidate in any elections. For the same reason, and in order to ensure the full independence of the Court from any political influence (or even suspect of influence), it is provided that the judges cannot take part in the activities of any association or political party.[44]

It has been noted that the 'appearance of impartiality' is a need that is valid both for ordinary judges and for constitutional justices.[45] This principle imposes on all judges the duty to ensure the freedom from any bond and to the suspension of any activity and expression relating to the status of member of a political party (e.g. attending party meetings or congresses, signing 'manifestos' or political programmes, etc.), in order to protect both the independence in the judgement and the prestige of the body, and therefore the trust of the citizens. As a result, the prohibition for constitutional justices to carry out political activities is considered to entail the prohibition to publicly reveal their political beliefs and raise doubts on their impartiality in the exercise of their functions, in addition to the duty of acting independently from the political parties.[46]

Again, as for the confirmation of the subjective satisfaction of the qualifications of the judges candidate to become members, the Court decides also (but in this case with the majority of the two thirds of the members taking part in the voting) on the incompatibility of the judges for the reasons listed above, as well as on the verification of the judges' compliance with their duty to take part in the activities of the Court.[47]

---

[44] Article 8 of Law no. 87/1953. A traditional discussion related to whether such prohibition also included the prohibition for the constitutional justices to register with a political party, which is a right of all citizens under Article 49 of the Constitution. The answer to this question depends on the extension of the scope of the notion of 'activities' and on how much the notion of independence of the Constitutional Court can in fact be linked to the notion of independence of the judiciary as a whole.

[45] Even the scholars who have opposed the idea that the position of the two categories of judges should be assimilated recognized that such principle applies to the Constitutional judges as well as to ordinary judges.

[46] Bin 2009, p 4019.

[47] Article 3 of Constitutional Law no. 1/1948; Article 7 of Constitutional Law no. 1/1953; Article 11 of Law no. 87/1953.

In addition, a further evidence of the autonomy of the Court is represented by the rule under which the judges are responsible for 'serious misconduct in the exercise of their functions'[48], which leaves to the Court itself to define both the functions of its members and how these should be correctly carried out.[49]

4.3.2.3 Irremovability of the Judges

For the same purpose of ensuring the independence of the Court, the applicable provisions also state the principle of irremovability of the judges, who cannot be dismissed unless there is a specific decision of the Court ordering their dismissal. Depending on the seriousness of the reason for such decision, the Court may decide to either remove the judge concerned (for more serious violations or for supervening inability), to suspend him (for minor or for temporary reasons), or to declare the loss of the title of judge of the Court (for not having taken part in the works of the Court for more than six months).[50]

4.3.2.4 Immunity

The legal framework defining the independence of the Court as described above is reinforced by another element of the status of the judges of the Court: the immunity they enjoy. The judges of the Court cannot be held accountable for the votes cast and for the opinions expressed in the exercise of their functions.[51]

The rules on the immunity of the judges of the Court has been for several years at the centre of a lively debate, because of the uncertainty regarding the interpretation of one of those rules,[52] which provides that they enjoy the same immunity and the same protection recognized to the members of the Parliament under Article 68, second paragraph, of the Constitution. This provision included a rule by which the judges could only be prosecuted if the Court authorized their prosecution on a case-by-case basis. The problem arose when (in 1993[53]) the corresponding provision relating to the members of the Parliament was amended, and the new rules did not contain any power for the Parliament to authorize or not authorize the prose-

---

[48] Article 3, para 1, of Constitutional Law no. 1/1948.

[49] Conti 2006.

[50] *Ibid*. This has never happened in practice, while there have been cases in which judges have resigned before the end of their tenure, not always for health reasons.

[51] Article 5 of Constitutional Law no. 1/1953.

[52] Article 3, second paragraph, of Constitutional Law no. 1/1948.

[53] Constitutional Law no. 3/1993.

cution of its members.[54] In particular, the doctrine started discussing whether the rule concerning the judges of the Court should have been considered automatically changed (due to the change of the provision to which it was referring) or whether the authorization should have been considered to be still necessary for the judges of the Court, because this was the original intention of the legislator.

Some scholars note that the authorization should be considered as still necessary for the judges of the Court, irrespective of the changes to the rules applicable to the members of the Parliament. In particular, this would be due to the fact that the very rationale of the rule on the authorization has traditionally been different for the judges (i.e. protecting their independence and impartiality) and for the members of the Parliament (i.e. protecting the autonomy of the institution).[55]

4.3.2.5 Title of 'Judge Emeritus'

Another element of the status of the constitutional judges which qualifies their independence relates to their title following the end of the mandate. In fact, once they cease to be members of the Court, all the former judges become 'judge emeritus' without the need of any act by the Court or by any other body (provided that they have served as judges of the Court for at least four years).[56] It has been observed that the automatic attribution of this title (as well as the pension rights of the judges) serves the purpose of further reinforcing the independence of the body as a whole, as well as ensuring that all the judges are at the same level.[57]

---

[54] Article 68, para 2, of the Constitution now states: 'In default of the authorisation of his House, no Member of Parliament may be submitted to personal or home search, nor may he be arrested or otherwise deprived of his personal freedom, nor held in detention, except when a final court sentence is enforced, or when the Member is apprehended in the act of committing an offence for which arrest flagrante delicto is mandatory'.

[55] Sandulli 1966. In addition, it has also been noted that the instrument of the required authorization to prosecute has a much more relevant role when it relates to the protection of the integrity of the Court (which is composed of only fifteen judges) rather than when it relates to the protection of the Parliament (composed of almost one thousand members). In the first case, the risk is considerably higher that a series of prosecutions could substantially paralyze the Court. For the reasons above, several scholars advocate for the maintenance of the required authorization to prosecute for the judges of the Court (Conti 2006). As regards in particular the President of the Constitutional Court, a law of 2003 had provided for the suspension of any criminal prosecution against him or her, as well as of the prosecution against the individuals holding the highest offices of the State (the President of the Republic, the President of the Council of Ministers, the Presidents of the Chamber of Deputies and the President of the Senate). Such law, however, has been declared in breach of the Constitution by the very Constitutional Court, which among other things considered it to be discriminatory, because it unduly differentiated between the Presidents and the members of those institutions (Decision of the Constitutional Court n. 24/2004).

[56] Article 20 of the Statute of the Constitutional Court.

[57] Conti 2006.

4.3.2.6 Salary

In order to ensure the full independence of the judges of the Court, together with the 'prestige' of the institution itself, it has been considered appropriate to ensure that the members receive an appropriate salary. Their economic treatment is calculated on the basis of the salary of the First President of the Supreme Court of Cassation and is not subject to taxation; in addition, the President of the Court is recognized a further allowance for his role, corresponding to one fifth of the salary. This mechanism has been considered as an adequate means to guarantee the independence of the Court, not only because it can ensure that the judges shall receive an adequate salary (and therefore be less inclined to be influenced) but also because the legislator will not be able to intervene on the economic treatment of the judges of the Court without also intervening on the economic treatment of the judges of the highest courts (and in particular of the Supreme Court of Cassation).[58]

4.3.3 Other Procedural and Organization Rules Aimed at Ensuring the Independence of the Court

4.3.3.1 Lack of Dissenting and Concurring Opinions and Lack of Appeal Against the Decisions of the Court

The decisions of the Constitutional Court are 'unsigned and without dissents, making partisanship difficult to measure'.[59] As mentioned, all decisions of the Court are adopted by a college of judges (the Panel), made of at least eleven of the fifteen judges. The college tends to reach unanimity on its decisions but, should this prove to be impossible in specific cases, decisions may be adopted by simple majority (the weight of the vote expressed by the President is doubled, in case there is a tie).[60]

The fact that the judgments of the Court are only attributable to the college as a whole removes the possibility of verifying the attitudes and 'political loyalty' of each judge, thus increasing the independence and the 'freedom' of the Court. On the other hand, however, some commentators have argued that the system adopted in Italy, which does not recognize the possibility for each judge to publicly express his individual opinions, may contribute to make the activity of the Court more

---

[58] *Ibid.*

[59] Volcansek 2006, where the author claims the absolute independence of the judges of the Constitutional Court, despite the so-called *'lottizzazione'*, i.e. the 'division whereby virtually all sectors of Italian civil life are allocated on the basis of political party affiliation'.

[60] Collegiate judgements are considered to be a common feature of continental European courts (except for Germany), as opposed to common law courts (where dissenting and concurring opinions are allowed) and serve the purpose of favouring judicial independence (Peri 2012, p 19).

'ambiguous' and more difficult to classify from a political point of view, thus also making it more difficult for the Court to establish a direct relationship with the people.[61]

In addition, pursuant to Article 137, para 3, of the Constitution '[n]o appeals are allowed against the decision of the Constitutional Court', thus further reducing the external influence which could be exercised on constitutional judges while voting on specific judgements.

4.3.3.2 The Special Rules on the Abstention and Objection

The rules on the abstention and the objection relating to ordinary judges do not apply to the justices of the Constitutional Court.[62] The rationale of such exclusion is that the composition of the college follows the rules provided in the Constitution, aimed at ensuring its effective operations and its independence, and therefore cannot be modified by the single judges or by the parties in the proceeding. In addition, it was noted that the abstention and the objection would lack any basis if applied to the Court, because it reviews acts issued by public bodies.[63]

In fact the very Constitutional Court recognized in the past that the abstention and the objection serve the purpose of ensuring the impartiality of the judge in relation to the specific dispute[64] and for this reason these instruments are regulated according to rules, which are specific to the type of proceedings (and for example differ between the criminal and the civil procedures).[65]

As a result, the rule preventing the application of the objection in proceedings before the Court could be interpreted as a limitation of the right of defence of the

---

[61] Peri 2012, p 19. However, it shall be observed that, in an increasing number of decisions, the judge rapporteur is replaced by another judge of the Court for the drafting of the final decision: this is considered as a sign of the dissent of the rapporteur towards the decision of the college.

[62] As stated in Article 29, *Norme integrative giudizi costituzionali* (OJ n. 261 of 7 November 2008), with the exception of the proceedings for charges brought against the President of the Republic for high treason and attempt to overthrow the Constitution (Article 25 of Law no. 20/1962).

[63] Bin 2009, p 4017, as well as Pertici 2004, 3105 and ff, where it is argued that the legislator should introduce a specific set of rules applicable to the judges of the Constitutional Court and aimed at preserving their impartiality.

[64] See for example decision of the Constitutional Court n. 103 of 1964.

[65] As noted by Bin 2009, p 4023, this might also explains why the abstention and the objection only apply, among the different proceedings that can be submitted to the Constitutional Court, to the criminal charges brought against the President of the Republic, which may be considered as the only case in which it is possible that real reasons for abstention or objection may arise, due to the concrete and specific nature of the dispute (very different from, for example, the review of the admissibility of a referendum, whose object is very abstract).

parties, should a judge put himself in a situation which would be in a different context be solved through an objection against him.[66]

However, it has been noted that the exclusion of the application of the objection in the proceedings before the Court should rather be interpreted as a 'diplomatic' way of imposing certain limits on the conduct of the constitutional justices in the form of a self-restraint. By stating that the parties are not allowed to object against the participation of any of the justices in the proceedings, the provision is indirectly pointing the justices' attention to the obligations they have assumed when they have accepted to become members of the Constitutional Court, i.e. to avoid any circumstance in which their 'appearance of impartiality' might be questioned and to abstain should such situation occur, in order to avoid any embarrassment for the Court itself.[67]

4.3.3.3 Duration of the Term of Office and the Rule Against the Re-election of the Judges

Generally, the tenure in office of the judges of the Supreme or Constitutional Courts is considered one of the features able to ensure their independence. In particular, common ways to ensure such independence include long terms in office and the exclusion of the possibility to reappoint a judge following his or her first term. Alternatively, it can be provided that the judges maintain their role for life.[68]

Both approaches are considered to serve the purpose of increasing the independence of the courts for two different reasons. First of all, because they substantially reduce the risk that the judges are influenced in their decision making by the interest in being reappointed (thus for example attempting to favour the powers which will decide on their reappointment). Secondly, providing for a long term of office avoids the risk that there is political homogeneity between the courts and the representative bodies.[69]

The duration of the term of office of the judges of the Italian Constitutional Court was initially set at twelve years and later reduced to nine years,[70] one of longest terms of office among Italian public offices. Most importantly, it has been provided that the judges of the Constitutional Court could not be re-elected. This is considered to be another important element of the constitutional architecture aimed at ensuring the independence of the Court: as mentioned above, if a judge cannot be re-elected, it is possible to assume that he or she will be less inclined to be

[66] For example, this would be the case if a judge issues a statement on the press where he takes position in relation to a delicate question of constitutionality currently pending before the Court.

[67] Bin 2009, p 4025.

[68] As it is for example for the judges of the Supreme Court in the U.S.; see Tega 2018, p 439.

[69] Peri 2012, p 11.

[70] Constitutional Law no. 2/1967, which amended Article 135, para 3, of the Constitution.

influenced by external factors in his decisions, including the desire to increase the chances of being re-elected.

4.3.3.4 Election of the President of the Court

The Constitution explicitly provides that it is for the Court itself to elect, by secret ballot, its President, who remains in office for three years and may be re-elected, 'respecting in all cases the expiry term for constitutional judges'.[71] This has traditionally been considered to be another instrument to ensure the independence of the Court, which enjoys the freedom to decide who - among its members - will preside over its works.

The rules provide that, should none of the candidates, receive the majority of the votes at the first ballot, a second ballot takes place and, if necessary, a runoff election between the two judges with the most votes occurs.

The rules relating to the election of the President of the Court should not be underestimated, considering the important role that he plays in shaping the decisions of the Court: he has the power to select the rapporteur for each case and in turn the rapporteurs produce their reports, which are one of the very few documents of the proceedings before the Court which are made known to the public. In addition, the President decides the Court calendar and several important procedural aspects.[72]

However, the Court has traditionally followed the practice of electing President the judge with most seniority, with the aim of reinforcing the collegial nature of the institution and of avoiding any competition between the judges for the role of President.

4.3.4 The Accountability of the Court

The activities of the Constitutional Court are inspired by the principle of transparency, both from the point of view of its organization and from the point of view of its decisional powers. The reasons for this are, first of all, that the Court - like any other institution of a democratic legal system - is accountable towards the citizens for its actions, both when it takes its decisions (because these are taken in the name of the people[73]) and when it manages the resources, which are needed for its functioning (because they are constituted by public money, and therefore taxation).

---

[71] Article 135 of the Constitution.

[72] However, it shall also be noted that the President of the Court does not enjoy the same considerable power, for example, of the Chief justices in the United States or Canada (Breton and Fraschini 2003, p 323).

[73] As mentioned above, Article 1, para 2 of the Constitution, states that 'Sovereignty belongs to the people and is exercised by the people in the forms and within the limits of the Constitution', thus providing both legitimacy and accountability to the Court.

It has been noted that the principle of accountability is somehow weakened, in relation to the Italian Constitutional Court, due to the lack of dissenting or concurring opinions (see above). The lack of such instruments - meant to disclose the whole rationale of a certain decision to the public - would prevent the dialogue internal to the Court from being known at the exterior. As a result, the judges would risk being perceived as an 'oracle' or as a 'judge-king', who know the truth and 'dispense' it to the people.[74]

4.4 The Independence and the Accountability of the Italian Constitutional Court in Light of Bipolar Constitutionalism

4.4.1 The Independence of the Italian Constitutional Court in Practice

Besides the analysis provided above of the constitutional rules governing the independence of the Court, it is now useful to see if the Court can in practice actually be considered independent.

Some commentators have stressed that an assessment of the degree of independence of a court can only be based on the empirical observation.[75] In constitutional law terms, it could be said that, having observed and analysed the Constitutional provisions regulating the independence of the Court (i.e. the so-called 'formal Constitution'), we should now examine how these rules play within the real context (i.e. the so-called 'material Constitution').

Studies on the independence of the Court in practice have in particular focused on its decisions of the Court in cases relating to constitutional illegitimacy. This choice is traditionally linked with the fact that those decisions are in fact the main means for the Court to oppose the decisions of the other public powers and to enforce the constitutional provisions against the will of the other institutions and therefore be independent.[76]

---

[74] De Vergottini and Frosini 2010, p 7.

[75] Breton and Fraschini 2003, p 319. It is therefore not surprising that these kind of studies have been carried out in the past by economists.

[76] Fiorino et al. 2007, p 694, where the authors highlight that these decisions modify the legislation, and therefore have a considerable impact. The authors reject the theory that the high rate of judicial invalidation is a consequence of the political miscalculation of the legislator or of strategic choices of the disputants. The first hypothesis is excluded on the basis that Italian politicians would enact a statute that the voters want in that specific moment, although they know the Court will strike it down; the second one because it is very difficult for the disputants to foresee the final decision of the Court, due to the fact that it is for the local tribunal to decide to submit the case of potential illegitimacy to the Court, and due to the fact that much depends on the rapporteur and the Panel that are appointed.

It has been observed that the independence of the Italian Constitutional Court is in practice ensured by the fact that the rules on its composition and on the collegiate nature of its decisions make extremely difficult to carry out the so-called log-rolling.[77] As a consequence, it seems that the application of the rules governing the composition and the operations of the Court produce in practice the result that 'even if every single judge chose not to be independent, the Court itself would still be independent'.[78]

It has been observed that two elements relating to the judges taking part in the decision-making for the single cases seem in particular to be positively correlated with the independence of the Court, i.e. the number of judges elected by the professional judiciary and the age of the judges.[79]

In Italy, as opposed to what happens in several other jurisdictions (where the tenure of constitutional judges is longer than the mandate of political institutions), the political system has traditionally been more stable[80] than the - quite short - duration of the tenure of the judges of the Constitutional Court (nine years). Since the end of World War II, the Italian political scenario was ruled for decades by the same coalition of parties, with a leading role attributed to the Christian Democrats (the so-called 'blocked political system'). Following the end of the so-called First Republic and the beginning of the Second Republic in the early 1990s, new parties emerged together with a sort of two coalition system, where the left and the right coalition alternated in taking power.[81]

The relative stability of the political system - especially compared with the rather short tenure of the Constitutional judges - created a situation in which the legislative and executive branches have a quite small possibility to influence the career of the judges, thus creating a situation in which 'it does not pay judges to be accommodating'.[82]

The observation of the career paths of the judges of the Constitutional Court following their tenure seems to confirm this statement. In particular, it has been recorded that the percentage of post-tenure appointments for Presidents and

---

[77] This is defined as a system in which judge A supports judge B in a decision aimed at (directly or indirectly) favouring judge B's interests in exchange for judge B's support in a decision which favours judge A's interests (Breton and Fraschini 2003, p 323). In particular, the functioning of this system within the Italian Constitutional Court is made extremely difficult by the fact that only a small number of the judges can be involved, by the special role of the rapporteurs in the decision-making process, by the importance and the weight of precedent decisions on similar cases, and by the rules on the adoption of the decisions (simple majority and lack of dissenting opinions) which make the decisions anonymous.

[78] Breton and Fraschini 2003, p 324.

[79] Fiorino et al. 2007, p 683.

[80] To be noted, anyway, that while political alliances have traditionally been stable, governments changed very often.

[81] In more recent years, we witnessed a switch towards a sort of three or four party system; however, it is probably too early to assess its impact on the whole checks and balances structure and on the independence of the Constitutional Court.

[82] Fiorino et al. 2007, p 686.

Vice-Presidents of the Court rather than for ordinary judges is much higher, that most of those receiving such appointments were university professors, and that younger judges have more chances of being appointed to other posts than older judges.

As a result, these data do not seem to lead to the conclusion that the conduct of the judges during their tenure could be considered as a way to favour certain interests and being rewarded for this favour. To the contrary, they seem to show a rather natural situation, which can be quite easily explained with the institutional role exercised during the mandate, with the age at the end of the tenure and with the professional qualifications held by the former judges. In particular, the high appointment rate for university professors could be explained by the fact that they possess a legal training and a preparation that make them natural candidate for further appointments.[83]

In conclusion, through the analysis of the decisional practice of the Court, it has been observed that the independence of the Court appears to be increased by certain elements of structural independence (in particular, the presence in the Panel deciding a specific cases of more justices elected by the judiciary rather than from the other bodies) and by the age of the judges. This has led to the conclusion that independence should not be considered as a constant feature, but as a characteristic depending on the role played from time to time by those variables.[84]

4.4.2 The Italian Constitutional Court in Light of Bipolar Constitutionalism

We aim now at understanding how the independence of the Italian Constitutional Court qualifies the Italian system as constitutionally bipolar and whether the current situation in Italy is healthy from the perspective of sound bipolar constitutionalism. In other words, it is now important to assess whether and how the independence of the Court allows it to be the 'other pole' to which legislation is subject (i.e. to be the judicial pole, in addition to the legislative one).[85]

In fact, as it has been noted, the main characteristic distinguishing the courts from the political institutions is judicial independence, and this means 'independence from government and from political leadership, independence from political

83 Breton and Fraschini 2003, p 325.

84 Fiorino et al. 2007, p 694.

85 As it occurs in the context of the bipolar constitutionalism, as explained in Van der Schyff 2010, p 5.

parties and the latest political fashion, independence from popular feelings'.[86] As a result, 'judicial independence is at the heart of the bipolar model'.[87]

4.4.2.1 The Court of Rights and the Court of Powers

First of all, we should analyse the position of the Court within the Italian form of government. It shall be noted, in fact, that the very creation of the Court modified that form of government, because it had the effect of making the law lose its position of 'absolute supremacy' that it used to enjoy.[88] In fact, before the establishment of the Court, a traditional principle would entail the prohibition to subject the law to review and the prohibition - for any subject other than the Parliament - to amend it. The Constitution introduced the principle that the law can be reviewed and annulled by an institution which is not directly representative of the people.

The role of the Court within the legal order and its impact on the form of government has changed over the years since its establishment. This evolution is traditionally classified in different phases which correspond to different periods of the history of the Italian Republic.

In the first fifteen years of its activity (between the 1950s and the end of the Sixties), the Court mainly played the role of promoting reforms and applying the Constitution. In this phase, the Court was mainly called to 'clean' the Italian legal order which had recently come out of the Fascist period. In order to do so, the Court was in particular called to not only reinforce and root the values of the new Constitution but also more in general to support the process of modernization of the whole legal system. In a way, the Court replaced the Parliament which was still reluctant to substantially intervene and change the existing system and assumed what has been defined as a 'didactic' function, in the sense that it 'explained' the values of the Constitution to the public (including the notions of personal liberty, freedom of expression, freedom of assembly and gender equality), thus acquiring its authority as guardian of the Constitution.[89]

In the Seventies and at the beginning of the Eighties, the Court served as an instrument of mediation in the social and political conflicts which characterized those years. During this phase, the Court promoted the recognition and the consolidation of new rights and focused its review and attention on the new legislation. It has been observed that in this phase the Court became more politicized and more involved in ensuring the balancing of the different interests and values concerned by the questions it was called to decide on, making sure that the choices taken by the

---

[86] Koopmans 2003, p 250.

[87] *Ibid.*

[88] Mortati 1949, 460.

[89] Groppi 2008, pp 110–111.

Parliament were able to ensure the best balancing possible among the different values.[90] In these years, the Court did not hesitate to take important decisions concerning very sensitive issues, such as divorce and abortion, as well as family rights and the relationship between the State and the Church.[91]

Since the end of the Eighties, the Court entered the so-called phase of the 'operational efficiency' (thus managing to eliminate the backlog, which was due to the mentioned increase in the intervention of the Court on several different issues), acquiring an important role within the process for the legislative and constitutional reforms, facing a more bipolar political system with a high level of conflict and political tension.

Following the elimination of the backlog, the Court entered into a new phase, in which the rapidity of the operational efficiency of the Court brought it to more and more often review laws which had been recently adopted (in some cases, when the Parliament that has adopted those laws was still in power). This inevitably determined that the Court got more and more involved in the political debate. The situation not only made more difficult to ensure that its decisions maintain full authority and the aura of full impartiality, but also forced the Court to take into account the economic consequences of its decisions, which had to be balanced with the need to protect and implement the principles embodied in the Constitution.[92]

The current role of the Court in the form of government is substantially influenced by the nature of the functions attributed to it according to the Constitution. While for many years, it has been almost exclusively the judge of the scrutiny of the legislation through an 'incidental' review, it progressively became the judge of conflicts among the powers of the State and between the State and the Regions.[93] As a result, the Court has become more and more a Court of rights (when exercising its control over the laws) and a Court of powers (when deciding on the disputes among the institutions). In other words it involuntarily assumed a role of an arbiter of political (as well as constitutional) conflicts.[94]

4.4.2.2 The Relationship Between the Constitutional Court and the Legislator

The relationship between the Court and the Parliament has been extensively debated, because the Court has exercised for many years what has been defined as a

[90] Celotto 2009, p 21.

[91] Franciscis and Zannini 1992.

[92] Groppi 2008, pp 113–114.

[93] In recent years, however, the Court's case-law on conflicts became more and more consolidated and decisions rarely include significant new statements of principle.

[94] Celotto 2009, pp 21–22.

'para-legislative' function.[95] In particular, what was considered particularly problematic, at the beginning, was the fact that the Court started adopting - and this habit became more and more consolidated with time - the so-called manipulative decisions, i.e. judgements amending the literal content of a law or regulation. The additive judgements in particular are decisions of the Court in which it declares a provision unconstitutional not for what it provides but for what it fails to provide and adds a norm to the legal order. As a result, the Constitutional Court stopped being a 'negative legislator' in accordance with the Kelsenian model of constitutional review and started exercising the powers of the legislator. This approach of the Court attracted heavy criticism that was based, in particular, on the limited democratic legitimation of the Court (legitimation which on the contrary is attributed to the Parliament).[96]

Not only has the Court increased such activity but this has been progressively accepted at all levels.[97] The Court in particular was able to successfully reduce the intensity of the criticisms and of the discussions by creating decisions known as *'additive di principio'*.[98] In other words, it created a new form of decisions in which the need to issue a decision of unconstitutionality is balanced with the need to respect the discretional powers of the Parliament in identifying one of the possible solutions, in order to make the norm compatible with the Constitution. In those decisions, the Court would still declare the unconstitutionality of a law 'because it does not provide that…' (as in the 'ordinary' additive judgements) but instead of inserting the new provision it would only state the principle, that the Parliament will have to follow in inserting the new provision.[99]

---

95 As noted by Groppi 2008, pp 106, this was made technically possible through the theoretical distinction between '*disposizione*' (the legal text) and *'norma'* (the norm) (Crisafulli 1956, pp 929–939). Such distinction allows to 'derive multiple norms from a single text or a single norm from multiple texts' and, therefore, allows the Court to 'operate with more surgical precision' and allows the system to evolve.

96 Groppi 2008, pp 108; Celotto 2009, p 23; Celotto 2004, pp 118–120. In order to avoid such criticism, the Court has traditionally followed the so-called theory of the '*rime obbligate*' (prescribed verses), by which the Court may add to the statutes only the rules required by the Constitution.

97 It was noted that the fact that the Constitutional Court may interfere in the activity of the legislator is obvious and represents a necessary consequence of the constitutional norms providing for forms of control on the legislation. The very fact that it is accepted - and explicitly allowed - that a judicial review is exercised on the constitutionality of the statutes means that the Constitution allows for a judgement to compete or to prevail over the law (De Vergottini and Frosini 2010, p 3).

98 However, the use of the *additive di principio* has also been subjected to criticism because they attribute to the judge the power to decide which rule shall be applied in the specific case, until the intervention of the Parliament.

99 Clearly, this type of decisions created problems in relation to their effectiveness, because, while in some instances ordinary judges would consider them to be directly applicable to the specific case, in most cases ordinary judges would rather prefer to wait for the Parliament to intervene and adopt the 'missing' provision.

Another tool used by the Court to mitigate the intrusiveness of its intervention into the remit of the legislator is represented by the so-called 'admonitory decisions', i.e. decisions by which the Court rejects the challenge to the law but warns the Parliament that – should it not intervene and amend the contested law – it will uphold a future challenge and declare the law unconstitutional.[100]

The decisional practice outlined above created a sort of 'dialogue' between the Court and the Parliament. However, such collaboration with the legislator has not always been fully implemented by the Court, especially in two sector, which can be considered as a counter-trend. The first one is represented by the additive judgments as described above, which use has been sometimes even worrying: in some cases, the Court has forced its will upon the Parliament, which is in theory the only institution with the legitimation of creating new rules.

The second trend is constituted by the more and more active scrutiny of reasonableness. Year after year, such form of review has been developed into a sort of scrutiny on the unfairness of the law. In other words, it has been observed, the Court feels that the law 'is not right' and, although it cannot identify any direct or indirect, explicit or implicit violation of the Constitution, the Court still finds that the Constitution has been breached.[101] It has been argued that, through this reasoning, the Court created a sort of *passe partout* which can be used in several different situations and cases and which could lead the Court to decide on the merits (and not on the legality) of the law and on political issues.[102] As a result, some commentators have concluded that the Court ended up controlling that the laws are 'just', as it was feared in the past and without having the legitimation to do so.[103]

4.5 Conclusive Remarks

In conclusion, looking at the different elements and the main features of the Constitutional Court it appears that the choices adopted by the Italian constitution seem to be strongly inclined towards a strong independence of the Court, with a

100 Groppi 2008, p 109, where the author also notes that the Court has over the years also attempted to mitigate the effects of its decisions declaring laws as unconstitutional, taking into account the needs connected with the social welfare state and the limits to public economic resources.

101 Ruggeri and Spadaro 2004.

102 Paladin 1998.

103 Luther 1997. On the other hand, others have argued that the Court had to adopt such an approach to 'fix' the defects of the Italian legislation.

rather low degree of accountability.[104] Moreover, it can be concluded that the rules aimed at ensuring the independence of the Court have effectively served their purpose in practice. The doctrine has traditionally considered the Italian Constitutional Court to be characterized by a high degree of independence[105] or stated that it is 'at least as independent as any other corresponding constitutional court of democratic countries'.[106] In particular, it has been observed that the independence of the Court and its independent decision-making have helped it 'counteract the greater cohesion of the other government branches', thus 'improving the effectiveness of the system of checks and balances'.[107]

In fact, this degree of independence, together with the peculiar mixed nature of the Court (i.e. at the same time legal and political[108]) allowed the Court to effectively play the role for which it was conceived by the Constituent Assembly, i.e. protecting the Constitution from possible manipulations by the dominant groups. If the values and the principles of the Constitution are still present and effective in the Italian legal system, this is also due to the activity and constant intervention of the Constitutional Court.[109]

Interestingly, the Court traditionally took very strict positions *vis-a-vis* the Parliament and the ordinary judges, while it opted for a 'softer' approach toward the abuses of the Government concerning the rules concerning sources of law (e.g.

---

[104] See in particular Peri 2012, pp 22–23, where the author has carried out a comparison among the Constitutional Courts of a number of jurisdictions, and has concluded that Italy opted for the highest level of independence and the lowest level of accountability.

[105] Peri 2012, p 17.

[106] Breton and Fraschini 2003, p 319.

[107] Fiorino et al. 2007, p 683.

[108] However, when compared to constitutional courts of other jurisdictions, the Italian Constitutional Court is often considered one of those with the smallest degree of politicization, at least as regards the norms provided for the appointment of the judges. In particular, this is derived from the following features: (i) two thirds of the judges are appointed by a college and not by a single person; (ii) a quite considerable number of judges are appointed by the judiciary and not by political powers; and (iii) all the powers of the State are involved in the appointment procedure (Peri 2012, p 16).

[109] However, it has also been noted that because of the delicate role it has been attributed by the Constitution, the Court has never been fully accepted and its authority recognized by politicians. It is in particular claimed that recently the decisions of the Court are often not followed by the legislator or are strongly criticized by policitians and public opinion: this is seen as a serious problem, considering that the Court does not have powers to impose its decisions, and its force lies with its prestige and the consensus it enjoys (Bin 2009, p 4028). It has been observed that the approach of the Court to such situation has been very cautious, in order to 'preserve its legitimacy and to defend itself against an increasingly aggressive political power', not trying to make a 'direct link with public opinion' but rather deciding to '"disappear" from the headlines, devolving a large part of its job to other actors' (Groppi 2008, p 116). According to the author, this is particularly achieved by decentralizing its work (i.e. involving ordinary judges in constitutional review) and increasingly looking at supranational jurisdictions.

legislative decrees whose content is not aligned with the delegating laws and decree-laws adopted in breach of constitutional rules on their adoption).[110] The reason for this reluctance is probably that the Court never wanted to intervene in the core of the relationship between the Parliament and the Government, and wanted to leave to the former the role of controlling the latter.

In any case, the Court demonstrated to be ductile over time and to adapt its role to the different phases of the history of the Italian Republic, always maintaining its independence, as well as its accountability, and therefore its prestige and authority. It was able over the years to 'clean' the legal order from laws and regulations of the Fascist time, to mediate in social and political conflicts, to promote progress in the legal system and to become more and more efficient in its activities, while at the same time affirming its legitimation within the legal order.

In other words, the initial role of the Court was that of the 'island of reasonableness in the chaos of the opinions',[111] i.e. the Kelsenian constitutional judge and rational guardian of the law not influenced by political considerations. With time, the Court more and more became a mediator of social conflicts and a political interlocutor. However, it never turned into a body of the political system but was rather able to 'measure politics with the meter of the law'.[112] It is so possible to fully understand the real role of the Court in the Italian legal system, also in the light of the notion of bipolar constitutionalism: it served as an intermediary between law and politics, 'jurisdictionalising' politics into the legal procedures and, at the same time, 'politicizing' its judicial role through the political nature of the matters examined and the political effects of its decisions. As a result, it can be said that the Court turned into the 'island of the most reasonable opinion',[113] based on the idea that constitutional cases shall be assessed with a discretion which is similar to that of political decisions.

References

Bin R (2009) Sull'imparzialità dei giudici costituzionali, Giurisprudenza costituzionale. 4015–4028

Breton A, Fraschini A (2003) The Independence of the Constitutional Court. Constitutional Political Economy 14:319–333

Celotto A (2004) La Corte costituzionale. Il Mulino, Bologna

---

110 It can be observed, however, that a similarly soft approach was adopted in cases relating to the breach of procedural rules on the ordinary legislative procedure.

111 Modugno 1970, p XI.

112 Cheli 1996, 13.

113 Elia 1984, p 163.

Celotto A (2006) Rappresentanza e Corte costituzionale. In: Chieffi L (ed) Rappresentanza politica. Gruppi di pressione. *Élites* al potere. Atti del convegno (Caserta, 6–7 maggio 2005). Giappichelli, Turin
Celotto A (2009) Questioni di giustizia costituzionale. Editoriale Scientifica, Naples
Cheli E (1996) Il giudice delle leggi. Il Mulino, Bologna
Conti G L (2006) Articolo 135. In: Bifulco R, Celotto A, Olivetti M, Commentario alla Costituzione. UTET Giuridica, Turin
Crisafulli V (1956) Questioni in tema di interpretazione della Corte Costituzionale nei confronti con l'interpretazione giudiziaria, Giurisprudenza costituzionale, 929
De Franciscis M E, Zannini R (1992) Judicial Policy-Making in Italy: The Constitutional Court. West European Politics 15:68–79
De Vergottini G, Frosini T E (2010) Sul mito della Corte costituzionale 'in-politica'. Percorsi costituzionali, 2/3
D'Orazio G (1966) Aspetti dello status di giudice costituzionale. Giuffrè, Milan
Elia L (1984) Relazione di sintesi sul tema Corte costituzionale e principio di eguaglianza. In: Occhiocupo N (ed) La Corte costituzionale tra norma giuridica e realtà sociale. CEDAM, Padua
Fiorino N, Padovano F, Sgarra G (2007) The Determinants of Judiciary Independence: Evidence from the Italian Constitutional Court (1956–2002). Journal of Institutional and Theoretical Economics 163:683–705
Koopmans T (2003) Courts and Political Institutions. A Comparative View. Cambridge University Press, Cambridge
Groppi T (2008) The Italian Constitutional Court: Towards a 'Multilevel System' of Constitutional Review? Journal of Comparative Law 3:100–117
Luther J (1997) Ragionevolezza (delle leggi). In: Digesto delle discipline pubblicistiche. UTET, Turin, 12:341–362
Modugno F (1970) L'invalidità della legge. Giuffrè, Milan
Mortati C (1949) Sull'eccesso di potere legislativo. Giurisprudenza Italiana, 1:457–461
Paladin L (1998) Diritto costituzionale. CEDAM, Padua
Peri A (2012) Judicial Independence vs. Judicial Accountability: Judicial Selection Models for Constitutional Courts. A Comparative Analysis. Comparative Law Review 3:1–24
Pertici A (2004) Astensione e ricusazione dei giudici costituzionali: ragioni e limiti della loro esclusione ed ipotesi di una loro introduzione. Giurisprudenza costituzionale, 3105
Ruggeri A, Spadaro A (2004) Lineamenti di giustizia costituzionale. Giappichelli, Turin
Russell P H (2001) Toward a General Theory of Judicial Independence. In: Russell P H, O'Brien D M (eds) Judicial Independence in the Age of Democracy. University Press of Virginia, Charlottesville/London
Sandulli A M (1966) L'indipendenza della Corte costituzionale. In: Maranini G (ed) La giustizia costituzionale. Vallecchi, Florence
Tega D (2018) Articolo 135. In: Clementi F, Cuocolo L, Rosa F, Vigevani G E (eds) La Costituzione italiana: commento articolo per articolo. Il Mulino, Bologna, pp 438–443
Van der Schyff G (2010) Judicial Review of Legislation: A Comparative Study of the United Kingdom, the Netherlands and South Africa. Springer, New York
Volcansek M (2006) Judicial Selection in Italy: A Civil Service Model with Partisan Results. In: Mallerson K, Russell P H (eds) Appointing Judges in an Age of Judicial Power. University of Toronto Press, Toronto/Buffalo/London
Zagrebelsky G (1992) Il diritto mite. Legge diritti giustizia. Einaudi, Turin
Zagrebelsky G, Marcenò V (2018) Giustizia costituzionale. Il Mulino, Bologna

Alfonso Celotto is Professor of Constitutional Law at 'Roma Tre' University and lawyer admitted to plead before the Court of Cassation. He was visiting professor at the universities of Buenos Aires and Warsaw and at the McGill University of Montreal. He authored more than 400 books, articles, comments and encyclopaedia entries, as well as novels. He coordinates the Editorial Board of the journal *Giurisprudenza Costituzionale* and of www.giustamm.it, and is a member of the Steering Committee of the journal *Giurisprudenza Italiana*. He is co-editor of the 'Dictionary of public law' and coordinates the *Commentario alla Costituzione* and the *Digesto delle discipline pubblicistiche*.

Chapter 5
Bipolar Constitutionalism in The Netherlands and Its Consequences for the Independence and Accountability of the Judiciary

Geerten Boogaard

Contents

Abstract The expansion of the constitutional function of the judiciary in the Netherlands necessitates a perpetual review of its independence. Should it be reinforced in order to better protect judges from the possible repercussions of politically unwelcome judgments? Or should the safeguards be weakened in order to legitimize judicial interventions in political processes? This chapter analyses the historical expansion of the constitutional function and provides an overview of the current formal and informal constitutional safeguards relating to the legal status and institutional and functional independence of the judiciary in the Netherlands. The conclusion is that in particular the informal safeguards for independence such as the convention of co-optation and the *sub judice* principle can help to strike a balance between legal protection and democracy.

G. Boogaard (✉)
Leiden University, Leiden, The Netherlands
e-mail: g.boogaard@law.leidenuniv.nl

Hirsch Ballin, Van der Schyff & Stremler (eds.), *European Yearbook of Constitutional Law 2019*, European Yearbook of Constitutional Law 1,
https://doi.org/10.1007/978-94-6265-359-7_5

Keywords Administrative Jurisdiction Division of the Dutch Council of State · constitutionalism · Dutch Supreme Court · judicial accountability · judicial independence

5.1 Introduction

Any jurisdiction with some history has court judgments which in hindsight are referred to with great pride, or which one would rather were forgotten. Judgments where the court did what it had to do, and choices that turned out to be on the wrong side of history. The same is true in The Netherlands. At the end of the 19th century, the feminist Aletta Jacobs brought a case contesting her exclusion from the right to vote. She relied in the court proceedings on the literal text of the Netherlands Constitution. In 1848, the constitutional legislature had apparently found it so self-evident that only men would be called to the ballot box, that it had simply omitted stating this explicitly in the text. In the case of suffrage based on ownership of property, the only requirement was full Dutch citizenship.[1] And were women, Jacobs argued before the Supreme Court, not also full Dutch citizens? Not entirely, the Supreme Court ruled; at least not in the relevant sense of the meaning in this case.[2] Without providing any further critical reasoning, the Supreme Court left the issue to the constitutional legislature, which waited until 1917 before giving women the right to vote. This thorny issue and the evasive response of the Court brings to mind the *Dredd Scott* case in 1857.[3] Scott was a slave who had applied to the American Supreme Court for his freedom, only to have the door slammed in his face. Afro-Americans were not *citizens* in the sense of the American Constitution and therefore had no standing in federal courts. They only received this after the civil war by virtue of the fourteenth amendment to the American Constitution. In terms of legal protection of minorities or the attainment of individual fundamental rights, terms often used to defend the constitutional function of the courts in a democracy, both cases bestow little honour on the highest courts. Thankfully, there are judgments that do so. In American literature, the case *Brown v. Board of Education* in 1954[4] is placed opposite *Dredd Scott*. Miss Brown was refused enrolment by the school of her choice because of her dark skin colour and she, too,

---

[1] More precisely: 'The members of the House of Representatives will be elected in the electoral districts, into which the Kingdom is divided, by the Dutch residents of majority age, in the full enjoyment of civil and citizenship rights', Article 76 Dutch Constitution 1848 (author's translation).

[2] Supreme Court of the Netherlands, 18 May 1883, *Weekblad van het recht*, 45, No. 4917. See on this case Pessers 1983.

[3] Supreme Court of the United States, *Dred Scott v. Sandford*, 6 March 1857, 60 U.S. 393.

[4] Supreme Court of the United States, *Brown v. Board of Education*, 17 May 1954, 347 U.S. 483.

turned to the Supreme Court. In this case the Court responded positively. Not only was Brown's claim upheld, the Supreme Court proceeded to rule against all segregation in public schools since separate facilities were considered inherently unequal. From an institutional point of view, this was a courageous judgment and assistance from marines would be required to actually implement the decision. The Netherlands Supreme Court also made peace with the women's movement. Instead of being left out in the cold like Aletta Jacobs, there was a warm reception for the *Proefprocessenfonds Clara Wichmann* (Clara Wichmann Foundation for Test Cases) in its case against the State concerning the *Staatkundig Gereformeerde Partij* (Political Reformed Party) (SGP).[5] The SGP is a small orthodox Protestant political party that refused to include women on its list of candidates because it believes this to be incompatible with the position of women in society. The Foundation claimed that if the State did not act to halt this practice, it would be unlawful because the Netherlands is party to the UN Women's Convention. The Netherlands is thus obliged to ensure that men and women are *equally* electable in representative bodies. The Supreme Court accepted this argument and upheld a declaratory Statement, which required the State to take legislative measures against a political party represented in parliament. Though no marines were needed in this case, it was a politically sensitive judicial intervention that had a number of constitutional complications; a good example, thus, of how far the Supreme Court is now prepared to go to safeguard legal rights and fulfil fundamental rights.

There are many differences between *Brown v. Board of Education* and the *SGP* case; but there are also similarities. One of the most interesting similarities from a scholarly point of view is that both cases are examples of *public interest litigation* with which the American Supreme Court and the Netherlands Supreme Court fulfil their constitutional function compared to other state authorities.[6] Public interest litigation is characterized by its typical structure in a legal dispute. Often cases are involved where interest groups strive to implement fundamental rights via the courts. This is in direct contrast to the classic model upon which the division of powers is based. The archetype of civil law justice is the settlement of a dispute between two individual citizens concerning a conflict that has arisen between them. The victim and the offender are claimant and defendant; the issue is an unlawful act, which occurred in the past, the resulting damage of which must be compensated. Public interest litigation cases are less involved with individuals, but more with groups who are focussed on the general interest. Claimants are sometimes not even a victim: in the *SGP* case, not the SGP women had gone to court but a foundation that stood up for the general interest that would be served by proceedings against the SGP. In the way that the claimant does not necessarily have to be the victim, the defendant does not have to be the actual offender. The *SGP* case was brought against the State and not the SGP. Finally, the focus of public interest litigation is

---

[5] Supreme Court of the Netherlands, *SGP*, 9 April 2010, ECLI:NL:HR:2010:BK4549. See on this case: Van den Brink and Ten Napel 2013.

[6] Uzman and Boogaard 2015.

not primarily redress for a past injustice, but is aimed more at extra measures in the future. In the *SGP* case, no payment or compensation was required; it was all about measures to prevent the SGP acting in such a manner again in the future. All things considered, public interest litigation is an important element of what Koopmans refers to as bipolar constitutionalism: political institutions, understood as the executive and the legislature of a constitutional entity, are held to account not only through elections and political checks and balances, but also through review performed by national and supranational courts.[7]

The constitutional function of the courts in bipolar constitutionalism gives rise to new questions concerning the independence of the judiciary. Should the safeguards against interference be reinforced in order to strengthen the constitutional function? A court which directly corrects political bodies could, after all, expect repercussions. An illustration of this is the politicization of appointments to the American Supreme Court since the growth of public interest litigation. Or is the opposite true, and should the safeguards be weakened to legitimize the constitutional function? Or is the situation just fine as it is? This chapter will discuss these questions in relation to the Netherlands legal system. More specifically, in relation to the two most important courts with a constitutional function: the Supreme Court and the Administrative Jurisdiction Division of the Council of State (the Division). The Supreme Court has always been independent and only in the course of time acquired a constitutional function. The Council of State, on the other hand, has had a constitutional function for years, but its independent Administrative Jurisdiction Division is of a later date. In the Netherlands, there are a few other highest administrative courts that officially also have a constitutional function, but little can be added to this contribution by giving these separate attention.

The background and development of bipolar constitutionalism in the Netherlands will be analysed in Sects. 5.2 to 5.4. Sections 5.5 and 5.6 will deal with the official and unofficial constitutional safeguards for the independence of these courts. Section 5.7 will close with an evaluation of whether these safeguards should be reinforced, weakened, or whether they should remain as they are. This chapter deals with classic constitutionalism. The implications of various factual developments, such as the growth of digital technology, on the functioning and position of the judiciary will only be dealt with briefly. This is not because they are irrelevant for the independence of the judiciary, but because such developments have little particular relevance to the question of whether the growth of the constitutional function of the judiciary must lead to a new appraisal of the safeguards for independence.

Certainly, from a theoretical point of view, there is a difference between the independence of the courts and their impartiality. The first difference is institutional: is the court in an optimal position to do what it thinks the law requires of it? The second is individual: does the court have any special interest, which coincides with that of one of the parties? Of course, marginal cases do exist. For example, the

---

[7] Koopmans 2003, pp 248–251.

institutional setting of a court can create the appearance of partiality, which is prohibited, as will become clear in relation to the Division. This chapter, however, will deal mainly with the independence of the judiciary. The rules on the 'blood' relationships between courts and parties etc. will not be considered; the topic of independence is already large enough as it is. It is even so large, that it would be helpful at the outset to make certain distinctions. In this chapter, independence takes (at least) three forms: in relation to the institution, its legal position and its function[8] Institutional independence relates to the organization of the judiciary as a whole; it concerns systematic safeguards. For example, the structural underpayment of judges, or specific powers for the executive to intervene in proceedings at a certain court which threaten the institutional independence. In addition, there is independence in relation to the legal position of the courts. In an independent judiciary, judges need not fear individual repercussions if their decisions possibly go down badly with other state authorities. Consider, for example, protection from dismissal, or the policy on promotions or lowering the retirement age in order to sidetrack certain judges. Finally, functional independence concerns the absence of any form of legal authority to issue instructions to individual judges, but goes much further than that. True functional independence exists when all judges feel free to decide in accordance with what they believe the law requires of them. For example, if a judge on a criminal court has the freedom to acquit a suspect who was deemed guilty by the public of child abuse because he found that the evidence, though valid, was unconvincing. Such functional independence is not just a matter of judicial standards, it is perhaps in particular a question of a collective mentality: an *ésprit de corps* within the judiciary and the constitutional understanding of this outside the judiciary. As Böckenförde put it, a state, which is based on the rule of law, exists on conditions, which it cannot secure itself. Meaningful evaluations of the independence of the judiciary cannot ignore this. I have therefore noted this here at the outset.

5.2 Historical Introduction to the Netherlands Judiciary

The history of the current Netherlands judiciary starts in 1811, when the Emperor Napoleon had had enough of the squabbling in the Low Countries and annexed them by decree to his empire. This led to the implementation here of the existing French judicial system.[9] Just like in France, the Netherlands was divided into *arrondissementen* and *departementen*, each with its own district court and court of assizes. In The Hague, an Imperial High Court of Law was established for all Dutch *departementen* combined. An appeal could be brought against the judgments of the

[8] Van den Eijnden 2011; Van Emmerik et al. 2014, pp 16–18.

[9] Van Boven 2011.

Imperial High Court of Law in The Hague before the existing *Cour de cassation* in Paris. As a result, three Dutch judges were appointed to that Court. And so Napoleon succeeded where the patriots had failed: transforming the 1579 confederal Republic of the Seven United Provinces of the Netherlands into a modern unitary state. The administration of justice in the Republic had been a matter for the provinces, and the various provincial aristocracies resisted centralization of the influential competences wholeheartedly. That was, until Napoleon lost his patience and dispatched an army of French officials to the North to get matters organized centrally. At the same time, the French kept a close eye on stability. For the new judicial functions, they recruited the same regents as had previously been in office in the Republic; therefore, in the end, the same group of judges remained. But from 1811 onwards, a professional judicial organization existed that had functional requirements with regard to education and age, procedures for appointments, protection from dismissal and also included a number of incompatibilities; and this would remain so.

After the French period, the Netherlands became a Kingdom under King Willem I in 1815. The judiciary formed according to the French example, remained an important pillar in the unitary state. 'Throughout the Kingdom, justice will be done in the name of the King', the Constitution declared in 1815. A return to the old provincial jurisdiction was therefore absolutely out of the question. However, instead of the French *departementen*, the old provinces and their Provincial Courts of Appeal did return. This was hardly efficient. At the Court of Appeal in Assen, the capital of the sparsely populated province Drenthe, between 1838 and 1875 on average there was one criminal case a week and one civil case every six weeks.[10] One concession to the old provincial aristocracy were the Provincial Courts of Appeal. Appointments were made upon the nomination of three persons, done by the Provincial Council of the province in question. Once again, the same regents therefore still called the judicial shots, so to speak. But they did have a court of cassation above them. This task was given to the new Supreme Court in The Hague which could first only set aside a judgment because of a breach of procedural rules, but soon also because of a violation of law. In this way, uniformity of law was safeguarded in the new Kingdom. One typical compromise with which the French legacy became reconciled with Dutch history in 1815, was the constitutional requirement to select members of the Supreme Court as far as possible from all the different provinces. These types of proportionality requirements are taken very seriously in the Netherlands. A justice was even appointed from the abovementioned province Drenthe after a long search.[11]

Not only did the organization of the judiciary remain more or less intact during the regime change between 1813 and 1815, the French safeguards for independence survived for the most part. The 1815 Constitution required that officers of the judiciary would be appointed for life and when appointing new justices to the

[10] Brood 2011, p 243.

[11] Van Koppen and Ten Kate 2003.

Supreme Court, the King had to choose between three persons nominated by the House of Representatives. As a result, a certain degree of independence for the judiciary was safeguarded in relation to the government: it was not possible to easily appoint friends, and enemies could also not easily be removed from office. In addition, a degree of independence of the judiciary as an institution was safeguarded by virtue of the instruction from the constitutional legislature to the ordinary legislature to establish the organization of the judiciary in general and the remuneration of judges in particular in an Act. Therefore, in principle, the executive could not intervene at the individual level. Setting up the judiciary, however, remained problematic. It took until 1838 before the Judiciary (Organization) Act took effect. Of relevance in relation to judicial independence is the prohibition on justices of the Supreme Court to become a member of the House of Representatives included in this Act. And the members of the Provincial Courts of Appeal may not also be a member of the Provincial Council. The background to this incompatibility was a safeguard against a conflict of interests, since the House of Representatives and the Provincial States nominated the candidates for these posts. At that time, it was not generally incompatible for judicial officers to have a political post. What is more, until the end of the 19th century it was even not unusual that judges were appointed to representative bodies as well. Between 1849 and 1888, 15 percent of the members of the House of Representatives came from or were still active in the judiciary.[12] Later, this combination of offices gradually disappeared, while at the same time the States General became more democratic and political. Until recently, there were only a few members of the Upper House who also presided as judge.[13] Today, the internal rules of the judiciary advise against membership of the States General, since 'a judge should not at the same time be a (co)legislator'.[14] Recently, a senator therefore resigned when she was appointed as a judge.[15] In this way, the factual division of the legislature and the judiciary from a staffing perspective has been accomplished; a conclusion which the Group of States against Corruption (GRECO) of the Council of Europe would like to see laid down in the Constitution.[16]

---

[12] Brood 2011, pp 229–256.

[13] From 2007 to 2011 senator E.F. Lagerwerf-Vergunst was a senator for the ChristenUnie party and a judge at the District Court Rotterdam. See www.parlement.com/id/vhjogfpxq4zz/e_f_flora_lagerwerf_vergunst. Accessed 1 March 2019.

[14] See https://www.rechtspraak.nl/SiteCollectionDocuments/Leidraad-onpartijdigheid-en-nevenfuncties-in-de-rechtspraak-januari-2014.pdf, p 14. Accessed 1 March 2019.

[15] In April 2018 senator J. Beuving became a justice at the Court of Appeal in Arnhem-Leeuwarden and as a result resigned from her position at the Senate. See https://www.eerstekamer.nl/nieuws/20180326/senator_beuving_pvda_vertrekt_uit. Accessed 1 March 2019.

[16] Group of States against Corruption 2012, p 49 (Recommendation V).

However, not everything from the French period was adopted in full in the new Kingdom. A crown jewel of the French revolution - trial by jury - was repealed as soon as possible. There is no reason to suppose that so much had gone wrong between 1811 and 1813 at trials by jury in the courts of assizes. It is more likely that the democratic origin of a system of trial by jury was distrusted. The Dutch regents judged faith in themselves to be greater than that of the French people in the judges of their *ancien régime*.[17] Moreover, trial by jury does not fit in the elitist tradition, which has never entirely disappeared in the Netherlands. The reintroduction of trial by jury was something that regularly returned to the agenda, but never became a serious option. The Constitution in 1922 ruled out the introduction of trial by jury.[18] In 1971, the Cals/Donner Government Committee considered the ordinary citizen to be too emotional when it came to criminal justice.[19] However, for many years now, there have been a few specialist courts where laypersons do have a part in judicial proceedings.[20] This is more to do with specific expertise than democracy.

What remains in relation to the history of the judicial organization can be concluded as being more of the same: further centralization and professionalization. By 1875, the unitary state had become so self-evident that the authority of the provinces could finally be broken. The inefficient eleven provincial Courts of Appeal were abolished and the judicial map for appeals was divided into five areas of jurisdiction, each with its own court of appeal. At the same time, the number of district courts was reduced from 34 to 23. The 1983 Constitution deleted the slogan that throughout the entire Kingdom, justice was administered in the name of the King. The confusion that such a slogan could give rise to in relation to the independence of the judiciary, outweighed the necessity to reinforce the unitary state. Nevertheless, the custom has remained to hang a portrait of the reigning monarch behind the judges in all courtrooms. In 2013 the judicial map was completely revised so that the Netherlands now has eleven district courts, four courts of appeal and one Supreme Court.[21] Their relationship to each other has never changed: district courts pass judgment mainly at first instance, courts of appeal in appeal cases and the Supreme Court in appeals in cassation.

---

[17] Bossers 1987.

[18] Technically because Article 116(3) Dutch Constitution refers to 'partial participation' of laypersons in the judicial system. *A contrario*, it can thus be deduced that a judicial system with full implementation via laypersons can be considered to be excluded.

[19] Staatscommissie-Cals/Donner 1971, pp 247–249. See for a recent reiteration: De Roos 2013.

[20] Jansen 2014.

[21] See for a useful introduction to the current judicial organization the English web pages on rechtspraak.nl: www.rechtspraak.nl/English and on the website of the national government: www.government.nl/topics/administration-of-justice-and-dispute-settlement/the-dutch-court-system. Accessed 1 March 2019.

5.3 The Development of the Constitutional Function of the Supreme Court

When the Netherlands inherited the French judicial system, it also inherited something of the French revolutionary distrust of the judiciary. The Dutch tradition falls under *the French deviation*: the desire to protect the law from the judges.[22] If trial by jury was found in the Netherlands to be a bit of an insult to the professional administration of justice, this certainly did not mean that the judiciary was seen as *the least dangerous branch of government*. Illustrative of this is the General Provisions (Kingdom Legislation) Act of 1829, parts of which are still in effect today. The Act emphasizes to judges that they must 'rule in accordance with the law' and 'on no occasion may judge the inherent value or fairness of the law'. They are also prohibited from delivering judgment 'by way of general regulation, disposition or rule'.[23] In particular, the prohibition on so-called *arrêts de règlement* (regulatory judgments) is striking since this is clearly superfluous. Contrary to France, this has never existed in the Netherlands. These are purely prohibited to be on the safe side.

In line with this distrust towards judges, the Supreme Court did not fulfil a constitutional function from the start. The independent administration of justice was mainly limited to the adjudication of criminal offences and the settlement of private disputes. Between 1822 and 1844, a so-called Conflict Decree even existed in which the King could remove a case against the executive power from the jurisdiction of the judiciary. In 1848, the Constitution added a prohibition on constitutional review. This article prohibits the courts from reviewing the constitutionality of an Act. Of all the degenerate types of government, the government of judges was the worst, so it was thought on that occasion, and therefore the formal Act had to be placed outside any suspicion.[24] So the fact that the Supreme Court in 1883 did not consider itself to be the correct institution to introduce the vote for women may be disappointing from the perspective of human rights, but it is not entirely inexplicable in light of the institutional context.

Since 1900, the civil courts have increasingly acquired a constitutional function. The starting point of this process is often viewed to be a ruling in 1915 in which the Supreme Court finally dealt with the thought behind the Conflict Decree: that the civil courts should not be involved in disputes in which the government is a party.[25] Ever since, the Supreme Court has ruled that the civil courts at all times have jurisdiction when a citizen requests protection against a violation of a civil right, even if protection against the State is requested. Given the possibility to bring all

---

22 Merryman 1996; Pieterman 1990.

23 Respectively Articles 11 and 12 of the General Provisions (Kingdom Legislation) Act (Act 15 May 1829, Bulletin of Acts and Decrees 829/28) (author's translation).

24 Adams and Van der Schyff 2006; Boogaard and Uzman 2018.

25 Supreme Court of the Netherlands, *Guldemond/Noordwijkerhout*, 21 December 1915, ECLI: NL:HR:1915:AG1773.

government action which is alleged to be unlawful before the courts, since 1915 an independent court has always had jurisdiction in disputes against the government. A second relevant development is the recognition of group actions. Originally developed as a way for environmental activists to bring court proceedings, the general interest action has now acquired its own place in the Civil Code. As a result, not only can government actions be put to the civil courts, but the possibilities to do so are almost infinite. A further important impetus for the constitutional function is the development of international human rights since the Second World War. The European Convention on Human Rights (ECHR) is central here, where an individual right of complaint is possible before the European Court of Human Rights (ECtHR) in Strasbourg. Because of the traditional openness of the Dutch Constitution towards international law, an alternative arose for testing an Act against the Constitution, which is still prohibited.[26] Citizens seeking legal protection against the government or wishing to invoke their fundamental rights against the legislature, can achieve via a human rights convention what is not possible via the Constitution. The Dutch courts may be prohibited from performing a constitutional review of Acts, but they are obliged to not apply 'provisions applicable in the Kingdom' on the grounds of directly applicable treaty law. From an uncertain start in the 1960s and 1970s, the application of international human rights has risen dramatically since the 1980s. The reason for this was not just the uncertainty of lawyers and the cold feet of the courts, the unpleasant prospect of actually being held to account in Strasbourg also played a role.

And so in the course of time, all building blocks for public interest litigation were in place and the approach of the Supreme Court also changed. It still cannot be called activist, but the Supreme Court has certainly become more self-confident in the past hundred years.[27] If the Supreme Court wishes to intervene, it does so. Even if this means coming opposite the other State authorities or finding itself in politically sensitive waters. The *SGP* case is the most striking example of this. In spite of the lack of constitutional review – the debate about which continues in full[28] – the constitutional function of the Supreme Court has reached adulthood.

5.4 The Independence of Administrative Jurisdiction

Parallel to the development of the constitutional function of the civil courts, the administrative jurisdiction became independent. This was no easy process.[29] For a long time the notion prevailed that, legal protection against the government had to be organized within the government. Finally, a single citizen requested protection

---

[26] Efthymiou and De Wit 2013; Martens 1998; Ten Kate and Van Koppen 1994.

[27] Uzman et al. 2010.

[28] Adams and Van der Schyff 2006.

[29] For a general overview of Dutch administrative law, see: Seerden and Wenders 2012.

against policy that was applied to him in the name of all citizens. An important spokesman for this line of thought was the Leiden professor of constitutional law Struycken. In a modern parliamentary democracy, he claimed in 1910, the executive authority does not stand opposite the citizens, but emanates from among the citizens.[30] Disputes between the government and individual citizens are in fact disputes among citizens themselves. So they can be better dealt with by other administrators than by independent civil courts. It is the distance between the administration and the judiciary which exists because of this independence, that makes the court, according to this line of thought, unfit to fulfil a constitutional role. More shelter was expected from the administrative appeal. Here, a higher administrative authority rules on the legitimacy of the actions of the lower administrative authority.

The most familiar form of administrative appeal was the *Kroonberoep* (appeal to the Crown) against government action and brought before the Constitutional King, so the King acting under the aegis of one or more ministers. Since 1861, the Crown was obliged in its handling of such appeals to the Crown, to request advice from the Council of State, the oldest advisory body of the government which had assisted Emperor Charles V and which has since reinvented itself in new functions. To provide advice in appeals to the Crown, the Council of State in line with the model of the French *Conseil d'Etat*, was given a separate Administrative Disputes Division. Members of this Division were appointed for life. This Division heard the parties and drew up its advice in the form of a draft Royal Decree which the government merely had to sign. In practice, the government always did so. In this way, the Disputes Division had *de facto* a constitutional function. But officially, it remained an advisory practice and therefore the ECtHR ruled in 1985 in the *Bentham* case that the Disputes Division was not an impartial and independent tribunal in the sense of Article 6 ECHR.[31] The Netherlands, against all expectations at the time when it became party to the Convention, was found to be in violation of a human right.

The impact of the *Benthem* ruling was considerable. It stimulated the uniformisation of administrative law which the constitutional legislature had already decided on in 1983, and the independence of administrative jurisdiction even more so. In 1994 the General Administrative Law Act came into being.[32] The opportunity for administrative appeal remained, but splitting up the appeal was given a definite preference. First, there is a full administrative review by the administrative authority which has taken the primary decision, and then there is a review of the lawfulness by an independent administrative court. Administrative jurisdiction in first instance was held at the courts of the ordinary judiciary. In 1994 the appeal remained divided over the specialized courts which had developed in part within the judiciary, but mainly outside it. This arrangement still applies. The final judgment in tax

---

[30] Struycken 1910.

[31] European Court of Human Rights, *Benthem v. Netherlands*, 23 October 1985, ECLI:CE:ECHR:1985:1023JUD000884880. See on this case Van Dijk 1987.

[32] Barkhuysen et al. 2012.

cases is given by the Supreme Court, disputes concerning social security are handled before the Central Appeals Tribunal[33] and appeals concerning economic administrative law are handled before the Trade and Industry Appeals Tribunal. In the case of an appeal concerning general administrative law, environmental law and immigration law, the Administrative Jurisdiction Division of the Council of State is authorized to pass judgment itself.[34]

Maintaining an Administrative Jurisdiction Division at the Council of State has not led to the Netherlands being found in violation of Article 6 ECHR again. The independence of the Division has not been challenged directly again in Strasbourg. However, doubts do exist about the combination of administrative jurisdiction and the provision of legislative advice in relation to institutional independence and its close relation: the objective impartiality or the absence of the appearance of partiality. A court, according to the ECHR, can never be objectively impartial when it advises and adjudicates in the same case or on the same legal issue (same case, same decision).[35] Partly in response to this, the legislature in 2010 made the division of staff at the Council of State clearer by dividing staff into state councillors and adjudicating state councillors. The number of staff who fulfil both functions at the Council of State (the 'members' in the proper sense) has been reduced to just ten out of the current sixty members and state councillors. The criticism of the combination of the advising and adjudicating task of the Council of State has not completely disappeared with this tightening of the rules. It is certainly still a possibility that eventually the entire administrative jurisdiction will be integrated in the ordinary judiciary, as intended in the 1980s.[36] Swift reform of the judicial organization was not a feature of the Dutch system in 1800, and that still applies today.

5.5 The Formal Safeguards for the Independence of the Supreme Court and the Administrative Jurisdiction Division of the Council of State

The Constitution contains a number of safeguards for the independence of the judiciary.[37] The Constitution does not determine which courts are part of that judiciary. The constitutional legislature leaves this to the ordinary legislature in the

---

[33] See www.rechtspraak.nl/Organisatie-en-contact/Organisatie/Centrale-Raad-van-beroep/English-summary. Accessed 1 March 2019.

[34] See https://www.raadvanstate.nl/talen/artikel/. Accessed 1 March 2019.

[35] European Court of Human Rights, *Procola v. Luxembourg*, 28 September 1995, ECLI:CE:ECHR:1995:0928JUD001457089; European Court of Human Rights, *Kleyn v. Netherlands*, 6 May 2003, ECLI:CE:ECHR:2003:0506JUD003934398.

[36] *Kamerstukken II* 1980/ 81, 16 162, no. 3, pp 2–3.

[37] For an English translation of the Dutch constitution, see https://www.government.nl/topics/constitution. Accessed 1 March 2019. On the judicial organization and its independence in particular, see: Van den Eijnden 2011; Bovend'Eert 2008.

expectation that it will designate 'all judicial institutions which within our legal system fulfil a judicial task in the long term' as courts of the judiciary.[38] This expectation has only materialized to a certain extent. Article 2 of the Judicial Organization Act currently only designates district courts, courts of appeal and the Supreme Court. The Administrative Jurisdiction Division of the Council of State therefore is not part of the judiciary. As it is only involved in administrative law, though contrary to the expectation of the constitutional legislature, this is not in conflict with the actual wording of the Constitution. The Constitution stipulates that civil jurisdiction and criminal jurisdiction must be incorporated in the judiciary, but administrative law *may* also be assigned to courts outside the judiciary. So the Constitution contains no general safeguard that all jurisdiction with a constitutional function must be assigned to the officially independent judiciary. This is one of the points where the Constitution gives priority to room for developments in the judiciary above codifying safeguards itself.

Compared to the Division, the Supreme Court, being part of the judiciary, does share in the safeguards for the judiciary. Institutional independence, in particular, is anchored in Article 116 of the Constitution. This article instructs the ordinary legislature to regulate the structure, composition and competence of the judiciary in an Act of Parliament. Thus the former safeguard is retained which required that the organization of the judiciary is regulated in a general Act. Delegating regulatory competence to the government is not excluded, but must remain very limited. The legislature may also not create administrative competences with which the government can interfere in details, for example in the duties of a President or the finances of a particular court. The Council of State also has similar protection from rushed administrative interventions. By virtue of Article 75 of the Constitution, its structure, composition and competence must also be regulated by a general Act.

In spite of this institutional independence, any judiciary remains unavoidably dependent on the executive for the actual conditions under which it operates. Someone has to provide the resources. Institutional independence moreover does not reach to the extent that the management boards of the courts simply submit their receipts to the ministry and the budget legislature approves what the courts have spent. The legislature can expect the judiciary to be efficient in the way it spends what boils down to taxpayer's money. At the same time the legislature, via this connection, could actually threaten the functional independence of the judiciary. The so-called Council for the Judiciary was founded in 2002 to deal with this dilemma.[39] The Council is intended to function as a buffer between the large Ministry of Justice and Security and the individual courts. It is composed mainly of judges appointed for life, and is supplemented by a minority of administrators

---

[38] *Kamerstukken II* 1980/81, 16 162, no. 3, p 2.

[39] See www.rechtspraak.nl/English/The-Council-for-the-Judiciary. Accessed 1 March 2019. See also part 6 of the Judicial Organization Act.

without a life appointment. In the case of the judiciary as a whole, every three years the Council negotiates a budget with the ministry, after which the Council allocates funding to the courts. This funding is not provided without accountability. With a view to good management, the Council for the Judiciary is authorized to provide the court boards with general guidelines. In relation to this, the Council itself may receive general guidelines from the minister. At no time, though, may the minister use this authority to interfere 'in the proceedings, assessment or the decision of a specific case or categories of cases', as prescribed by law. The Council itself may decide *whether* such a situation arises. As a result, an attempt is made to avert a threat to functional independence.[40] Moreover, the Division and the Supreme Court are not linked in an official sense to the Council for the Judiciary. The Council of State, as High Council of State has a separate budget over which the Council of State itself negotiates with the Minister of the Interior and Kingdom Relations. Nor can the Supreme Court be given guidelines for its operational management from the Council for the Judiciary, but it is part of the department budget of the Ministry of Justice and Security. Rules have been drawn up on this in a separate covenant between the Minister and the Supreme Court. Thus, the Supreme Court is more or less in the same position as the Council of State. In this way, the institutional independence of both courts is safeguarded in relation to finance.

The independence of the legal position of the judiciary is laid down in Article 117 of the Constitution. A central feature of this provision is appointment by the Government for life. Dismissal by the Government can, and must, be done if a judge so requests or when a judge reaches the statutory retirement age; since 1932 this has been 70 years old. The Constitution does not rule out delegation of the competence to set the retirement age. It is after all a constitutionally precarious competence, in particular for courts of law with an important constitutional function. In a system where the more experienced career judges at the end of their career reach the top of the pyramid, the judiciary can be relatively simply 'decapitated' by lowering the retirement age by a few years. This is exactly what Seyss-Inquart did when he was appointed by the Nazis as the *Reichskommissar* at the beginning of the German occupation of the Netherlands in the Second World War. He lowered the retirement age from 70 to 65 and thus straight away could replace six of the seventeen justices with persons who were more sympathetic to the Germans.[41] Judges may be dismissed as a result of incompetence in office. This can only be done in narrowly worded cases by a court of appeal which is part of the judiciary; this is the Supreme Court, on the application of the Procurator General at the Supreme Court. Judges, including the justices of the Supreme Court itself, can therefore be dismissed by the Supreme Court. A legislative proposal is being processed to extend judicial disciplinary law with more instruments to respond to inadequate performance. To bridge the gap between a written warning from the President and punitive dismissal, measures have been proposed such as a transfer,

[40] Langbroek 2010.
[41] Jansen 2005.

withholding salary and other such options; always within the judiciary and always regulated by law. The members of the Council of State and the state councillors entrusted with the administration of justice have the same independence in relation to the substance of their legal position. Only the former, however, are protected by the Constitution (by virtue of Article 74); the latter derive safeguards against involuntary dismissal from an ordinary Act.

The Constitution does not contain specific requirements for the appointment of a judge. The ordinary Act requires for the appointment of a judge to the judiciary the successful completion of academic training in law, and delegates the further selection of judges to the aforementioned Council for the Judiciary. This Council has established a full recruitment system including an extensive job profile, a broadly composed selection committee and its own four-year training programme.[42] To become a judge, it is not sufficient just to have completed this national procedure. Judges are not assigned by 'The Hague' to the courts of law. In the end, the individual court boards select candidates for an appointment. This combination of a national suitability assessment and a decentral placement sometimes gives rise to tension. A well-known judge recently signalled that court boards are frequently confronted with highly suitable candidate judges with excellent references, whom they would very much like to be appointed, being rejected because of the outcome of a psychological *assessment* in the national procedure. Candidates who for years had objectively produced top quality legal work, for some reason failed the intelligence test. The judge called for these tests to no longer be interpreted in absolute terms and to always have the possibility to deviate from negative test results on the grounds of reasonableness.[43] The plea hit a raw nerve, since the House of Representatives called for a response from the Minister who proceeded to refuse to commit himself and referred to an ongoing evaluation of the national selection procedures.[44]

In the case of the appointment of a justice, the involvement of the House of Representatives is regulated in the Constitution. The Supreme Court even has a committee that checks out academic circles and professional practice for potential candidates. If a vacancy becomes available, the Supreme Court selects suitable candidates from its own files using a self-made job profile.[45] When the President of the Supreme Court informs the House of Representatives of a vacancy, he also nominates six persons as the potential successor. The nominations are ranked in order of suitability. Number one is the candidate whom the Supreme Court would prefer to see appointed and the five other candidates are deemed to be future frontrunners. The President, the Procurator General at the Supreme Court and the

---

[42] See https://www.rechtspraak.nl/SiteCollectionDocuments/judicial-refrom-in-the-Netherlands-2014.pdf. Accessed 1 March 2019.

[43] Hofhuis 2018.

[44] *Kamerstukken II* 2017/18, 29 279, No. 452.

[45] See https://www.rechtspraak.nl/Organisatie-en-contact/Organisatie/Hoge-Raad-der-Nederlanden/Over-de-Hoge-Raad/Raad/Paginas/Profiel-raadsheer-en-groepsprofielen-kamers.aspx. Accessed 1 March 2019.

candidates appear at a closed meeting of the Standing Committee for Justice and Security of the House of Representatives. The House of Representatives then puts forward three candidates to the Government which has no obligation to follow the nomination of the Supreme Court. The Government is bound by the nomination of the House of Representatives. In the practice of recent history, the favoured candidate of the Supreme Court is appointed. The House of Representatives strikes through the names of the lowest three candidates and the Government chooses the first nominee from the remaining three names and appoints this person to the position of justice by Royal Decree. Becoming a state councillor at the Administrative Jurisdiction Division also occurs via Royal Decree, but is not a question of just applying to the Government. The Council of State has drawn up a document with quality requirements and controls recruitment and selection. When a vacancy arises, the Council of State puts forward a single, non-binding nomination to the Minister of the Interior and Kingdom Relations.[46] This procedure does not include any official involvement by the House of Representatives. If the House want to interfere, then it would have to make use of parliamentary means. Full ministerial responsibility ultimately applies to the appointment of state councillors and justices.

Where institutional independence in particular is evident from Article 116 of the Constitution and the independence of the legal position in particular from Article 117, the functional independence is not as such included in the Constitution. Its existence is evident from the law in particular in the negative sense: there are no authorities to issue instructions with respect to the judiciary such as those that exist towards the Procurator General; the instructions from the Council for the Judiciary can never be related to the content of the administration of justice; the internal disciplinary law only deals with the incumbency of judges, etc. In each case, the functional independence is respected. This is a conscious choice. In line with the observation made at the end of the introduction above, that the functional independence ultimately can only be anchored in the law to a very limited degree, the constitutional legislature found in 1983 that the official constitutional safeguards were primarily intended as a means of support for the judiciary. So the Constitution refers onwards to a higher ideal. At the same time, the Constitution also actually limits functional independence. This, after all, would be absolute if adjudication, like elections, took place in secrecy. In that case, the judge, just like the voter, would be left to rely on his own conscience. The Constitution clearly does not choose this option. By virtue of Article 121 of the Constitution, judges are obliged to pass judgment in public and to motivate what led to their judgment. A judge is therefore subjected to the monitoring and criticism of the general public. This standard includes the requirement to reflect this public access in a way that public control is optimal. This does not mean that the judge always has to do his work *live*

---

46 See https://www.raadvanstate.nl/publish/library/10/notitie-kwaliteiten-staatsraden.pdf. Accessed 1 March 2019.

on the internet, but the digital publication of all judgments, for example, comes close.

The lack of a positive codification of the functional independence of the judiciary in the Constitution is partially compensated for through the international codification of human rights. These are part of the Dutch Constitution. The most important standard here is Article 6 ECHR, which lays down a substantive ultimate outcome: the dispensation of justice must be done by an independent and impartial court established by law. Via this substantive international standard, the gaps left by the procedural standards in particular in the Constitution, can still be closed. The *Benthem* case referred to above is an example of this in relation to the Administrative Jurisdiction Division. In connection with the Supreme Court, limits to the interference of the House of Representatives in the appointment of state councillors to the Supreme Court could be considered. The Constitution only arranges the procedure, but in the case law of the ECtHR it is clear that political bodies may only play a role in the appointment of judges, provided they do not make use of *improper motives*.[47] The disadvantage of this approach by the ECHR and the ECtHR is that the standard is very case-based. For a full overview of what has now been developed under Article 6 ECHR, see the overviews elsewhere.[48]

5.6 The Informal Safeguards for the Independence of the Supreme Court and the Administrative Jurisdiction Division of the Council of State

The official safeguards for the independence of courts that have a constitutional function are a combination of a limited number of concrete constitutional rules plus elaboration through international case law concerning a human right (Article 6 ECHR). The functioning of the official safeguards can therefore not be viewed separately from informal safeguards. These are not a question of enforceable constitutional law, nor strictly a question of political culture. They concern the intermediate category of political appropriateness standards: conventions. Conventions arise when an existing practice and a normative conviction coincide. These are constitutional practices, which can no longer be departed from without being reproached from all sides. At the same time, they are not unwavering standards or parts of a *rigid constitution* which can only be departed from in a more serious official procedure. When it comes to judicial independence, two conventions in particular are important: the convention of co-optation and the *sub judice* convention. These conventions support the independence of the judiciary because they both increase the distance between politics and the judiciary and thus help prevent individual judges or individual decisions becoming a political football.

---

[47] Van den Eijnden 2011, pp 73–78.

[48] Kuijer 2004; Van den Eijnden 2011; Van Emmerik et al. 2014, pp 28–38.

The convention of co-optation is practice-based and arises from the conviction that judges, in principle, are best suited to appoint one another: it takes one to know one.[49] This follows in the first instance from the large degree to which the legislature generally leaves the selection of new judges to the Council for the Judiciary. This choice is not accidental, as appeared from the abovementioned response by the House of Representatives to a claim by the judiciary about national test results being interpreted too strictly. The sensitivity concerning these kinds of issues shows that the House of Representatives actually believes that experienced judges are the best people to select other suitable judges. Secondly, the convention of co-optation is seen in the passiveness of the House of Representatives in the appointment of judges to bodies with a constitutional function. Even in cases in which the Constitution requires interference from the House of Representatives in the nomination for the Supreme Court, the belief has always prevailed that the Supreme Court itself knows best who is appropriate to reinforce the ranks. The Supreme Court and the Administrative Jurisdiction Division also propagate this themselves. An example of this is the document referred to by the Council of State concerning the recruitment of new state councillors. In the composition of the Advisory Division, an explicit attempt is made to achieve a good reflection of mainstream politics. At many other bodies concerned with Dutch constitutional law, it is customary to share the top positions proportionally among the large political parties. But this is explicitly not the case in the recruitment of state councillors to the Administrative Jurisdiction Division, in accordance with the same document. The only aim there is to achieve 'a broad variation in backgrounds, both legal, administrative and other'. This also applies to the Supreme Court. Long ago an attempt was made to have a good representative spread from the provinces; between 1838 and 1970 a minimum number of Catholic justices was aimed for; and currently the proportion of men to women must be in balance. Taking into account non-legal factors is therefore permitted, but the political background of a candidate is never officially deemed to be a relevant criterion. Thus, politicians generally do not regard themselves as the most appropriate persons to assess the suitability of a judge.

The expansion of the constitutional function of the Supreme Court has of course put pressure on the convention of co-optation.[50] Cracks are already visible in places. Generally speaking, the convention of co-optation has hardly led to a judiciary which from an ethnical point of view somehow resembles society in the Netherlands at present. As a result, it is now sometimes argued that the time has come for politics to get involved in the selection of judges. More concretely, now and then the political background of the judges does sometimes enter the political debate. A survey shows that a relatively high number of members of the judiciary vote for the pragmatic social liberal party D66 and that there are relatively few

---

[49] This convention is described (and criticized) by Bovend'Eert 2000, pp 19–21. Likewise on the appointment of judges in the Netherlands, see: De Werd 1994 and Van Koppen 1990.

[50] Van Koppen 1990.

supporters of the Socialist Party (SP) and the Party for Freedom (PVV) active in dispensing justice. Not surprisingly, judges are more moderate and pragmatic, instead of having a clear political profile on the edges of the political spectrum. But as a result of the news concerning the overrepresentation of D66 supporters, it is often argued that there should be more political diversity in the judiciary, though this does not generally lead to concrete action.[51] This did however happen recently in two incidents concerning appointments to the Supreme Court. Both concerned objections from the PVV led by Geert Wilders.[52] In 2011, the party protested against the Supreme Court's choice to nominate professor of criminal law Buruma to be appointed to the Criminal Division. Buruma was active in the Labour Party (PvdA) and had spoken very critically in an opinion piece about Wilders, when Wilders at that time had been called to appear before the criminal court. The convention of co-optation was too weak then to prevent the PVV from opposing the appointment to a judicial body of a known critic who themselves might possibly be dealing with an appeal to the Supreme Court of Geert Wilders in the future. Likewise, in 2011 it became known that the PVV in a closed meeting of the Standing Committee for Justice and Security had been able to block the appointment of a different justice by once again threatening to cause commotion. Then, again, there was a court case pending against Wilders. A document in the past had been leaked in which the proposed justice had legally 'filleted' a judgment that had been given in Wilder's favour. At that time, the Supreme Court opted to make the best of a bad job by amending the original nomination and keeping the candidate who had been challenged for a later moment. This caused quite some outrage, particularly from the core of the Supreme Court. These incidents are cracks in the convention of co-optation and proof that informal safeguards should not be underestimated. On the other hand, these are incidents specifically related to a criminal case against a well-known politician. The widespread criticism of the PVV's actions shows that the normative belief that the judiciary itself should fill its own ranks has not disappeared yet.

The second convention that supports the independence of the judiciary, is the rule that politicians should not speak on cases that are still being heard in the courts.[53] The term in the legal tradition is *sub judice*. In the Netherlands, the term itself has no history or right of existence. The rule is connected to the prevention of members of a jury becoming influenced by inappropriate commentary from parliamentarians and so the term *sub judice* is pre-eminently not applicable in the Netherlands. The Chairman of the Dutch Lawyers' Association expressed the sentiments of his members by saying that anyone who calls themselves a professional judge can take a 'punch'.[54] The term, therefore, may not be entirely appropriate, though the same chairman also believed that politicians should observe

[51] Ten Kate and Van Koppen 1994, p 147.

[52] Bovend'Eert 2015, pp 94–101.

[53] Transparency International 2012, p 93.

[54] Hoekstra 2017, pp 1975–1979.

certain limits when commenting on ongoing legal proceedings. Members of the House of Representatives do increasingly confront one another with this norm.[55] This is also confirmed in the courts. In the case against Volkert van der Graaf, the murderer of Pim Fortuyn, ministers and MPs had commented harshly on what they perceived to be a sentence that was too low being passed in first instance. During the appeal proceedings, the Court of Appeal considered, in relation to Article 6 ECHR, that public authorities such as ministers and MPs could indeed endanger a fair trial for Van der Graaf through their comments.[56] All in all, there is discussion about the nature, extent and desirability of the *sub judice* convention, but its practice and a certain level of normative conviction have been established.

The benefit of the restraining effect of the *sub judice* convention in relation to the independence of the judiciary is demonstrated when the convention is not observed, and indignant MPs immediately latch on to news items. A good example of this occurred in 2009 when the dangerous criminal Şaban Baran, who had been found guilty in first instance, fled to Turkey. Pending his appeal, the Court of Appeal had given him temporary leave to visit his newly-born child. When the human trafficker did not return, it was clear that the Court had made a huge mistake. The justifiable public outrage in response, led in the media to less the justifiable identification of the individual judges involved in the case and subsequently in politics to the totally inappropriate call to have these justices immediately dismissed. The Minister of Justice was able to calm the debate by shifting the discussion to his own proposal to leave these kinds of decisions about leave to prison directors, with a remedy at the independent Council for the Administration of Criminal Justice and Protection of Juveniles. In this way, he channelled the criticism away from mistakes by judges without dealing with their dismissal. The Procurator General later gave a detailed explanation to the Supreme Court, the body which had been approached by the public to demand the dismissal of the justices, giving his reasons for not doing so. His letter reads: ‘If a judge runs the risk of being fired in the event he passes a judgment which he believes to be in accordance with the law, but which in political and/or social circles is seen to be wrong, the parties to the proceedings will rightly place question marks against an independent assessment of their case’.[57] Dismissal due to an *honest mistake* would be inconsistent with the functional independence of the judiciary. Ideally, the House of Representative would rather have waited till this

---

[55] See extensively on the Anglo-Saxon background and the history and the use of the *sub judice* principle in The Netherlands Gommer 2008. Gommer himself disputes the existence of a *sub judice* convention in the Netherlands since he believes that not enough cohesion in its use can be discerned. However, in doing so he has raised the threshold for the existence of a convention too much.

[56] Court of Appeal Amsterdam 18 July 2003, ECLI:NL:GHAMS:2003:AI0123. The Court found this to have been ‘risky’ and ‘in the danger zone’, but not serious enough to be unlawful.

[57] As cited in NRC Handelsblad, ‘Ontslaggronden voor rechters’, 25 November 2009 (author’s translation).

moment to comment on the issue. It was already known at that point that Baran had been arrested in Turkey and sentenced to a long term of imprisonment.

The above example underlines not only the benefit of the *sub judice* convention for the independence of a judiciary with a constitutional function, but also its limits. Repercussions to politically unwelcome court judgments can also be targeted towards the powers of the judge and thus form a threat to functional independence. Politics has more means to get rid of what it sees as difficult jurisdiction besides politicizing appointment policy or commenting on ongoing court proceedings. For example, it can attempt to settle certain offences by placing them with the executive power, or raising the court fees. The courts then remain independent but no longer deal with the matter or access to the courts becomes very difficult. In that sense, the formal and informal safeguards for the independence of the rule of law are not set in stone.

5.7 Conclusion: Bipolar Constitutionalism and Democratic Legitimacy

Nothing in constitutional law is absolute, except perhaps the prohibition of torture. Everything else has limits, and that even applies to the most important and vulnerable principle of the state based on the rule of law: that judges ought to be independent. This is because judges are no exception to the ancient question *quis custodiet ipsos custodes*? Judges are subject to various forms of monitoring. The most important mechanisms have already been discussed. The institutional independence of the judiciary, for example, is tempered by the responsibility the executive retains for the organization of the judiciary. In the end, the judicial system must account for the expenditure of public money and the Council for the Judiciary monitors the material administration. Likewise, the independence of the judiciary's legal position is tempered by the possibility to be dismissed by the Supreme Court for dereliction of duty. Neither judges nor courts of law are inviolable. The most important check on judges, however, is formed by the requirement to clearly and publicly motivate their judgments. Both norms are laid down in the Constitution and they subject everything a court does to the critical eye of fellow professionals, the media, politics and the general public. This check is a moderation of the functional independence of the judiciary, because a good judge who does what the law asks can often predict how his judgment will be received in the public opinion. For example, all judges will be aware what the reactions will be if an escaped forensic patient, who has brutally raped and murdered a random innocent young girl, is discharged from prosecution because he was threatened with torture during his arrest. This, however, may be what the law requires of him. And so it is at such times that the independence of the judiciary must prove its worth. And so in such cases, the judge relies on two conventions in particular: the convention of co-optation and the *sub judice* convention. The former prevents a judge from constantly having to fear damage to his career in the case of politically unwelcome judgments, because his professional colleagues will ultimately assess his promotion. And the latter convention reduces the chance that politicians start applying pressure on an individual judge prior to the final judgment.

It is striking that in this way the most important area of judicial independence is afforded the weakest protection under constitutional law. The functional independence of the judge, which is the main issue, is only 'supported' in the Constitution and relies most on non-legally binding conventions. This leads to vulnerability of the constitutional function of the Supreme Court and the Administrative Jurisdiction Division of the Council of State because they perhaps do not feel sufficiently secure by applying conventions to do what the law requires of them. But this vulnerability can also be valued as a special form of democratic legitimacy. Judges, more than anyone, have an interest in the continued existence of the conventions and this makes them sensitive to the threats they can create. For example, judges see that surveys on the one-sided political and cultural composition of the judiciary can lead to proposals to politicize appointment procedures. This will make them particularly alert to avoiding the accusation of one-sidedness and to stimulating internal diversity policies. And these are good things. Likewise, judges will be able to appreciate the real value of the *sub judice* principle. But they also know that the convention can only survive if judges do not constantly tread on the toes of the general public. This realization stimulates a kind of institutional hesitancy which is a good safeguard against judicial activism 'gone wild'. The conventions give the judiciary a certain responsiveness to the resilience of the democratic bodies. This contributes to the legitimacy of the constitutional function of the courts. And moreover, it fits with the recognition that the independence of the judiciary cannot only exist as a result of 'tough' principles in the Constitution, but must also be cherished from within the judiciary itself and respected outside it. Vulnerable conventions are a continual reminder of this. This does not just concern what is laid down in the Constitution, but more in particular about how sturdy the conventions remain.

References

Adams M, Van der Schyff G (2006) Constitutional Review by the Judiciary in the Netherlands. A Matter of Politics, Democracy or Compensating Strategy. Zeitschrift für ausländisches öffentliches Recht und Völkerrecht 66:399–413

Barkhuysen T, Den Ouden W, Schuurmans Y E (2012) The Law on Administrative Procedures in the Netherlands. NALL, http://www.nall.nl/tijdschrift/nall/2012/06/NALL-D-12-00004 Accessed 1 March 2019

Boogaard G, Uzman J (2018) Commentaar op artikel 120 van de Grondwet. In: Hirsch Ballin E M H, Leenknegt G (eds) Artikelsgewijs commentaar op de Grondwet. https://www.nederlandrechtsstaat.nl/module/nlrs/script/viewer.asp?soort=commentaar&artikel=120 Accessed 1 March 2019

Bossers G F M (1987) Welk eene natie, die de jurij gehad heeft, en ze weder afschaft! De jury in de Nederlandse rechtspraktijk 1811–1813. Eburon, Delft

Bovend'Eert P P T (2000) Benoeming en ontslag van rechters. Kluwer, Deventer
Bovend'Eert P P T (2008) Rechterlijke organisatie, Rechters en rechtspraak. Kluwer, Deventer
Bovend'Eert P P T (2015) Terugkerend rumoer over benoemingen door de regering en de Tweede Kamer. Nederlands Juristenblad 2015/90:94–101
Brood P (2011) Rechters in de politiek. In: Van Boven M W et al (eds) Tweehonderd jaar rechters. Verloren, Hilversum, pp 229–256
De Roos Th A (2013) Democratischer strafrechtspraak? De betekenis van de inbreng van leken, Ars Aequi, 7(8):560–565
De Werd M F J M (1994) De benoeming van rechters: constitutionele aspecten van de toegang tot het rechtersambt in Nederland en in de Amerikaanse deelstaat New York. Gouda Quint, Arnhem
Efthymiou N S, De Wit J C (2013) The Role of Dutch Courts in the Protection of Fundamental Rights. Utrecht Law Review 9(2):75–88
Gommer H (2008) Onder de rechter. Wolf, Nijmegen
Group of States against Corruption (2012) Evaluation Report Netherlands. https://rm.coe.int/CoERMPublicCommonSearchServices/DisplayDCTMContent?documentId=09000016806c799a Accessed 22 February 2019
Hoekstra J (2017) De rechter kan tegen een stootje, ja zelfs tegen een beuk, maar behoeft zich stoten onder de gordel niet te laten welgevallen. Nederlands Juristenblad 2017/1515:1975–1979
Hofhuis H F M (2018) De selectie voor rechters geanalyseerd. Nederlands Juristenblad 2018/999:1431–1433
Jansen C J H (2005) De spagaat van de leden van de Hoge Raad in de Tweede Wereldoorlog. Nederlands Juristenblad 17:880–886
Jansen C J H (2014) The Participation of Laymen in the Dutch Judiciary 1811–2011. Fundamina 20(1):427–436
Koopmans T (2003) Courts and Political Institutions: A Comparative View. Cambridge University Press, Cambridge
Kuijer M (2004) The Blindfold of Lady Justice. Judicial Independence and Impartiality in Light of the Requirements of Article 6 ECHR. Wolf, Nijmegen
Langbroek P M (2010) Organization Development of the Dutch Judiciary. Between Accountability and Judicial Independence. International Journal for Court Administration 2(2):1–10
Martens S K (1998) Incorporating the European Convention. The Role of the Judiciary. European Human Rights Law Review 3:5–14
Merryman J H (1996) The French Deviation. The American Journal of Comparative Law 44 (1):109–119
Pessers D (1983) 100 jaar na de zaak Aletta Jacobs. Nederlands Juristenblad 58:663–664
Pieterman M (1990) De plaats van de rechter in Nederland 1813–1920. Gouda Quint, Arnhem
Seerden R J G H, Wenders D W M (2012) Administrative Law in the Netherlands. In: Seerden R J G H (ed) Administrative Law of the European Union, its Member States and the United States. A Comparative Analysis. Intersentia, Antwerp, pp 101–175
Staatscommissie-Cals/Donner (1971) Eindrapport van de Staatscommissie van advies inzake de Grondwet en de Kieswet. http://resources.huygens.knaw.nl/watermarker/pdf/cc/scans/1967a_cie_cals-donner/verslag/plenair/data/1971-03-29/1971-03-29.pdf Accessed 1 March 2019
Struycken A A H (1910) Administratie of rechter? Gouda Quint, Arnhem
Ten Kate J, Van Koppen P (1994) Judicialization of Politics in The Netherlands: Towards a Form of Judicial Review. International Political Science Review 15(2):143–151
Transparency International (2012) National Integrity System Assessment. http://files.transparency.org/content/download/282/1132/file/2012_NetherlandsNIS_EN.pdf Accessed 1 March 2019
Uzman J, Barkhuysen T, Van Emmerik M L (2010) The Dutch Supreme Court: A Reluctant Positive Legislator? In: Van Erp J H M, Van Vliet L P W (eds) Netherlands Reports to the Eighteenth International Congress of Comparative Law. Intersentia, Antwerp/Oxford/Portland, pp 423–468

Uzman J, Boogaard G (2015) Make It a Better Place. Transnational Public Interest Litigation and the Separation of Powers. In: Ten Napel H M T D et al (eds) The Powers That Be. Rethinking the Separation of Powers. Leiden University Press, Leiden, pp 295–319

Van Boven M W (2011) Rechters en regenten. De benoemingen van de leden van de nieuwe rechterlijke macht in 1811. In: Van Boven M W et al (eds) Tweehonderd jaar rechters. Verloren, Hilversum, pp 159–202

Van den Brink J, Ten Napel H M T D (2013) The Dutch Political Reformed Party (SGP) and Passive Female Suffrage. A Comparison of Three High Court Judgments From the Viewpoint of Democratic Theory. Utrecht Journal of International and European Law 29(77):29–41

Van den Eijnden P M (2011) Onafhankelijkheid van de rechter in constitutioneel perspectief. Kluwer, Deventer

Van Dijk P (1987) The Benthem Case and its Aftermath in the Netherlands. Netherlands International Law Review 34(1):5–24

Van Emmerik M L, Loof J P, Schuurmans Y E (2014) Systeemwaarborgen voor de kernwaarden van de rechtspraak. Raad voor de Rechtspraak Research Memoranda 2/2014

Van Koppen (1990) The Dutch Supreme Court and Parliament: Political Decision Making versus Non-political Appointments. Law and Society Review 24(3):745–780

Van Koppen P J, Ten Kate J (2003) De Hoge Raad in persoon. Benoemingen in de Hoge Raad der Nederlanden 1838–2002. Kluwer, Deventer

Geerten Boogaard is Assistant Professor in Constitutional Law and holds the Thorbecke Chair in regional law and politics at Leiden Law School. He published extensively on the constitutional role of the judiciary and on (local) democracy. His current scholarship can be divided into two strands: decentralization and the evolution of a political question-theory in Dutch case law.

Chapter 6
'… destroy all sense of dependence': On the Selection and Independence of the Judiciary in Norway

Eivind Smith

Contents

Abstract Notwithstanding its bicentennial system of judicial review, the constitutional system of Norway does not seem to justify a shift from a triangular to a bipolar perspective. In the single-tiered judicial system, the courts have competence in any legal matter, including administrative and constitutional law. Some lacunae in the constitutional protection have not given rise to serious concerns about its independence. However, judicial appointments by the executive give rise to some particular questions. The author argues that appointment completely isolated from the political branches of government, as sometimes advocated, undermines the legitimacy of judges with a permanent status to undertake constitutional and other norm-setting functions.

E. Smith (✉)
University of Oslo, Oslo, Norway
e-mail: eivind.smith@jus.uio.no

Hirsch Ballin, Van der Schyff & Stremler (eds.), *European Yearbook of Constitutional Law 2019*, European Yearbook of Constitutional Law 1,
https://doi.org/10.1007/978-94-6265-359-7_6

Keywords bipolarity · career systems · judges as norm-setters · judicial development of the law · judicial review · Norwegian Constitution of 1814 · political appointments · precedent · social trust · Supreme Court of Norway · the constitution as positive law

6.1 Introduction

Within most constitutional democracies, the judiciary is regarded as the third among three branches of government. At regular intervals, Parliament is exposed to the evaluation of the electorate. In systems with elements of parliamentary government, the executive is responsible towards Parliament and indirectly, thus, towards the electorate. By contrast, independence from the electorate as well as from the other branches of government is generally regarded as a prerequisite for a judiciary able to conveniently fulfil its tasks.

The requirement of independence applies, of course, towards the parties of any cases submitted to judicial decision-making. It applies both when the parties are natural or legal persons belonging to the private sector and when public entities, the legislative or executive powers included, as such are involved because the legality or the constitutionality of their acts are challenged. In other words, the public-private divide is immaterial to the basic requirement that both courts and the individual judges act independently and in manners likely to make their independence apparent to the parties as well as to the public at large.

Towards the legislative and executive powers, however, the quest for judicial independence extends beyond the individual cases. If the judiciary constitutes one of the prime institutions of the traditional *trias politica*, it appears in many ways as the feeble part. Money and other resources essential for a proper administration of justice come from the other state powers. In different ways, even the answer to questions like who shall become or stay judges and what is their security of office depend on them. They may well be tempted to use such sources of influence to facilitate the realisation of their own views about how to apply and develop the law in general as well as about the outcome in particular cases in other ways than by adopting or amending the Constitution itself and other legal norms enjoying binding effect under the Constitution.

This way, the judiciary's fundamental dependence on the political branches of government may be detrimental to the freedom of judges to adopt the solutions they find most suitable in a society governed by law. In legal systems where the judiciary has the power to curtail the interests of the other state powers by setting their proper acts aside on constitutional or other grounds, the risk of undue influence may increase further.

Norway counts among the states where the judiciary enjoys similar powers. In contrast to the numerous polities that have established special institutions for constitutional affairs, namely constitutional courts, however, the task of judging the constitutionality of formal legislation and other acts of Parliament belongs to courts of general jurisdiction. The present essay will pay particular attention to some of the questions that the inclusion of constitutional jurisdiction in the overall judicial capacity is likely to give rise to.

This chapter will first offer a paramount look at the role of the judiciary in the constitutional system of a country (and a part of the world) impregnated by a high level of social trust (Sect. 6.2). Turning to the legal-institutional pattern, the Norwegian judiciary and its judges will be introduced (Sects. 6.3–6.5). The remaining parts of the chapter (Sects. 6.6–6.8) will be devoted to the appointment of judges with constitutional and other norm-setting functions as a possible aspect of the independence of the judiciary.

6.2 Constitutional Bipolarity?

Traditionally, we study constitutional systems as a triangle. This inaugural volume of the *European Yearbook of Constitutional Law*, however, purports to study judicial independence as a prerequisite for 'the proper functioning of bipolar constitutionalism'.[1] This responds to the suggestion that a *bipolar* constitutional model is actually emerging.[2]

The adjective bipolar may carry different institutional designs. Immediately, it seems to point at a system with just two key players, opposing the judiciary to the political branches of government. Even if the different systems of triangular separation of powers around the world rarely function according to the recipes of *Montesquieu* and some other thinkers, however, it seems exaggerated to talk about a general shift from a triangular to a bipolar approach to constitutional systems. In most countries of a somewhat democratic character, important elements of power sharing still operate between the legislative and executive branches of government. At the same time, no judiciary comes close to equalising the two other state powers' functions to set norms and ensuring that they are generally observed. There is a powerful move in many European states towards conferring important decision-making functions on independent administrative agencies more or less sheltered from day-to-day politics without being parts of the judiciary. Similar developments in the EU further underpin doubts about the sustainability of a purely bipolar understanding of the distribution of public power.[3]

Against this background, it seems that a concept about bipolarity has more to it if used in a way 'essentially' meaning that judicial review of both legislation and executive acts form part of the relevant system of government.[4] The appearance of

---

[1] Editor's guidelines. As current literature tends to use the word 'constitutionalism' in different ways that are not always made apparent, it will not be further called upon in this chapter.

[2] For a prominent example, see Koopmans 2003, pp 248–251.

[3] See for instance Trondal 2012.

[4] Van der Schyff 2010, p 5.

specialised constitutional courts in a large number of political systems in Europe and beyond after the end of World War II, in Europe supplemented by powerful international courts, seems to be the factor that has most heavily inspired the formation of the concept. Many of these institutions have adopted less deferential attitudes when reviewing statutes and other fruits of political action than those that used to prevail in most of our societies.

To what extent could the constitutional system of Norway be characterised as bipolar? Insofar as we use the presence of judicial review as the key criterion, it seems to fit well; in fact, review of both administrative and legislative acts has been around for two centuries, i.e. since the very first years following the adoption of the Constitution (1814). It should be noted, however, that judicial review remains with the ordinary courts with no institutional specialisation and that the numerical importance of such cases remains remote.

When it comes to understanding the role of the judiciary within the relevant *trias politica*, however, it is worthwhile taking into account that Norway, like its Scandinavian neighbours but different from most other parts of the world, enjoys a very high level of social trust towards other people as well as political institutions.[5] The resulting social climate helps understanding why discussion and compromise are often preferred to clear-cut antinomies in political decision-making and that legislation is generally preferred to judicial action. Few would regard courts as prime political actors in a way likely to justify recourse to a bipolar perspective on the system at large.

This observation fits even in the field of human rights. Deliberate political action during a century or more in the form of ordinary legislation and appropriate financial measures adopted by virtue of the Constitution provides the core explanation for the comparatively high level of rights' protection. It is true that Norway's extensive adherence to international covenants and its recent adoption of a quite updated catalogues of human rights in the Constitution (2014) have given rise to an increasing number of court cases. But their outcome rarely appears as dramatic from a political point of view. Frequently, the cases boil down to questions about the interpretation of statutory law in the relevant field within the limits laid down by the Constitution or relevant treaties. In short, thus, the Norwegian system of government does not seem to fit into an image of the judiciary as one of only two (sets of) key players.

There are nevertheless no reasons to presume that the judiciary may not be called upon in cases of tension or conflict with political connotations, nor that violation of fundamental rights may never be perpetrated by public authorities. The increasing heterogeneity of modern western societies and the political responses to it contribute to substantiate the *memento*. Whatever overarching concept one chooses as a point of departure, we thus cannot avoid addressing basic questions about judicial

---

[5] See for instance Ortiz-Spinosa and Roser 2017 and OECD 2017, Fig. 3.14.

independence and accountability. The following remarks regarding Norway will cast a particular eye on the importance for such questions as prerequisites for proper review of political and administrative action.

6.3 The Norwegian Judiciary

The long period when the rulers of the ancient kingdom of Norway sat in Copenhagen has been qualified as the '400 years' night'.[6] From 1661, Denmark-Norway was ruled by one of Europe's most absolute monarchies, following the King's successful exclusion of the high nobility from formalised political power. Breaking up from the double monarchy, the 1814 Constitution of Norway opted for a constitutional monarchy as a critical part of the new state institutions. In Denmark, *l'ancien régime* remained until the adoption of the country's first modern constitution in 1849.

According to the new constitution of Norway, pre-constitutional legislation should remain in force until replaced by statutes adopted by virtue of the new procedures. Their applicability, however, depended on their substantive conformity with the new basic law. In the last resort, it thus became for the judiciary to decide on the conformity of a contested legal norm with the Constitution. This way, one of the precursors for the following emergence of a general system of judicial review was established.

In other ways as well, the Danish-Norwegian legal heritage impregnated the first steps of the new constitution apparatus of Norway. In the absence of a separate university, for instance, the judicial staff held diplomas from the University of Copenhagen. Only little by little, appointees trained at the Royal Frederik's university (since 1939 known as the University of Oslo), established a few years before the adoption of the Constitution (1811) were at hand for gradually taking over the judiciary. For similar reasons, the bulk of the legal literature remained Danish-Norwegian with a clear pre-eminence for books and other publications printed in Copenhagen.

Starting its activity (1815) more or less from scratch, even the Supreme Court of Norway followed in the footpaths of the Copenhagen-based apex court,[7] an institution that was established simultaneously with the absolute monarchy (1661) and actually remains the World's oldest of its kind. This makes it important to underscore that the monarchy's absolute character did not stand in the way for the Supreme Court of Denmark-Norway to gradually conquer a high degree of *de facto* independence from the royal power in the name of which it decided.[8] During the

[6] The expression, forged by the playwright Henrik Ibsen during the nation-building years of the late 1800s, has been contested by historians.

[7] Cf. Langeland 2005.

[8] Cf. Christensen et al. 2015.

last decades of absolutism, it even started to review the legality of administrative acts by virtue of royal consents formally needed, but almost systematically granted.

The fact that specialised collegiums of civil servants that were not necessarily of noble origin but increasingly chosen for their skills, run the administrative apparatus largely facilitated this development. In fact, the Supreme Court was one of these collegiums. Together, they administered justice and most other matters in the name of absolute monarchs who were not always devoted to the dull task of exercising their power and sometimes even squarely insane.

This way, the Supreme Court of Norway emerged from an institution already enjoying a considerable degree of independence as a court. In addition, the Constitution of 1814 formalised the guarantee of independence that a judge was ensured to keeping his office unless a court decided otherwise. This guarantee was important even if it was enjoyed not only by the judges, but by a number of other high civil servants appointed by the King in Council.

In the absence of particular provisions on the independence of the judiciary, its position as one of the key creatures of a new constitution that (unlike most others in the epoch of the *bourgeois* revolutions) succeeded in founding a new political regime,[9] no doubt contributed to enhancing its strength as an independent actor. In fact, the Constitution of 1814 rapidly established itself as a positive symbol for the nation.[10]

It is true that the distribution of the branches of government between separate chapters in the Constitution reflects the basic *trias politica.* By substance, however, the text only carries remote testimony to the comparatively strong status of the new judiciary. In fact, Chapter D on the judiciary was – and remains – rather succinct, and most of its few provisions dealt with the specialised court for judging ministers, etc. in the first and last instance (*Riksretten*, the National Court). The key element regarding the ordinary courts was the establishment of a single instance for deciding in the last resort.

Determining that the Supreme Court has the last word, the Constitution explicitly presupposes the existence of lower courts. Within this framework, the judicial system is organised by virtue of ordinary statute. Somewhat simplifying, it now consists of three levels where some 60 first instance courts and 6 regional courts of appeal join the supreme instance. An extensively oral procedure places the bulk of responsibility for the preparation of the cases on the parties – in practise, thus, on their attorneys.

Appeal to the Supreme Court requires leave from an Appeals Committee composed of three members of the Court that serve for a few weeks in a row. Since

---

9 Among several hundred constitutions adopted during the last years of the 18th and the first years of the 19th centuries, only few actually succeeded in constituting a new state and/or a new political regime.

10 On the symbolic functions of constitutions, see Smith 2012c, pp 767–795.

2008, leave is granted in principle only if the case raises questions of importance beyond the case itself or is regarded as particularly important for other reasons. This way, its role as a court of precedent instead of as a supreme court of appeal supposed to correcting misled choices by inferior instances is emphasised to a much higher degree than during the first couple of centuries of its existence.[11] In accordance, the number of judgments handed out on the merits of the case (as opposed to decisions on procedure, etc.) has considerably diminished; in 2017, for instance, only 71 civil and 50 criminal cases were heard in chamber.[12]

By establishing a single Supreme Court, the Constitution indirectly closes the door towards establishing judicial instances not submitted to the jurisdiction of the apex instance, like administrative or constitutional courts. Instead, the jurisdiction of the Supreme Court extends to all fields of the legal order not explicitly exempted.[13] The lower courts possess the same broad powers of adjudication as the Supreme Court itself. In principle, no court is specialised in particular legal matters, and the members of each court circulate at short intervals between all kinds of lawsuits in a way supposed to keep them updated on any kind of legal matters (administrative, civil, criminal …).

Questions related to administrative and constitutional law are handled under the auspices of either civil or criminal procedure with very few accommodations for the specificity of such cases. For instance, someone convicted under criminal law may claim his acquittal because applying the relevant sub-constitutional provision would be contrary to the ban on retroactivity under Article 97 of the Constitution. In civil proceedings, you might similarly sustain your case by arguing, for instance, that a governmental decree has been adopted without the legal basis required by the Constitution or that the measure could be applied only insofar as the right to financial compensation in case of expropriation under Article 105 of the Constitution is observed.

The Constitution was silent about what kinds of lawsuits should fall under the jurisdiction of the Supreme Court as the last instance. The judiciary nevertheless followed the path laid down by its Danish-Norwegians forerunners by reviewing administrative acts, including those inherited from the absolute monarchy (see above). Moreover, it started to review the constitutionality of legislation adopted by virtue of the new Constitution (see further Sect. 6.6 below).

[11] For a comparative look at the doctrine of precedent in Norway, see Eng 2000.

[12] Supreme Court of Norway 2017.

[13] In addition to the provisions on the National Court, Articles 55 and 64 of the Constitution, which confer the resolution of disputes over parliamentary elections to Parliament, provide examples.

6.4 The Judges

Many European countries entertain formal career systems for judges of different kinds. Such systems typically enrol new judges at their exit from the relevant law or professional school and administer their career during most of their professional life, possibly all the way up to a position within the supreme instance. In order to avoid the kind of dependence of the judges that would too easily follow if such a system were run or supervised by the executive alone, those tasks are frequently carried out by some kind of 'supreme judicial councils' with a high degree of formal independence from the other state powers.

Formal career systems are typically supposed to produce judges with a high level of legal-technical skills in the relevant fields of law. By contrast, they are commonly regarded as less well fitted for providing judges with experience from other fields of the society or from the political life. This has served as one of the main arguments for recurring to other procedures for the selection of members of constitutional courts, typically including elements of openly political appointments.

While Denmark and Sweden entertain different versions of judicial career systems, no similar system has ever existed in Norway. Instead, permanent judges are appointed by the King in Council (at present, thus, *de facto* by the government) upon advice from the Minister of justice. Over time, this has contributed to keeping the selection relatively open. New judges have typically been appointed at the age or 40 or beyond, after having served in other sectors of the society, such as the public administration, the police or prosecution departments and law firms.

Sometimes, local or appellate judges apply for and obtain positions in a higher instance, but relatively few members of the appellate and supreme instances are chosen among judges at lower levels. In particular, most new members of the Supreme Court are picked from outside the judiciary, and throughout most of the 19th and the first part of 20th centuries, its membership counted persons with a distinctive political or academic past.[14] Together with the founding character of the Constitution, this profile certainly contributes to explaining the development of constitutional justice in Norway several decades before similar phenomena appeared in other parts of Europe.

This opening towards the political world *stricto sensu* was not systematically used, however, for picking judges sympathetic to the political views of the government in a way similar to those best known from the federal judiciary in the USA. Notwithstanding a few exceptions, the point is rather that quite a few of the Supreme Court judges throughout history have been involved in political or other societal activities before entering the bench in a way that must have influenced their attitude as judicial actors towards the political branches of government.

That pattern is now changing, however. In fact, the last member of the Supreme Court with a distinctive political past at National level, actually a former minister of justice, left the Court some 30 years ago (1990).

---

[14] Cf. Langeland 2005 and Sandmo 2005.

The movement is further enhanced by the establishment of an independent administrative body charged with selecting new permanent judges at all three levels (except the position of president of the Supreme Court). In operation since 2002, the collegium holds seven members including three judges, one practising lawyer, one legally trained civil servant, and two people not trained as lawyers, all appointed by the King in Council. When a position as permanent judge is open, it presents a prioritised list of applicants to the Ministry. As the Constitution confers the power of appointment to the King in Council, the government is free to choose another name than the one ranked first by the administrative body. Should it consider appointing someone not already ranked, however, it must first invite the collegium to consider the relevant candidate. With a few exceptions regarding the choice between a man and a woman, however, the position always goes to the top name on the list.

Under the present system, thus, the task of selecting new judges has effectively been taken away from the minister carrying the political responsibility and handed over to a group of people where judges and other legally trained members outweigh the 'popular' element by five to two. The remote possibility of active parliamentary control *ex post* in such matters set aside, Parliament has no say.

As mentioned, systems where new members of the judiciary are selected by independent administrative bodies with a strong presence of people already admitted to the bench first developed as a part of formal career systems. For the selection of members of specialised constitutional courts, however, no career system takes care of the recruitment, as judicial action in the field of constitutional law and by necessity, thus, in that of politics *lato sensu* is commonly thought to require or at least to legitimise other procedures of selection than those established for the management of formal career systems. Leaving it to collegiums dominated by members of the legal professions or by their colleagues-to-be to select new judges would quite evidently lack the legitimacy required for selection according to political considerations.

In systems where 'ordinary' courts exercise constitutional functions, similar techniques would hardly be better suited for safeguarding that sufficient attention is paid to elements like broad socio-political experience and a credible equilibrium between political currents. In Norway, the judiciary precisely exercises such functions, with the Supreme Court as the final instance. Moreover, permanent judges are appointed for the rest of their professional life, i.e. until the general age of retirement fixed by law. In such systems, it is far from obvious that the need of judicial independence towards the executive requires that judges are selected in complete isolation from the political branches of government. Neither could we take for granted that selection in the hands of independent bodies constructed with an aim of widening the distance between legal and political institutions is best suited for ensuring the judges a sufficient degree of legitimacy for tasks like reviewing acts of Parliament.

6.5 The Independence of the Judiciary[15]

Throughout the first 200 years, the Constitution of Norway held no general clause on the independence of the supreme and other courts. Instead, the main provisions of relevance for the independence were common to judges and other kinds of high civil servants, university professors, etc. As already mentioned, the particular status enjoyed by high civil servants appointed as *embetsmann* implies that before reaching the general age of retirement fixed by statute, a judge may involuntarily lose his or her position only by virtue of a court order.[16] For members of the Supreme Court, the order must be issued by the National Court (*Riksretten*, see above), an event that has never been close to materialise.

Other items critical for the protection of judicial independence, such as a ban on reduced salaries in the course of the mandate or the certainty of a decent pension level after retirement, however, have never been addressed by the Constitution of Norway. In a comparative perspective, thus, the formal protection is far from being complete.

The legal situation may have somewhat changed with the inclusion of a new constitutional provision in a package of human rights provisions adopted at the Constitution's bicentennial in 2014. According to Article 95, 'everyone has the right to have their case tried by an independent and impartial court within reasonable time'.[17] Together with its second part on 'fair and public' legal proceedings, the text obviously represents an adaptation of Article 6(1) of the European Convention on Human Rights. In that sense, it may not be qualified as genuinely new in the domestic law, as Norway has been a party to the Convention from the very beginning and made it directly applicable *en bloc* at statutory level in 1999.

The similarity between the two provisions is not perfect. In one direction, the constitutional clause extends the right to justice beyond 'civil rights and obligations' and 'criminal charge'. By contrast, it limits the right to have your case tried to 'courts' only, thus seemingly excluding a number of administrative complaints bodies and other tribunals that no doubt satisfy the basic requirements about independence and impartiality under Article 6 of the Convention. The legal implications of such differences remain unclear.

What remains, however, is that for the first time since Article 1 on National independence was adopted in 1814, the Constitution of Norway now consecrates the word independent (*uavhengig*). But it is far from clear that this step strengthens the formal independence of the judiciary. In fact, the catalogue of human rights of

[15] On the independence of judges with a particular eye on Norway, see Engstad et al. 2014.

[16] Articles 21 and 22(2) of the Constitution.

[17] The Constitution of the Kingdom of Norway 2018, https://lovdata.no/dokument/NLE/lov/1814-05-17/ (unofficial translation). Accessed 1 March 2019.

which it is a part was adopted under Parliament's clear presupposition that its aim was to strengthen the formal status of the human rights selected by 'exposing' them in the text of the Constitution without extending a level of protection that had already been realised in domestic law by other means.

Whatever the signification of the new provision might be, the existing lacunae in the constitutional protection of judicial independence has not given rise to major concerns in a system where the personal independence of judges has never been challenged by financial means. In fact, nobody seems to claim that the independence of the judiciary is under serious threat.[18]For instance, none of the papers presented in an anthology prepared at the occasion of the 100th anniversary of the Norwegian Association of Judges is devoted to particular concerns regarding the independence of the judiciary in Norway.[19] To the contrary, the ideology underpinning judicial independence seems firmly rooted with the judicial professions as well as in the Norwegian society in general.

The adoption of measures further restricting the possibility for judges to take up non-judicial tasks is likely to further enhance their image of independence during the last few decades. An official register that makes publicly available information about the judges' commercial and other personal interests supplements the measures.

In the same direction, disciplinary complaints against judges are now handled by an independent administrative collegium of two judges, one practising lawyer and two 'representatives from the public', all appointed by the King in Council. Established in 2001, the institution may issue disciplinary sanctions when a judge 'either wilfully or negligently breaches the obligations that are incumbent on the position or otherwise acts in breach of proper conduct of judges' under the current legislation and a number of ethical principles for judicial conduct. However, the possible sanctions only extend to 'warnings' and 'critical assessments'. So far, few complaints have been successful; in 2016, for instance, only two 'critical assessments' were issued. More importantly, complaints regarding case processing, decisions and assessments made by judges as well as the content of judicial decisions fall outside the collegium's scope of action.[20] In conformity with basic requirements of judicial independence, such questions can only be addressed by way of appeal to a superior court.

[18] Of course, the statement about the absence of 'serious threats' does not exclude that a number of other concerns merit discussion. See further in the anthology published in Norwegian at the occasion of the centennial of the Norwegian Association of Judges (Engstad et al. 2012), including Smith 2012a (on the use of short-term appointments for filling vacancies, including the use of retired judges in short-term positions within the collegial formations of the courts of appeal).

[19] Engstad et al. 2014.

[20] The Supervisory Committee for Judges 2016.

6.6 The Norwegian Judge as a Constitutional Judge[21]

As already noted, the Norwegian judiciary holds general jurisdiction including juridical review of statutes. Because the appointment of judges with constitutional functions may give raise to particular questions regarding independence, an overview of the development of the Norwegian system of judicial review of legislation seems appropriate.

The Norwegian system is actually the World's oldest next to that of the United States of America. Both systems emerged with no explicit basis in the text of the Constitution. In Norway, this gradually happened after the adoption of the Constitution, and one had to wait a few years only (1821) before the Supreme Court started referring to the Constitution[22] as a seemingly decisive argument for solving issues at stake. Most fundamentally, this implies acceptance of the Constitution as positive law.[23]

Even if the number of cases was limited in a society where the legislative activity was sparse and therefore created few opportunities for constitutional litigation, the following decades provided several.[24] Some of them sparked public debate as early as in the 1840s.[25]

Departing from a situation where the opinions of the Supreme Court were kept secret, individual public voting with the obligation for each member to give reasons for his vote was imposed by a statute adopted in 1863. The aim was to increase the Court's accountability in the aftermath of a number of controversies over its jurisprudence in constitutional and other matters.[26]

Shortly afterwards (1866), the first case appeared where the Supreme Court ruled against the government on the basis of reasons discussing and justifying its own power to review.[27] According to Court President Lasson speaking for the majority, established doctrine implied that the Constitution must be preferred when the relevant constitutional and statutory provisions cannot apply simultaneously.[28] This way, he not only confirmed the hierarchical character of the legal system as such,

---

[21] In English, see Smith 2018 and Kierulf 2018. In Norwegian, the literature on the past and present of judicial review is extensive.

[22] Since the very beginning, the generally framed non-retroactivity clause in Article 97 has constantly been the constitutional provision attracting the highest number of court cases.

[23] On the emergence of the Constitution of Norway as positive law, see Smith 1999.

[24] On the emergence of judicial review of legislation in Norway, see namely Holmøyvik 2007; Kierulf 2018; Langeland 2005 and Smith 1993.

[25] Slagstad 1995 and Langeland 2005.

[26] Cf. Langeland 2005, pp 369 ff.

[27] UfL 1866, p 165 (Wedel Jarlsberg) on a question of non-retroactivity.

[28] It is no surprise that Lasson's core reasoning leans heavily on a kind of hierarchical argument close to those called upon by US Chief justice Marshall in the famous *Marbury v Madison* case (1802).

but implicitly reaffirmed the Constitution's character as positive law as a prerequisite for judicial review.

The empoisoned question about the personal union with Sweden was brought to an end by Norway's unilateral breaking out in 1905. This left considerable room for government to enhance its activity regarding economic and social affairs. The frequency of constitutional case law increased correspondingly, and the Supreme Court set aside a number of legislative provisions as unconstitutional during a few years from 1909. This jurisprudence sparked growing political reaction, and the Supreme Court took a step back in a much-commented case in 1918.[29]

To some extent, the period appears as a Norwegian version of a 'New Deal' battle almost two decades before the far better known conflict between US President Roosevelt and the Supreme Court unfolded in the 1930s. In any case, however, what has often been regarded as a period of judicial activism eventually evaporated during the next 20 years. During the 'everyone together' reconstruction period after the end of the German occupation (1940–1945), no piece of legislation was set aside on constitutional grounds. In some cases, it may rather be argued that the Supreme Court gave too much leeway to Parliament.

Arguably, a judgment handed out in 1976 was the first instance after World War II where the Supreme Court set a piece of legislation aside on constitutional grounds. The relevant statutory provision was adopted with the aim of reducing the level of 'full compensation' in cases of expropriation according to Article 105 compared to the level established by previous case law in the absence of relevant legislation.[30] The issue had been heatedly debated in the society at large. Within the Supreme Court itself, the judges, sitting in plenary, split in two almost equal fractions about the constitutionality of the contested provision.

When deciding against the government, however, the majority presented the outcome as an instance of constitutional-conform interpretation rather than as an open setting-aside. Moreover, the fractions joined in introducing a doctrine about setting aside legislative provisions in cases only where the understanding of the Constitution on which Parliament had based its adoption of the relevant statute falls outside the scope of 'reasonable doubt'. Both elements convey an impression of care for avoiding confrontation with Parliament.

More than 40 years later, the climate regarding judicial review has changed considerably. After a number of precursors, including a 2007 case on property rights,[31] the shift in judicial attitude strikingly appears in three plenary cases adjudicated in 2010. In the first one, the key issue was the retroactive character of new legislation regarding taxation in a case the outcome of which would entail huge financial consequences either for a limited group of ship-owners or for the

[29] Supreme Court of Norway, 'den store konsesjonssak', 19 October 1917, Rt. 1918, p 1.

[30] Supreme Court of Norway, 'Kløfta', 27 January 1976, Rt. 1976, p 1.

[31] Supreme Court of Norway, 'tomtefeste III', 21 September 2007, Rt. 2007, p 1308. On the recent history of the Supreme Court of Norway, see Sunde 2005.

government.[32] In the second, the Court was faced with legislation that opened up for using parts of the fortune allotted to church affairs in a way deviating from those authorised by a constitutional clause unaltered since 1814.[33] In the final case, the key question was the constitutionality of applying penal law on war crimes and crimes against humanity on acts committed years before the relevant provisions had been adopted (Yugoslavia in the early 1990s).[34]

In all three cases, Parliament had devoted considerable attention to the constitutional aspects of the reform. The Court nevertheless decided against the government in all of them. This happened under sharp dissents while nevertheless qualifying the relevant provisions as 'clearly' or 'manifestly' unconstitutional. Visibly, the caution apparent in the 1976 opinions and other cases has faded away.

The change seems clearly interiorised by a majority of the members of the Court at least. Not surprisingly, however, tensions sometimes permeate from within the Supreme Court itself about which stance to adopt towards Parliament as the highest detainee of popular sovereignty. Tensions even appear in some of the cases adjudicated on the basis of the Constitution's extended bill of human rights (2014). If all agree that the new provisions should be used as positive law, full agreement on what judicial attitude to adopt does not seem established. Should the Court, for instance, depart from the relevant legislation and intervene only when needed for avoiding outcomes that it finds unconstitutional, or rather draw the outcome directly from the Constitution?[35] The question is important, of course, because reasoning by way of 'principle' would tend to extend the judicial freedom of appreciation more than reasoning primarily with an eye on the relevant pieces of legislation, in accordance with the inherited approach in Norway.

The relative weight judges allot to the tasks of clarifying the law or 'developing' it may even reflect the position they adopt on the scale between 'principle' and 'statute'. By way of interpretation, 'balancing', etc., the judiciary cannot avoid determining the meaning of the law they are supposed to apply in each case. But the function of developing the law may be cultivated in different ways. A deliberately active role necessarily implies that the judiciary takes part in the law-making power that the Constitution otherwise confers on the legislative and executive branches of government.

According to the mission, it has defined for itself, the 'main function of the Supreme Court of Norway is to ensure clarity and development of the law'.[36] As a chief task of the system's apex court, clarifying the law is not surprising. As interpretation necessarily commands a minimum of creative activity, one may even

---

[32] Supreme Court of Norway, 'rederiskatt', 12 February 2010, Rt. 2010, p 143.

[33] Supreme Court of Norway, 'Opplysningsvesenets fond', 12 May 2010, Rt. 2010, p 535.

[34] Supreme Court of Norway, 'krigsforbrytelse', 3 December 2010, Rt. 2010, p 1445. On the 2010 cases, see Smith 2011, pp 180–190 and Smith 2012b, pp 577–578.

[35] For a telling example, see Supreme Court of Norway, 'Maria', 29 January 2015, Rt. 2015, p 93 on the legality of expulsing a Nigerian woman whose small daughter had obtained Norwegian citizenship.

[36] Supreme Court of Norway 2018.

regard clarification and development of the law as identical features. The more the task of 'developing' the law is stressed as an autonomous or even primary task, however, the supreme instance takes upon itself an eminently political function.

This makes advocacy of judicial development of the law by some Supreme Court judges even more interesting. For example, one of them has stressed that 'the Court is prepared to apply a contemporary perspective to constitutional adjudication – the Constitution is not dead, it is alive'.[37] In other words, thus, the basic law would be dead if the judges did not insufflate life according to their own ideas about what would fit the societal needs at the time of adjudication. Not surprisingly, the most outspoken advocate of a dynamic approach to constitutional interpretation has spent most of his pre-judicial career publishing on the jurisprudence of the European Court of Human Rights.[38]

Even if the bulk of jurisprudence does not necessarily bear testimony to adherence to a deliberately dynamic stance by a plurality within the Court, a similar attitude nevertheless seems adopted in a number of recent cases. Suffice it here to mention the Acta judgment handed out in 2014.[39] In short, the reason why it has sparked debate is that the Court preferred deducing the outcome from a general 'principle' of the Constitution in a case where the relevant statutory provision (regarding criminal procedure) in itself might have provided a clear and perfectly defendable answer.[40]

6.7 Judicial Appointment and Independence

In the absence of serious concern over the independence of the judiciary in contemporary Norway (see Sect. 6.5 above), possibly negative effects on judicial independence of keeping judicial appointments with the executive is nevertheless ventilated in the current debate in and around the judiciary itself.[41]

Whatever system is used for the selection of new judges, genuine dependence may result from pressure against someone who, for instance, has accepted a bribe. We must therefore turn to other possible effects of preferring one kind of recruitment system to another.

Appointment systems likely to influence the independence of those appointed are easy to design. Renewable terms provide evident examples; in extreme cases (as in some extra-European polities), the future career of a judge even depends on

---

[37] Bårdsen 2017.

[38] See further Smith 2017.

[39] Supreme Court of Norway, 24 November 2014, Rt. 2014, p 1105.

[40] See further Kinander 2016.

[41] A governmental commission appointed in 2017 is currently discussing whether the administration of the judiciary should turn to an even stronger version of encapsulation from the political branches of government; see also www.domstolkommisjonen.no. Accessed 1 March 2019.

re-election by popular vote. Appointment for a fixed term or until a general age of retirement, like in Norway, does not give rise to the same kind of concerns. In general, we may even suggest that insofar as permanent and secure judicial positions are not for sale, the way you are selected will not influence your independence on the bench.

This implies that there is no reason to think that judicial nomination or election by a political body (like Parliament or the government) in itself makes the judge dependant on the person or the political party that had the decisive word in the selection. The status and position once installed on the bench is far more important than the way the judges arrived there. For the 'judiciary department … the permanent tenure by which the appointments are held … must soon destroy all sense of dependence on the authority conferring them'.[42]

That your independence primarily depends on where you stand, not on where you come from does not contradict, of course, that our previous personal experiences may influence the way we think. However, such influences do not equalise being dependent of someone else than yourself. A high-profiled judicial actor like late Justice Antonin Scalia of the US Supreme Court may serve as an example. Knowing his way of reasoning frequently gave some hold on his position in upcoming cases. Nobody would seriously claim, however, that his opinions were due to some kind of dependence on the authority that appointed him or on the political party (the Republicans) to which the appointing person (actually, president Reagan) belonged. What Scalia was dependent on, was his own convictions about how to interpret the Constitution, and so on. Dependence on oneself could not possibly be in conflict with our ideals of the rule of law.

6.8 Selecting Judges with Constitutional Functions

Adopted on the bicentennial of the Supreme Court (2015), the first constitutional clause on the bicentennial system of judicial review may contribute to comforting the re-established self-confidence of the Court in the field of constitutional law. Article 89 reads as follows: 'In cases brought before the Courts, the Courts have the power and the duty to review whether Laws and other decisions made by the authorities of the State are contrary to the Constitution.'[43] In conformity with the inherited system, the provision makes clear that the judiciary cannot itself initiate cases ('brought before the Courts'), that 'the power and the duty' to review 'Laws and other decisions' belong to courts at any level and that both statutory law, other acts of Parliament and administrative acts may be reviewed. On the other side, review of administrative acts on behalf of ordinary legislation is not spelled out

[42] Madison 1961.

[43] The Constitution of the Kingdom of Norway 2018, https://lovdata.no/dokument/NLE/lov/1814-05-17/ (unofficial translation). Accessed 1 March 2019.

even if of far greater practical importance than review on constitutional grounds only. This omission clearly disregards an uncontested part of the heritage. Luckily enough, however, nothing leaves us to believe that this lacunae implies that this part of the tasks of the Norwegian judiciary has been eradicated.

The provision's most problematic element is that the text seems to indicate that the scope of review is no longer the constitutionality of the application of the relevant legal norms in individual cases (*concrete* review), but of those 'laws and other decisions' as such. This way, it seems to establish (or confirm) a system of *abstract* judicial review, an understanding that would uncontestably modify the firmly established system of *ex post* review in Norway.

As the provision was adopted with the aim of making judicial review apparent in the text of the fundamental law without changing the system itself, it must be understood in light of the patterns appearing from jurisprudence throughout a couple of Centuries. But these patterns are not immutable. To the contrary, the Supreme Court of Norway now cultivates its role as a court of precedent much more than in any former period and in a way marked by a growing appetite for 'developing' the law.

This tendency is enhanced by the judges' growing willingness to issue general statements about the law in their opinions far beyond what would be needed in order to determine the relationship between the parties to the case. To the extent that such statements are counted as more than pure *obiter dicta*, the recourse to this technique tends to extend the norm-setting role of the Supreme Court beyond what necessarily follows from its function as a court of precedent obviously in need of giving meaning to legal provisions.

In any case, even genuinely concrete *ex post* review according to the inherited system may indirectly have effects *de facto* close to those created by abstract norm control. This appears most clearly in cases where the relevant provision concerns only few subjects or the conflict may be situated somewhere in the middle of the scope of the relevant norm, but even because the two other branches of government in Norway invariably take account of Supreme Court rulings in a way lending them a kind of *erga omnes* effect.

Together, such elements represent authoritative settling of general norms for the *polis* in a way that cannot avoid making the Court an increasingly political actor.[44] The political aspect of its activity is further enhanced when the norms pronounced are of a constitutional kind, thus supposedly binding the hands of majorities in Parliament that would otherwise be entitled to make and to change the law through the adoption of statutory provisions.

Genuinely abstract norm review with general effect constitutes a prominent part of the activities of specialized constitutional courts. Recalling that the Supreme Court of Norway shares with such institutions the power to review legislation, some of its own members have recently argued that it should be seen as a constitutional

[44] For a political science perspective, see Grendstad et al. 2015.

court.[45] However, a similar proposition tends to ignore (or omit) that members of both constitutional courts and other courts with important constitutional functions outside Norway are selected in ways that leave considerable freedom of appreciation according to openly political criteria.[46] Selection by Parliament, a combination of political bodies or a mixture of political and professional actors are typical features.

Elements of open political appointments are commonly regarded not only as legitimate but even as necessary for ensuring a sufficient level of legitimacy for political actors even when swathed in a judges' mantle. For almost 200 years, the Constitution of Norway has given considerable leeway to the executive when selecting new judges. Since 2002, however, an independent administrative body established by statute and dominated by members of the legal professions effectively selects nearly 100 per cent of new permanent judges for formal appointment by the executive.

As mentioned, however, this reform has not stood in the way for leading members of the judiciary to argue that the appointment system remains insufficient for taking care of the independence of the judiciary. In support, recommendations from different international bodies are frequently called upon. Most prominently, a 2010 recommendation from the Council of Europe's Committee of Ministers prescribes the establishment of a 'Judicial Council' at least half of the members of which should be elected from within the judiciary.[47] New judges should be appointed by that council itself or by another body independent from the political branches of government. If the formal appointment remains with the executive power, like in Norway, the council should have the decisive word. In any case, the selection should take place according to 'objective criteria pre-established by law' and in a way ensuring that candidates are not discriminated against in any way, including on the basis of their 'political or other opinions'.

An increasing number of European countries have established collegial bodies of the kind initially developed for the management of formal career systems where judges ought to be selected on more or less purely legal-technical grounds. None, however, seems to have followed the Council of Europe's recommendation when it comes to appointing members of specialised constitutional courts, and the appointees' 'political or other opinions' are not regarded as foreign to the selection. Even other judges vested with important constitutional functions in Europe appointed on purely legal-technical grounds would be difficult to find.

We may here leave open whether professional encapsulating of the recruitment process for the selection of members of jurisdictions with typical legal tasks (like penal or family law) is wise in the long run for the judiciary itself. In this respect, suffice it to mention the risks of creating or comforting an impression of a

---

45 See for instance Bårdsen 2015, commented upon by Smith 2017.

46 See for instance Stone Sweet 2012.

47 Council of Europe 2010.

self-sufficient judiciary and of mental streamlining along predominating states of mind within the legal world itself.

In any case, a *memento* seems allowed because similar steps are not decisive for ensuring a sufficient degree of judicial independence. According to European Court of Human Rights jurisprudence, for instance, a multitude of different recruitment systems may satisfy the requirements of independence according to Article 6 of the Convention. More generally, thus, your status on the bench is more important than where you come from (see Sect. 6.7 above).

The question thus becomes why Norwegian judges would enjoy a degree of legitimacy for constitutional adjudication that is not recognised to ordinary 'judicial' instances with members selected on the basis of their presumed legal-technical skills elsewhere in Europe. To what extent may an insofar-as-possible 'apolitical' procedure for selecting new judges be justified in a situation where the Supreme Court increasingly seems willing to take upon itself the eminently political task of authoritative norm-setting, generally as well as in matters of constitutional law?

In the years to come, Norway might have to choose between a judiciary with important constitutional and norm-setting functions comforted by a recruitment system that is likely to ensure that societal experiences and political balance are taken into account, and judges recruited on purely legal-technical grounds and primarily focusing on the uncontestably important tasks as a legal-technical court that has motivated the authors of the Council of Europe's recommendation and similar instruments. Should the future appointment system be constructed entirely according to the Council of Europe's and similar recommendations, it is hard to see how a genuinely political profile for the Supreme Court could be defended.

References

Bårdsen A (2015) The Nordic Supreme Courts as Constitutional Courts. Main Features as Seen From the Norwegian Perspective. https://www.domstol.no/globalassets/upload/hret/artikler-og-foredrag/nordic-constitutional-courts—vienna-29102015.pdf Accessed 1 March 2019

Bårdsen A (2017) The Norwegian Supreme Court as the Guardian of Constitutional Rights and Freedoms. https://www.domstol.no/globalassets/upload/hret/artikler-og-foredrag/supreme-court—constitutional-rights—bardsen18092017.pdf Accessed 1 March 2019

Christensen J P, Erichsen J, Tamm D (2015) The Supreme Court of Denmark. DJØF Publishing, Copenhagen

Council of Europe (2010) Recommendation CM/Rec(2010)12 of the Council of Ministers of the Council of Europe. https://rm.coe.int/16807096c1 Accessed 1 March 2019

Eng S (2000) The Doctrine of Precedent in English and Norwegian Law. Some Common and Specific Features. Scandinavian Studies in Law. Stockholm Institute for Scandinavian Law, Stockholm

Engstad N, Frøseth A L, Tønder B (eds) (2012) Dommernes uavhengighet. Den norske dommerforening 100 år. Fagbokforlaget, Bergen

Engstad N, Froseth A L, Tonder B (eds) (2014) The Independence of Judges. Eleven International Publishing, The Hague

Grendstad G, Shaffer W R, Waltenburg E (2015) Policy Making in an Independent Judiciary. The Norwegian Supreme Court. ECPR Press, Colchester

Holmøyvik E (2007) Årsaker til utviklinga av prøvingsretten i Noreg og Danmark. Tidsskrift for rettsvitenskap pp 718–779
Kierulf A (2018) Judicial Review in Norway. A Bicentennial Debate. Cambridge University Press, Cambridge
Kinander M (2016) Fra tilbakeholdenhet til aktivisme: Nyere utviklingslinjer i forholdet mellom rett og politikk i Høyesterett. Lov og rett 2016 pp 141–164
Koopmans T (2003) Courts and Political Institutions. A Comparative View. Cambridge University Press, Cambridge
Langeland N R (2005) Siste ord. Høgsterett i norsk historie. Bind I, 1814–1905. Cappelen, Oslo
Madison J (1961) The Federalist Papers. No. 51. The New American Library, New York
OECD (2017) How's Life? Measuring Well-Being. https://read.oecd-ilibrary.org/economics/how-s-life-2017_how_life-2017-en#page1 Accessed 1 March 2019
Ortiz-Spinosa E, Roser M (2017) Trust. https://ourworldindata.org/trust Accessed 1 March 2019
Sandmo E (2005) Siste ord. Høyesterett i norsk historie. Bind II, 1905–1965. Cappelen, Oslo
Slagstad R (1995) The Breakthrough of Judicial Review in the Norwegian System. In: Smith E (ed) Constitutional Justice under Old Constitutions. Kluwer Law International, The Hague, pp 81–112
Smith E (1993) Høyesterett og folkestyret. Prøvingsretten overfor lover. Universitetsforlaget, Oslo
Smith E (1999) On the formation and development of constitutional justice in a democratic society. In: Marcusson L et al (eds) Festskrift till Fredrik Sterzel. Iustus, Uppsala, pp 289–305
Smith E (2011) Norway. Supreme Court strongly reaffirms supremacy of constitution by striking down controversial legislative provisions. Public Law, London, pp 188–190
Smith E (2012a) Høyesterett som statsmakt: Innordnet, men uavhengig? In: Engstad N et al (eds) Dommernes uavhengighet. Den norske dommerforening 100 år. Fagbokforlaget, Bergen, pp 149–179
Smith E (2012b) Norway. Supreme Court on non-retroactivity of new legislation regarding crimes of war. Public Law, London, pp 577–578
Smith E (2012c) Les fonctions symboliques des constitutions. In: Troper T, Chagnollaud D (eds) Traité international de droit constitutionnel. Tome I: Théorie de la Constitution. Dalloz, Paris
Smith E (2017) Er Høyesterett en konstitusjonsdomstol? Jussens Venner (Oslo) 2/2017, pp 98–121
Smith E (2018) Judicial Review of Legislation. In: Krunke H, Thorarensen B (eds) The Nordic Constitutions. A Comparative and Contextual Approach. Hart Publishing, Oxford, Ch. 5
Stone Sweet A (2012) Constitutional Courts. In: Rosenfeld M, Sajó B (eds) The Oxford Handbook of Comparative Constitutional Law. Hart Publishing, Oxford, Ch. 38
Sunde J Ø (2005) Høgsteretts historie 1965–2015. Fagbokforlaget, Bergen
Supreme Court of Norway (2017) Annual Report 2017. https://indd.adobe.com/view/1bc9c6b9-75c2-4d3d-8af2-c950e08fff40 Accessed 1 March 2019
Supreme Court of Norway (2018) The Supreme Court. https://www.domstol.no/en/Enkelt-domstol/-norges-hoyesterett/ Accessed 1 March 2019
The Supervisory Committee for Judges (2016) Annual Report. https://www.domstol.no/globalassets/upload/tu/arsmelding-2016_eng.pdf Accessed 27 November 2018
Trondal J (2012) The Agency Phenomenon in the European Union. Manchester University Press, Manchester
Van der Schyff G (2010) Judicial Review of Legislation. A Comparative Study of the United Kingdom, the Netherlands and South Africa. Springer, Heidelberg

Eivind Smith is Professor of Public Law at the University of Oslo. He has published extensively in several languages on domestic and comparative public (administrative and constitutional) law. He is a member of several learned societies and an honorary doctor in Denmark, France and Sweden. Enjoying extensive international experience, he has chaired a number of commissions appointed by the Norwegian Parliament, the government and other bodies and acts as chair of the Norwegian tribunal on political party financing. Together with a number of articles in Norway and abroad, he has recently published books on both administrative and constitutional law.

Chapter 7
Judicial Independence and Accountability in the British Constitution

Paul Daly

Contents

Abstract The principal objective of this chapter is to describe the present state of judicial independence and accountability in the British Constitution. The chapter also takes, however, a critical view of Britain's constitutional arrangements for securing judicial independence and accountability, drawing on recent controversies to demonstrate the potential frailty of these arrangements. Underlying the description is a broader message, that Britain's constitutional arrangements are best understood as a series of pragmatic responses to such challenges as happen to arise from time to time. Given the nature of Britain's uncodified constitution, which is neither supreme nor entrenched, the norms that exist in and constitute the British Constitution do not lie, ultimately, in the hands of the judiciary. Significant constitutional change can happen very quickly – as with the transformation of the office

P. Daly (✉)
University of Cambridge, Cambridge, UK
e-mail: pd309@cam.ac.uk

Hirsch Ballin, Van der Schyff & Stremler (eds.), *European Yearbook of Constitutional Law 2019*, European Yearbook of Constitutional Law 1,
https://doi.org/10.1007/978-94-6265-359-7_7

of Lord Chancellor. There is reason to fear, therefore, that the protection of norms (including those of judicial independence and accountability) will be less robust than in jurisdictions with a codified, entrenched, supreme constitutional document.

Keywords British Constitution · financial security · judicial accountability · judicial appointments · judicial independence · judicial pensions · security of tenure

7.1 Introduction

The principal objective of this chapter is to describe the present state of judicial independence and accountability in the British Constitution.[1] I also take, however, a critical view of Britain's constitutional arrangements for securing judicial independence and accountability, drawing on recent controversies to demonstrate the potential frailty of these arrangements.

Underlying my description is a broader message, that Britain's constitutional arrangements are best understood as a series of pragmatic responses to such challenges as happen to arise from time to time. As the United Kingdom Supreme Court recently reminded us, the British Constitution has 'developed over time in a pragmatic as much as in a principled way, through a combination of statutes, events, conventions, academic writings and judicial decisions'.[2] An observer of the landscape of British constitutional law will peer in vain for pristine examples of principles such as 'separation of powers', 'judicial independence' or 'accountability'. Britain's constitutional law is, after all, common-law in nature. Quite unlike the coherent, self-contained codes of the civilian tradition, the common law is 'chaos with a full index'.[3] The point is not that Britain's constitutional arrangements are chaotic, but that they have not emerged from a mapping exercise conducted by learned jurists or a constituent assembly: Britain's is a 'political constitution', which 'lives on, changing from day to day for the constitution is no more and no less than what happens'.[4]

Accordingly, the responses to the challenges posed by judicial independence and accountability have taken multiple forms:[5] Acts of Parliament; delegated legislation; non-statutory instruments; constitutional conventions; constitutional

[1] For those who wish to delve further into the subject matter there are two excellent texts of recent provenance: Gee et al. 2015 and Shetreet and Turenne 2013.

[2] UKSC, *Miller v Secretary of State for Exiting the European Union*, 24 January 2017, UKSC 5; [2017] 2 WLR 583, [40].

[3] Holland 2001, p 171, cited by Postema 2004, p 1.

[4] Griffith 1979.

[5] See also Le Sueur 2013, p 215: 'In the absence of a written constitution, the constitutional framework of the judicial system has to rest on ordinary legislation (primary and secondary), "soft law" and constitutional conventions'.

principles; day-to-day practice; and even 'often unarticulated understandings'.[6] I do not expect that Britain is unique in this regard,[7] but the British approach to judicial independence and accountability cannot be understood without having regard to the wide variety of norms that exist in and constitute the British Constitution. However, given the nature of Britain's uncodified constitution, which is neither supreme nor entrenched, these norms do not lie, ultimately, in the hands of the judiciary. There is reason to fear, therefore, that the protection of norms (including those of judicial independence and accountability) will be less robust than in jurisdictions with a codified, entrenched, supreme constitutional document. A comparative enterprise like the collection of essays in the present volume assists in assessing whether the British approach is better or worse than those followed by other European polities – but any such assessment must at least take into account the potential frailty of the United Kingdom's constitutional arrangements for securing judicial independence and accountability.

In Sect. 7.2, I will discuss judicial independence, describing how the security of tenure, financial security and institutional independence of judges are ensured in the British Constitution. Particularly prominent in this account will be the Lord Chancellor, with the radical change in the nature of this office providing a vivid illustration of the way in which (and how rapidly) constitutional change can occur in Britain. In Sect. 7.3, I will turn to judicial accountability, describing how British judges respond to the challenges of ensuring accountability, both by engaging in discussion with the other branches of government (and, to a lesser extent, the wider public) and by developing an understanding of their place in the British constitutional order.[8]

In both Sects. 7.2 and 7.3, I will use some recent controversies to provide a critical perspective on the British approach to securing judicial independence and accountability. In Sect. 7.2, I will discuss the difficulties that have been experienced in recruiting qualified judges to the bench, in the wake of reforms to judicial pensions. I will also highlight the failure of the Lord Chancellor to offer a robust defence of judicial independence subsequent to the vituperative criticism levelled at

---

[6] Oliver 2011, p 99.

[7] See e.g., on Canada, Walters 2008, and on the United States of America, Reed Amar 2012.

[8] The United Kingdom comprises three separate jurisdictions – England and Wales; Scotland; and Northern Ireland. These jurisdictions, though distinct, operate within the framework of the British Constitution. Accordingly, although the particular arrangements that exist in respect of judicial independence and accountability differ in some respects between the jurisdictions, the same constitutional framework applies. With a view to keeping this contribution to a reasonable size, my focus will be on the judiciary of England and Wales. I will occasionally refer to material from Scotland and Northern Ireland, comprehensive treatment of which can be found elsewhere (Gee et al. 2015, chapter 9) but my primary goal is to describe how judicial independence and accountability are secured in the British Constitution by particular reference to the judiciary of England and Wales. Going into more detail on Scotland and Northern Ireland would not be feasible without an extended discussion of the nature of the devolution of legislative power in the contemporary British Constitution, which is beyond the parameters of a chapter on judicial independence and accountability.

the first-instance judges who held that Parliament would have to authorise Britain's departure from the European Union.[9] In Sect. 7.3, I will observe that the judges' means of avoiding trespassing in what is perceived to be the domain of politics have been inadequate to protect them from being drawn into political controversy, especially in respect of the Human Rights Act 1998, which domesticates many of the rights set out in the European Convention on Human Rights.

7.2 Independence

My framework for analysis in this section comprises the criteria for judicial independence enunciated by the Supreme Court of Canada in *Valente v The Queen.*[10] I recognise, of course, that judicial independence is a large concept[11] and that different conceptions of it may exist in different legal and judicial cultures at different times.[12] Moreover, as I suggested in the introduction, understanding judicial independence in Britain – as with understanding any of its constitutional arrangements – is easier without resort to neatly-packaged abstract concepts. Nonetheless, one must start somewhere and the 'much cited'[13] *Valente* factors are as good a starting point as any. In *Valente*, Le Dain J described the 'essential conditions of judicial independence' as:[14] security of tenure; financial security; and institutional independence. I use these criteria as a guide to analysis only, for as will become clear they do not exist in a pure form in respect of the British judiciary.

First, the 'essence' of security of tenure involves 'a tenure, whether until an age of retirement, for a fixed term, or for a specific adjudicative task, that is secure against interference by the Executive or other appointing authority in a discretionary or arbitrary manner'.[15] If exposed to the risk of removal from office, a judge

---

[9] UKSC, *R (Miller) v Secretary of State for Exiting the European Union*, 2016, HRLR 23.

[10] SCR, *Valente v. The Queen*, 19 December 1985, 2 SCR 673.

[11] See, e.g., Lord Hodge 2016, para 4: 'To do right, that is to decide cases impartially and in accordance with the law, judges must be independent of all litigants and also of all who might directly or indirectly seek to influence the outcome of a legal action, including their fellow judges who are not sitting on the particular case.' Lord Hodge went on to identify 10 'pillars' of judicial independence: (1) A clear constitutional commitment to the independence of the judiciary and the rule of law; (2) Exclusion, or at the very least, minimisation, of political considerations as an influence on the appointment and promotion of judges; (3) Adequate finance; (4) Personal immunity from suit from acts and omissions in the exercise of judicial functions; (5) Security of tenure; (6) The separation of powers; (7) Accountability; (8) 'Role recognition' by judges; (9) Performance and moral authority; (10) Maintaining political and public understanding and support. See also International Association of Judicial Independence and World Peace, *Mount Scopus International Standards of Judicial Independence* (19 March 2008).

[12] See, e.g., Bell 2001.

[13] Lord Justice Beatson 2017.

[14] *Valente*, [25].

[15] *Ibid.*, [31].

is (all things being equal) relatively more likely to favour in his or her decisions the interests of those who hold the removal power.

Second, at the core of financial security is that 'the right to salary and pension should be established by law and not be subject to arbitrary interference by the Executive in a manner that could affect judicial independence'.[16] Control of the purse strings, such that they could be tightened or loosened from time to time, will exercise the mind of a judge who will naturally be concerned that his or her salary might be docked for failing to please his or her financial masters, or alternatively that his or her salary might be increased in response to decisions favourable to his or her financial masters.

Third, the 'essentials' of institutional independence can 'be summed up as judicial control over the administrative decisions that bear directly and immediately on the exercise of the judicial function',[17] in particular (having regard to the fact that court facilities are typically provided by the political branches of government) matters such as the 'assignment of judges, sittings of the court, and court lists – as well as the related matters of allocation of court rooms and direction of the administrative staff engaged in carrying out these functions'.[18] As with control of the purse strings, control of judicial administration allows officials variously to threaten judges with the withdrawal of services when decisions are unfavourable and promise enhanced services for favourable decisions.

7.2.1 *Security of Tenure*

Senior judges have benefitted, since the Act of Settlement 1701, from formalised protection for their security of tenure. Provision is made for removal of a sitting judge by s. 11(3) of the Senior Courts Act 1981:

> A person appointed to an office to which this section applies shall hold that office during good behaviour, subject to a power of removal by Her Majesty on an address presented to Her by both Houses of Parliament.[19]

Whilst the Act of Settlement 'has been at the basis of judicial protection in all common law countries', it is worth emphasising that the impetus for the inclusion of security of tenure in the Act came from contemporary political events; the provision was designed to ensure that the interferences with the administration of justice that had pockmarked the constitutional history of late-17th century England

---

16 *Ibid.*, [40].

17 *Ibid.*, [52].

18 *Ibid.*, [49].

19 See also Scotland Act 1998, s. 95(6)–(7) (Scottish judges); Constitutional Reform Act 2005, s. 33 (Supreme Court judges); Tribunals, Courts and Enforcement Act 2007, sched. 1, para 6 (Senior President of Tribunals).

would not recur.[20] What has become a cornerstone of judicial independence in the United Kingdom was designed as a pragmatic response to a set of challenges that happened to arise at a particular point in time.

Today's legislative framework for judicial discipline was created by the Constitutional Reform Act 2005, a piece of legislation born of the then-government's 'obsession with modernisation'.[21] Chapter 3 of the Act empowers the Lord Chancellor and, in particular, the Lord Chief Justice to put in place procedures leading to the taking of disciplinary action against judges; delegated legislation has been adopted to this effect.[22] Most judicial offices are now regulated entirely, as to discipline, under the framework of the 2005 Act.[23] Members of the senior judiciary of England and Wales can still be removed only upon an 'address' to Parliament, but the decision of the Lord Chancellor to 'move' an address is now to be taken only after the prescribed procedures have been followed.[24] An address has only ever been moved once,[25] but judges embroiled in controversy may choose to step down quietly before matters ever get that far.[26]

Many complaints are received each year by the Judicial Conduct Investigations Office established by delegated legislation under the auspices of the 2005 Act. Most are unsubstantiated and the occasions requiring disciplinary action 'are in proportion very low'.[27] Of relevance in setting the standards against which judges' behaviour is measured is a non-statutory *Guide to Judicial Conduct*.[28] To the provisions of the *Guide* must be added the terms of the Magna Carta 1215 ('To none will we sell, to none deny or delay right or justice') and the judicial oath ('I will do right by all manner of people, after the law and usages of this realm,

---

[20] Stevens 2001, p 266.

[21] Lord Windlesham 2005, p 809. Loughlin 2013, p 3, describes the reforms under the New Labour government in the late 1990s and early 2000s as a 'more radical set of constitutional reforms' than those enacted by any government since the First World War.

[22] See now The Judicial Discipline (Prescribed Procedures) Regulations 2014; The Judicial Conduct (Judicial and other office holders) Rules 2014; The Judicial Conduct (Tribunals) Rules 2014.

[23] See Schedule 14 to the 2005 Act, as amended by Schedule 13, Part 4 of the Crime and Courts Act 2013 for a full list of judicial offices covered by its provisions. Separate legislation exists in respect of Scotland, which has a separate legal system and judiciary presided over by the Lord President: Judiciary and Courts (Scotland) Act 2008. See also, in relation to Northern Ireland, the Justice (Northern Ireland) Act 2002.

[24] The Judicial Discipline (Prescribed Procedures) Regulations 2014, Article 2(1).

[25] In respect of Sir Jonah Barrington, in 1830.

[26] A recent example is provided by Sir Peter Smith, a former High Court judge who retired before disciplinary proceedings against him concluded: 'Conduct probe into High Court judge ends with retirement', *The Law Society Gazette*, October 27, 2017. See generally, Shetreet and Turenne 2013, pp 339–354 for other examples.

[27] Shetreet and Turenne 2013, p 291.

[28] Courts and Tribunals Judiciary 2018. This is 'a set of core principles which will help judges reach their own decisions' about their conduct (p 5) and to which the disciplinary bodies 'may have regard' (p 6).

without fear or favour, affection or ill will'),[29] also instruments of great constitutional importance despite their non-statutory basis.

In short, the mechanisms for the protection of security of tenure in the British Constitution are found partly in legislation (enacted in response to political conditions that happened to prevail from time to time), delegated legislation and non-statutory instruments.

The flipside of removal from office is appointment to office, the fear here being that judicial appointees will favour, in their decisions from the bench, those who sent them there. Historically, in both form and substance, appointments to the senior judiciary have been in the hands of the executive: judicial appointments are made under the royal prerogative, by the Crown, but – by constitutional convention – on the advice of ministers.[30] Until recent times, judicial appointments were in substance made by the Lord Chancellor. As the volume of work in the Lord Chancellor's department increased, he was supported to a greater extent by civil servants,[31] though much still depended on the informal 'soundings' taken from members of the legal profession and existing judges.[32]

Modernisation did not occur overnight. Even before the era of the Constitutional Reform Act 2005, significant transparency had been injected into the process of judicial appointments, as a matter of practice, not as a matter of statute law or delegated legislation:

> Lord Mackay of Clashfern, had introduced a good deal of modernisation: posts were advertised, job descriptions and statements of eligibility were introduced as were selection criteria for each judicial office. Candidates were required to complete application forms designed to elicit information to enable them to be assessed against the published selection criteria.[33]

Now, most judicial appointments in England and Wales are made, in substance, by the Judicial Appointments Commission established by s. 62(1) of the Constitutional Reform Act 2005. For instance, the JAC recommends candidates for the High Court and Court of Appeal to the Lord Chancellor. The 2005 Act imposes some substantive and procedural requirements: for instance, selection must be on merit and appointees must be of good character;[34] and selection panels for

---

[29] Shetreet and Turenne 2013, p 185.

[30] Cabinet Office 2011, para 3.33.

[31] Shetreet and Turenne 2013, p 105: 'Under the supervision of the Permanent Secretary, the Lord Chancellor's Department used to maintain records of potential candidates for the High Court and for the lower judicial offices. At any given time the Lord Chancellor's Office had a list of qualified candidates who could be considered for judicial vacancies. The Lord Chancellor's staff also processed the applications for Queen's Counsel, which enabled them to follow up the advancement of leading members of the Bar from among whose ranks judges were drawn.'

[32] See the account in Darbyshire 2011, pp 90–95. On the increasingly professionalised approach in the 1980s and 1990s see Lord Mackay of Clashfern 2010.

[33] Stephens 2018, p 22.

[34] Constitutional Reform Act 2005, s. 63.

higher-level appointments must comprise at least five members.[35] The composition of the Judicial Appointments Commission is set out in delegated legislation.[36] A separate process exists for Supreme Court appointments.[37]

Within the statutory parameters, there is a great deal of space for the Judicial Appointments Commission to develop its own criteria to evaluate candidates for judicial office, to elaborate '[a] continuing programme of work [...] to ensure that JAC selections are fair, made solely on merit, and open [...]'[38] Similarly, criteria against which to evaluate potential additions to the UK Supreme Court bench are not to be found in legislation, which has 'little to say about how the commissions should go about their work',[39] but in non-statutory documentation.[40] Indeed, though the creation of statutory appointments bodies seemed to herald a new era of transparency, with lay members to play a key role and in which existing judges would have less influence, it is clear that as a matter of practice the judiciary continues to exert significant sway in shaping the choices of the statutory appointments bodies,[41] with the Lord Chancellor playing a minimal role notwithstanding his formal powers.[42] In general,

> [...] a highly informal system in which ministerial discretion was lightly regulated by non-legal conventions has been replaced with a formal statutory scheme in which the Lord Chancellor is entirely removed from lower-level appointments and where ministerial discretion for top appointments is, in practice, exceptionally limited.[43]

Therefore, in order to understand how judicial appointments function in the United Kingdom, and support judicial independence, one must look not only to statute but also to delegated legislation, non-statutory instruments and practice.

---

[35] Constitutional Reform Act 2005, ss. 70, 75B, 80.

[36] The Judicial Appointments Commission Regulations 2013, Article 4. There are to be 15 members: a lay Chair, seven judicial members, five lay members and two legal practitioners. The Judicial Appointments Board for Scotland has a lay majority: see https://www.judicialappointments.scot/about/meet-our-team/board-members, accessed 1 April 2019.

[37] Constitutional Reform Act 2005, ss. 25–27B, as amended by the Crime and Courts Act 2013, Schedule 13. Promotions fall outside the ambit of the 2005 Act. Promotions within the judiciary are shrouded in relative secrecy, in no small part because '[t]here is currently no comprehensive system for appraisal for courts or tribunals': Shetreet and Turenne 2013, p 137.

[38] Stephens 2018, p 25.

[39] Lady Hale 2018, p 309.

[40] See, e.g., 'Information Pack – Vacancies for Appointment as Deputy President of the Supreme Court and Justice of the Supreme Court', pp 5–7 (https://www.supremecourt.uk/docs/judicial-vacancies-2018-information-pack.pdf, accessed 1 April 2019).

[41] Gee 2018.

[42] See, e.g., The Judicial Appointments Regulations 2013, Articles 9(3), 15(3), 21(3) and 27(3) (powers not to follow recommendations, but coupled with obligations to provide reasons).

[43] Gee et al. 2015, p 164.

7.2.2 *Financial Security*

It is (again) to the Act of Settlement 1701 that we can trace the principle that judicial salaries should be 'ascertained and established' by statute. In modern times, judicial salaries are 'determined by the Lord Chancellor with the concurrence of the Minister for the Civil Service'[44] and 'charged on and paid out of the Consolidated Fund',[45] the significance of which 'is to prevent any routine or frivolous discussion of the conduct of judges by Parliament in financial debate'.[46] Once more, flesh is put on the bones of the skeleton of the statute by non-statutory means, with the Lord Chancellor's determinations heavily influenced by the recommendations of the Review Body on Senior Salaries, an independent review body, which advises the government on remuneration for senior public servants.

Notwithstanding this generally rosy picture, there is no entrenched protection for judicial salaries. They could be reduced by Act of Parliament. Indeed, orthodox British constitutional theory holds that Parliament cannot bind its successors and so would be incapable of entrenching a statutory provision preventing the reduction of judicial salaries.[47] It is relevant, however, that judicial independence is a recognised constitutional principle. Indeed, s. 3(1) of the Constitutional Reform Act 2005 provides:

> The Lord Chancellor, other Ministers of the Crown and all with responsibility for matters relating to the judiciary or otherwise to the administration of justice must uphold the continued independence of the judiciary.

A minister who introduced or supported legislation providing for a reduction in judicial salaries would be in breach of this principle. Even though such a principle is likely to be non-justiciable in a court of law,[48] it imposes an important political restraint on what political actors may legitimately do: in light of s. 3(1), an attempt

---

[44] Senior Courts Act 1981, s. 12(1).

[45] Senior Courts Act 1981, s. 12(5). This can be traced to 1 Geo. III, c. 23 (1760). The Consolidated Fund: 'is the Government's general bank account at the Bank of England. Payments from this account must be authorised in advance by the House of Commons. The Government presents its "requests" to use this money in the form of Consolidated Fund Bills.' https://www.parliament.uk/site-information/glossary/consolidated-fund/, accessed 1 April 2019.

[46] Lederman 1956, p 792.

[47] See UKHL, *Jackson v Attorney General,* [2006] 1 A.C. 262, [113], *per* Lord Hope of Craighead: '[I]t is a fundamental aspect of the rule of sovereignty that no Parliament can bind its successors. There are no means by whereby, even with the assistance of the most skilful draftsman, it can entrench an Act of Parliament. It is impossible for Parliament to enact something which a subsequent statute dealing with the same subject matter cannot repeal.'

[48] See, e.g., UKSC, *Miller v Secretary of State for Exiting the European Union*, 24 January 2017, UKSC 5; [2017] 2 WLR 583, at [145], describing the Sewel Convention – a constitutional convention relating to the need for the Westminster Parliament to seek the consent of the devolved legislatures in Northern Ireland, Scotland and Wales before legislating on certain matters – as non-justiciable notwithstanding the fact that it had been put on a statutory basis in the Scotland Act 2016.

by ministers to reduce judicial salaries would be unconstitutional, as would legislation to that effect (though not necessarily illegalities which a court of law could invalidate).[49]

In summary, the financial security of British judges is protected by statute, non-statutory means, constitutional principle and shared understandings about what it is appropriate for political actors to do vis-à-vis judicial salaries.

However, the efficacy of these arrangements, which relies heavily on members of the political branches actively ensuring that judges are adequately remunerated, has been called into serious question by recent developments. Judicial salaries were not always especially handsome:[50] in previous times, they were often supplemented by various other sources of income, many derived from judicial office.[51] Although English judges 'are among the highest paid public officials',[52] judicial salaries are rarely as attractive as the income high-flying barristers or solicitors can earn in private practice, which may have had an impact on the recruitment of judges.[53] In recent recruitment exercises run by the JAC, there have been 'shortfalls' in judicial appointments: for instance, in 2016–2017, it was possible only to fill eight of 14 vacant positions in the High Court.[54] Indeed, '[t]he percentage of candidates assessed as outstanding or strong compared to the number of selections in key salaried roles has been decreasing overall since 2012–2013'.[55] In short, a career in the judiciary has become less attractive to qualified candidates.[56] Moreover, according to the Lord Chief Justice of England and Wales, there is 'undoubtedly a growing phenomenon of judges retiring a little earlier than they need'.[57]

The background is a 'serious loss of morale across the judiciary and continuing dissatisfaction over (1) working conditions, (2) the volume of work, and (3) pay and

---

[49] For the distinction between illegality and unconstitutionality in the British constitutional tradition, see JCPC, *Madzimbamuto v Lardner-Burke and George* [1969] 1 AC 645, at p 723, *per* Lord Reid: 'It is often said that it would be unconstitutional for the United Kingdom Parliament to do certain things, meaning that the moral, political and other reasons against doing them are so strong that most people would regard it as highly improper if Parliament did these things. But that does not mean that it is beyond the power of Parliament to do such things. If Parliament chose to do any of them the courts could not hold the Act of Parliament invalid.'

[50] Beloff 2006.

[51] See, e.g., Poser 2013.

[52] Shetreet and Turenne 2013, p 156.

[53] See, e.g., Review Board on Senior Salaries 2017, noting at para 6.91 the 'low morale' in the judiciary and recommending that 'the government should carefully explore the scope for pay and pension flexibilities, as found in the private sector, in order to support recruitment and retention within the judicial workforce'.

[54] Judicial Appointments Commission 2018a, paras 26–27.

[55] Judicial Appointments Commission 2018b, p 1.

[56] 'LCJ warns of "lasting damage" to High Court through judge shortage', *Law Society Gazette*, 5 July 2018.

[57] House of Lords Select Committee on the Constitution 2018, p 6.

pensions'.[58] Pensions has been a particular flashpoint.[59] On foot of a government review of public sector pensions in the wake of the financial crisis of the 2000s, the existing scheme of judicial pensions was phased out and replaced by a new scheme,[60] which is 'considerably less valuable' to its members.[61] In addition, a reform to the taxation treatment of judicial pensions in 2015 had a 'very, very serious unintended effect on the judiciary';[62] post-2015 judges are treated much less favourably than their pre-2015 counterparts, and, in practice, much less favourably than other public servants.[63] Indeed, newly appointed judges found themselves 'forced into' a much less favourable pension scheme than they had anticipated when accepting their appointment, which in the view of the House of Lords Select Committee on the Constitution constituted 'a breach of the principle of security of tenure'.[64] Litigation before the Employment Tribunal ensued, with younger judges claiming they were directly discriminated against on the basis of age and indirectly discriminated against on other grounds (on the basis that younger judges are more likely to come from vulnerable social groups). At first instance and on appeal, the judges were successful.[65] A further appeal to the Court of Appeal is pending.[66]

The lesson of this controversy is that the financial security of British judges depends to a very great extent on the willingness of government to fund adequate pay and pensions. In times of fiscal hardship, it is unlikely that an elite group, such as judges, will be excluded from a general government policy of austerity. Despite warnings from the Review Body on Senior Salaries, and senior members of the judiciary, no measures have been taken to counter the effects of recent reforms. A major review of judicial salaries is being conducted by the Board, but it expressly excludes the issue of 'levels of pay'.[67] Whilst the barriers to reductions in judicial pay are relatively robust (though perhaps also liable to come under strain in straitened economic times), there is no mechanism to ensure that British judges' pay and pensions increase in line with the needs and expectations of prospective new judges. This can only hurt the financial security of the judiciary.

---

58 Judiciary of England and Wales 2017, p 12.

59 Review Body on Senior Salaries 2017, p 85.

60 See generally Ministry of Justice 2017.

61 *The Lord Chancellor v McCloud and others* [2018] UKEAT /0071/17/LA, [21] (Employment Appeal Tribunal).

62 House of Lords Select Committee on the Constitution 2016, p 1.

63 Review Body on Senior Salaries 2017, p 35.

64 House of Lords Select Committee on the Constitution 2017a, p 10.

65 *The Lord Chancellor v McCloud and others* [2018] UKEAT /0071/17/LA, para 21 (Employment Appeal Tribunal), holding in particular at para 167 that the first-instance decision-maker was justified in concluding that 'the extremely severe impact of the transitional provisions on the Claimants far outweighed the public benefit of applying the policy consistently across the whole public service pension sector'.

66 'Government continues to fight judges' pension case', *Financial Times Adviser*, 1 February 2018.

67 Review Body on Senior Salaries 2018, p 4.

7.2.3 Institutional Independence

Prior to the constitutional tumult of the 17th century, there was little or no meaningful separation of functions in the British Constitution. What comparative constitutional lawyers now tend to describe as legislative, executive and judicial functions were concentrated in the monarch:[68] 'the hallmarks of the sixteenth century were a strong monarch, a subservient parliament and a non-interventionist judiciary'.[69] Judges were 'servants of the king', who held their offices at pleasure and, as such, were 'no more secure in office than government ministers'.[70]

Even after the tumult had subsided and an identifiably distinctive judicial function emerged, it was not separated from politics: 'Lord Mansfield CJ was, for a time, a highly influential cabinet Minister. Lord Ellenborough CJ was a member of the Cabinet in 1806. Sir John Trevor was simultaneously Master of the Rolls and Speaker of the House of Commons at the end of the seventeenth century'.[71] Until the late 20th century, the law lords, who sat in the United Kingdom's apex court, actively contributed to parliamentary debates.[72]

Emblematic of the British approach to separation of powers was the Lord Chancellor,[73] simultaneously Speaker of the House of Lords, a member of the cabinet and the head of the judiciary.[74] Having regard to the dignity of the office, the Lord Chancellor was expected to be 'of the highest standing and eminence in the profession'.[75] In his capacity as head of the judiciary, the Lord Chancellor had significant responsibilities for the administration of justice:

> The Lord Chancellor's role was central. The initiative lay with him. He would have had ready access to the judiciary, and particularly the senior judiciary. He could take soundings from them as to the need for reform. If the need for action became apparent, the Lord Chancellor could act and make an appointment to carry out a review or chair a Royal Commission. Equally, he might not.[76]

As a leading member of the legal profession, the Lord Chancellor's views carried great weight with cabinet colleagues, helping to ensure the smooth operation of the machinery of the administration of justice. He was both a link and a buffer between the judges and the politicians.[77]

---

68 See generally Cane 2016.

69 Brooke 2015, p 449.

70 Baker 2002, p 166.

71 Lord Thomas of Cwmgiedd 2015, para 11.

72 See generally Blom-Cooper and Drewry 1972, chapter 7; Hope 2011.

73 See generally Woodhouse 2001.

74 The latter expression is a convenient shorthand for: 'President of the Supreme Court, *ex officio* member of the Court of Appeal, and President of the Chancery Division of the High Court': Oliver 2011, p 98.

75 Heuston 1964, p xxi.

76 Lord Thomas of Cwmgiedd 2015, para 13.

77 Oliver 2011, pp 106–108.

There was thus a concentration of power in the hands of the Lord Chancellor, who was responsible not only for appointing judges, but also for managing them.[78] As the judicial system grew, the Lord Chancellor's Department also grew. Increased professionalisation and centralisation[79] of an expanding system unsettled the previously cosy relationship between the appointer and his appointees.[80] There were tensions in the 1980s, indeed, 'mutual suspicion between the judges and the Lord Chancellor's Department'.[81] The Department was not untouched by the rise of the *New Public Management*,[82] which sharpened the focus on the achievement of efficiencies in government and more effective means of service delivery; in 1995, the Department's management responsibilities were vested in the Courts Service, an executive agency within the Department.[83]

Although the manner of the announcement left much to be desired,[84] it was not especially surprising that abolition of the office of Lord Chancellor was mooted in a 2003 White Paper, with a view to modernising the relationship between the branches of government.[85]

Subsequent to the White Paper, the then Lord Chief Justice, Lord Woolf M.R., negotiated a 'Concordat' with the Lord Chancellor.[86] This document of 'great constitutional importance'[87] though evidently non statutory in nature has come to shape the relations between the executive and the judiciary.[88] Indeed, it reads almost as an embryonic Constitutional Reform Act 2005, with many of its key provisions reproduced in that statute. However, given that the management of the judiciary in England and Wales has evolved as much by non-statutory means as by statutory means, it is unsurprising that one central commitment agreed in the Concordat – that the Secretary of State would create a 'Unified Courts Agency'[89] – has no statutory basis.

The 2005 Act makes the Lord Chief Justice of England and Wales the 'head of the judiciary'.[90] Various functions, especially in relation to the making of rules and

---

78 Shetreet and Turenne 2013, p 7.

79 See the Courts Act 1971, which vested significant administrative responsibilities in the Lord Chancellor's Department, following the recommendations in Lord Beeching's *Report of the Royal Commission on Assizes and Quarter Sessions* (Cmd. 4153, 1969).

80 On the scale of the expansion, see Lord Thomas of Cwmgiedd 2017, paras 18–19.

81 Browne-Wilkinson 1988, p 50.

82 See generally Hood 1991.

83 For background, see Freedland 1996.

84 See generally Lord Windlesham 2005.

85 Department for Constitutional Affairs 2003.

86 Department for Constitutional Affairs 2004.

87 House of Lords Constitution Committee 2007, para 13.

88 See especially Concordat, para 4, setting out the respective responsibilities of the Secretary of State for Constitutional Affairs and the Lord Chief Justice.

89 Concordat, para 20.

90 Constitutional Reform Act 2005, s. 7(1).

the giving of directions, are vested in the Lord Chief Justice,[91] but the 2005 Act has little or nothing to say on how the Lord Chief Justice should exercise these functions. Non-statutory administrative arrangements have filled the legislative silence in the 2005 Act on the management of the judiciary (much of which had been, in any event, a matter of practice within the Lord Chancellor's Department). The judiciary has developed its 'own leadership and governance'.[92] Indeed, '[t]he intention was to enable the judiciary to devise and, when necessary, reform its own internal governance structure without recourse to Parliament'.[93]

The constitutional tumult of the 2000s did not end with the enactment of the 2005 Act.[94] Just two years later the Department of Constitutional Affairs, which had negotiated the Concordat and the passage of the legislation, was abolished, its functions to be assumed by a new Ministry of Justice. This new Ministry, presided over by the Lord Chancellor, was responsible 'not only for constitutional issues, civil and administrative justice, the courts and legal aid, but for criminal justice policy as well'.[95] But the expanding remit of the Lord Chancellor prompted concerns on the part of the judiciary that the Lord Chancellor's responsibilities for the implementation of criminal justice policy might come into conflict with his responsibilities for management of the courts system. These concerns led to the negotiation of yet another non-statutory agreement, the HM Courts Framework Document, concluded in 2008 and updated in 2011 and 2014 to take account of the

---

[91] Constitutional Reform Act 2005, ss. 12–15; Scheds. 1–4.

[92] See Lord Thomas of Cwmgiedd 2015, para 33.

[93] Lord Thomas of Cwmgiedd 2017, para 26. Management of the judiciary of England and Wales is accomplished through three bodies: the Judicial Executive Board; the Judicial Office for England and Wales; and the Judges' Council. Of the Board, whose members are for the most part the heads of division of the courts of England and Wales, it is said (on the Board's website): 'The Lord Chief Justice exercises executive and leadership responsibilities through, and with the support of, the Judicial Executive Board (JEB)'. https://www.judiciary.gov.uk/about-the-judiciary/the-judiciary-the-government-and-the-constitution/how-the-judiciary-is-governed/judicial-executive-board/, accessed 1 April 2019. The *raison d'être* of the Office is to 'support the judiciary in upholding the rule of law and in delivering justice impartially, speedily and efficiently', a task to which it brings 'a range of skills and experience – the team includes professional trainers, legal advisers, HR and communication experts, policy makers and administrators'. https://www.judiciary.gov.uk/about-the-judiciary/training-support/jo-index/, accessed 1 April 2019. Meanwhile, '[t]hough the English judiciary lacks any union activity, the Judges' Council traditionally transmits the collective views of the judiciary'. Shetreet and Turenne 2013, p 71. It was initially a legislative creation, under the Judicature Act 1873, but the relevant provisions were repealed by the Supreme Court Act 1981. Its subsequent and current instantiations are non-statutory. On the antecedents to the Council, see Lord Justice Thomas 2005. According to its website, 'The primary function of the present Judges' Council is to be a body broadly representative of the judiciary as a whole which will inform and advise the Lord Chief Justice on matters as requested from time to time'. https://www.judiciary.gov.uk/about-the-judiciary/the-judiciary-the-government-and-the-constitution/how-the-judiciary-is-governed/judges-council/, accessed 1 April 2019.

[94] For a useful overview, see Gee et al. 2015, pp 41–45.

[95] *Ibid.*, p 45.

creation of a unified tribunals system.[96] The most recent version, 'reflects an agreement reached by the Lord Chancellor, the Lord Chief Justice and the Senior President of Tribunals on a partnership between them in relation to the effective governance, financing and operation of HM Courts & Tribunals Service'.[97] So far, relations have proved harmonious.[98] For instance, the Office worked closely with HMCTS on a £700m overhaul of the court and tribunal system, whilst the Board and Council were also involved.[99]

Therefore, we can say, the institutional independence of the British judiciary is secured in part by a statutory framework but also by non-statutory agreements.[100]

Going slightly beyond the third *Valente* factor, it is useful to have regard in considering institutional independence to the general legal and political culture of a given jurisdiction. Of course, there is a risk in ascribing a particular spirit to the members of a particular political community that one's analysis will be 'oversimplified and overstated'.[101] Nonetheless, the judiciary does not exist in a hermetically sealed container, separate and apart from the other organs of government and wider society, and its institutional independence depends at least to some extent on its protection from outside influence from political actors, the media, civil society and members of the public. At the very least, in terms of protecting judicial independence there is an 'interdependency' between the judiciary and the other organs of government,[102] as well as other outside actors. Again, constitutional conventions, or simply understandings, are very important. For instance, criticism of judges in Parliament is thought to be improper, *Erskine May* (the (non-statutory) bible for parliamentarians) providing that 'reflections must not be cast on the conduct of […] judges of the superior courts […]'[103] In this respect, changes in the wider environment, especially in the media, have provoked new challenges:

---

[96] See Tribunals, Courts and Enforcement Act 2007.

[97] HM Courts and Tribunals Service 2014, para 1.5.

[98] See also Judicial Executive Board 2016, especially at para 4: 'Engagement between the judiciary and the Executive can be beneficial to both branches of the State, whilst permissible comment on proposed policy and legislation can be in both the interests of the public and the administration of justice. However, it is crucial that the constitutional conventions are adhered to. Identifying the constitutionally appropriate boundaries or "red lines" will need to be carefully considered by the Lord Chief Justice and senior leadership judges before agreeing to engagement. Whilst the judiciary will strive to assist the Executive, there will nonetheless be some areas where they simply cannot comment.'

[99] See Lord Thomas of Cwmgiedd 2015, paras 29–32, 36–37.

[100] It is useful to mention, for the sake of completeness, that the administration of justice in Scotland is entirely in the hands of the judges: see Judiciary and Courts (Scotland) Act 2008, Part 4, establishing the Scottish Courts and Tribunals Service.

[101] Dicey 2013, p xxv.

[102] Lord Thomas of Cwmgiedd 2017.

[103] Quoted in Le Sueur 2013, p 220. See also *ibid.*, pp 220–221.

> [...] one of the most dramatic changes that has taken place over the past thirty years or so has been the increasing freedom felt by newspapers, in particular, to attack judges with a vigour [...] that was formerly quite unknown.[104]

Effective discharge of the responsibility to 'uphold the continued independence of the judiciary' imposed on ministers by s. 3(1) of the Constitutional Reform Act has, as far as relations between the judiciary and the media are concerned, been secured in part by parliamentary scrutiny. For instance, shortly after the coming into force of the 2005 Act, the House of Lords Constitution Committee expressed concern about ministerial comment on judicial decisions adverse to the government's political interests,[105] which had a salutary effect on ministers' perception of the appropriate scope of comment on judicial decisions.[106]

However, the recent changes to the office of Lord Chancellor seem to have had the effect of weakening a bulwark against media attacks on the judiciary. A recent vigorous attack, of some notoriety, occurred in the wake of the Divisional Court's decision in *Miller v Secretary of State for Exiting the European Union* to the effect that the royal prerogative could not be used to trigger article 50 of the Treaty on European Union and thereby precipitate Britain's exit from the European Union.[107] 'Enemies of the People', trumpeted the *Daily Mail* the following day, whilst the *Daily Telegraph* led with 'The judges versus the people' and the *Sun* asked, 'Who Do EU Think You Are?'[108] The message of these headlines was clear: the judges were acting to thwart the will of the people as expressed in the 2016 referendum on Britain's membership of the EU. Such a charge could have the effect of undermining public confidence in the judiciary's even-handedness in disputes between citizens and government officials. The day after the decision had been released, the Secretary of State for Communities, Sajid Javid M.P. described the case as 'an attempt to frustrate the will of the British people and it is unacceptable'.[109] Although Javid's comments were aimed at those who initiated the court challenge and not the judges themselves, they highlight the febrile contemporary atmosphere. There was, accordingly, an expectation that the Lord Chancellor, Elizabeth Truss MP would intervene to call for calm.

Yet instead of delivering a measured statement in support of the independence of the judiciary, the Lord Chancellor remained silent. Her silence was condemned by the Bar Council, one of England and Wales' legal regulatory bodies, which publicly expressed its regret at 'the lack of public statement by the Lord Chancellor

---

[104] Sir Derek Oulton, former Permanent Secretary to the Lord Chancellor's Department, quoted in Lord Bingham 1996, p 7.

[105] House of Lords Select Committee on the Constitution (2007).

[106] House of Lords Select Committee on the Constitution (2008).

[107] [2016] HRLR 23.

[108] See generally The Guardian (2016) 'British newspapers react to judges' Brexit ruling: "Enemies of the people"', 4 November 2016, https://www.theguardian.com/politics/2016/nov/04/enemies-of-the-people-british-newspapers-react-judges-brexit-ruling, accessed 1 April 2019.

[109] BBC News (2019) 'Brexit case "attempt to block will of people" says Sajid Javid', https://www.bbc.co.uk/news/uk-politics-37866411, accessed 1 April 2019.

condemning these attacks' and called for a supportive statement to be released 'as a matter of urgency'.[110] She finally broke her silence on the weekend following the decision:

> The independence of the judiciary is the foundation upon which our rule of law is built and our judiciary is rightly respected the world over for its independence and impartiality. In relation to the case heard in the high court, the government has made it clear it will appeal to the supreme court. Legal process must be followed.[111]

Plainly, the Lord Chancellor did not seek, in her remarks, to condemn in any way the sensationalist coverage of the decision – even the implication that the judges had been engaged in an act of treason went unchallenged. Subsequently, the Lord Chancellor has, in evidence to the House of Lords Constitution Committee, attempted to justify her position by reference to the importance of defending the freedom of the press.[112] Her justification drew a sharp response from the outgoing Lord Chief Justice of England and Wales, who described her view as 'completely and utterly wrong'.[113] I favour the latter view:[114] the question for the judges was one of law; and the Lord Chancellor's statutory obligation to uphold judicial independence does not make any exception for freedom of the press which, in any event, hardly extends to insinuations of treason against judges adjudicating on the merits of an important point of constitutional law.

According to a journalistic account of the event, produced by the reputable *Sunday Times* political editor, Tim Shipman, the Lord Chancellor wrote to her fellow ministers the morning after the decision to remind them of their obligation to uphold judicial independence. But she was dissuaded from releasing a statement by the Prime Minister's office, where staff were especially concerned about further provoking the media. By the weekend, feeling the pressure of public criticism, the Lord Chancellor proposed issuing a 'bland quote defending the integrity of the Lord

---

[110] The Bar Council (2016) Bar Council calls on Lord Chancellor to condemn attacks on the judiciary". https://www.barcouncil.org.uk/media-centre/news-and-press-releases/2016/november/bar-council-calls-on-lord-chancellor-to-condemn-attacks-on-judiciary/, accessed 1 April 2019.

[111] The Guardian (2016) 'Liz Truss defends judiciary after Brexit ruling criticism'. https://www.theguardian.com/law/2016/nov/05/barristers-urge-liz-truss-to-condemn-attacks-on-brexit-ruling-judges, accessed 6 November 2016.

[112] House of Lords Select Committee on the Constitution 2017b, p 5: 'I will always speak out and say how important having an independent judiciary is. I have also said that the individuals involved in both cases – the High Court and the Supreme Court – are people of integrity and impartiality, and that is very important. Where perhaps I might respectfully disagree with some who have asked me to condemn what the press are writing, is that I think it is dangerous for a government Minister to say this is an acceptable headline and this is not. I am a huge believer in the independence of the judiciary; I am also a very strong believer in a free press and the value it has in our society. In defending the judiciary, it is very important that I speak out about the valuable work it does. I want to work with the judiciary so that we have more from the judiciary explaining to the public the work that it does and the process of appointment, but I draw the line in saying what is acceptable for the press to print or not. For me, that goes too far.'

[113] House of Lords Select Committee on the Constitution 2017c, p 6.

[114] Contrast Gee 2016.

Chief Justice'.[115] Even this was too much for the Prime Minister's political officials. They only relented when the Lord Chancellor revealed that she had already told the Lord Chief Justice that a statement was coming. One doubts that Truss's predecessors would have been so pusillanimous in the face of such venom from the media and intransigence from political officials. One can attribute this unfortunate event to the reforms to the office of Lord Chancellor.[116]

Under the Constitutional Reform Act 2005, there is no obligation to appoint a lawyer as Lord Chancellor. Section 2(1) of the 2005 Act provides that the Prime Minister may only recommend for appointment a person who is 'qualified by experience'.[117]

Although the first incumbents of the reformed office of Lord Chancellor were lawyers (Charles Falconer MP, Jack Straw MP and Kenneth Clarke MP), in 2012 the first non-lawyer was appointed (Chris Grayling MP) and subsequent holders of the office have also not had a legal background.

It is true that a non-lawyer political heavyweight might be a very effective Lord Chancellor, especially if they 'have a high rank in cabinet and sufficient authority and seniority amongst his or her ministerial colleagues to carry out this duty effectively and impartially'.[118] With the expanding range of functions discharged by the Lord Chancellor, political heft can be as valuable an asset as legal acumen. But the existence of political heft is, as the 'Enemies of the People' row indicates, insufficient; it must actually be used. Where the Lord Chancellor has hopes of higher ministerial office in the future, however, they may be cowed by the media or political officials, as Truss clearly was.

There has, then, been a sea change in the office of Lord Chancellor. Only twenty years ago it was expected that the Lord Chancellor would be a distinguished lawyer, responsible for the smooth administration of justice and for maintaining good relations between the judges and the political branches of government. This

---

[115] Shipman 2017, p 52.

[116] In a thoughtful contribution, Professor Gee has defended Truss's discharge of her duties: Gee 2016. Gee observes that the 2005 Act creates a 'post-2005 Lord Chancellor [which] is not the same office as the pre-2005 Lord Chancellor'. Having laid out the attributes of the post-2005 office, Gee suggests: 'Truss could reasonabl[y] conclude that her statutory duty was not engaged, or that the duty was best discharged by taking action behind the scenes, or even that the most prudent course was to take action at a later date once the heat of the moment has passed…' Shipman's account of Truss's actions in the wake of the Divisional Court decision undermines Gee's defence of the Lord Chancellor, however. Far from thinking that her statutory duty was not engaged, or that she could best take action behind the scenes, it is clear that Truss herself believed it was necessary to release a statement supportive of the Lord Chief Justice but was dissuaded from doing so by the Prime Minister's Office. This supports my argument that the reaction to the Divisional Court decision demonstrates a weakening of a bulwark against media attacks on the judiciary.

[117] The Prime Minister is to bear in mind the factors laid out in s. 2(2) of the Constitutional Reform Act 2005: (a)experience as a Minister of the Crown; (b)experience as a member of either House of Parliament; (c)experience as a qualifying practitioner; (d)experience as a teacher of law in a university; (e)other experience that the Prime Minister considers relevant.

[118] House of Lords Select Committee on the Constitution 2014, para 117.

functions as a reminder of how quickly fundamental constitutional change can occur in the British Constitution: a legal system which was not so long ago in the hands of a distinguished lawyer/politician who took 'soundings' from the judges is now managed by the judiciary in partnership with Whitehall, under the auspices of a hotchpotch of statutory provisions, non-statutory instruments, constitutional principles and various practices. This is a vivid illustration of how constitutional change occurs in the United Kingdom, but also of the risks of rapid, informal constitutional change. In the space of a decade, one of the norms that the Lord Chancellor protected (independence of judges from personal criticism) has been eroded; the norm is now subject to being traded off against political considerations.

7.3 Accountability

Although accountability 'is a central value of modern constitutions',[119] the term has an elusive, 'catch-all' quality,[120] 'one of those evocative political words that can be used to patch up a rambling argument, to evoke an image of trustworthiness, fidelity and justice, or to hold critics at bay'.[121] Nonetheless, there is a well-known distinction between two different senses of accountability, between accountability in the sense of 'giving an account' and accountability in the sense of 'taking responsibility', sometimes described as the distinction between explanatory accountability and sacrificial accountability.

In this section, I will focus on the first, explanatory, sense of accountability: 'giving an account'. The second, sacrificial, sense has, for the most part, been addressed in the previous section, in relation to security of tenure. Grave failures of judicial ethics would have to occur for a judge to be formally removed from office. Beyond removal from office, however, it is difficult to see how judges otherwise 'take responsibility' for their judgments.[122] Judicial error is not a resigning matter: the appropriate mechanism for correcting mistakes is provided, in the British system, by appellate review.[123] When a High Court judge errs, he or she may be corrected by the Court of Appeal, which in turn is subject to review by the Supreme Court.[124] It is true that there is no higher authority than the Supreme Court – which, to borrow Robert Jackson's quip, is not final because it is infallible but infallible

---

[119] Davies 2008, p 92.

[120] Harlow 2002, p 23.

[121] Bovens 2007, p 449.

[122] Bogdanor 2009, p 85.

[123] See, e.g., *Hansard* HC vol 416, col 1448, January 22, 2004 (Chris Leslie MP): 'Judicial decisions are taken and explained in public (save where the circumstances of a case demand confidentiality) and any decision which a judge makes is liable to be scrutinised, and if necessary overturned, on appeal, which is also a public process. Judges are therefore fully accountable for their judicial decisions through the appeal system.'

[124] See, e.g., *R v Bentley* (2001) 1 Criminal Appeal Reports 307.

because it is final[125] – but this does not detract from the general point that errors of law, and even manifestly unreasonable findings of fact, are not grounds for resignation.

Accordingly, my focus will be on the 'giving an account' sense of accountability. At this point, a further nuance is necessary. As far as judicial accountability is concerned, there are two further senses in which 'giving an account' can be understood, which Mark Tushnet labels 'political accountability' and 'accountability to "the law"'.[126] In the first, political accountability, sense, judges in Britain now do 'give an account' of their activities.[127] Annual reports are filed[128] and judges make appearances before parliamentary committees.[129] With 'radical reforms to the office of Lord Chancellor […] the traditional notions of ministerial responsibility are no longer adequate to secure accountability for leadership roles, budgets, and decision-making powers that have been transferred or shared beyond the government department responsible for the legal system'.[130] Indeed, parliamentary committees 'can play an important role in holding the judiciary to account by questioning the judges in public'.[131] Interactions between judges and parliamentary committees are regulated by non-statutory guidance.[132] Beyond giving an account to Parliament, some judges even give press conferences.[133] The obvious effect of these developments is to make the courts more visible, 'giving an account' of their activities in public. In summary, the political accountability of British judges is secured through non-statutory means: appearances in select public venues, regulated by non-statutory guidance.

In another sense, judges 'give an account' of their activities in their reasons for judgment, explaining their accountability to the law. Contemporary British judges have considerable power to shape the laws governing relationships between private individuals and between individuals and the state; their accountability for this considerable power lies in the reasons they give to justify its exercise. To put it bluntly, there is a 'democratic deficit that confronts us',[134] for the judges cannot be

[125] *Brown v Allen*, 344 US 443 (9 February 1953), p 540. Though one should mention the possibility that a subsequent panel of the Supreme Court might well depart from a decision of a previous panel.

[126] Tushnet 2013.

[127] See, e.g., Lord Thomas of Cwmgiedd 2017, paras 20–33.

[128] See, e.g., Judiciary of England and Wales 2017; Constitutional Reform Act 2005, s. 5(1).

[129] Turenne 2016, pp 52–55.

[130] Le Sueur 2013, p 203.

[131] House of Lords Select Committee on the Constitution 2007, para 124.

[132] Judicial Executive Board 2012.

[133] See, e.g., Lord Burnett of Maldon 2017.

[134] Paterson 2013, p 306. See similarly Malleson 1999, p 37: 'A dominant feature of the current developments in the judiciary is the increasing pressure for increased accountability. This trend is not unique to England and Wales but is evident in many other judiciaries around the world. As the role of judges has expanded in liberal democracies in consequence of their increasing numbers and

voted out of office should they encroach too far on the territory of the political branches or take decisions that run counter to the desires of the electorate.

Both in the areas of private law and public law British judges in setting out the 'limits of the judicial role' have been influenced by – or, at least, can be understood as having been influenced by – the concepts of institutional and constitutional competence.[135] In terms of constitutional competence, sometimes the judiciary will not possess as much democratic legitimacy relative to the other organs of government in respect of a particular type of decision (to legislate or not to legislate; to take a particular type of executive action, or not to take it). On other occasions, judges will lack institutional competence relative to other organs of government:

> [Judges] do not have the resources of the Law Commissions to study an area of law in the round, to consult interested parties, and reach decisions with the benefit of that consultation, having had regard to the knock-on effects of the changes which they recommend. They are required to focus on the particular legal problem that parties have brought to the court. Nor do they have the resources of the elected branches of government to develop policy and obtain through the democratic process a form of public consent for their proposals.[136]

The 'declaratory theory' – that judges find the law and never make the law; as Blackstone put it, 'the decisions of courts are the evidence of what is the common law'[137] – reigned supreme for many centuries. But judges 'do not believe in fairy tales any more'[138] and now follow a 'more realistic approach', because 'we all know that in reality, in the common law as in equity, the law is the subject of development by the judges – normally, of course, by appellate judges'.[139] Institutional competence has exercised the minds of judges considering whether to change the common law.[140] Sometimes, judges will feel that they are competent to make a particular change: 'The common law is moulded by the judges and it is still their province to adapt it from time to time so as to make it serve the interests of those it binds. Particularly is this so in the field of procedural law'.[141] Lord Reid referred similarly to a distinction between '"lawyer's law" and matters which directly affect the lives and interests of large sections of the community'.[142] Here, however, the implication is that the former can be left to lawyers but the latter is best addressed by elected representatives. Sure enough, one finds references in the decided cases to the understanding that some types of change in the law would call

---

influence on policy-making, the demands for greater social and political accountability have grown.'

[135] Jowell 1999, p 451.

[136] Lord Hodge 2015, p 479.

[137] Blackstone 1775, pp 88–9.

[138] Lord Reid 1972, p 22.

[139] *Kleinwort Benson v Lincoln City Council* [1999] 2 AC 349, p 377, *per* Lord Goff of Chieveley.

[140] A power formally recognised by the House of Lords in 1966: *Practice Statement (Judicial Precedent)* [1966] 3 All ER 77.

[141] *Myers v Director of Public Prosecutions* [1965] AC 1001, p 1047, *per* Lord Donovan.

[142] *Pettitt v Pettitt* [1970] AC 777, pp 794–795.

'for social, financial, economic and administrative decisions which only the legislature can take'.[143] Constitutional competence also exercises the judicial mind. In some areas of law, raising sensitive moral and political issues, the role of the judges 'should be to apply the principles which society, through the democratic process, adopts, not to impose their standards on society'.[144] More generally, whilst judges may 'adopt and modernise the common law', any such judicial developments 'must be consistent with legislative policy': 'The courts may proceed in harmony with Parliament but there should be no discord'.[145]

In the field of public law, judicial power has become greater still in recent decades.[146] Under the European Communities Act 1972, judges can disapply legislation that is inconsistent with European Union law norms.[147] With the advent of the Human Rights Act 1998, judges have been asked to opine on controversial areas of public policy.[148] And judges have asserted an increasingly more intensive review jurisdiction over an ever-larger area of public (and sometimes private) administration.[149] Accordingly, it 'is incumbent on judges to see with clarity the limits of the judicial role'.[150]

Here, institutional competence and constitutional competence have purchase in determining the degree of deference to be accorded by the courts to decisions of elected officials. In terms of constitutional competence, the identity of the decision-maker might have an effect on the degree of deference due, because 'in a democracy a person charged with making assessments of [a political] kind should be politically responsible for them. Ministers are politically responsible for the

143 *Lim Poh Choo v Camden and Islington Area Health Authority* [1980] AC 174, p 183, *per* Lord Scarman. As Lord Pearce put it in a case involving vicarious liability: 'It seems to me that these innovations, whether or not they may be desirable, are not suitable to be introduced by judicial decision. They raise difficult questions of policy, as well as involving the introduction of new legal principles rather than extension of some principle already recognised and operating. The questions of policy need consideration by the government and Parliament, using the resources at their command for making wide inquiries and gathering evidence and opinions as to the practical effects of the proposed innovations.' *Morgans v Launchbury* [1973] AC 127, pp 142–143. See also *Gregg v Scott* [2005] 2 AC 176, para 90, *per* Lord Hoffmann.

144 *Airedale NHS Trust v Bland* [1993] AC 789, p 880, *per* Lord Browne-Wilkinson.

145 *Johnson v Unisys* [2003] 1 AC 518, [37], *per* Lord Hoffmann.

146 See, e.g., Masterman 2010.

147 See, e.g., Wade 1996.

148 Of course, judges have long been opining on matters of public policy. See generally Griffith 1997. Nonetheless, it is important in the present context that the 1998 Act has given the judges an even more prominent role in such matters: 'as the role of the judiciary expands in the field of human rights the scope for reaching controversial or political judgments which incur the disapproval of one group or another will increase significantly' (Malleson 1999, p 73).

149 See generally Forsyth 2000; Varuhas 2016; Heydon 2018. For vigorous defences, see Craig 2015; Daly 2018; Elliott 2001.

150 Lord Hodge 2016, para 28.

consequences of their decision. Judges are not'.[151] Thus, '[t]he formulation and the implementation of national economic policy are matters depending essentially on political judgment' such that the relevant decisions 'are for politicians to take' and to be debated 'in the political forum of the House of Commons'.[152] In terms of institutional competence, elected officials often have greater expertise relative to courts in respect of the subject matter falling within their jurisdiction. A minister has access to the 'collective knowledge, experience and expertise of all those who serve the Crown in the department',[153] which helps to explain why ministerial decisions on matters within departmental expertise are typically accorded significant deference by the courts. Polycentricity,[154] according to which problems 'cannot be resolved independently and sequentially' but are 'interdependent and a choice from one set of alternatives has implications for preferences within other sets of alternatives',[155] will also call for deference,[156] as will complex situations that require evaluative judgement on the part of decision-makers.[157]

Institutional competence and constitutional competence influence how British judges exercise the considerable powers they possess in respect of private law and public law. These concepts form part of judges' understanding of their role in the British Constitution, justifying judicial restraint in areas where caution is appropriate. They are not written down in statute law, still less in a written constitution, but perform nonetheless an important accountability function, allowing judges to 'give an account' of their decisions in order to justify their exercise of the considerable power they now possess and ensure they remain – in Tushnet's terms – 'accountable to "the law"'.

However, the efficacy of these means of ensuring judicial accountability may be doubted. British judges have been accused, since before the advent of the Human Rights Act 1998, of taking decisions motivated by political considerations[158] and personal values about public administration.[159] Of the decision of the House of Lords in *Roberts v Hopwood*,[160] for instance, it was said that the judges' speeches

[151] *R (Lord Carlile) v Secretary of State for the Home Department* [2015] AC 945, [32] [*Lord Carlile*].

[152] *R v Environment Secretary, ex parte Hammersmith and Fulham London Borough Council* [1991] 1 AC 521, p 597, *per* Lord Bridge of Harwich.

[153] *Bushell v Environment Secretary* [1981] AC 75, p 95, *per* Lord Diplock.

[154] Fuller 1978.

[155] Ogus 1994, p 117.

[156] See, e.g., *R v Cambridge Health Authority, ex parte B* [1995] 1 WLR 898, p 906.

[157] See, e.g., *(Lord Carlile)* at [32]; *Youssef v Secretary of State for Foreign and Commonwealth Affairs* [2016] 2 WLR 509, [50].

[158] See generally Griffith 1997.

[159] See, e.g., Feldman 1990.

[160] [1925] AC 578.

'were loaded with class assumptions'.[161] In the modern era the role of the judiciary has become even more hotly disputed, with commentators warning of a 'legitimacy crisis'[162] as judges allegedly stray into the domain of politics and various 'myths' being developed by the media and politicians about the operation of the Human Rights Act[163] to drive a campaign to repeal it.[164]

The persistent controversy about the judicial role in the British Constitution and the ease with which political actors have been able to whip up dissatisfaction with judges' exercise of their powers under the Human Rights Act suggest that reliance on institutional and constitutional competence is not sufficient to shield judges from accusations of improper use of their powers. In some ways, British judges have the worst of both worlds. With only their sense of constitutional and institutional competence to guide them, the judges often end up in controversial territory, just like their counterparts in jurisdictions with codified, supreme, entrenched constitutions. Yet they lack a basis in a written constitutional document to which they can refer as the source of and limit on their powers. Britain's constitutional arrangements for securing judicial accountability seem thus destined to produce persistent controversy about the limits of the judicial role.

7.4 Conclusion

In Sect. 7.2, I described the current state of judicial independence in Britain before turning in Sect. 7.3 to judicial accountability, with the focus in both sections on the judiciary of England and Wales. Running through these descriptions is a broader theme about the nature of the British Constitution, namely that it consists of a body of norms, written and unwritten, developed as pragmatic responses to different challenges that have occurred from time to time. Significant constitutional change can happen very quickly – as with the transformation of the office of Lord Chancellor.

As we have seen, in the British Constitution, judicial independence and accountability are secured by a variety of means: *statute law*, such as the Act of Settlement 1701 and the Constitutional Reform Act 2005; *delegated legislation*, such as the 2014 regulations relating to judicial discipline; *non-statutory instruments*, such as the 2004 Concordat, the Framework Agreements between the judiciary and HMTCS and the guidance documents on judicial interactions with Parliament and the executive; *constitutional conventions*, such as the norms in

161 Stevens 2005, p 23; 'It is an easy step from [this] judgment to the conclusion that the House of Lords is, in entire good faith, the unconscious servant of a single class in the community' (Harold Laski, cited in Stevens, *ibid.*)

162 Varuhas 2016.

163 Department for Constitutional Affairs 2006, chapter 4.

164 Conservative Party 2010, p 79.

respect of the exercise of prerogative powers; *constitutional principles*, such as judicial independence; *day-to-day practice*, such as the setting of judicial salaries; and *understandings*, such as judicial reliance on the concepts of institutional competence and constitutional competence in deciding private law and public law cases. All of the items on the foregoing list, despite their sometimes modest provenance, are constitutional in nature. Taken together, they secure judicial independence and accountability in the British Constitution.

We have also seen, however, that the lack of a codified, supreme, entrenched constitutional document can make British judges vulnerable to changes in the political climate. Judicial pay and pensions (and thus recruitment to the bench) have been hit by a policy of government austerity. Changes to the role of the Lord Chancellor seem to have weakened a bulwark against personalised political and media criticism of individual judges. And the limits on the judicial role in the British Constitution are so ill defined as to invite persistent controversy about the scope of the judges' power. A written constitution would not necessarily solve or avoid these problems, which have of course arisen in many jurisdictions, but they need to be taken into account in any comparative assessment of the strengths and weaknesses of the means used in different constitutional traditions for securing judicial independence and accountability.

References

Baker J H (2002) An Introduction to English Legal History, 4th edn. Butterworths, London

Bell J (2001) Judicial Cultures and Judicial Independence. Cambridge Yearbook of European Legal Studies 4:47–60

Beloff M J (2006) Paying Judges: Why, Who, Whom, How Much. Denning Law Journal 18:1–36

Blackstone W (1775) Commentaries on the Laws of England, 6th edn. The Company of Booksellers, Dublin

Blom-Cooper L, Drewry G (1972) Final Appeal: A Study of the House of Lords in its Judicial Capacity. Clarendon Press, Oxford

Bogdanor V (2009) The New British Constitution. Hart Publishing, Oxford

Bovens M (2007) Analysing and Assessing Accountability: A Conceptual Framework. European Law Journal 13:447–468

Brooke H (2015) The History of Judicial Independence in England and Wales. European Human Rights Law Review 446–458

Browne-Wilkinson N (1988) The Independence of the Judiciary in the 1980s. Public Law 44–57

Cabinet Office (2011) The Cabinet Manual: A guide to laws, conventions and rules on the operation of government, 1st edn. (October 2011)

Cane P (2016) Controlling Administrative Power: An Historical Comparison. Cambridge University Press, Cambridge

Conservative Party (2010) Invitation to Join the Government of Britain

Courts and Tribunals Judiciary (2018) Guide to Judicial Conduct (March 2018)

Craig P (2015) UK, EU and Global Administrative Law: Foundations and Challenges. Cambridge University Press, Cambridge

Daly P (2018) Administrative Law: Characteristics, Legitimacy, Unity. In: Elliott M, Varuhas J, Stark S (eds) The Unity of Public Law? Doctrinal, Theoretical and Comparative Perspectives. Hart Publishing, Oxford

Darbyshire P (2011) The Working Lives of Judges. Hart Publishing, Oxford
Davies A (2008) The Public Law of Government Contracts. Oxford University Press, Oxford
Department for Constitutional Affairs (2003) Constitutional reform: Reforming the Office of the Lord Chancellor, CP/03 (September 2003)
Department for Constitutional Affairs (2004) Constitutional Reform: The Lord Chancellor's judiciary-related functions: Proposals (January 2004)
Department for Constitutional Affairs (2006) Review of the Implementation of the Human Rights Act
Dicey A V (2013) Lectures on Comparative Constitutionalism. In: Allison JWF (ed). Oxford University Press, Oxford
Elliott M (2001) The Constitutional Foundations of Judicial Review. Hart Publishing, Oxford
Feldman D (1990) Public Law Values in the House of Lords. Law Quarterly Review 106:246–276
Forsyth C (ed) (2000) Judicial Review and the Constitution. Hart Publishing, Oxford
Freedland M (1996) The Rule Against Delegation and the Carltona Doctrine in an Agency Context. Public Law 19–30
Fuller L (1978) The Forms and Limits of Adjudication. Harvard Law Review 92:353–409
Gee G (2016) A Tale of Two Constitutional Duties: Liz Truss, Lady Hale, and Miller. Judicial Power Project, Policy Exchange. https://judicialpowerproject.org.uk/graham-gee-a-tale-of-two-constitutional-duties-liz-truss-lady-hale-and-miller/ Accessed 1 April 2018
Gee G (2018) Judging the JAC: How much judicial influence over judicial appointments is too much? In: Gee G, Rackley E (eds) Debating Judicial Appointments in an Age of Diversity. Routledge, London
Gee G et al (2015) The Politics of Judicial Independence in the UK's Changing Constitution. Cambridge University Press, Cambridge
Griffith J A G (1979) The Political Constitution. Modern Law Review 42:1–21
Griffith J A G (1997) The Politics of the Judiciary, 5th edn. Fortuna, London
Harlow C (2002) Accountability in the European Union. Oxford University Press, Oxford
Heuston R V F (1964) Lives of the Lord Chancellors (1885–1940). Clarendon, Oxford
Heydon D (2018) Enclaves and Exclaves: Limits and Exceptions to the Doctrine of Judicial Review. Policy Exchange, London
HM Courts and Tribunals Service (2014) Framework Document (July 2014)
Holland T E (2001) Essays on the Form of Law. Butterworths, London
Hood C (1991) A Public Management for All Seasons? Public Administration 69:1–19
Hope D (2011) Law Lords in Parliament. In: Blom-Cooper L et al (eds) The Judicial House of Lords, 1876–2009. Oxford University Press, Oxford
House of Lords Select Committee on the Constitution (2007) Relations between the Executive, the Judiciary and Parliament, Report with Evidence, 6th Report of Session 2006–07. HL Paper 151 (26 July 2007)
House of Lords Select Committee on the Constitution (2008) Relations between the Executive, the Judiciary and Parliament: Follow-up Report, 11th Report of Session 2007–08. HL Paper 177 (16 October 2008)
House of Lords Select Committee on the Constitution (2014) The Office of the Lord Chancellor, 6th Report of Session 2014–15. HL Paper 75 (11 December 2014)
House of Lords Select Committee on the Constitution (2016) Revised transcript of evidence: The Lord Chief Justice, 27 April 2016
House of Lords Select Committee on the Constitution (2017a) Judicial Appointments: Follow-up, 7th Report of Session 2017–19. HL Paper 32 (2 November 2017)
House of Lords Select Committee on the Constitution (2017b) Corrected oral evidence: Oral evidence session with the Lord Chancellor and Secretary of State for Justice, 1 March 2017
House of Lords Select Committee on the Constitution (2017c) Corrected oral evidence: Oral evidence session with the Lord Chief Justice, 22 March 2017
House of Lords Select Committee on the Constitution (2018) Corrected oral evidence: The Lord Chief Justice, 25 April 2018

Jowell J (1999) Of Vires and Vacuums: The Constitutional Context of Judicial Review. Public Law 448–460
Judicial Appointments Commission (2018a) Evidence from the Judicial Appointments Commission to the Senior Salaries Review Body (February 2018)
Judicial Appointments Commission (2018b) Update from the JAC to the Senior Salaries Review Board (26 April 2018)
Judicial Executive Board (2012) Guidance for Judges appearing before or providing written evidence to parliamentary committees
Judicial Executive Board (2016) Guidance to the judiciary on engagement with the Executive (July 2016)
Judiciary of England and Wales (2017) The Lord Chief Justice's Report 2017. Judicial Office, London
Lady Hale (2018) Appointments to the Supreme Court. In: Gee G, Rackley E (eds) Debating Judicial Appointments in an Age of Diversity. Routledge, London
Le Sueur A (2013) Parliamentary Accountability and the Judicial System. In: Bamforth N, Leylands P (eds) Accountability in the Contemporary Constitution. Oxford University Press, Oxford
Lederman W R (1956) The Independence of the Judiciary. Canadian Bar Review 34:1139–1179
Lord Bingham (1996) Judicial Independence. Judicial Studies Board, London
Lord Burnett of Maldon (2017) Press Conference held by the Lord Chief Justice of England and Wales. https://www.judiciary.gov.uk/wp-content/uploads/2017/12/lcj-press-conference-20171205.pdf Accessed 1 April 2019
Lord Hodge (2015) Judicial Law-Making in a Changing Constitution. Stellenbosch Law Review 26:471–485
Lord Hodge (2016) Upholding the Rule of Law: How we preserve judicial independence in the United Kingdom. Lincoln's Inn Denning Society
Lord Justice Beatson (2017) Judicial Independence: Internal and External Challenges and Opportunities. Atkin Lecture, 14 November 2017
Lord Justice Thomas (2005) The Judges' Council. Public Law 608–630
Lord Mackay of Clashfern (2010) Selection of Judges Prior to the Establishment of the Judicial Appointments Commission in 2006. In: Judicial Appointments: Balancing Independence, Accountability and Legitimacy. Judicial Appointments Commission, London
Lord Reid (1972) The Judge as Lawmaker. Journal of the Society of Public Teachers of Law 3:1–15
Lord Thomas of Cwmgiedd (2015) Judicial Leadership. University College London Constitution Unit, 22 June 2015
Lord Thomas of Cwmgiedd (2017) The Judiciary Within the State – Governance and Cohesion of the Judiciary. Hebrew University Jerusalem, 15 May 2017
Lord Windlesham (2005) The Constitutional Reform Act 2005: Ministers, judges and constitutional change: Part 1. Public Law 806–823
Loughlin M (2013) The British Constitution: A Very Short Introduction. Oxford University Press, Oxford
Malleson K (1999) The New Judiciary: The Effects of Expansion and Activism. Ashgate, Aldershot
Masterman R (2010) The Separation of Powers in the Contemporary Constitution. Cambridge University Press, Cambridge
Ministry of Justice (2017) Fee-Paid Judicial Pension Scheme: Scheme Guide (August 2017)
Ogus A (1994) Regulation: Legal Form and Economic Theory. Clarendon Press, Oxford
Oliver D (2011) The Lord Chancellor as Head of the Judiciary. In: Blom-Cooper L et al (eds) The Judicial House of Lords, 1876–2009. Oxford University Press, Oxford
Paterson A (2013) Final Judgment: The Last Law Lords and the Supreme Court. Hart Publishing, Oxford
Poser N (2013) Lord Mansfield: Justice in the Age of Reason. McGill-Queen's University Press, Montreal/Kingston

Postema G (2004) Introduction: Search for an Explanatory Theory of Torts. In: Postema G (ed) Philosophy and the Law of Torts. Cambridge University Press, Cambridge
Reed Amar A (2012) The Unwritten Constitution: The Precedents and Principles We Live By. Basic Books, New York
Review Body on Senior Salaries (2017) Thirty-Ninth Annual Report on Senior Salaries 2017 (report no. 87)
Review Body on Senior Salaries (2018) Major Review of the Judicial Salary Structure Consultation on Job Placement (20 April 2018)
Shetreet S, Turenne S (2013) Judges on Trial: The Independence and Accountability of the English Judiciary, 2nd edn. Cambridge University Press, Cambridge
Shipman T (2017) Fall Out: A Year of Political Mayhem. William Collins, London
Stephens C (2018) The JAC's first ten years. In: Gee G, Rackley E (eds) Debating Judicial Appointments in an Age of Diversity. Routledge, London
Stevens R (2001) The Act of Settlement and the Questionable History of Judicial Independence. Oxford University Commonwealth Law Journal 1:253–267
Stevens R (2005) The English Judges: Their Role in the Changing Constitution. Hart Publishing, Oxford
Turenne S (2016) Judicial Independence and Judicial Accountability: Two Sides of the Same Coin. In: Shetreet S, McCormack W (eds) The Culture of Judicial Independence in a Globalised World. Brill Nijhoff, Leiden
Tushnet M (2013) Judicial Accountability in Comparative Perspective. In: Bamforth N, Leyland P (eds) Accountability in the Contemporary Constitution. Oxford University Press, Oxford
Varuhas J (2016) Judicial Capture of Political Accountability. Policy Exchange, London
Wade W (1996) Sovereignty: Evolution or Revolution? Law Quarterly Review 112:568–575
Walters M (2008) Written Constitutions and Unwritten Constitutionalism. In: Huscroft G (ed) Expounding the Constitution: Essays in Constitutional Theory. Cambridge University Press, New York
Woodhouse D (2001) The Office of the Lord Chancellor. Hart Publishing, Oxford

Paul Daly is Senior Lecturer in Public Law at the University of Cambridge. His scholarship in the broad field of public law, especially administrative law, has appeared in journals in Britain, Canada and Ireland and has been cited by courts and tribunals including the Supreme Court of Canada and the Irish Supreme Court. He is the author of *A Theory of Deference in Administrative Law: Basis, Application and Scope* (Cambridge University Press, 2012) and maintains the internationally read, award-winning blog Administrative Law Matters.

Chapter 8
Independence and Accountability of the South African Judiciary

Francois Venter

Contents

Abstract The history of the South African judiciary reaches back over centuries to colonial times. Until 1994, South African courts did not have clear or influential constitutional jurisdiction. The constitutional renewal of the country in the early 1990s brought about dramatic changes in the structure, operation and constitutional influence of the courts. The newly established Constitutional Court has played a

---

F. Venter (✉)
North-West University, Potchefstroom, South Africa
e-mail: francois.venter@nwu.ac.za

Hirsch Ballin, Van der Schyff & Stremler (eds.), *European Yearbook of Constitutional Law 2019*, European Yearbook of Constitutional Law 1,
https://doi.org/10.1007/978-94-6265-359-7_8

particularly important role in this process that amounted to the reconfiguration of the legal order as a whole. The constitutional work of the courts has not been free of challenges, including political interference or attempts at such interference and non-compliance with adverse judgments against state institutions. The judiciary needed to establish new principles of adjudication and accountability, in the process developing constitutional doctrine regarding essential elements such as the separation of powers, the rule of law and constitutionalism. Not surprisingly, progress has not always been smooth, but much has been achieved. In fact, the role of constitutional adjudication in the concretisation of South African constitutionalism can hardly be underestimated, but it seems likely that the challenges to the independence of the judiciary will increase, rather than abate.

Keywords accountability · Constitutional Court of South Africa · constitutionalism · corruption · rule of law · separation of powers · transformation

8.1 Introduction

The history of the South African judiciary weaves through some three centuries of Dutch and British colonial, 19th century republican, British Commonwealth, pre-constitutional 20th century republican and post-constitutional routes. Over time unique and admirable mores and institutions were established, great judicial minds (and some others) were at work, occasional instances of dubious integrity relieved by incidents of brilliance and creativity came and went, and the courts survived political onslaughts, moral battles and reconfigurations. Before 1994, the courts' constitutional jurisdiction was the subject of a few landmark decisions and controversial political responses. Since the historical entrenchment a quarter of a century ago of the constitutional status of the judiciary as a pillar of constitutionalism, remarkable progress has been made – but not without challenges and setbacks along the way.

In the next section, the history and the constitutional and statutory foundations of the judiciary, primarily focused on the Constitutional Court, are described, followed by a discussion in the third section of the challenges to the independence of the judicial branch with reference to politics, non-compliance with judgments and 'transformation'. In the fourth section, the direction of development is addressed in the context of accountability, separation of powers and the rule of law, the impact of constitutional judgments and the need for the courts to deal with corruption. Some comparative observations are made in the fifth section before concluding remarks are offered in the last section.

8.2 Constitutional and Statutory Foundations

8.2.1 History

8.2.1.1 Colonial Times

In the build-up to the establishment of South Africa as a distinct state in 1910, the sources of influence on the development of the judiciary were various. The era of Dutch colonial rule (1652–1795; 1803–1806) ensured the founding of South African (private) law on the Roman-Dutch law. This was not fundamentally changed during the period of British colonialism (1795–1803; 1806–1910). Inevitably, with the political and economic control of the country came the introduction of British colonial constitutional law and elements of English commercial and procedural law. The nature of the legal order required judicial knowledge and skills suited to it. In the second half of the 19th century the constitutional jurisdiction of the courts of the Orange Free State and Transvaal republics was based on republican constitutions, but the influence that lawyers, judges, administrators and leading politicians with backgrounds in the forensic practice of the Cape Colony exerted in the republics, was significant.

8.2.1.2 From Union to Constitutionalism

The Supreme Court of South Africa, composed of the Appellate Division, the Provincial and Local Divisions, was established in 1910 in terms of the first constitution of the country.[1] Until 1994, the Supreme Court structure remained essentially the same. The tenets of British colonial constitutional law regarding jurisdiction survived the transition from (nominal ex-colonial) monarchy to republic in 1961. The implications were that the courts produced profound jurisprudence in many areas of the law, but very little of a constitutional nature. The impediment was the colonial heritage of parliamentary sovereignty.

Until 1994, the courts were constitutionally precluded from reviewing legislation for constitutionality, which gave the executive free rein to legitimise conduct that contravened the ordinary demands of Western constitutionalism for accountability. After a brief, and eventually unsuccessful attempt by the judiciary to assert a degree of constitutional authority in the 1950s,[2] the judges were left with little more than making critical *obiter* remarks, or to take refuge in literalism and positivism in judgments involving the legality of government conduct.

[1] See The South Africa Act 1909, pp 95–98.

[2] See *Harris v Minister of the Interior* 1952 (2) SA 428 (AD), *Minister of the Interior v Harris* 1952 (4) SA 769 (AD) and *Collins v Minister of the Interior* 1957 (1) SA 552 (AD).

8.2.1.3 1994 Onward

The advent of constitutionalism in 1994 removed the Common Law notion of parliamentary sovereignty completely. The introduction of a constitution elevated to the level of 'supreme law of the Republic' gave powerful transformational meaning to the provision that the 'judiciary shall be independent, impartial and subject only to this Constitution and the law'.[3]

Initially the court structure was retained unchanged, with the addition only of the newly established Constitutional Court. Although the other divisions of the Supreme Court were also given constitutional jurisdiction under the new arrangements,[4] the Constitutional Court, headed by its 'President',[5] was awarded exclusive jurisdiction on some constitutional matters,[6] and final jurisdiction on all other matters of a constitutional nature.[7]

In terms of the 1993 Constitution, the Supreme Court of Appeal, still led by the Chief Justice, retained final jurisdiction in all non-constitutional matters, but all matters within the jurisdiction of the Constitutional Court were excluded.[8] Significantly, Johannesburg, 400 km from Bloemfontein where the Appellate Division has been situated since 1910, was made the seat of the Constitutional Court.[9]

The dualism of two final appeal courts was obviously not sustainable, nor was it intended to be. In a few steps taken between 1997 and 2013, the configuration of the courts was adapted and consolidated. The first step was taken in 1997 when the 'final' (current) Constitution of the Republic of South Africa 1996 (the Constitution) came into effect. Since then the Supreme Court of Appeal could also exercise constitutional jurisdiction, subject however to appeals to the Constitutional Court.

In 2001, the head of the Constitutional Court became the Chief Justice and the designation of the head of the Supreme Court of Appeal was changed to 'President'. This step signified a shift from the pre-constitutional concept of a non-constitutional judicial hierarchy to the re-aligned primacy of constitution-based adjudication. It was also significant in the sense that the concept of two parallel, potentially concurrent jurisdictions was replaced with a clear move towards the elevation of the Constitutional Court to the pinnacle position. This was finally achieved in 2013 when the restructuring was completed by constitutional amendment,[10] thus bringing about the consolidation of the historical court structure with one which was better

[3] S 2 and 96(2) of the *Constitution of the Republic of South Africa*, 1993 (the 1993 Constitution).

[4] S 101(3) of the 1993 Constitution.

[5] S 97(2)(a) of the 1993 Constitution.

[6] S 98(3) of the 1993 Constitution.

[7] S 98 of the 1993 Constitution.

[8] S 101(2) and (5) of the 1993 Constitution.

[9] S 106 of the 1993 Constitution.

[10] Constitution Seventeenth Amendment Act, 2012.

suited to the transition to a constitutional state. The Chief Justice now became 'the head of the judiciary' to exercise 'responsibility over the establishment and monitoring of norms and standards for the exercise of the judicial functions of all courts.'[11]

8.2.2 *The Constitution*

8.2.2.1 Jurisdiction

When the current court structure was finalised in 2013 the limitation of the jurisdiction of the Constitutional Court to 'constitutional matters' was removed by rendering it 'the highest court of the Republic'.[12]

The Constitution is unequivocal when it comes to the constitutional jurisdiction of the courts. In addition to the provision in section 2 that law or conduct inconsistent with the Constitution is invalid, section 172(1) explicitly requires courts deciding constitutional matters within its jurisdiction to declare that any law or conduct that is inconsistent with the Constitution is invalid to the extent of its inconsistency.

All divisions of the High Court have constitutional jurisdiction. Such jurisdiction may be curtailed by the Constitutional Court by agreeing, on application, to hear a matter directly 'in the interests of justice'.

Currently judgments on constitutional matters by a High Court may, if not appealed, be final, except in cases where the court makes an order declaring national or provincial legislation or conduct of the President to be constitutionally invalid. Such orders must be confirmed by the Constitutional Court, but the High Court may grant temporary relief pending the final decision of the Constitutional Court.[13]

The jurisdiction of the Constitutional Court is primarily, but not exclusively, to adjudicate on constitutional matters. Since 2013 the Constitutional Court may (as pinnacle court) decide any matter if it grants leave to appeal 'on the grounds that the matter raises an arguable point of law of general public importance which ought to be considered by that Court.'[14] The Court may also grant direct access to itself as first and last instance or a direct appeal from any other court.[15] Thus, the positioning of the Constitutional Court at the top of the judicial hierarchy has had the

---

[11] S 165(6) of the Constitution

[12] S 167(3)(a) of the Constitution as amended by the Constitution Seventeenth Amendment Act, 2012.

[13] S 169(1) and 172 of the Constitution.

[14] S 167(3)(b) and (c) of the Constitution.

[15] S 167(6) of the Constitution.

effect of allowing it to select causes on the basis of the impact that their resolution may have on the development of the law in general.

8.2.2.2 Composition and Appointment of Judges

The Constitutional Court is composed of eleven judges, including the Chief Justice and the Deputy Chief Justice. In the event of a vacancy on the bench or the absence of a judge from the Court, the President of the Republic may, on the recommendation of the Minister of Justice and with the concurrence of the Chief Justice appoint an acting judge to fill the vacancy temporarily.[16]

The 1993 Constitution provided for the establishment of the Judicial Service Commission (JSC) to make recommendations regarding the appointment of judges and to render advice on all matters relating to the judiciary and the administration of justice.[17] The current Constitution continued this arrangement with some necessary changes.[18]

The JSC is presided over by the Chief Justice, and the other members are the President of the Supreme Court of Appeal, a Judge President designated by the Judges President of the Provincial Divisions of the High Court, the Minister of Justice, two practising advocates and two practicing attorneys nominated by the professions for appointment by the President, one teacher of law designated by teachers of law at South African universities, six persons designated by the National Assembly from among its members, at least three of whom must be members of opposition parties represented in the Assembly, four permanent delegates to the National Council of Provinces designated by the Council, four persons designated by the President after consulting the leaders of all the parties in the National Assembly, and, when considering matters relating to a specific Division of the High Court, the Judge President of that Division and the Premier of the province concerned. The six members of the National Assembly and the four members of the National Council of Provinces participate in the proceedings of the JSC only when the appointment of judges is considered.[19]

The appointment of the Chief Justice and the Deputy Chief Justice is entrusted to the President as head of the national executive. The President must, before making the appointment, consult the JSC and the leaders of political parties represented in the National Assembly.[20] In practice, the President nominates a person for appointment, after which the JSC interviews the candidate, sometimes quite rigorously, before making a recommendation. Although the involvement of the JSC ostensibly allows for objective considerations to come in play, the influence of

---

[16] S 175(1) of the Constitution

[17] S 105 of the 1993 Constitution.

[18] S 178 of the Constitution.

[19] S 178(5) of the Constitution.

[20] S 174(3) of the Constitution.

politicians evident in the composition of the JSC dominates the recommendations for appointment to the bench. Since 1994, the JSC has consistently endorsed every nominee put forward by the President.

Judges of the Constitutional Court must be South African citizens, and at all times at least four of the eleven must have been judges prior to their appointment.[21] Although the President also appoints the other nine judges on the bench, the Constitution provides for a framework for the procedure whereby political influence is rendered less obvious than when a Chief Justice or Deputy Chief Justice must be appointed, but it is still present.[22] Where vacancies occur, the JSC must prepare a list of nominees with three names more than the number of appointments to be made. Preparation of such a list involves calling for nominations and shortlisting nominated candidates, followed by public interviews of the candidates. This list is then submitted to the President, who makes the appointments from the list after consulting the Chief Justice and the leaders of parties represented in the National Assembly. The President may however find nominees to be 'unacceptable' and must then inform the JSC accordingly, providing reasons. The JSC must then supplement the list, after which the President must make the required appointments from it.

8.2.2.3 Independence

The Constitution seeks to ensure the independence and authority of the judiciary as a whole by means of the unambiguous provisions of section 165(2)–(5). Sub-section (2) states that 'the courts are independent and subject only to the Constitution and the law, which they must apply impartially and without fear, favour or prejudice.' This is supported by the wording of judicial officers' oath of office, in that they are required, before beginning to perform their judicial functions, to swear or solemnly affirm that they 'will be faithful to the Republic of South Africa, will uphold and protect the Constitution and the human rights entrenched in it, and will administer justice to all persons alike without fear, favour or prejudice, in accordance with the Constitution and the law.'[23]

Section 165(3) prohibits any interference with the functioning of the courts, sub-section (4) requires all organs of state to take measures to 'assist and protect the courts to ensure the independence, impartiality, dignity, accessibility and effectiveness of the courts'. In sub-section (5) all orders and decisions issued by the courts are rendered binding on everyone and every organ of state.

[21] S 174(1) and (5) of the Constitution.

[22] S 174(4) of the Constitution.

[23] Item 6 of Schedule 2 to the Constitution.

8.2.3 *Legislation*

8.2.3.1 Superior Courts

The Superior Courts Act 1994 replaced the key pre-constitutional legislation regulating the superior courts, such as the Supreme Court Act 1959, in order, in terms of its long title '[t]o rationalise, consolidate and amend the laws relating to the Constitutional Court, the Supreme Court of Appeal and the High Court of South Africa; to make provision for the administration of the judicial functions of all courts; [and] to make provision for administrative and budgetary matters relating to the Superior Courts.' Significantly, in the opening statement of the preamble, Parliament 'noted' that 'section 1 of the Constitution of the Republic of South Africa, 1996, provides that the supremacy of the Constitution and the rule of law form part of the founding values of the Republic'.

The Act regulates, consonant with the provisions of the Constitution concerning the judiciary, a range of matters such as the composition and seats of the various superior courts, the management of judicial functions, access to the courts, the appointment of executive officers of the courts, the manner of arriving at decisions and resolving conflicting decisions in different divisions of the High Court, the making of rules of court, some evidentiary and procedural matters, etc.

8.2.3.2 Office of the Chief Justice

As part of the process of restructuring the superior courts and ensuring the independence of the judiciary, the need for administrative support for the Chief Justice to perform the duties as head of the judiciary, and the desirability of removing court administration from the executive and placing it in the hands of the judiciary itself, provision was made in 2010 for the establishment of the Office of the Chief Justice (OCJ). This was done by proclaiming the OCJ to be a 'department' in terms of the Public Service Act 1994.[24]

Various other pieces of legislation govern the extra-forensic work of the Chief Justice assisted by the OCJ. In terms of the Superior Courts Act, 2013 the Chief Justice is responsible for the establishment and monitoring of norms and standards of judicial functions for all courts and may issue written protocols, directives, guidance and advice regarding the implementation of such norms and standards. This Act also stipulates that the Secretary-General of the OCJ is its accounting officer, indicating where the responsibility for the management of especially the

---

[24] A national department is established by presidential proclamation in terms of which the name of the department and its head is listed in Schedule 1 of the Public Service Act. Most departments are placed under the political authority of members of cabinet, with directors-general as their administrative heads. The head of the OCJ has the designation of 'Secretary-General: Office of the Chief Justice'.

financial resources is vested. As all departments of state, the OCJ is operated subject to the provisions of the Public Finance Management Act 1999.

For the performance of a range of other functions of the Chief Justice, the OCJ must provide support. These functions include chairing the council of the South African Judicial Education Institution,[25] the Judicial Service Commission[26] and to convene and chair a panel to process nominations for the Electoral Commission Board.[27]

8.3 Challenges to Judicial Independence

As final arbitrators of disputes between a government and the citizenry, courts will inevitably be exposed to close scrutiny of their compliance with the constitutional requirements of objectivity and independence. It is also to be expected that a powerful national executive whose actions and conduct are frequently scrutinised by the judiciary, causing it political discomfort, will tend to attempt to circumvent or decrease the risk of being constrained in pursuing its political agenda. Over the past two decades, executive office bearers have indeed often resisted the authority of the courts.

8.3.1 Political Challenges

8.3.1.1 'Transformation' of the Judiciary

'Transformation' has been developed by the ANC government into an important and pervasive rallying call for the shaping of policies, legislation and practices in all aspects of state governance. Due to its generality and vagueness, the manner in which the notion is utilised, justified and interpreted, varies. Regarding the 'transformation' of the judiciary, much has been written,[28] but pinning down a single purpose and intent of the campaign is difficult. That it is heavily burdened with veiled ideological motivations, is nevertheless clear.[29]

---

[25] In terms of the South African Judicial Education Institute Act 2008.

[26] In terms of the Judicial Service Commission Act 1994.

[27] In terms of the Electoral Commission Act 1996.

[28] See, e.g., Klaaren 2015. It is evident that the racial composition of institutions such as the judiciary is a key consideration of the 'transformation' project. Thus, e.g., one finds the following government assessment of March 2017 at https://www.gov.za/about-government/judicial-system#transform. Accessed 24 April 2018: 'The department has made significant strides in its quest to transform the judiciary. (…) Regarding racial demographics, there were 39 black judges, 11 coloured judges, 11 Indian judges and 25 white judges.'

[29] See, e.g., Venter 2018b.

The basic political philosophy of the ANC is known as the 'National Democratic Revolution' (NDR) whose core purpose is expressed as 'the liberation of Africans in particular and Blacks in general from political and socioeconomic bondage' and 'liberating the white community from the false ideology of racial superiority and the insecurity attached to oppressing others'.[30] Although a clear definition of 'transformation' is not to be found in the Constitution or legislation, one may assume that it is founded on the ethos of the NDR.

As an indication of the importance of the notion of transformation in political thinking, the transformation of the judiciary has often been the subject of political and policy documents generated by the ANC and the government. The National Development Plan (NDP)[31] for instance states:

> Although the Constitution stipulates general criteria for the appointment of judicial officers; it is important for the JSC to elaborate further guiding principles to build consensus on the qualities and attributes of the "ideal South African judge". The criteria should include a progressive philosophy and an understanding of the socioeconomic context in which the law is interpreted and enforced. While the JSC published a broad list of criteria for judicial appointments in September 2010, they require further development and a clear understanding of their meaning and application.[32]

In a recent policy document of the ANC, it was indicated that the ANC must

> influence the development of a criteria (sic) for the appointment of judicial officers with progressive credentials and transformative judicial philosophy and expertise as required by the NDP and ensure that adequate steps are taken to eliminate the risk of appointing candidates who are not loyal to the Constitution and are beholden to racial and oppressive policies of the past regime to the bench.[33]

The desired criteria 'progressive philosophy', 'progressive credentials' and 'transformative judicial philosophy' for appointment to the bench are vague enough to allow for subjective and ideologically prejudiced choices to be made by the JSC. That a degree of apprehension in this regard is justified is borne out by various occurrences regarding the restructuring of the judiciary and actions surrounding the JSC.

8.3.1.2 Executive Interference

Following behind the scenes discussions over a number of years between the judiciary and the executive, the government published a draft Bill shortly before the Christmas holidays of 2005 for public comment within the inordinately short period

---

[30] ANC (2013) 24, para 39.

[31] The NDP was compiled between 2010 and 2012 by an official National Planning Commission appointed by the President.

[32] National Planning Commission 2012, p 453.

[33] ANC 2017, para 137.

of thirty days.[34] This draft generated strong reaction from the public, the judiciary and the legal profession, especially due to the impression that it created that the intention was to allow the executive to interfere in the affairs of the judiciary. This was to be achieved by inter alia empowering the Minister of Justice to exercise authority over the administration and finances of all courts, the removal of the courts' jurisdiction to hear a matter dealing with, and to order the suspension of the commencement of, an Act of Parliament or provincial Acts, and the weakening of the role of the Chief Justice in the appointment of acting judges by requiring mere consultation instead of concurrence in such appointments.[35]

At a conference organized by the Human Rights Committee of the General Council of the Bar held in Johannesburg on 17 February 2006 former Chief Justice Chaskalson (who had retired the previous year) and the newly appointed Chief Justice Langa made their and the rest of the judiciary's surprise over and opposition to the government's proposed incursions very clear.[36] Fortunately, the public response led to the withdrawal of the draft Bill, and eventually to the milder constitutional amendments and the establishment of the OCJ discussed above. This may indeed be seen as a victory at the time over an overbearing executive, but no guarantee against similar attempts in future.

There have been many instances where politicians expressed their opposition to judicial restraints on government conduct. In the run-up to the adoption of the Constitution Seventeenth Amendment Act, 2012, for instance the following statements were reported:[37]

- The then Deputy Minister of Correctional Services said, 'In the past 17 years (…) we have witnessed sustained and relentless efforts to immigrate the little power left with the executive and the legislature to civil society and the judiciary. Power (is) systematically taken out of the legislature and the executive to curtail efforts and initiatives aimed at inducing fundamental changes.'
- The then ANC Secretary General was of the opinion that the judiciary was becoming a form of opposition and said, 'You can't have a judiciary that seeks to arrest the functioning of government.'
- The then President Zuma said in an interview: 'We don't want to review the Constitutional Court, we want to review its powers.'
- The then ANC national spokesperson stated that 'It is clear that democracy can be undermined by simply approaching courts to reverse any decision arrived at by a qualified organ of state.'

---

[34] The draft was named the *Constitution of the Republic of South Africa Fourteenth Amendment Bill* and was published in General Notice 2023 *Government Gazette* 28334 of 14 December 2005. Some elements of this Bill eventually emerged in the *Constitution Seventeenth Amendment Act* of 2012.

[35] For a thorough discussion of the draft Bill and the issues surrounding it, see Albertyn 2006.

[36] See, e.g., Spilg 2006.

[37] Tumukamoyo 2012.

- The then ANC Chief Whip said that the organisation would do everything in its power, 'to prevent government's attempts to deliver services to the people' being derailed by the courts.

In an analysis of the Constitutional Court's 'position of relative institutional security' in 2009, Roux found that the Court had not been in a position to concern itself much with public opinion because 'the ANC political elite has shielded the Court from the political repercussions of its most unpopular decisions, allowing it to build its legal legitimacy through principled decision making', and that this was achieved by 'lending considerable legitimacy to the ANC's social transformation policies'.[38] Since then however, the Court has been confronted with increased government challenges of its authority amidst growing private appeals for the protection of constitutional propriety and fundamental rights.

8.3.2 *Non-compliance*

The most evident form of political and executive challenge to the authority of the courts is the frequent refusal of state institutions to give effect to negative outcomes against them in the cases in which they are parties.

Where the fulfilment of the ideals of constitutionalism becomes a matter for concern, an essential consideration is whether the public administration, the legislature and executive consistently fulfil their constitutional obligations, including those brought about by section 165(5) of the Constitution in terms of which all orders and decisions issued by the courts bind everyone, including the organs of state. This has been a concern for some time against which the courts, including the Constitutional Court, have waged an enduring battle. It has been the subject of numerous cases and academic commentary.[39]

8.3.2.1 Enforcing Orders Against the State

Circumstances under which this problem has arisen have typically been where courts issued orders against the state for payments to be made to private applicants sounding in money, findings that legislation was unconstitutional warranting an order for rectification of the legislation within a set period of time, and determination of executive or administrative laxity or default requiring corrective steps to be taken.

---

[38] Roux 2009, p 138.

[39] See, e.g., Roos 2006; De Vos 2009 and Malherbe and Van Eck 2009 for analyses of many of the relevant cases.

The judgments of the Constitutional Court in 2008 and 2009 in the *Nyati* cases[40] may be considered to represent an important beacon in this process. In 2008, Madala J remarked:

> In more recent years, and in particular the period from 2002 onwards, courts have been inundated with situations where court orders have been flouted by state functionaries, who, on being handed such court orders, have given very flimsy excuses which in the end only point to their dilatoriness. The public officials seem not to understand the integral role that they play in our constitutional state, as the right of access to courts entails a duty not only on the courts to ensure access but also on the state to bring about the enforceability of court orders.[41]

At stake in these cases was the validity of a provision of the pre-constitutional State Liability Act of 1957 (fashioned on the English Crown Liabilities Act) which placed mere moral obligations on the state to satisfy debts incurred by judgments made against it. The Court declared the relevant section of the Act to be inconsistent with the Constitution to the extent that it does not allow for execution or attachment against the State and that it does not provide for an express procedure for the satisfaction of judgment debts. The declaration of invalidity was suspended for a period of 12 months to allow Parliament to pass legislation providing for the effective enforcement of court orders.

One day before the expiry of the 12-month period allowed for the rectification, a draft of the required amending legislation was officially published for public comment, and the responsible minister urgently applied to the Court for an extension of the suspension of invalidity for another year. The Court granted the request for extension but made an order to remedy the shortcomings of the old law in the interim. The Court ruled that, if a final order against a national or provincial department for the payment of money is not satisfied within thirty days of the date of the judgment, the judgment creditor may serve the court order on the relevant national or provincial treasury, the state attorney, the accounting officer of the relevant national or provincial department, as well as the executive authority of the department concerned who had to cause the judgment debt to be settled within fourteen days of service of the order, failing which movable property of the state could be attached, removed and sold in execution of the judgment debt.

8.3.2.2 Executive and Administrative Procrastination

An amendment to the 1957 Act was eventually adopted in 2011 to conform to the requirements of the Constitution as indicated by the Constitutional Court. More

---

[40] *Nyati v Member of the Executive Council for the Department of Health, Gauteng* 2008 (5) SA 94 (CC) and *Nyathi v Minister for Justice and Constitutional Development* 2010 (4) SA 567 (CC).

[41] *Nyati v Member of the Executive Council for the Department of Health, Gauteng* 2008 (5) SA 94 (CC), para 60.

recently, the Court however found it necessary to deal with executive negligence not only judicially, but also administratively.

In accordance with government policy a massive scheme for the provision of financial support to indigent persons was developed, involving the monthly disbursement of social welfare grants to seventeen million beneficiaries. Initially the grants were paid out by the nine provincial governments, but due to their inefficiency, the task was centralised. For this purpose, the South African Social Security Agency (SASSA) was established in 2005 to administer the payment of social security grants. Lacking the capacity to do the actual disbursement, SASSA awarded a tender to a private company (Cash Paymaster) to undertake the task. In 2013, the Constitutional Court determined that the tender was invalidly awarded but suspended the order of invalidity pending determination of a just and equitable remedy.[42]

In a follow-up case, the Court found that SASSA's contract with Cash Paymaster was invalid, but, in order not to interrupt the distribution of the grants essential for the subsistence of many recipients, the invalidity was suspended to allow for the tender process to be conducted properly. The Court issued a structural (supervisory) order requiring regular reports at each stage of the new tender process to be submitted to the Court itself to ensure effective monitoring, accountability and impartiality.[43]

It soon emerged that the new tender process was also flawed, causing the Court to intervene again.[44] SASSA indicated late in 2015 that it would undertake the distribution of the grants itself when the Cash Paymaster was to stop its services on 31 March 2017, but the SASSA officials soon discovered that the agency would not be up to the task. The matter again came before the Constitutional Court, where the responsible Minister stated that the officials told her of SASSA's inability to perform the function only by October 2016. Neither SASSA nor the Minister did anything to rectify the situation and confronted the Court with their opinion that Cash Paymaster was the only entity capable of administering the disbursement of the grants. Various NGO's approached the Court to intervene, and in its judgment severe judicial frustration was expressed:

> This Court and the country as a whole are now confronted with a situation where the executive arm of government admits that it is not able to fulfil its constitutional and statutory obligations to provide for the social assistance of its people. Moreover, in the deepest and most shaming of ironies, it now seeks to rely on a private corporate entity, with no discernible commitment to transformative empowerment in its own management structures, to get it out of this predicament.[45]

---

[42] *AllPay Consolidated Investment Holdings (Pty) Ltd v Chief Executive Officer, South African Social Security Agency* 2014 (1) SA 604 (CC) (AllPay 1).

[43] *AllPay Consolidated Investment Holdings (Pty) Ltd v Chief Executive Officer, South African Social Security Agency* 2014 (4) SA 179 (CC) (AllPay 2).

[44] *AllPay Consolidated Investment Holdings (Pty) Ltd v Chief Executive Officer of the South African Social Security Agency* 2015 (6) BCLR 653 (CC).

[45] *Black Sash Trust v Minister of Social Development* 2017 (3) SA 335 (CC), para 8.

At the time of writing (April 2018), it would appear that a portion of the grant payments will in future be undertaken through the South African Post Office, but the process for the due award of the tender to deal with the rest has not been concluded.

8.3.3 *'Transformation'*

The degree of independence of the judiciary is closely related to the nature and quality of the legal professions serving the courts. The structure of the legal professions in South Africa has its roots in the English tradition introduced in the colonial era of the 19th century. Although the English designations of 'barrister' and 'solicitor' have long since been replaced by 'advocate' and 'attorney', the split nature of the broad profession has survived. Both the advocates and the attorneys have for many years been self-regulating professions with strict ethical standards enforced in the case of the advocacy by voluntary associations known as 'bar councils', and for the attorneys, regional societies of attorneys known in the vernacular as 'law societies'.

Over a period of more than a decade, politically driven planning for the 'restructuring' of the legal professions has been afoot. The development of a system of centralisation of control over the professions and direct executive involvement as a means of restructuring the existing legal professions, has ominous implications for the independence of the legal profession and by strong implication also for the judiciary. A brief review of the history of the process is necessary to illuminate its implications.

In 1999 the bar councils approached the courts for a review of the Competition Commission's refusal to grant advocates exemption from certain statutory requirements concerning restrictive horizontal practices. When the matter reached the Supreme Court of Appeal, it became clear that the government wished to take steps to radically 'transform' the legal professions and the judiciary. In the judgment of the Supreme Court of Appeal the Commission's explanation of its refusal was strongly criticised because not the relevant statutory grounds were proffered, but the fact that the government was preparing legislation to effect the desired 'transformation'.[46]

When the Legal Practice Act, 2014 was passed twelve years later, the preamble stated the primary purpose to be '[t]o provide a legislative framework for the transformation and restructuring of the legal profession in line with constitutional imperatives so as to facilitate and enhance an independent legal profession that broadly reflects the diversity and demographics of the Republic'. A key feature of the Act is the dissolution of the self-regulating associations and societies of the

---

[46] *Commissioner, Competition Commission v General Council of the Bar of South Africa* 2002 (6) SA 606 (SCA), para 11 at 616.

advocates and attorneys and their replacement with a 'Legal Practice Council', which is to report to and render advice to the Minister of Justice.

Significantly, the explanatory memorandum attached to the Bill when it was introduced in Parliament stated that '[t]raining is recognised in the Bill as a key transformational imperative, as legal practitioners are the main source of candidates for the judiciary, the transformation of which is of paramount importance.'[47] The Act purports to be founded on the need to 'embrace the values underpinning the Constitution'[48] and requires the Council to create a mechanism to 'provide appropriate legal education and training, having due regard to our inherited legacy and new constitutional dispensation.'[49] The Act is however silent on the meaning that should be attached to the expressions 'constitutional imperatives' linked to 'transformational imperatives', which leaves ample room for arbitrary influence of legal education and training aimed at achieving the government-prescribed goals of 'transformation'. The gradual implementation of the Legal Practice Act is currently underway.

8.4 Development and Direction: An Assessment

Given the constitutional and legislative foundations on which the Constitutional Court is built, its history since 1995 and the body of jurisprudence produced over this period by the apex court and other South African courts with constitutional jurisdiction, there is sufficient data on which an assessment can be made of the accountability of the judiciary, its positioning in the scheme of separated state powers and the impact of its judgments.

8.4.1 Accountability

8.4.1.1 Political Predilection

Against the background of the constitutional arrangements regarding the independence and binding judicial authority of the courts, their primary accountability is to the 'Constitution and the law.' This standard may be understood to justify and provide the overall measure for the system of review and appeal from the lowest courts through the full hierarchy up to the Constitutional Court. When cases are adjudicated by the apex court, accountability to the Constitution and the law can become abstract, because the judgments of the Constitutional Court are final and

---

[47] *Legal Practice Bill* [B 20D-2012] 3.5.8 of the Memorandum on page 65.

[48] S 3(a).

[49] S 6(5)(f)(i).

they bind all, in effect implying that the law and the Constitution means what the Constitutional Court says it means, subject only to the possibility of parliamentary amendment of legislation or of the Constitution itself in accordance with the procedural requirements entrenched in the Constitution itself.[50]

Very early in the career of the Constitutional Court it was established that it was not appropriate for the Court to be guided by popular sentiment or opinion. In the iconical death penalty case, actually the very first case heard by the new court in February 1995, the President of the Court made this point in the following *dictum* poignantly providing direction for the future, therefore warranting full citation here:

> Public opinion may have some relevance to the enquiry, but in itself, it is no substitute for the duty vested in the Courts to interpret the Constitution and to uphold its provisions without fear or favour. If public opinion were to be decisive, there would be no need for constitutional adjudication. The protection of rights could then be left to Parliament, which has a mandate from the public, and is answerable to the public for the way its mandate is exercised, but this would be a return to parliamentary sovereignty, and a retreat from the new legal order established by the 1993 Constitution. By the same token the issue of the constitutionality of capital punishment cannot be referred to a referendum, in which a majority view would prevail over the wishes of any minority. The very reason for establishing the new legal order, and for vesting the power of judicial review of all legislation in the courts, was to protect the rights of minorities and others who cannot protect their rights adequately through the democratic process.[51]

The positioning of public opinion below the courts' understanding of the demands of the Constitution is more readily justifiable where it concerns opinions on the death penalty than in cases where political dogma comes into play. It would appear that judges have lately become less restrained in giving expression in their judgments to their personal predilections regarding sensitive social issues such as racial equality. Thus, in a judgment that condoned the non-appointment of a white police officer to a position for which she was better qualified than any of the other applicants, the Constitutional Court cited a judgment of the Supreme Court of Appeal that described the Constitution as a generous gift of the majority to the minority to justify its findings:

> It was because the majority of South Africans had experienced the humiliating legal effect of repressive colonial conceptions of race and gender that they determined that henceforth the role of the law would be different for all South Africans. Having themselves experienced the indignity and pain of legally regulated subordination, and the injustice of exclusion and humiliation through law, the majority committed this country to particularly generous constitutional protection for all South Africans[52]

---

[50] Sections 73–82 of the Constitution provide for these procedures in minute detail. Compliance with these procedures is subject to adjudication by the Constitutional Court in terms of section 167 (4) and (5).

[51] *S v Makwanyane* 1995 (3) SA 391 (CC), para 88.

[52] *Dictum* of the Supreme Court of Appeal in *Fourie v Minister of Home Affairs* 2005 (3) SA 429 (SCA) cited in *South African Police Service v Solidarity obo Barnard* 2014 (6) SA 123 (CC), para 31.

More recently profound differences in dogmatic preference was alarmingly demonstrated in acrimonious exchanges between judges in their formal judgments in a case concerning the changing of street names in Pretoria. Two judges on the Constitutional Court bench took the position that '[i]t is not consonant with the values of the Constitution to deny constitutional protections to people because of the content of their beliefs, views and aspirations'[53] to which another judge retaliated with the following heated statement:[54]

> How can that unquestionably transformative Constitution be expected to recognise cultural traditions rooted in the racist past? The answer must be, if there is such expectation, that it is misplaced. The fact that the oppressive racist history exists at the level of fact does not mean that it deserves any recognition in the Constitution.[55]

These examples of increasing variation in the dogmatic stances among the justices (more of which have occurred recently)[56] raise the concern that some judges of the apex court are developing a penchant for interpreting the Constitution, especially in certain types of cases, more in accordance with the policies of the government than with the dictates of the Constitution. Such a tendency may suggest a shift in the courts' understanding of accountability.

8.4.1.2 Formal Censure

On a formal level, judges may be held accountable by the JSC for their conduct. The Judicial Service Commission Act 1994 provides for the establishment of the Judicial Conduct Committee, composed of the Chief Justice, the Deputy Chief Justice and four judges designated by the Chief Justice in consultation with the Minister. The Committee is tasked to deal with complaints lodged by anyone against a judge based on grounds such as gross incapacity, misconduct and negligence. Lesser complaints may be summarily dismissed, 'serious, non-impeachable complaints' may lead to reprimands, warnings, etc. by the Committee, but if the chairperson (normally the Chief Justice) is satisfied that the complaint may lead to a finding of serious misconduct, the Committee may decide to refer the matter to a Judicial Conduct Tribunal.

Such a tribunal is appointed by the Chief Justice at the request of the Judicial Conduct Committee composed of two judges and one other 'suitable' person. The President of the Tribunal (designated by the Chief Justice) may arrange for a member of the NPA to collect evidence on behalf of the Tribunal. The Tribunal

---

[53] *Tshwane City v Afriforum* 2016 (6) SA 279 (CC), para 159.

[54] *Ibid.*, para 151.

[55] The 'implication' referred to here was that 'any reliance by white South Africans, particularly white Afrikaner people, on a cultural tradition founded in history, finds no recognition in the Constitution.'

[56] See, e.g., the separate judgments of Mogoeng CJ and Froneman J in *Economic Freedom Fighters v Speaker of the National Assembly* 2018 (2) SA 571 (CC).

reports its findings to the JSC. If the Commission finds that judge concerned is suffering from an incapacity, is grossly incompetent or is guilty of gross misconduct, the JSC (on which the ten parliamentary members do not serve for this purpose) must submit its findings to the Speaker of the National Assembly.

The purpose of reporting the findings against a judge to the National Assembly is for that democratically elected body to consider, in terms of section 177(1) of the Constitution the removal of the judge. Section 177(1)(b) requires a resolution supported by at least two-thirds of the members of the National Assembly for a judge to be removed ('impeached'[57]), where after the President is bound to formally remove the judge.

The JSC's record regarding judicial discipline has, to say the least, been mottled.[58] It is significant that many of the activities of the JSC relating to judicial discipline and accountability have led to litigation in which the courts consistently called the Commission to order.[59] Commenting on the manner in which the serious allegations against the Judge President of the Western Cape High Court have been dealt with by the JSC, Corder concluded that

> [p]erhaps the most striking point of this long-running saga is that the courts' repeated reversal of the JSC's decisions, as well as the manner in which the JSC attempted to justify its actions, has betrayed a degree of incompetence as well as an arrogant pursuit of political interests by the majority in the JSC rather than the fulfilment of its constitutional duty to ensure judicial accountability.[60]

At the time of writing it would however appear that the JSC may soon take decisions that can lead to 'impeachment' procedures being launched. In the Hlope matter a tribunal was set up in 2013, and after much prevarication and litigation, it has been announced that the Tribunal will sit early July 2018.[61] In a report of the Judicial Conduct Tribunal dated 17 April 2018 'in re: Judge NJ Motata' it was concluded that the impugned conduct of the judge was 'racist and that they impinge on and are prejudicial to the impartiality and dignity of the courts', that 'the lack of integrity in the manner in which Judge Motata allowed his defence to be conducted at his trial, in our view is incompatible with or unbecoming of the holding of judicial office' and it was suggested that, if the judge was to retain his position as judicial officer, it would 'negatively affect the public confidence in the judicial

---

[57] Although the Judicial Service Commission Act 1994 uses the term 'impeachable complaints' in ss 16 and 17, the term 'impeachment' does not occur in the Constitution.

[58] See, e.g., Corder 2014, pp 212–221.

[59] Cf., e.g., *Langa CJ v Hlope* 2009 (4) SA 382 (SCA), *Motata v Nair* 2009 (1) SACR 263 (T), *Acting Chairperson, Judicial Service Commission* v *Premier, Western Cape* 2011 (3) SA 538 (SCA), *Freedom Under Law v Acting Chairperson, Judicial Service Commission* 2011 (3) SA 549 (SCA) and *Hlope v Premier of the Western Cape Province; Hlope v Freedom Under Law* 2012 (6) SA 13 (CC).

[60] Corder 2014, p 219.

[61] See https://city-press.news24.com/News/john-hlophe-faces-risk-of-impeachment-20180415. Accessed 25 April 2018.

system.' The Tribunal recommended the institution of the constitutional procedure for the removal ('impeachment') of the judge.[62]

In April 2018, the Constitutional Court handed down a judgment pertaining to the transparency of the proceedings of the JSC.[63] The case concerned 'private deliberations' held by the JSC in 2012 regarding recommendations for the appointment of judges to the Western Cape Division of the High Court. The appellant in the case wished the decision on the recommendations to be declared unlawful and irrational. The JSC withheld the recordings of its deliberations from the courts and both the provincial High Court and the Supreme Court of Appeal held that the JSC was entitled to withhold the recordings. The Constitutional Court however set aside this holding, ordering that the recordings and transcripts of the relevant proceedings be delivered to the appellant. In the majority judgment, the Court stated:

> If a public functionary can withhold information relevant to the decision, there is always a risk that possible illegalities remain uncovered and are thus insulated from scrutiny and review. That is at variance with the rule of law and our paramount values of accountability, responsiveness and openness. This affects not only the individual litigant, but also the public interest in the exercise of public power in accordance with the Constitution.[64]

8.4.2 *Separation of Powers and the Rule of Law*

The introduction of constitutional review jurisdiction to South African constitutional law inevitably required the judiciary to attend to issues relating to the *trias politica* and the rule of law. References to this doctrine abound in the judgments of the Constitutional Court. Thus, for instance, the Court stated in 1998 that the right not to be detained without trial was 'the pre-eminent, if not the only, guarantee against arbitrary administrative detention and is indispensable for the upholding of the rule of law and the separation of powers in a constitutional state.'[65]

In a case concerning the extension of the term of office of the Chief Justice by the President in 2011, the Court reiterated that '[t]he principles of the rule of law, the separation of powers and judicial independence, underscored by international law, are indispensable cornerstones of our constitutional democracy.'[66]

---

[62] Published online at http://www.politicsweb.co.za/documents/nkola-motata-should-be-impeached–judicial-conduct. Accessed 25 April 2018, paras 58–60.

[63] *Helen Suzman Foundation v Judicial Service Commission* [2018] ZACC 8.

[64] *Ibid.*, para 67.

[65] *De Lange v Smuts* 1998 (3) SA 785 (CC), para 89.

[66] *Justice Alliance of South Africa v President of Republic of South Africa* 2011 (5) SA 388 (CC), para 40.

The frail position of the judiciary in relation to the executive and the legislature was expressed by a judge given to flowery language in a judgment of 2008:

> In our constitutional order, the judiciary is an independent pillar of state, constitutionally mandated to exercise the judicial authority of the state fearlessly and impartially. Under the doctrine of separation of powers, it stands on an equal footing with the executive and the legislative pillars of state; but in terms of political, financial or military power, it cannot hope to compete. It is in these terms by far the weakest of the three pillars; yet its manifest independence and authority are essential. Having no constituency, no purse and no sword, the judiciary must rely on moral authority. Without such authority it cannot perform its vital function as the interpreter of the Constitution, the arbiter in disputes between organs of state and, ultimately, as the watchdog over the Constitution and its Bill of Rights — even against the state.[67]

The progressive inclusion in the Bill of Rights of socio-economic rights enforceable against the state has particularly caused the judiciary to test the boundaries of the separation of powers. The basic justification adhered to by the Constitutional Court to intervene in the exercise of legislative and executive powers has been that 'the courts are the ultimate guardians of the Constitution'.[68] That the doctrine will always be theoretically vague, has also been acknowledged: 'that although there are no bright lines that separate the roles of the legislature, the executive and the courts from one another, there are certain matters that are pre-eminently within the domain of one or other of the arms of government and not the others'.[69]

In quite a few instances, especially in recent years during the Zuma presidency, the Constitutional Court was called upon to resolve hotly contested political issues involving the constitutional delinquency of the executive and the executive-dominated Parliament. In a judgment in which the Court found that the failure by the National Assembly to make rules regulating the removal of a President was a violation of the Constitution and ordered the making of such rules without delay, the separation of powers inevitably came up again. The Court set out its position as follows:

> The order proposed does not involve the exercise by this Court of the Assembly's powers. On the contrary, it requires the Assembly itself to exercise those powers and perform its constitutional functions without delay. This cannot be and is not a breach of the principle of separation of powers but consists in no more than the Court fulfilling its constitutionally assigned duty.[70]

---

[67] *S v Mamabolo* 2001 (3) SA 409 (CC), para 16.

[68] See, e.g., *Glenister v President of the Republic of South Africa* 2009 (1) SA 287 (CC), para 33.

[69] See *Minister of Health v Treatment Action Campaign* 2002 (5) SA 721 (CC), paras 98–99.

[70] *Economic Freedom Fighters v Speaker of the National Assembly* 2018 (2) SA 571 (CC), para 220.

8.4.3 *Impact of Constitutional Judgments*

8.4.3.1 Concurrence and Dissent

A key element in the nature (and success) of the Constitutional Court is the arrangement that it has only one bench. In principle, this means that when the Court sits to hear and decide every case that comes before it, all the judges sit together. For various reasons, such as being on leave, temporary illness or legitimate absence from the Court, it is not always possible for all eleven justices to attend all the sittings of the Court. A quorum consists of eight judges.[71]

As may be expected, *en banc* judgments are not always unanimous, and minority judgments either supporting or dissenting from the judgment of the majority, which is binding on all, often occur. The requirement implied by the configuration of the Court that at least a majority of the members of the Court must agree on its decisions has a constructive consequence: prior to the delivery of a judgment the judges must discuss, and debate if necessary, and therefore carefully consider its outcome and justification.[72]

Minority judgments are not always dissenting in nature but intended to add the minority judges' perspectives and reasons for the Court's findings. As in all judgments of the Constitutional Court dissenting minority judgments are consistently supported by judges' justificatory arguments. These arguments may be useful for the Court and counsel in future cases to assist in the justification of arguments in similar or related matters. It stands to reason that minority judgments in support of the majority will be more persuasive, but the arguments and justifications found in minority judgments may also carry weight in the process of the judicial development of the law.

8.4.3.2 Precedent

The pre-constitutional judge-made doctrine of *stare decisis* survived the constitutional transition of 1994, although it is not regulated constitutionally or statutorily. The Constitutional Court has, however clearly confirmed it in the following terms:

> [P]recedents must be respected in order to ensure legal certainty and equality before the law. This is essential for the rule of law. Law cannot "rule" unless it is reasonably predictable. A highest court of appeal – and this Court in particular – has to be especially cautious as far as adherence to or deviation from its own previous decisions is concerned. It is the upper guardian of the letter, spirit and values of the Constitution. The Constitution is the supreme law and has had a major impact on the entire South African legal order – as it was intended to do. But it is young; so is the legislation following from it. As a jurisprudence develops, understanding may increase and interpretations may change. At the same time though, a

---

[71] S 167(2) of the Constitution.

[72] See, e.g., O'Regan 2014, pp 409–11.

> single source of consistent, authoritative and binding decisions is essential for the development of a stable constitutional jurisprudence and for the effective protection of fundamental rights. This Court must not easily and without coherent and compelling reason deviate from its own previous decisions or be seen to have done so. One exceptional instance where this principle may be invoked is when this Court's earlier decisions have given rise to controversy or uncertainty, leading to conflicting decisions in the lower courts.[73]

8.4.3.3 Confronting Corruption

Over time, but especially during the Zuma presidency (2009–2018) constitutional adjudication of matters concerning the stemming of corrupt practices and abuse of government powers have taken much time and judicial energy. An exposition and analysis of the resulting jurisprudence requires extensive discussion.[74] For present purposes, the citation of a few *dicta* should suffice to obtain an impression of the flavour of the judicial attitude in this regard:

> There can be no gainsaying that corruption threatens to fell at the knees virtually everything we hold dear and precious in our hard-won constitutional order. It blatantly undermines the democratic ethos, the institutions of democracy, the rule of law and the foundational values of our nascent constitutional project. It fuels maladministration and public fraudulence and imperils the capacity of the state to fulfil its obligations to respect, protect, promote and fulfil all the rights enshrined in the Bill of Rights. When corruption and organised crime flourish, sustainable development and economic growth are stunted. And in turn, the stability and security of society is put at risk.[75]

> All South Africans across the racial, religious, class and political divide are in broad agreement that corruption is rife in this country and that stringent measures are required to contain this malady before it graduates into something terminal.[76]

> (…) public-office bearers ignore their constitutional obligations at their peril. This is so because constitutionalism, accountability and the rule of law constitute the sharp and mighty sword that stands ready to chop the ugly head of impunity off its stiffened neck.[77]

> Taking all the circumstances sketched and the considerations made we are of the view that the President was ill advised and reckless in launching the challenge against the remedial action of the Public Protector. He is aware that since allegations of "State Capture" initially surfaced and more so, after the Public Protector's report the matter remains in the public domain and requires decisive action and resolution. His Court challenge has resulted in further delaying the resolution of the "State Capture" allegations.[78]

---

[73] *Gcaba v Minister for Safety and Security* 2010 (1) SA 232 (CC), para 62.

[74] See, e.g., Venter 2018a and 2018b.

[75] *Glenister v President of the Republic of South Africa* 2011 (3) SA 347 (CC), para 166.

[76] *Helen Suzman Foundation v President of the Republic of South Africa* 2015 (2) SA 1 (CC), para 1.

[77] *Economic Freedom Fighters v Speaker, National Assembly* 2016 (3) SA 580 (CC), para 1. For an analysis of the judgment, see Venter 2017.

[78] *President of the Republic of South Africa v Office of the Public Protector* 2018 (2) SA 100 (GP), para 189.

8.5 Some Comparative Observations

At least in Sub-Saharan Africa South African constitutional law and jurisprudence are regularly cited. The draftsmanship of the Constitutions of Kenya of 2010[79] and of Zimbabwe of 2013[80] show clear signs of the influence of the South African Constitution of 1996, and the courts of countries such as Botswana, Kenya and Namibia regularly cite the South African Constitutional Court in their judgments. This may in general terms be ascribed to the impact that the global precepts of constitutional democracy have had on African constitution-writing and jurisprudence in recent decades.[81]

Because of the influence that the German and Canadian constitutions had on the drafting of the South African Constitution, it is not surprising that the Constitutional Court has, especially in its early years, made extensive use of the jurisprudence of those countries,[82] but authority from a wide range of other jurisdictions, including the USA, the EU, the UK and India have also been sourced by constitutional judges.[83]

8.6 Concluding Remarks

The South African judiciary, and specifically the Constitutional Court has established itself as the most important and effective institution capable and able to develop and protect the precepts of constitutionalism expressed in the Constitution. Especially in its first decade the Constitutional Court took the responsibility essentially to reconfigure the South African legal order as a whole and excelled in breaking new ground in which the values and principles of the new dispensation could sprout.

In time, the Court has undergone a number of severe challenges and has survived them by consistently providing well-reasoned and accessible judgments. Inevitably the courts have been embroiled in a number of distasteful and even alarming political struggles between champions of and aggressors against constitutionalism, and there is an ongoing executive-led programme to 'transform' the judiciary in

---

[79] See, e.g., Kaguongo 2018, p 6.

[80] See, e.g., Banda 2014, p 491.

[81] Cf., e.g., the tenor of the preamble to the African Charter on Democracy, Elections and Governance adopted by the African Union in 2007, including phrases such as 'to deepen and consolidate the rule of law, peace, security and development in our countries'; 'to strengthen and consolidate institutions for good governance, continental unity and solidarity' and 'committed to promote the universal values and principles of democracy, good governance, human rights and the right to development'.

[82] See, e.g., Rautenbach and Du Plessis 2013.

[83] See, e.g., Lollini 2007.

order to secure a larger degree of judicial amenability to majority politics. That this programme is having consequences is apparent from judgments providing legitimacy to the ANC's policies aimed at 'social transformation' and in the ongoing process of obtaining executive control over the legal professions.

Despite these indications that there may be cause for concern, the momentum of the judicial culture that was developed independently in the first years following the introduction of constitutional supremacy still prevails. The legitimacy of the judgments of especially the Constitutional Court continues to be buttressed by mechanisms such as *en banc* adjudication, comprehensive (sometimes exhaustive) justificatory argumentation and commitment to the defence of the integrity of the Constitution.

References

African National Congress (2013) Strategy & Tactics of the ANC December 2012. http://www.anc.org.za/docs/pol/2013/strategyp.pdf Accessed 18 April 2018

African National Congress (2017) Peace and Stability – Discussion Paper towards the 5th National Policy Conference. http://www.anc.org.za/sites/default/files/National%20Policy%20Conference%202017%20Peace%20and%20Stability.pdf Accessed 18 April 2018

Albertyn C (2006) Judicial Independence and the Constitution Fourteenth Amendment Bill. SAJHR 22:126–143

Banda F (2014) The Constitution of Zimbabwe 2013: Constitutional Curate's Egg. International Survey of Family Law 491–503

Corder H (2014) Judicial Accountability. In: Hoexter C, Olivier M (eds) The Judiciary in South Africa. Juta, Cape Town, pp 200–244

De Vos P (2009) Between Moral Authority and Formalism: Nyati v Member of Executive Council for Dept of Health, Gauteng. 2 Constitutional Court Review 409–427

Kaguongo W (2018) Introductory Note on Kenya. http://www.icla.up.ac.za/images/country_reports/kenya_country_report.pdf Accessed 26 April 2018

Klaaren J (2015) Transformation of the Judicial System in South Africa, 2012–2013. The George Washington International Law Review 47:481–508

Lollini A (2007) Legal argumentation based on foreign law: An example from case law of the South African Constitutional Court. Utrecht Law Review 3:60–74

Malherbe R, Van Eck M (2009) State Non-compliance with Legal Duties: The Constitutional Court Finally Cracks the Whip. TSAR 191–198

National Planning Commission (2012) Our future: Make it work. National Development Plan 2030. https://nationalplanningcommission.files.wordpress.com/2015/02/ndp-2030-our-future-make-it-work_0.pdf Accessed 18 April 2018 Accessed 19 April 2018

O'Regan K (2014) The Constitutional Court: A Judge's Perspective. In: Hoexter C, Olivier M (eds) The Judiciary in South Africa. Juta, Cape Town, pp 403–413

Rautenbach C, Du Plessis L (2013) In the Name of Comparative Constitutional Jurisprudence: The Consideration of German Precedents by South African Constitutional Court Judges. German Law Journal 14:1539–1577

Roos R (2006) Executive Disregard for Court Orders: Enforcing Judgments against the State. SALJ 123:744–766

Roux T (2009) Principle and Pragmatism on the Constitutional Court of South Africa. I-CON 7:106–138

Spilg B (2006) Conference on judicial independence. Advocate 19:5–7

Tumukamoyo H (2012) Double Speak About Judicial Reform In South Africa Raises Alarm Bells. ISS Today 23 March 2012. https://issafrica.org/iss-today/double-speak-about-judicial-reform-in-south-africa-raises-alarm-bells Accessed 18 April 2018

Venter F (2017) Economic Freedom Fighters and Others v Speaker of the National Assembly and Others Cases (S Afr). In: Grote R, Lachenmann F, Wolfrum R (eds) Max Planck Encyclopedia of Comparative Constitutional Law. Oxford University Press, Oxford http://oxcon.ouplaw.com/view/10.1093/law-mpeccol/law-mpeccol-e759. Accessed 27 April 2018

Venter F (2018a) South Africa: The State of Liberal Democracy. In: Albert R et al (eds) The I·CONnect-Clough Center 2017 Global Review of Constitutional Law 260

Venter F (2018b) The limits of transformation in South Africa's constitutional democracy. SAJHR 34:143–166

Francois Venter is a constitutional scholar who was closely involved in the drafting of the South African constitutions between 1990 and 1995. He was the founding editor of *PER/PELJ* (Potchefstoom Electronic Law Journal), served as dean of the Faculty of Law in Potchefstroom between 1990 and 2012, and has published widely on constitutional comparison and constitutionalism, e.g. *Constitutionalism and Religion* (Edward Elgar, 2015) and 'Rethinking the Language of Constitutional Comparison' (*South African Journal on Human Rights*, 2017). He is a regular visitor and alumnus of the Max Planck Institute for Comparative Public Law and International Law in Heidelberg.

Chapter 9
Judicial Independence and Accountability in the Council of Europe and the European Court of Human Rights

Jörg Luther

Contents

Abstract This chapter assesses various aspects of judicial independence, judicial accountability and the election and selection of judges as reflected by the experiences of the European Court of Human Rights (ECtHR). History shows that independence is a common principle and tradition of European constitutionalism. It has been implemented and balanced with accountability through reforms conditioned by standards of soft law from the Council of Europe and by case law of the ECtHR. The puzzle of rules that frame personal and institutional independence and accountability shows remaining problems and differences between international and constitutional judges. Election procedures balance personal independence with

J. Luther (✉)
University of Eastern Piedmont Amedeo Avogadro, Alessandria, Italy
e-mail: joerg.luther@uniupo.it

Hirsch Ballin, Van der Schyff & Stremler (eds.), *European Yearbook of Constitutional Law 2019*, European Yearbook of Constitutional Law 1,
https://doi.org/10.1007/978-94-6265-359-7_9

institutional accountability, but the supporting European consensus suffers populist threats to human rights protection.

Keywords accountability · comparative law · constitutionalism · European Court of Human Rights · independence · selection of judges

9.1 The Relevance of the Common European Constitutional Heritage

The design of judicial power in a democratic society might have been improved by the European models of constitutional and international jurisdiction. European constitutional and international judges worked on principles and rules of independence and accountability, two polysemous and potentially antithetic topics that need to be accurately contextualised in different legal and political cultures. This chapter focusses on the Council of Europe and the European Court of Human Rights (ECtHR), institutions where the contexts are frequently compared and both the construction of ideals of a common constitutionalism and the maintenance of cultural differentiation are performed.

The Council of Europe is 'safeguarding and realising the ideals and principles which are their common heritage' (Article 1a, 3 Statute), including the common European constitutional heritage of the rule of law and 'genuine democracy' (preamble).[1] Generally spoken, judicial independence and legal or political accountability are principles necessary for the 'maintenance and further realisation of human rights and fundamental freedoms' (Article 1b) and for the separation of powers, a fundamental principle common to the law of the member states of the Council of Europe. The Council of Europe's Statute did not establish a judiciary, but the European Convention of Human Rights (ECHR) created the Court for inter-state litigation and applications from any person, non-governmental organisation or group of individuals who claim to be victims of a violation of the conventional rights, including the entitlement to 'a fair and public hearing within a reasonable time by an *independent* and impartial tribunal established by law' (Article 6(1) ECHR).

This source of European human rights law is binding for States as national and international lawmakers for a democratic society. The normative value and the concrete rules may vary within the relevant legal orders, but in a comparative perspective judicial independence seems to be a consolidated common constitutional tradition. Meanwhile, common features of judicial accountability are still *in fieri* (1) and the transfer of both principles to constitutional and international courts, especially the ECtHR, needs further comparative analysis (2).

---

[1] Pizzorusso 2002, p 144 ff.

(1) Judicial accountability has a common law background and is translated in different ways. It is used less in Council of Europe sources and more in economic management and political theory.[2] For purposes of comparative analysis, a broad concept could include all mechanisms of personal responsibility and liability of judges as well as of control over efficient performance of the institution, including the mechanisms of judge selection.

A general constitutional idea might be that all powers can be independent and accountable through mechanisms of 'checks and balance' as well as of electoral accountability. All powerholders need to be ensured against violence, threats and corruption and to be held accountable for crimes, torts and lack of discipline. Their institutions need to respect the rule of law, but public powers in a democratic society also need control through public opinion framed by differentiated media. Administrations need control by a government accountable to the lawmakers and by judges accessed by the people. Judges, even of last resort, need to be independent from governmental control and mechanisms of political confidence, but subject to impartial law-making and to judicial remedies and responsibilities. Democratic discontinuity of parliaments and governments justifies forms of sacrificial accountability to the electors; the continuity of administrations and jurisdictions could require more forms of explanatory accountability.[3]

(2) The principles of independence and accountability could be applied also to constitutional and international judges, but there are relevant structural and functional differences regarding the different but interdependent legal orders and the national and transnational contexts of democracy. Unlike the EU, the Council of Europe is more rarely identified with a European society and might be expected to pay still more attention to the nation state than to popular sovereignty. National constitutional courts and the ECtHR rely on different but complementary value communities:[4] on the one hand on a national consensus on principles of democratic constitutionalism, on the other hand on a European consensus over universal values of a human-rights-civilization and peacebuilding principles of the international rule of law. While constitutional judges have to fear more the hegemony of political parties, the tyranny of populist leaders and clashes within national societies, the principle 'one state, one judge' makes the ECtHR more vulnerable for national pressure and international tensions not (counter-)balanced by international institutions, especially in countries and moments of authoritarian involution.

---

[2] Von Bogdandy and Venzke 2014, p 191. For a political concept, see Tushnet 2013 and Schmitter 2007, p 3: 'Accountability is first a relationship between two sets of actors (actually, most of it is played out not between individuals, but between organizations) in which the former accepts to inform the other, explain or justify his or her actions and submit to any pre-determined sanctions that the latter may impose'.

[3] Bogdanor as quoted by official UK documents under: https://www.judiciary.uk/wp-content/uploads/JCO/Documents/Consultations/accountability.pdf Accessed 1 April 2019.

[4] Von Bogdandy and Venzke 2014, p 85 ff.

ECtHR-judges are empowered by international parliamentary elections, but their work faces more governments than parliaments and a public sphere hardly able to represent humanity as a whole. Further democratic legitimacy of the institution could nevertheless be derived from increased popular and global demand for human rights justice and un-fragmented law-making, but depends upon the conjuncture of rights discourses and leads to conflicts with national constitutional and other international courts.[5] Constitutional courts decide more on constitutional review of legislation and inter-branch litigation and give not necessarily direct access to rights holders. By contrast, the ECtHR is designed for subsidiary adjudication of human rights and related interstate litigation.[6] The ECtHR cannot declare null and void acts of state legislation and administration or Council of Europe treaties and decisions of the Council of Europe-administration. Furthermore, the execution of the judgments is entrusted to the Committee of Ministers (CoM), making it sometimes subject to threats of noncompliance and Court reform attempts.

The Brighton and the Copenhagen Declarations on the reform of the ECHR-system adopted by High Level Conferences in 2012 and 2018[7] stressed a new concept of 'shared responsibility' for effective human rights protection. Sharing requires dialogues that might favour cooperation more than conflict, but can produce informal dependence that is something less than full independence and complicates accountability. Synthetizing all these comparative aspects, *prima facie* the independence of the ECtHR seems to be *de jure* less protected[8] and/or *de facto* more endangered than constitutional courts.

In order to analyse how the ECtHR deals with principles of judicial independence and accountability within the Council of Europe, this chapter first explores their historical roots in European constitutionalism (Sect. 9.2) and their gradual implementation within the Council of Europe (Sect. 9.3). Special attention is drawn to the interaction of the ECtHR-case law with ECHR-amendments and Council of Europe-soft law, because of the auto-poietic value of judgments that favour the search for a rational system of rules ensuring independence and accountability (Sect. 9.4). A more analytical approach therefore distinguishes between the personal and institutional aspects of both. The former are related to individual rights (Sect. 9.5) and duties (Sect. 9.6), the latter to the power relations of the ECtHR to the Council of Europe and member states (Sect. 9.7) and a weak European public opinion threatened by national veto plays (Sect. 9.8). The main balance between independence and accountability is made in the judge-(s)election procedures (Sect. 9.9). A final conclusion is that public confidence in judicial independence and accountability is endangered (Sect. 9.10).

---

5 Benvenisti and Downs 2017, p 105 ff.

6 Guarnieri 2013, p 356. Andenas 2007, p 12 distinguishes the 'judicial culture' of European judges from the 'diplomatic culture' of other international judges.

7 https://www.echr.coe.int/Documents/2012_Brighton_FinalDeclaration_ENG.pdf; https://www.echr.coe.int/Documents/Copenhagen_Declaration_ENG.pdf. Accessed 1 April 2019.

8 Posner and Yoo 2005, p 66 praise a higher dependence and efficiency of international judges.

9.2 Why the History of European Constitutionalism Matters

Judicial independence is a classical ideal of European constitutionalism that was prepared, over the long run of history, through the transformation of political into legal accountability. Plato's *Nomoi* designed justice to be participated by the people, with judges of a court of last resort to be elected by the highest officers for short terms 'in the most incorruptible form of which human things admit'.[9] A judge that decided wrong intentionally was held accountable by the guardians of the laws. [10] The corrupted judge was harshly punished also in ancient Rome,[11] but a separation of *jurisdictio* from *gubernaculum* was prepared by the republican *praetor*. Justinian codified the principle that no one can be judge of himself.[12]

In premodern times, Henry II created a distinct judicial council 'to do right' and hear all complaints (1178), but medieval pluralism supported feudal, ecclesiastical and corporate bounds of judges with disciplinary forms of accountability favoured by professionalization. Jean Bodin recommended kings to do no more the job of a judge ('*faire mestier d'estre juges*') and to prefer officers to commissioners. The Sacred Roman Empire's *Kammergerichtsordnung* (1521) provided sanctions for corruption and incompetence and proceedings for the removal of judges that never applied. Edward Coke was dismissed when he refused to stop or delay a proceeding as requested by the king (1616). Under proposition 12 (1642), independence rendered accountability of judges exceptional: 'That all the Judges, and all the officers placed by approbation of both Houses of Parliament, may hold their places *quam diu bene se gesserint*' (during good behaviour).[13]

The Enlightenment promoted further the ideals of the rule of law and meekness, with judicial independence construed as an additional guarantee of impartiality and of the subjective right to have rights and freedoms ensured even against the State.[14] As Montesquieu pointed out, any form of royal '*justice retenue*' was despotism, but the power of judging, being so 'terrible among man', should be zero and just the 'mouth of the laws', otherwise freedoms could be threatened by the fear of judicial tyranny.[15] While the US Constitution conserved the impeachment for judges, the parliament of Paris vindicated security of tenure ('*inamovibilité*'), the power to not

[9] Plato, Laws, VI, 13, 767–768.

[10] *Ibid.*

[11] Tabula IX, 2: 'Duram esse legem putas, quae iudicem arbitrumve iure datum, qui ob rem [iu] dic[a]ndam pecuniam accepisse convictus est, capite poenitur?'

[12] C. 3.5.1.: 'Generali lege decernimus neminem sibi esse iudicem vel ius sibi dicere debere.'

[13] Act of Settlement 1701: 'That after the said Limitation shall take Effect as aforesaid Judges Commissions be made Quam diu se bene Gesserint and their Salaries ascertained and established but upon the Address of both Houses of Parliament it may be lawfull to remove them.'

[14] Grove 2018, p 465; Zimmermann 2014, p 56 ff; Pasquino 2010, p 195.

[15] Spirit of the Laws (1748), XI, 6: '… one fears the magistracy, not the magistrates?'

take into account a royal will contrary to the fundamental laws of the State and the right of citizens to have 'natural judges designed by the law' (1788).[16]

Article 19 of the first short French constitution of 1789 implemented the insurance of rights and separation of powers promised by Article 16 of the Declaration through a symbolic delegation: '*Le pouvoir judiciare ne pourra, en aucun cas, être exercéee par le Roi, ni par le Corps législatif; mais la Justice sera administrée au nom du Roi par les seuls Tribunaux établis par la Loi, suivant les principes de la Constitution, et selon les formes déterminées par la Loi*.'[17] The law of 16–24 August 1790 adapted the ancient '*référé législatif* (*relatio ad principem*)' to the new law-making mechanism, but promised that 'those to be judged may not be distracted from their natural judge by any commission, nor by competences or call back different from those established by law'. The constitution of 1791 created a '*tribunal de cassation, établi auprès du corps législatif*' (Article XIX) and the constitutional charter of 1815 determined that no judges can be removed (Article 58) and nobody should be removed from natural judges (Article 62). The senates' proposal in 1814 to declare 'the independence of the judicial power guaranteed' was realised only in 1958 (Article 64).

Until 1848, judicial independence did not enter into European constitutional texts, but practices of political accountability became inconvenient.[18] A failed German constitution (1849) declared jurisdiction and administration separated and independent from each other (§ 181), the Prussian constitution (1850) promised 'independent courts' (Article 86) and the Austrian *Staatsgrundgesetz* on judicial power (1867) ensured judges to 'stand for themselves and to be independent' (Article 6), while it also was a starting point for the idea of the constitutional court.[19] The ideal of judicial independence could prevail over political accountability only in the last century when constitutional and international justices were institutionalised. A new international judicial power was created in the Permanent Arbitration Court (1899) and the Permanent International Court of Justice (1922) as a 'body of independent judges, elected regardless of their nationality from amongst persons of high moral character'.

The experiences of dictatorial despotism and totalitarianism in the twentieth century pushed for a general recognition of judicial independence as a fundamental principle of the European constitutional heritage and of the international law of 'civilised nations'.[20] The constitutions of France (1946) and Italy (1947) constitutionalized the Higher Council of the Judiciary and the German Basic Law (1949)

---

[16] Quoted by Alvazzi dal Frate 1999, p 124.

[17] 'The judicial power can in no case be exercised neither by the king, nor by the legislature, but justice will be administrated in the name of the King by the sole tribunals established by law, respecting the principles of the Constitution and the forms determined by the law.'

[18] Article 102 Constitution Belgium 1831 added that remunerations shall be defined by law.

[19] Hayo and Voigt 2014, p 189: 'countries with a British legal origin and a Scandinavian legal origin are less likely to have implemented [judicial independence] in their constitutions.'

[20] Kotuby and Sobota 2017, p 163 ff. For the relevance of general principles see *Golder v. United Kingdom* (1975).

echoed Article 10 of the Universal Declaration of Human Rights (UDHR) of 1948: 'Everyone is entitled in full equality to a fair and public hearing by an independent and impartial tribunal, in the determination of his rights and obligations and of any criminal charge against him.'[21] Article 6(1) ECHR (1950) restricted this to civil rights, but added a requirement of legality ('established by law') and a guarantee against *iustitia denegata vel protracta* ('within a reasonable time').

The ECtHR developed an international human rights jurisdiction that can impact on or be impacted by constitutional justice and qualified the ECHR as 'a constitutional instrument of European public order'.[22] The Council of Europe-Secretary denied that the convention could be intended as a European Constitution, but the ECtHR president prospected a 'European quasi-constitutional court' working on minimal common standards of constitutionalism.[23] Scholars might still disagree on whether the ECtHR is *de facto* or has to be similar to a constitutional court,[24] but they can recognize that the Council of Europe-law synthesizes common legal principles of judicial independence and legal accountability even for constitutional and ECtHR-judges.

9.3 How Judicial Independence and Accountability Were Developed Within the Council of Europe

Since 1945, the constitutionalisation and internationalisation of law worked hand in hand for constitutional and international courts. Independence and impartiality were transformed from professional and institutional duties into justiciable rights. Judicial independence was extended from the person of the judge to the institution of the court and balanced by accountability. The principles were implemented and strengthened by national reforms and ECHR amendments supported both by the ECtHR case law and the soft law produced within the Council of Europe.

In the original design, the ECtHR was a non-permanent institution separated from the Council of Europe. The duration of office was nine years, re-election allowed and no provisions for removal of judges provided. Article 21(3) ECHR required that during their terms of office judges shall not engage in activities 'incompatible with their independence, impartiality or with the demands of a full-time office.' To exercise the 'functions as a judge honourably, independently and impartially' became part of the oath of the judges of the ECHR (rule 3). The ECtHR did not get a formal statute, but the Plenary Court was empowered to elect (vice-) presidents and (deputy-)registrars, to 'draw up its own rules' and to 'determine its

---

[21] Similar Article 14 Covenant of Civil and Political Rights (CCPR) 1996. Article 26 OAS-Declaration 1948: just impartiality.

[22] *Loizidou* 1995, para 75.

[23] Wildhaber 2007, p. 521 ff; Greer and Wildhaber 2012, p. 655 ff.

[24] Favoreu 2002, p 35 ff.

own procedure' (Article 55 original version). Advisory opinions could be asked in non-jurisdictional procedures under protocol n. 2 (1963).

The academic question of whether the ECtHR has become a *de facto* organ of the Council of Europe or a judicial institution common to the member states[25] can be left open, because it was subject to powers of both the Council of Europe and state institutions that agreed various amendments to the ECHR. The Steering Committee for Human Rights (CDDH) established in 1976 was assisted by the ECtHR – without vote – when preparing the amendments to the control machinery under protocols n. 5 (packaging elections), 8 (criteria of office, chambers), 9 (individual complaints), 11 (abolition of the Commission (EComHR),[26] terms of office), 14 (judicial formations, criteria of admissibility) and 15 (age limits). The increasing acceptation of the ECtHR-jurisdiction by member states, the raising demand for judicial human rights protection and the enlargement from 22 to 47 member states after 1989 accelerated the growth of its powers and independence.

Under protocol 11, the Plenary Court received a competence for procedures of dismissal and adopted a resolution on judicial ethics (2008). For the explanatory report, the reform was made 'in order to ensure the independence of the Court', moving perhaps from distrust in the judges of the new member states to an element of trust. The term of duration of judges was reduced without any explanation to six years, but the original term was re-established in 2009 and re-election was excluded. High rates of inadmissibility and threats of noncompliance pushed the Brighton Declaration of 2012 for further structural reforms and a shared responsibility for efficiency that seems to be less driven by the ECtHR.

These changes were conditioned by a general context of standard setting and institution building within the Council of Europe for judicial reforms all over Europe. CoM Recommendation Rec (1994) 12 to member states 'on the independence, efficiency and role of judges' was followed by Rec (2010) 12 on 'independence, efficiency and responsibilities of judges' that is 'applicable to all persons exercising judicial functions, including those dealing with constitutional matters'. The CoM created an *ad hoc* Consultative Council of European Judges (CCJE, 2000) and a European Commission for the Efficiency of Justice (CEPEJ, 2002).[27] CEPEJ has a Statute that allows the ECtHR to ask for opinions. The CCJE's website does not publish rules of composition, but informs that national judicial members are 'chosen in contact, where such authorities exist, with the national authorities responsible for ensuring the independence and impartiality of judges and with the national administration responsible for managing the judiciary.' Upon

---

25 Zimmermann 2014, p 449 ff.

26 The Commissioner for Human Rights was admitted to third party intervention ex Article 36 (3) ECHR.

27 The Directorate of Legal Affairs launched a multilateral conference with the European Association of Judges (EAJ) and the European Association of Judges for Democracy and Freedom (MEDEL) adopting a 'European Charter on the Statute of Judges' (1998).

proposal of the Secretary, the CCJE drafted a 'Report on judicial independence and impartiality in the Council of Europe member States in 2017'.[28] The standards of judicial independence were translated in guidelines of the CoM and resolutions of the Parliamentary Assembly (PACE) for the recruitment of judges.[29]

The Council of Europe recruited further 'independent experts' *inter alia* for the Committee ex Article 25 of the European Social Charter (1961), the European Committee for the Prevention of Torture (ECPT 1987), the European Commission against Racism and Intolerance (ECRI 1993), the European Commission for Democracy through Law under the Statute of 2002 (Venice Commission), the Group of experts on action against violence against women and domestic violence (GREVIO) under the Istanbul Convention (2011), the 'Group of Independent Experts' for the Congress of Local and Regional Authorities (2017), et cetera. They can deliver opinions in matters relevant for the ECtHR-jurisdiction to be presented through the Human Rights Commissioner.

The Venice Commission included judicial independence in the 'Report on the Rule of Law'[30] and delivered a 'Report on the Independence of Judicial Systems' (2010)[31] that makes reference to the ECtHR-case law, but not to the ECtHR as a case. The ECtHR has an observer status in the European Conference of Constitutional Courts as one of the 'supranational European Courts' (5 of Regulations) and participates in all World Conferences on Constitutional Justice, both hosted by the Venice Commission. The ECtHR itself launched a 'Superior Courts Network', today including 67 courts of 35 states, but not yet participated by the constitutional courts of Austria, Germany and Italy.

In conclusion, the Council of Europe increased independence of national judiciaries and of the ECtHR, building a European consensus on independence balanced by accountability for efficiency supported by soft-law standards, supranational monitoring institutions and networks. Legal positivists will warn that soft law is not legally binding,[32] while political realists have to acknowledge that the consensus is not merely judge-self-made but also based on overlapping cultural and economic interests.[33] The ongoing dialogues allow weak forms of informal *peer support* and self-coordination between courts. This does not lead to global juristocracy, but implies a shift from judicial independence to judicial interdependence.

---

[28] See the appendix of the 'Framework global action plan for judges in Europe' https://www.coe.int/fr/web/ccje/-/report-on-judicial-independence-and-impartiality-in-the-council-of-europe-member-states-in-2017 Accessed 1 April 2019.

[29] Resolutions 1082 (1996), 1295 (1996), 1200 (1999), 1646 (2009), 2002 (2014), recomendations 1429 (1996), 1649 (2009).

[30] CDL-AL (2001)003-rev, par. 41.

[31] CDL-AD (2010)004.

[32] Wittreck 2015, p 148 ff.

[33] Voigt 2017, p 51.

9.4 On the Autopoietic Value of the ECtHR Case Law

The ECtHR is a court for applications based on the entitlement to be heard by an independent, impartial and lawful judge ex Article 6(1) ECHR. One could argue that the Court itself is bound by this rule, but impartiality implies also a '*nemo judex in causa sua*' principle. Nevertheless, these international judges selected by democratic states produce judgments to be implemented under constitutions that protect judicial independence. Therefore the consistent case law of the ECtHR[34] regarding even supreme and constitutional courts of the Council of Europe-states could also apply at least indirectly to the ECtHR itself. It would be unrealistic to say that this case law was irrelevant for the amendments and has no value for the authority and legitimacy of the ECtHR itself.

Independence, impartiality and lawfulness under Article 6(1) ECHR indicate different principles and aspects distinguished by theory, but integrated in practice. Independence was first referred both to the parties of the case and to the executive power (*Neumeister* 1968, *Ringeisen* 1971) and based on a public confidence that 'justice must not only be done; it must also be seen to be done' (*Delcourt* 1971).[35] In order to distinguish judicial from administrative powers, independence associated even to legal rules defining terms of office, procedural guarantees and the power to determine rights and obligations are as elements constitutive for a functional concept of judiciary.

In *Crociani* (1980), the Commission (EComHR) decided 'that the same independence must be established in respect of the Legislature, i.e. Parliament.' The applications concerned a decision of the Italian Constitutional Court in a criminal jurisdiction over former ministers accused by a parliamentary committee of enquiry, taken with additional judges elected by the parliament and appointed for a fixed period with guarantees of ineligibility and immunity. They were 'subject to no authority and (could) exercise the power conferred on them without any interference by the Executive or Parliament'.[36] In an unpublished decision of 1981, the Commission considered parliamentary election of judges a common feature of various Council of Europe member states.[37] The election mechanism of the ECtHR was justified when *Le Compte* (1981) held that a term of office of six years was a sufficient 'further guarantee' of independence. In *Sramek* (1984), even a term of

[34] *Neumeister* 1968, *Delcourt* 1970, *Ringeisen* 1971, *De Wilde* 1971, *H. v. Belgium* 1979, *Schiesser* 1980, *Le Compte* 1981, *Piersack* 1982, *Sramek* 1984, *Campbell* 1984, *Benthem* 1985, *Ettl* 1987, *Belilos* 1988, *Langborger* 1989, *Padovani* 1993, *Bryan* 1995, *Findlay* 1997, *Lauko* 1998, *Incal* 1998, *Wille* 1999, *Silfirdingur* 1999, *Kyprianou* 2001, *Morris* 2002, *Kleyn* 2003, *Meznaric* 2005, *Flux* 2007, *Micallef* 2009, *Urban* 2010, *Maktouf* 2013, *Baka* 2016.

[35] Overruled in Borgers (1991), the participation without vote of the Belgian Procurateur Général to a deliberation of the Cour de Cassation was only criticised as 'unusual' and compared with the better system of the Court of Justice of the European Union. On impartiality, see Steinfatt 2012.

[36] EComHR, application no. 8603/79, 8722/79, 8723/79, 8729/79, 18 December 1980.

[37] EComHR, application no. 8866/80, 5 October 1981, quoted by Schermers and Kuijer 2005, application no. 12952/87, 6 November 1990.

three years was justified, at least if the judge was not remunerated. Such shorter terms were provided by Article 40 ECHR for the first composition of the ECtHR.

In *Piersack* (1982), judges needed a 'shield from outside pressures'. The confidence in independence and impartiality was compromised by acts of internal organisation that allowed a public prosecutor to sit as a judge when his department dealt with the case. *Sramek* (1984) added that 'appearances may also be of importance' and strengthened disciplinary accountability.

In contrast to the Austrian Constitutional Court, the ECtHR denied the independence of a civil servant acting as judge 'who is in a subordinate position, in terms of his duties and of the organisation of his service, vis-à-vis one of the parties'. That was the case of most judges who held only an additional office in the Court (until 1998). *Campbell & Fell* (1984) upheld the appointment by the executive of judges of a board that performed both adjudicatory and supervisory functions: 'to hold otherwise would mean that judges appointed by or on the advice of a Minister having responsibilities in the field of the administration of the courts were also not independent'. Self-administration became an indicator for judicial independence.

Independence required judicial discretion and neutrality when judges exercise freedom of expression. In *E. v. Switzerland* (1984), the Commission held 'for maintaining the authority and impartiality of the judiciary' in a democratic society necessitates a disciplinary sanction for political opinions on pending criminal proceedings expressed by a judge who claimed that 'for a party member to be elected judge and re-elected to the same office after six years, he must be politically active within the party to which he belongs'.[38] In *H. v. Belgium* (1987), the ECtHR accepted the appointment of lay judges by peers in disciplinary proceedings, but in *De Moor* (1993), the EComHR held that the French Conseil de l'Ordre did not offer sufficient impartiality as a judge on the admission to the bar.

The ECtHR was initially reluctant to face questions regarding independence and impartiality of constitutional and international judges. During the negotiations of the 11th protocol, the EComHR found in *Ruiz-Mateos* (1990) 'that it is not part of its function to exercise general scrutiny over the system for electing members of the Spanish Constitutional Court.' In *Wille* (1999), the ECtHR censured a letter of the prince of Liechtenstein that announced to the President of the Administrative Court the intention to not appoint him again to a public office because of his opinions expressed in a conference on the constitutional court's powers. *Kleyn* (2003) added that 'although the notion of the separation of powers between the political organs of government and the judiciary has assumed growing importance in the Court's case law […] neither Article 6 nor any other provision of the Convention requires States to comply with any theoretical constitutional concepts regarding the permissible limits of the powers' interaction'.

In *Meznaric* (2005), the prior involvement of a constitutional judge as a counsel in civil law litigation raised legitimate doubts in respect of its impartiality in the

[38] EComHR, application no. 10279/83, 7 May 1984.

constitutional review of the judgment. In *Steck-Risch* (2005), a member of the Constitutional Court of Liechtenstein could decide on an application against a judgment of the Administrative Court in which his law-office colleague acted as presiding judge, because no evidence for a specific friendship and for any form of dependence, be it professional, financial or hierarchical was offered. In *Maktouf* (2013), the ECtHR shared the view of the Constitutional Court of Bosnia-Herzegovina that the international judges in war crime chambers appointed by the High Representative were sufficiently independent, being recommended by 'the highest judicial figures in Bosnia and Herzegovina' and being required to perform their judicial duties in accordance with national law and rules of professional conduct.

In *Ivanovski* (2016), the applicant was President of the Constitutional Court of the former Yugoslav Republic of Macedonia when he was dismissed from office in lustration proceedings brought against him. The Court stated that an open letter of the Prime Minister accusing the applicant of having been a collaborator of the secret police of the former regime was detrimental for the appearance of impartiality. In *Baka* (2016), the ECtHR decided finally that the premature termination of the applicant's mandate as President of the Supreme Court of Hungary through a legislative act violated his freedom of expression and a principle of the rule of law that requires 'intervention of an authority independent of the executive and legislative powers in respect of every decision affecting the termination of office of a judge'.

This ECtHR case law has auto-poietic value and shows that the general principles of increasing judicial independence can be applied also to constitutional and international judges, but it cannot surrogate a rational system of rules defining independence and accountability compatible to the ECHR.

9.5 How Rights and Duties Safeguard Personal Independence

From an analytical legal point of view, independence and accountability can be construed as an individual status of personal rights and duties of service of the judge and as institutional positions of the court, aspects that are intertwined but shall be well distinguished. The independence of the tribunal (Article 6(1)) is a necessary condition for the independence of the judge (Article 21(3)), but not a sufficient one, it being possible that internal interferences and hegemonies and external pressures more easily bear on single judges than on the Court.[39]

[39] European Network of Councils for the Judiciary, 'Independence, Accountability and Quality of the Judiciary', available at http://njb.nl/Uploads/2017/6/encj-report-ia-2017-adopted-ga.pdf Accessed 1 April 2019.

Individual independence is in the interest of the functioning of the Court and a service related duty declared in the resolution on judicial ethics of 2008,[40] but the judge is always personally entitled to all rights and freedoms of the ECHR and granted by the national legal order including *habeas corpus*, privacy, freedom of conscience, free speech, travel and association (*status negativus*), health care, work, salary and pension (*status positivus*), the right to access selection procedures, *jus ad officium* of the elected judge and access to justice in the relevant legal order (*status activus*). Personal rights need to be defended personally, but legal defence could allow other judges to investigate and collide with the duty of the court to protect the judge's and the institution's independence.

Personal independence shall be a cultural outcome of the 'high moral character' and acknowledged qualifications and competence (Article 21(1) ECHR). Sitting in the court 'in their individual capacity' (Article 21(2)), judges do neither represent the governments that advanced their candidature nor the state that is claimed to violate human rights.[41] Earlier empirical studies found that ECtHR-judges do not necessarily, but more frequently vote in favour of the fatherland, but at that time re-election was still not excluded.[42] A specific incompatibility was introduced for single-judge formations to examine applications against the State in respect of which that judge has been elected (Article 26(3)), but *ad hoc* judges are still allowed (Article 26(4), 28(3) ECHR).

Qualifications and competences are presumed for the whole term. The fixed retirement age of 70 years (Article 23(2)) is a synthesis of most domestic rules that distinguish judges from other public servants, not a permission to exclude candidates over 61 years[43] or to prefer more ambitious younger candidates. If 'senior' is also *sanior pars*, the age could be on the contrary an indicator for better qualification and more competence and offer some Presbyterian charisma to the Court. The 15th protocol preferred fixed retirement, a requirement that judges be aged less than 65 at the time of the call for nominations by PACE. Raising life expectations in the ageing societies and a gradual evolution of retirement rules could oblige to revise and adapt these rules from time to time in order to avoid discrimination based on age.

Incompatibilities protect both independence and full-time office of the judge (Article 21(3)). Rule 4 specifies that judges cannot engage 'in any political or administrative activity or any professional activity which is incompatible', but leaves the decision on what is effectively incompatible to the President and, only in

---

[40] 'In the exercise of their judicial functions, judges shall be independent of all external authority or influence. They shall refrain from any activity or membership of an association, and avoid any situation, that may affect confidence in their independence.' Similar 'The Burgh House Principles on the Independence of the International Judiciary', available at https://www.ucl.ac.uk/international-courts/sites/international-courts/files/burgh_final_21204.pdf Accessed 1 April 2019.

[41] AS/Jur (2014) 17 'Reinforcement of the independence of the European Court of Human Rights'.

[42] Voeten 2009 and 2011, p 70 ff.

[43] Zimmermann 2014, p 497 ff.

cases of disagreement, to the Court.[44] The judge has the duty to give notice to the President of facts relevant for disqualifications provided by Rule 28(2) – amended in 2002, 2004 and 2006 – in situations of personal interest or prior involvement in the case, public expression of opinions 'objectively capable of adversely affecting' impartiality, or when 'independence or impartiality may legitimately be called into doubt'. The Judicial Ethics explain that confidence in independence and impartiality could be compromised by conflicts of interest, gifts and honours and additional activities such as individual advisory opinions rendered *extra moenia*, the exercise of academic powers in examinations, recruitment procedures and peer review. A strict interpretation could exclude statements in parliaments or public celebrations managed by governments unless the authorisation is not justified through a specific mandate of representation of the Court for purposes of institutional accountability.

9.6 Mechanisms that Grant Personal Accountability

ECtHR judges shall be entitled during their term to the privileges and immunities provided for in Article 40 of the Statute of Council of Europe (Article 51 ECHR) as defined by the Sixth Protocol to the General Agreement on Privileges and Immunities of the Council of Europe (1996). This international immunity is 'not for the personal benefit of the individuals themselves but in order to safeguard the independent exercise of their functions'. Even if minor compared to the immunity of a judge of the International Court of Justice, it is extended to spouses and minor children (Article 1) and beyond the expiration of the term (Article 2). Diplomatic passports should be issued. Post-term immunity was at stake in the case of the Moldavian judge *Tudor Pantiru* (2001) who refused to justify in a separate vote the position of the government and was put under a criminal proceeding regarding the property of his house in order to exclude re-election. The President granted first an administrative job in the ECtHR and later a nomination for constitutional judge in Bosnia-Herzegovina and Kosovo.[45]

The aforementioned protocol allows the plenary court to waive the immunity of judges. The Court is under a duty to waive it in any case where, in its opinion, the immunity would impede the course of justice, and where it can be waived without prejudice to the purpose for which the immunity is accorded. No procedural rule has been established whether a waiver can be requested directly by national judges, by the ECtHR judge involved or only by the national government to the General

[44] Article 4 amended in 2010 precludes representation in ECtHR proceedings for a period of two years from expiration.

[45] Engel 2003, p 130. Pantiru became President of the Constitutional Court of Moldavia.

Secretary. In a precedent, the Court requested a national government 'to indicate whether they have grounds for asking the Court to waive a judge's immunity.'[46]

The judge can decide at any time to resign (Rule 6) or withdraw from taking part in sittings until an official request of waiver has been decided. A procedure of removal under Article 23(4) ECHR can be started internally and a majority of two-thirds can decide that the judge 'has ceased to fulfil the required conditions.' All procedures regarding the request of waiver, the temporary withdrawal and the removal have to respect the conventional rights, including the right of the judge to be heard (Rule 7) and to have a fair trial by the plenary Court as an independent and impartial judge. Similar proceedings of self-purification exist also in national constitutional courts and provide a limited personal accountability to the benefit of the Court.

Could this happen if the judge does not work enough or with sufficient diligence? Full employment is a required condition, but the new management strategies of the Court do not provide any quantitative and qualitative standards for individual work. The rapporteur of the registry supervised by the President and the colleagues in the committee could help, but create internal dependencies and asymmetries between more and less efficient judges.[47] The case allocation power of the President aims at a 'fair distribution' of workload (Article 52) and allows to take into account specific personal shortcomings, but cannot avoid peer pressure and reputation stress. 'Judicial ethics' could justify further peer pressure and presidential investigation mechanisms.

In any case, judges are accountable to the Court, but could also give account to their governments, for example through separate opinions and criticising the Court at least at the end of the mandate. Personal independence does not need golden pensions and privileges, but adequate social security. The ECtHR welcomed the Resolution 'On the status and conditions of service of judges of the ECtHR'[48] that provided their affiliation to the contribution based pension, medical and social insurance schemes for staff members of the Council of Europe.[49] The CoM called upon States 'to address appropriately' the situation of judges after expiration of the term of office. Social rights to work and social protection – family included – have to be respected and any perception should be avoided that the social security or career of former ECtHR judges could be conditioned by their judgments. A report of the Committee on Legal Affairs and Human Rights (2014) urged for more flexible solutions and recommended the sending state to assist former judges in finding employment upon the expiration of their mandate.

---

[46] Statement of the ECtHR President 19 October 2011.

[47] Follesdal 2017, p 500.

[48] CoM Res (2009) 5.

[49] Engel 2010, p 148 ff.

9.7 How the Court's Powers Grant Institutional Independence from the Council of Europe and Member States

The institutional independence of the ECtHR as a permanent court requires further structural guarantees against interferences of institutions of the Council of Europe and member States, counterbalanced by forms of public accountability. The institutional foundations and the subjection of the ECtHR to law have stable conventional sources that can be changed only by unanimity of (majorities in) Council in Europe states in coherence with supreme constitutional principles, even without referenda. The legal framework has been frequently changed, but leaves a modest normative autonomy to the Court.[50]

All discretionary powers of the plenary Court under Article 25 ECHR can be functional to independence, including those of internal rulemaking, (re-)electing (vice-)presidents for the representation and direction of works and Court-administration (Rule 9), setting up Chambers (sections) and electing their Presidents and the (Deputy) Registrars.

By virtue of the obligatory participation of the national judge, the competence of the judicial formations is sufficiently pre-determined by law, but the rules of allocation of the cases are not sufficiently transparent and explained and the CoM decides at the request of the ECtHR whether to reduce exceptionally to five the number of chamber members (Article 26). The Court rules define further details of organisation and procedure, including the calculation of term of office, incompatible activities, resignation and dismissal and the election of the Court's president. The President can give further general practice directions binding for the judges (Rule 32). The Court can fix general criteria for the determination of the order of dealing with cases that have been laid down in a priority catalogue (Rule 41).

Independence is limited through administrative powers directed by the Secretary General. There have been tensions between Secretary Schwimmer and President Wildhaber regarding the power over the administrative staff of the court.[51] Interferences can be mitigated by the president's co-decision power on the appointment of the officials of the Registry (Rule 18(3)) and the plenary court's power to dismiss the Registrar (Rule 15(2)). A PACE-document observed that the policy of non-renewability of the B-lawyers contracts in the registry could generate further risks of dependency for the Court.[52] The court could not avoid to be subject to the jurisdiction of the administrative tribunal of the CoE and to be represented in this jurisdiction by the Secretary. Finally, the Secretary may request a member State to 'furnish an explanation of the manner in which its internal law ensures the effective implementation of the provisions of the Convention' (Article 52). This

[50] Lambert Abdelgawad 2017a, p 246 ff.

[51] Engel 2003; De Boer-Buquicchio 2003.

[52] AS/Jur (2014) 17.

discretionary power could defend judicial independence, but interfere with pending proceedings or adopted judgments.

The most critical issues to be considered are the financial aspects. The expenditure of the Court, legal aid included, shall be borne by the Council of Europe (Article 50). Only costs for translations (Rule 34(3)) and for witnesses, experts or persons under detention (Rule A 5) can be transferred to others. The ECtHR does not have its own budget like some constitutional court and no specific provision in the financial regulations of the CoM allows it to make proposals for additional funds.[53] Financial independence is safeguarded only by informal consultations in a Liaison Committee of the CoM and good customs in budgeting practices.

The ECtHR is subject to the internal and external auditing system of the Council of Europe with an internal auditor appointed by the Secretary General – whose reports are reviewed by national parliaments – and an external report of a national audit office chosen by the CoM. The auditing through independent authorities favours quantitative evaluation over qualitative criteria for the court's performance and shows how independence can be combined with accountability.[54]

9.8 Whether Institutional Accountability in Europe Can Avoid National Veto Plays

What happens if countries like Turkey or Russia threaten to stop financing the Council of Europe and executing judgments? The Copenhagen Declaration (2018) stresses 'the importance of retaining a sufficient budget for the Court, as well as the Department for the Execution of Judgments, to solve present and future challenges' (para 52) and calls upon the States Parties to 'consider making voluntary contributions to the Human Rights Trust Fund and to the Court's special account' (para 53), but the ECtHR does not have equal distance from unwilling and voluntary contributors. In the long run, the original idea that recourses need to be costless for all, not just in cases of (risk of) poverty but even for legal persons, could be revised at least in favour of a punitive tax for abuse of the right to make applications.

The mechanisms of institutional accountability designed by the law of the Council of Europe seem to prefer weak forms of explanatory accountability towards a European public opinion to the aforesaid stronger forms of national resistance. They are based first of all on the rule of publicity of hearings. Publicity can be excluded only for interests of public order and justice or national security, to be verified by the Court (Rule 63). The representation of applicants and Contracting parties as well as the interlocution of third party interventions even from civil society (Rule 44) produce not always a well-informed European public opinion.

---

53 Zimmermann 2014, p 490 ff.

54 Critical Lamber Abdelgawad 2017b.

Nevertheless, the judgments have to answer all of them in order to prevent repetitive applications and to improve legitimacy.

'Answerability' inspires the duty to give reasons for judgments and decisions on admissibility (Article 45(1)). The customary rituals of annual reports presented in press conferences, press releases and on the website produce practices that allow supervision and critics at least within a special professional and academic public sphere. The separate opinion is a special form of accountability similar to 'peer review' that safeguards not only the freedom of conscience and personal independence of single judges (Article 45(2)). If supported not only by academic comments, the dissenting opinion could condition judge selection and become a future majority opinion of the Court.

Another weak form of transnational accountability derives from the standard setting and monitoring powers of PACE. Resolution 1685/2009 encourages the ECtHR 'to consider giving priority to applications pertaining to alleged violations of the independence of judges and politically motivated abuses of the criminal justice system', a friendly interference in the power of case management. Assembly members should not be allowed to submit written questions on pending procedures of the ECtHR, but all committees shall 'follow the activities of, and maintain working relations' with the ECtHR. The terms of reference of the Committee on Legal Affairs and Human Rights refer to 'all matters concerning the human rights treaties and mechanisms of the CoE', 'the state of human rights and fundamental freedoms and the rule of law in Europe' and the 'functioning of national and international judicial institutions'.[55] A 'Sub-Committee on the implementation of judgments of the ECtHR' has been set up. The Court's President can be invited as a guest speaker and held recently an 'exchange of views' with the standing committees, suggesting new forms of mediation with national parliaments in order to prevent conflicts over subsidiarity: 'To fulfil its mission, the Court needs your Assembly'.

National mechanisms of accountability could lead to a refusal of Contracting Parties to implement judgments like *Greens* and *MT* on the right to vote for serving prisoners in UK. Like some constitutional court, the ECtHR has no power to command or use coercion and must respect the principle of subsidiarity when indicating individual or general measures to be taken, but risks to face repetitive applications and noncompliance under the principle of subsidiarity. The supervision power of the CoM (Article 46 ECHR) as revised by protocol 14 includes now the faculty to refer with a majority of two thirds questions of 'interpretation of the judgment' or of 'failure to fulfil' the obligations deriving from a final judgment. But when a simple majority finds a violation and a third of the members of the CoM decide that no question of failure should be referred to the ECtHR, is it not 'condemned' to a silent loss of authority and a trumping state sovereignty? In such a scenario, the confidence not only in the unaccountable State, but even in the independence of the ECtHR and in European accountability could suffer.

---

[55] Resolutions 1842 (2011) and 2002 (2014).

The accounts of former judges addressed to the public sphere of a member state can accompany initiatives for amendments and threats of exit through denunciation (Article 58), if not incompatible with existing constitutional commitments to human rights protection. National legislators and constitutional courts can also try to strengthen subsidiarity and sustain the primacy of fundamental principles of the national constitution.[56]

In order to avoid shortcomings, the Brighton Declaration (2012) encouraged 'the States parties, the CoM and the Court to work together to find ways to resolve the large numbers of applications arising from systemic issues identified by the Court'. The recent Court's Bureaus observation on the draft Copenhagen declaration highlights 'the need for dialogue and participation', expecting them to be intensified through the new advisory opinion procedures and warning that dialogues at the political level should respect the Court's independence and the binding character of its judgments. Dialogue remains a concept open for transnational forms of accountability and consensus building, but the judicial dialogues favoured by the last protocols and the dialogues with politicians have a different nature and impact on judicial independence. At the moment, the accountability of the ECtHR towards the member states has been institutionalised mainly in the procedure of judge (s)election.

9.9 How ECtHR Judges Get (S)elected

The parliamentary election of ECtHR judges under the 'one state one judge' rule (Article 20 ECHR) is a ritual that symbolizes the will of the States to be bound by the judgments and serves both expectations of personal independence and of a quasi-democratic accountability of the institution. The prohibition of re-election excludes any personal political responsibility, but the performance of a leaving judge and the Court can be evaluated and compared with elements of the qualification of the successor. And the governmental power over the presentation of candidates is still perceived as a risk to get less independent judges and as a chance to influence the Court's performance.

From a comparative point of view, the legal mechanism of the election of ECtHR judges is a mix between traditions of international judge selection by governments and constitutional judge election by parliaments. The advisory panel offers a third model of technocratic co-optation characteristic for most common judges in Europe and for the ECJ.[57] The mix aims to combine advantages, but risks to sum their disadvantages.

The aim of the mechanism is to find judges 'of high moral character' that 'either possess the qualifications required for appointment to high judicial office or be

---

[56] Lopez Guerra 2017, p 401 ff.

[57] Bobek 2015, p 281 ff.

jurisconsults of recognised competence' (Article 21). These concise but open concepts can neither be observed and measured in nature, nor presumed through sacralising rituals, but need to lead an international culture based on the pluralism of values, traditions and creativity in human rights. The promotion of judges and politicians could favour activism, the recruitment of diplomats and government advisers restraint. The Strasburg culture of selection and election of judges shows reasonable balancing, but was criticised for lack of transparency and accountability.[58]

The election being a competence of the Assembly (Article 22 ECHR), the aforesaid soft law documents developed standards and customs, including criteria for gender balance.[59] An advisory opinion of the ECtHR held in 2008 that 'the task of electing judges to the Court necessarily entails the ability to assess the candidates'. For this purpose the Assembly may devise 'a standard curriculum vitae for candidates, whom it also invites to take part in personal interviews before an ad hoc sub-committee set up for that purpose' and 'take account of additional criteria which it considers relevant for the purposes of choosing between the candidates put forward by a Contracting Party and may, as it has done in a bid to ensure transparency and foreseeability, incorporate those criteria in its resolutions and recommendations'. The opinion accepted as the required 'sufficient knowledge of at least one of the two official languages' – not yet specified by reference to the European Framework of Reference for Languages – but demanded for the gender-balance some exception if 'a Contracting Party has taken all the necessary and appropriate steps with a view to ensuring that the list contains a candidate of the under-represented sex, but without success, and especially where it has followed the Assembly's recommendations advocating an open and transparent procedure involving a call for candidatures'.

The criteria listed for the CV do not require certification, but reflect aspects of the court's performance and legitimacy. The 'knowledge and awareness of European Convention jurisprudence' could be derived from prior professional experience or from a training under the 'European Programme for human rights education for law professionals' (HELP Programme). The 'general legal knowledge and experience' refers to both national and international law, proved in temporal dimensions congruent to the standards of judges of last resort. Experiences as international human rights expert or constitutional judge should be privileged. 'Intellectual and analytical ability, decisiveness and authority', 'communication and listening skills', 'maturity and soundness of judgments' relating to preceding judicial activity should be evaluated only by structures that fully respect judicial independence. 'Understanding of people and society, courtesy and humanity, commitment to public service, conscientiousness and diligence' refers not only to national culture and society, but includes political and intercultural sensibility and

[58] Limbach 2003; Voeten 2009 and 2011; Schabas 2015, pp 658 ff; Lemmens 2015, pp 95 ff; Kosar 2015, pp 161 ff; Baade 2017, pp 481 ff.

[59] Resolution 1366 (2004), modified by resolutions 1426 (2005), 1627 (2008) and 1841 (2011).

competences in comparative legal and political sciences. The future judges' conscience has finally to interiorize 'integrity and independence, fairness and impartiality'.

All skills need to be assessed in a rational and fair election procedure with four sub-proceedings: (1) the nomination of candidates, (2) the examination of the advisory panel and the committee (3) the vote and (4) the taking up of office. At least one year before the term of a judge ends, the Secretary General calls the State affected to submit a list of three candidates and their curricula vitae within four months. The CoM-guidelines on selection of candidates (CM(2012)40) recommend sub-procedures of eliciting, interviews carried out by a national selection body and publication of the final list, but the selection procedure is governed only by national rules that could prescribe participation of a judicial council in order to prevent governmental interference in judicial structures. The CoM has few weeks for considering the list and sending it back if not fully complying with the requirements. Since 2011, an Advisory Panel[60] deciding by consensus or qualified majority (5 of 7) shall inform the national government whether candidates meet the criteria stipulated in Article 21 and can ask additional information and clarifications, also on facts spontaneously delivered by third parties. In case of negative advice (7 of 67 cases), the government is expected to submit new ones and always provided so. If the final list is submitted to PACE, it will be examined by the Committee on the Election of Judges to the ECtHR. Its 20 members shall have appropriate knowledge or practical experience in the legal field, interview all candidates and make a report with a recommendation decided by majority in secret ballot. A decision to reject a list of candidates or to admit a single-sex list of candidates requires a two-thirds majority of votes cast. In the light of the Committee's recommendations, the Assembly elects the judge with the absolute majority of votes cast, otherwise in a second ballot with relative majority. The office is taken up with the oath.

A significant exception is the appointment of ad-hoc judges when the elected judge is unable to sit or exempted has been delegated by the 14th protocol to the President of the Court, but a study of the Committee on Legal Affairs and Human Rights in 2011 criticized that the lists submitted by the States Parties are not controlled by PACE. The representation of the same list and a reappointment seem to be not precluded.

A 'Report on the Process of Selection and Election of Judges of the ECtHR' presented recently by the CDDH and welcomed by the Copenhagen Declaration (2018) has criticised a sensible lack of interaction between panel and committee. The panel-members should be allowed to be present at the interviews and illustrate their views in order to raise the quality of the reasons that support the recommendation. The interviews are too short (30 min), need better preparation and

[60] Members are geographically and gender balanced chosen by the CoM among members of the highest national courts, former judges of international courts and other lawyers of recognised competence.

effective presence of Committee members, with a composition undersized and unable to promote democratic legitimacy. If the Committee would be enabled to restrict the list to two candidates, a revision of Article 22 ECHR would be necessary. The Report does not offer a solution for the problem of small states to find three good candidates. Even the possible impact of EU accession on the judge selection has not yet been addressed. A participation of national parliaments as keepers of democratic accountability is not encouraged and the report does not mention other problems well known for parliamentary elections in constitutional courts. What happens if the time constraints do not work or more time for political compromise is needed? And what if a presidential government prefers to promote just friends? If criminal proceedings or media campaigns are started against candidates? If committee members transfer the discussion on social media? The Court's legitimacy is still ensured by the simple fact that judges get elected for interest of state reputation and can take care of their independence, giving account through fair and reasonable decisions. The best accountability could be realized *de facto* if they would be selected and their judgments be rendered in the name of a European humanity, but this is still a utopia.[61]

9.10 Conclusions

The general principles of judicial independence and legal accountability apply to international as well as to constitutional judges, but are concretised and balanced in different interdependent contexts. In the history of European constitutionalism, the ideal of independence prevailed over political accountability, but was implemented and shared only in the last century when constitutional and international courts were institutionalized. Judicial independence was gradually implemented through conventional and soft law of the Council of Europe and an ECtHR case law having an autopoietic value. Personal independence and accountability of ECtHR judges have been strengthened, but after expiration of their mandate they appear still less protected than constitutional judges. Institutional independence of the ECtHR is under pressure, because the increasing demand for human rights justice requires more cooperation with Council of Europe administration and member states. The dialogues envisaged by the last protocols and by the EU accession to the ECHR could lead from independence to interdependence. The rules of explanatory accountability of the ECtHR are devoted to ideals of a European public opinion, but national veto players have not yet been domesticated. Not yet sufficiently transparent procedures of (s)election of judges are balancing expectations of personal independence and institutional accountability. The legitimacy of the ECtHR derives still from a strong demand for subsidiary international human rights protection for all and from the

[61] Häberle 2016, p 95.

need of States to have a good reputation.[62] Nevertheless, the European consensus on stronger judicial independence balanced by weaker forms of accountability and the public confidence in European judges might not be eternal when populism threatens the future of rights universalism and ignores the need for reputation.

References

Andenas M (2007) A European Perspective on Judicial Independence and Accountability. The International Lawyer 1:1–20

Avazzi dal Frate P (1999) Il giudice naturale. Viella, Rome

Baade B (2017) Der Europäische Gerichtshof für Menschenrechte als Diskurswächter. Springer, Berlin

Benvenisti E, Downs G (2017) Between Fragmentation and Democracy? The Role of National and International Courts. Cambridge University Press, Cambridge

Bobek M (2015) Epilogue: Searching for the European Herkules. In: Bobek M (ed) Selecting Europe's Judges. Oxford University Press, Oxford, pp 279–309

De Boer-Buquicchio M (2003) Klarstellung zum Status des Europäischen Gerichtshofs für Menschenrechte und seine Beziehungen zum Europarat. Europäische Grundrechte Zeitschrift (EuGRZ) 561–563.

Engel N (2010) Strukturreformen zur Entlastung des EGMR. EuGRZ 37:148–149

Engel N (2003) Status, Ausstattung und Personalhoheit des Inter-Amerikanischen und des Europäischen Gerichtshofs für Menschenrechte. EuGRZ 30:122–133

Favoreu L (2002) Les Cours de Luxembourg et de Strasbourg ne sont pas des cours constitutionnelles. In: Mélanges en l'honneur de Louis Dubouis. Dalloz, Paris, pp 35–45

Follesdal A (2017) Independent yet accountable: Stress test lessons for the European Court of Human Rights. Maastricht Journal of European and Comparative Law 24: 484–510

Greer L, Wildhaber L (2012) Revisiting the Debate About 'Constitutionalising' the European Court of Human Rights. Human Rights Law Review 12:655–687

Grove T (2018) The Origins (And Fragility) of Judicial Independence. Vanderbilt Law Review 71:465–545

Guarnieri C (2013) Judicial independence in Europe: Threat or resource for democracy? Representation 49:347–359

Häberle P (2016) Vergleichende Verfassungstheorie und Verfassungspraxis. Duncker & Humblot, Berlin

Hayo B, Voigt S (2014) Mapping Constitutionally Safeguarded Judicial Independence — A Global Survey. Journal of Empirical Legal Studies 11:159–195

Kosar D (2015) Selecting Strasbourg Judges. A Critique. In: Bobek M (ed) Selecting Europe's Judges. Oxford University Press, Oxford, pp 120–161

Kotuby C, Sobota L (2017) General Principles of Law and International Due Process. Oxford University Press, New York

Lambert Abdelgawad E (2017a) European Court of Human Rights. In: Schmahl S, Breuer M (eds) The Council of Europe. Oxford University Press, Oxford, pp 227–268

Lambert Abdelgawad E (2017b) Measuring the Judicial Performance of the European Court of Human Rights. International Journal for Court Administration 8:20–29

Lemmens K (2015) (S)electing Judges for Strasbourg. A (Dis)appointing Process? In: Bobek M (ed) Selecting Europe's Judges. Oxford University Press, Oxford, pp 95–119

[62] Voigt 2017, pp 527 ff.

Limbach J et al (2003) Judicial Independence: Law and Practice of Appointments to the European Court of Human Rights. Interrights
Lopez Guerra L (2017) Dialogues between the Strasbourg Courts and National Courts. In: Müller A (ed) Judicial Dialogues and Human Rights. Cambridge University Press, Cambridge, pp 401–409
Pasquino P (2010) Prolegomena to a Theory of Judicial Power. Revista de Estudos Constitucionais, Hermeneutica e Teoria do Direito 2:193–200
Pizzorusso A (2002) Il patrimonio costituzionale europeo. Il Mulino, Bologna
Posner E, Yoo JC (2005) Judicial Independence in International Tribunals. California Law Review 93:1–74
Schabas W (2015) The European Convention on Human Rights. Oxford University Press, Oxford
Schermers H, Kuijer M (2005) Right to Lawful Judge. In: Weber A, Schermers H (eds) Fundamental Rights in Europe and North America: European Court of Human Rights. Nijhoff, Leiden
Schmitter P (2007) Political Accountability in 'Real-Existing' Democracies: Meaning and Mechanisms. European University Institute, Florence
Steinfatt G (2012) Die Unparteilichkeit des Richters in Europa im Lichte der Rechtsprechung des Europäischen Gerichtshofes für Menschenrechte. Nomos, Baden-Baden
Tushnet M (2013) Judicial Accountability in a Comparative Perspective. In: Maforth N, Leyland P (eds) Accountability in the Contemporary Constitution. Oxford University Press, Oxford, pp 57–74
Voeten E (2009) The Impartiality of International Judges: Evidence from the European Court of Human Rights. American Political Science Review 102:417–433
Voeten E (2011) Politics, Judicial Behaviour and Institutional Design. In: Cristofferson J, Rask Madsen M (eds) The European Court of Human Rights between Law and Politics. Oxford University Press, Oxford, pp 61–76
Voigt S (2017) The independence of international courts – making reputation work? Maastricht Journal of European and Comparative Law 24:511–530
Von Bogdandy A, Venzke I (2014) In wessen Namen? Suhrkamp, Berlin
Wildhaber L (2007) The European Court of Human Rights: The Past, The Present, The Future
Wittreck F (2015) Dritte Gewalt im Wandel – veränderte Anforderungen an Legitimität und Effektivität? Veröffentlichungen der Vereinigung Deutscher Staatsrechtslehrer 74:115–167
Zimmermann D (2014) The Independence of International Courts. Nomos, Baden-Baden

Jörg Luther is Professor of Public Law at the University of Eastern Piedmont Amedeo Avogadro. He holds a German and Italian PhD, teaches courses in Constitutional Law and Fundamental Rights in Europe at the University of Torino, directs a PhD programme on public, social and cultural institutions and has published on comparative public law, constitutional law and history, constitutional justice and fundamental rights, regional law and local autonomy, and bicameralism and the judicial system.

Chapter 10
Accountability Through Transparency and the Role of the Court of Justice of the European Union

Marios Costa

Contents

Abstract It is often alleged that the EU's decision-making is insufficiently transparent and that accountability deficits are even growing, something which compromises the Union's overall legitimacy. In this regard, the EU's access to documents regime can be considered as an on-going process capable of securing, through a set of binding rules, open performance of the decision-making process. It is here that the role of the Court of Justice of the EU (CJEU) comes into play. Tasked with interpreting the access regime, the CJEU imposed boundaries on the broad derogations to the right. Yet, in terms of accountability, the transparency friendly line of case law has creatively been interpreted in a way that now restricts the access right per se. On the whole, the chapter concludes that the CJEU, with all due respect, contributed to the accountability deficit of the EU's access to documents regime.

M. Costa (✉)
City, University of London, London, UK
e-mail: marios.costa.1@city.ac.uk

Hirsch Ballin, Van der Schyff & Stremler (eds.), *European Yearbook of Constitutional Law 2019*, European Yearbook of Constitutional Law 1,
https://doi.org/10.1007/978-94-6265-359-7_10

Keywords access to documents · accountability deficit · Court of Justice of the European Union · EU law · Regulation 1049/2001 · transparency

10.1 Introduction

This chapter examines the EU access to documents regime from the point of accountability. It argues that the latest judicial tendency creates a substantial accountability gap in the area. To substantiate this, the first part of the chapter examines whether the judicial process before the CJEU qualifies as a fully-fledged accountability relation whereas the EU organs can be held accountable by the CJEU on how they implemented the Transparency Regulation.[1] The chapter then outlines the EU's transparency framework and examines whether the contribution of the CJEU strengthens public accountability. The chapter adopts a historical perspective by examining the Code of Conduct of access to EU documents introduced in 1993 and considers the *initial* contribution of the EU Courts with regards to transparency. Additionally, the chapter examines the developments introduced by the Transparency Regulation. Finally, the chapter argues that as regards non-legislative documents, the net effect of judicial developments is to reduce the standards for public accountability.

10.2 Accountability

This section focuses on whether the judicial process before the Court can qualify as an accountability relation. Observing the contribution of the CJEU with regards to transparency, as well as assessing whether the EU's access to documents regime suffers from accountability deficits, along with examining alternatives on how to mitigate these deficits, presupposes a clear understanding of the meaning of accountability. This section therefore begins by explaining accountability to understand what is, and what is not, meant by the concept. The definition adopted and explained here is used to measure accountability (deficits) in relation to the EU's access to documents rules and conversely highlights why more accountability is being called for in this area.

Accountability is a term frequently used in EU documents: 'we live in the age of accountability, wherever one looks there is a discussion and debate over accountability';[2] the word 'crops up everywhere performing all manner of analytical and

[1] Regulation (EC) No 1049/2001 regarding public access to European Parliament, Council and Commission documents [2001] OJ L145/43. See also: Adamski 2009, 2012; Alemanno and Stefan 2014; Rossi and Silva 2017.

[2] Fisher 2004, p 495. See also: Arnull and Wincott 2002; Broberg 2002; Curtin 2000, 2013; Curtin and Hart 2010.

rhetorical tasks and carrying most of the burdens of democratic "governance."'[3] In its fundamental sense, accountability means being answerable for one's actions to some authority and, if necessary, having to suffer sanctions for actions not in accordance with the mandate granted by that authority. This form of accountability can be broken down into four major elements: the setting of standards, the obtaining of an account, the judging of such an account and a decision about the consequences that arise from such a judgment.[4] A suitable definition of the term is provided by Bovens where he describes accountability as a 'relationship between an actor and a forum, in which the actor has an obligation to explain and to justify his or her conduct, the forum can pose questions and pass judgment, and the actor may face consequences.'[5] In other words: 'A is accountable to B when A is obliged to inform B about A's (past or future) actions and decisions, to justify them, and to suffer punishment in the case of eventual misconduct.'[6]

Accountability is also closely related with the notion of independence. Indeed, most commentators focus on the challenge of finding the fine balance between accountability and independence. In doing so, the literature considers independence as a factor or rather as a threat which may have a negative impact upon accountability. The apparent consensus is that accountability cannot co-exist with independence and that independence overload leads to a non-accountable agent.[7] Similarly, when the accountability forum is constantly steering the behaviour of the agent the accountability gap is drastically diminished. Yet, the autonomy of the agent under these circumstances is equally reduced and the outcome is to have an 'accountable' but rather dependent agent. I therefore argue for the contrary and I consider that the person or the body under scrutiny, the actor, needs to be accountable and simultaneously independent throughout the decision-making process. Following from this, the accountability relationship can be effective so long as the delegator does not directly interfere in the decentralized decision-making process. After all, accountability can be meaningful if the agent takes decisions by relying on highly complicated and technical scientific knowledge and expertise.[8] When the actions of the agent are directed by the delegator, the *raison d'être* of delegation defeats its purpose. In consequence, I consider that conceptually accountability and independence are interrelated terms and not mutually exclusive. Overall, the whole essence of accountability calls for independence from politics while the actor executes the delegated tasks.

What role do the EU Courts play to the state of accountability in the EU? To address this, we need to focus on the field of access to documents since accountability's alter ego, transparency, ensures and requires accessibility of all the relevant

[3] Mulgan 2000, p 555.
[4] Davies 2001. See also: Mulgan 2003; Schedler 1997; Tomkins 1999; Vesterdorf 1998.
[5] Bovens 2007, p 447.
[6] Schedler 1997, p 17.
[7] Geradin 2005, p 231; Busuioc 2009; Costa and Peers 2012, 2016; Costa 2017.
[8] Busuioc 2013.

information by taking decisions out of the backroom.[9] In consequence, access to documents rules become a pre-requisite of the accountability relationship.[10] It has been argued, rightly, that 'no society can be considered truly democratic if its citizens are denied the possibility of vindicating their legal rights in judicial proceedings, whether against the oppressive acts of a powerful legislature – even a democratically elected one – or against the unlawful practices of an overweening administration.'[11] As a consequence, the EU Courts can play a crucial role in public accountability by bringing transparency cases to public attention. It has been noted that:

> The fact that the citizens are aware of what the administration is doing is a guarantee that it will operate properly. Supervision by those who confer legitimacy on the public authorities encourages them to be effective in adhering to their [citizens'] initial will and can thereby inspire their confidence, which is a guarantee of public content as well as the proper functioning of the democratic system.[12]

Overall, I consider that the status of accountability in the EU can only be properly understood through the lens of the access to documents rules. The public's right to hold decision-makers into account, by assessing the impact of the activities of the EU and by commenting upon those activities, can only effectively be exercised if there are rules in place which allow people to access the relevant information. 'After all, without information on what decisions are being taken and by whom, it will not be possible for various accountability forums to hold actors to account'.[13] In this way, transparency enhances awareness and understanding of the ultimate objectives that the decision-making processes aim to achieve.[14] 'Without maximum access to government information, citizens have no way effectively to evaluate and monitor the process by which laws and policies get made and enforced'.[15] In the words of the judiciary, 'the widest possible access to documents (…) is essential to enable citizens to carry out genuine and efficient monitoring of the exercise of the powers vested in the [Union] institutions (…)'.[16] Accountability is now clearly set out in the second recital in the preamble of the Transparency Regulation which states that 'openness (…) guarantees that the administration enjoys greater legitimacy and is more effective and more *accountable* to the citizen in a democratic system'. Consequently, the constitutional role of the Court to interpret the access to documents rules has a significant impact upon the status of

[9] Fisher 2004, p 503.

[10] Frost 2003, p 87; Curtin and Leino 2017; Curtin and Meijer 1995; Davis 1999, 2000.

[11] Mancini and Keeling 1994, p 181.

[12] Court of Justice (hereafter: ECJ), *Hautala v* Council, 10 July 2001, case C-353/99, ECLI:EU:C:2001:392, opinion of Advocate-General Leger at 52.

[13] Brandsma et al. 2008, p 819.

[14] Harden 2001, p 165.

[15] Kierkegaard 2009, pp 3–4.

[16] ECJ, *Interporc v Commission*, 7 December 1999, case T-92/98, ECLI:EU:T:1999:308, para 39.

accountability in the EU legal order since the access regime is used as a tool to assess and strengthen the EU's legitimacy and accountability.

The duty of the CJEU is to rule on whether the legal requirements stipulated in the Transparency Regulation have been respected and to issue binding judgments settling the dispute. The adjudication is based on a legal debate amongst the litigants. The Court, as the stereotypical accountability forum, assesses the performance of the litigants, the actors. The assessment also involves the giving of an account of the defendant's prior conduct on how they applied the Transparency Regulation. In the end, the Court has discretion to impose sanctions that take the form of the annulment of the contested measure and rule on the legal costs. This is consistent with the legislative framework which provides for a mere annulment of the contested decision rather than for a substantive entitlement of the citizenry to access official documents.

Pursuant to the accountability requirements, the actor is liable for giving an explanation for their actions and to suffer the consequences where appropriate. In that regard, the role of the Court is often understood as a process that operates retrospectively in the sense that it assesses the prior conduct of the actor, and as such it meets perfectly the accountability requirements which mainly deal with past wrongdoings. This is the core meaning of the accountability relationship: the liability to give an account or explanation of actions and, where appropriate, to suffer the consequences, take the blame or undertake to put matters right if it should appear that errors have been made. That is essentially the role of the Court in the access to documents litigation. In order for the Court to comply with the accountability requirements, it needs to ensure public awareness and participation in the decision-making process. To see whether this is the case, the remaining of the chapter outlines the EU's access to documents regime and assesses the role of the EU Courts in interpreting that regime.

10.3 Historical Overview of the Legislative Background

The main problems that occurred during the process of ratification of the Treaty of Maastricht[17] and particularly the negative response from Danish public opinion confirmed the widespread notion that the Union's decision-making process lacked accountability and legitimacy. In consequence, accountability was placed high on the political agenda and forced the Heads of States and Government as well the other EU institutions to find alternatives that would bring the Union closer to the citizens. Access to documents was believed to be the solution to the problem.

---

[17] The Danes rejected the ratification of the Maastricht Treaty in a referendum, while the French only voted to approve the treaty by a narrow majority. Lengthy discussions occurred in the UK Parliament and in Germany ratification was challenged before the Constitutional Court.

Declaration No 17 attached to the Final Act of the Maastricht Treaty stated that:

> The Conference considers that transparency of the decision-making process strengthens the democratic nature of the institutions and the public's confidence in the administration. The conference accordingly recommends that the Commission submit to the Council no later than 1993 a report on measures designed to improve public access to the information available to the institutions.

Declaration No 17, quoted above, illustrated the willingness for the establishment of a general 'right' of access to information. This non-binding political statement constitutes a type of soft law and not a rule of law of higher order which the previous rules would be invalid for not complying with.[18] Rightly, the Advocate General Maduro opined that declarations attached to the Treaties can be used as a basis in order to clarify Treaty provisions so long as they do not amend explicit stipulations provided in the Treaties.[19] This approach is in line with the case law which confirms that declarations can be used as a basis for interpretation of Treaty provisions.[20]

In response to Declaration No 17, the Commission first surveyed national law on access to documents and then released a communication on the issue.[21] These endeavours constitute the early steps that the EU has taken as an attempt for more openness and transparency in the decision-making process. Amongst these, clearly the most important was the Code of Conduct on access to documents which was later implemented by the Council[22] and the Commission.[23]

The accession of Austria, Finland, and Sweden in 1995 and the appointment of the first European Ombudsman, Mr. Jacob Soderman, also increased the state of transparency in the EU. In 1996, the Ombudsman began an own initiative inquiry regarding the adoption of access rules by the other EU institutions, bodies, offices and agencies and argued that as long as the Union legislature had not adopted general rules on access to documents, the institutions and bodies were obliged to adopt access rules as part of their internal organisation. This inquiry resulted in a draft recommendation that the other institutions and bodies should follow the example of the Council and the Commission and adopt their own internal rules on public access considering that failure to do so could be maladministration. The outcome of this attempt was that all the Union institutions, bodies, offices and agencies introduced rules regarding public access to their documents.[24]

---

[18] Peers 2002b.

[19] ECJ, *Kingdom of Sweden v Commission of the European Communities and Others*, 18 July 2007, case C 64/05 P, ECLI:EU:C:2007:433, opinion of Advocate-General Maduro, para 7.

[20] ECJ, *Agrana Zucker und Stärke* v *Commission*, 7 June 2001, case T-187/99, ECLI:EU:T:2001:149 and order of the Court in ECJ, *Agrana Zucker und Stärke* v *Commission*, 5 November 2002, case C-321/01 P, ECLI:EU:C:2002:635.

[21] [1993] OJ L 156/5 and [1993] OJ L 166/4.

[22] Decision 93/731 [1993] OJ L 340/43.

[23] Decision 94/90 [1994] OJ L 340/41.

[24] OJ 1998 C295/1 (Court of Auditors); OJ 1997 C243/13 (European Investment Bank); OJ 1999 L110/30 (European Central Bank); the European Agency for Health and Safety at work; Europol; OJ 1997 L339/18 (Economic and Social Committee); OJ 1997 351/70 (Committee of the

10.3.1 The Pre-Regulation Regime: The Code of Conduct

The basic principle enshrined in the joint Code of Conduct governing access to the Commission and the Council was the 'widest possible access to documents' and also the narrowest interpretation of the exceptions since the latter is a corollary of the former.[25] However, this did not mean that the Code guaranteed an absolute right. On the contrary, it provided for documents to be refused where disclosure 'could' undermine the protection of certain public and private interests. Although the Code started with the assurance that 'the public will have the widest possible access to documents held by the Commission and the Council' the openness criterion was not the rule. Rather paradoxically, the Code's exceptions were defined broadly with the effect of changing the presumption of disclosure from positive rights with negative exceptions to a text which treated access as the exception.[26]

The Code contained a non-exhaustive list of mandatory exceptions,[27] which meant that the institutions must refuse access to documents that came within one of the exceptions, if the relevant circumstances were shown to exist. The rules provided for a radical change into the hitherto situation which was secrecy, thus the grounds for refusing access were drafted generously. The Code exceptions that were covered:

- The protection of the public interest (exemplified by public security, international relations, monetary stability, court proceedings, inspections, and investigations);
- The protection of the individual and of privacy;
- The protection of industrial and commercial secrecy;
- The protection of the Union's financial interests; and
- The protection of confidentiality as requested by the natural or legal persons that supplied the information or as required by the legislation of the Member State that supplied the information.

Additionally, the institutions could refuse access to protect confidentiality of their proceedings.[28]

Regions); OJ 1998 L90/43 (European Monetary Institute); European Centre for the Development of Vocational Training (cadefop); OJ 1997 C282/5 (European Environment Agency); OJ 1998 C46/5 (Translation Centre for Bodies of the European Union); European Monetary Centre for Drugs and Drug Addiction; European Agency for the Evaluation of Medicinal Products.

[25] Peers 2002b.

[26] De Leeuw 2003.

[27] ECJ, *Carlsen v Council*, 3 March 1998, case T-610/97 R, ECLI:EU:T:1998:48. The President of the Court ruled that the mandatory exceptions regarding the protection of the public interest were not exhaustive and that an exception relating to the stability of the Community legal order which covers also the legal advice given by the legal service of the institutions existed.

[28] ECJ, *Carvel v Council*, 19 October 1995, case T-194/94, ECLI:EU:T:1995:183.

Even after the enactment of the Code, the institutions were reluctant to interpret the code in favour of transparency.[29] This attitude led to the refusal of access repeatedly. The Code's exceptions were indeed dangerously restrictive and in a Court case the legal basis of the Code was challenged.[30] It was argued that transparency constitutes an essential aspect of democracy and as such cannot be regulated by measures of internal organisation. The Court of Justice, however, dismissed the challenge on the grounds that the institutions could adopt those measures as part of their internal organisation.[31] At that time the Treaty of Amsterdam was not in force and thus the institutions were entitled to have access rules governing citizens' rights based solely on internal procedural rules.[32]

The Court of Justice and the Court of First Instance handed down several judgments interpreting the Council and the Commission decisions denying access. The Courts held, for example, that the institutions after having adopted their internal rules on access were abiding by them and any exceptions to the principle of the widest access must be justified on objective grounds and be applied strictly.[33] In addition to this, the Court ruled that the institutions were obliged to carry out a concrete and individual assessment of each of the requested document before deciding whether or not to release.[34] Also, as already explained above, if the institutions were relying on a discretionary exception they were required to balance the interest of the applicant against their interest in protecting confidentiality. Access should be granted if the applicant's interest outweighed institution's interest.[35] Finally, the institutions had to disclose the part of the documents not covered

---

[29] Harlow 2002. See also the open letter addressed to the Secretary General of the Council by the European Federation of Journalists dated 30 April 1996 mentioning 'grave reservations about the Council's interpretation and practice of the code of conduct concerning access to documents'.

[30] The Netherlands, Denmark, Sweden, and Finland have consistently hard-pressed for greater openness within the Union gaining strong inspiration from their national laws where the notion of citizens' rights is underscored.

[31] ECJ, *Netherlands v Council*, 30 April 1996, case C-58/94, ECLI:EU:C:1996:171.

[32] It must be noted here that it was only in 1997 that the EP adopted rules regarding access to its documents.

[33] ECJ, *WWF v Commission*, 5 March 1997, case T-105/95, ECLI:EU:T:1997:26. This was the first judgment on access to documents rules concerning the Commission. It established that the internal institutional rules on access to documents are capable of conferring rights on citizens and imposing obligations on the Commission. The CFI also ruled for the first time on the public interest exception concerning inspections and investigations and ruled that the documents relating to investigations which may lead to an infringement procedure according to Article 226 of the EC Treaty, now Art 258 TFEU, satisfy the conditions that must be met by the Commission in order to rely on the public interest exception according to Article 4(1) of the Code of Conduct.

[34] ECJ, *Svenska Journalistforbundet v Council*, 17 June 1998, case T-174/95 ECLI:EU:T:1998:127.

[35] ECJ, *Carvel v Council*, 19 October 1995, case T-194/94, ECLI:EU:T:1995:183 and ECJ, *WWF v Commission*, 5 March 1997, case T-105/95 ECLI:EU:T:1997:26.

by the exceptions. This is known as the principle of partial access which was firstly developed by the Courts as this possibility was not provided by the Code.[36]

Under the Code, there is consistent jurisprudence that 'the legal rule is that the public is to have access to the documents of the institutions and the power to refuse access is the exception'.[37] At the same time, the exceptions needed to be interpreted and applied restrictively so as not to defeat the general principle of the widest possible access found in the Code.[38] To implement this, the institutions were required to examine concretely and individually the documents and to state reasons if access was to be refused.[39] The risk of the public or private interest being undermined must be reasonably foreseeable and not purely hypothetical.[40] This exercise was aimed to help the applicant to assess the reasons on which access was denied and to enable the Court to exercise its power of review. The Court ruled that in exceptional cases the requirement of concrete and individual examination could be limited under the 'administrative burden rule'.[41] Pursuant to that rule, the document by document examination could be abandoned. The institutions were allowed to balance the work that they will have to bear against the public interest in gaining access. In other words, excessive administrative work could allow an institution to derogate from the access requirement.[42]

10.4 The Transparency Regulation and the Relevant Case Law

The Transparency Regulation governs, at the time of writing, the right of citizens and residents in the EU to access, in principle, all the documents drawn or held by the EP, Council and the Commission.[43] The pre-Regulation case law has, to a large

---

[36] ECJ, *Hautala v Council*, 6 December 2001, case C-353/99 P, ECLI:EU:C:2001:661.

[37] ECJ, *Kuijer (II) v Council*, 7 February 2002, case T-211/00, ECLI:EU:T:2002:30, para 55.

[38] ECJ, *Svenska Journalistforbundet v Council*, 17 June 1998, case T-174/95, ECLI:EU:T:1998:127; ECJ, *WWF v Commission*, 5 March 1997, case T-105/95, ECLI:EU:T:1997:26; ECJ, *Interporc (I) v Commission*, 6 February 1998, case T-124/96, ECLI:EU:T:1998:25.

[39] ECJ, *Van der Wal v Commission*, 19 March 1998, case T-83/96, ECLI:EU:T:1998:59; ECJ, *Interporc (I) v Commission*, 6 February 1998, case T-124/96, ECLI:EU:T:1998:25.

[40] ECJ, *Kuijer (II) v Council*, 7 February 2002, case T-211/00, ECLI:EU:T:2002:30.

[41] ECJ, *Hautala v Council*, 6 December 2001, case C-353/99 P, ECLI:EU:C:2001:661; ECJ, *Hautala v Council*, 19 July 1999, case T-14/98, ECLI:EU:T:1999:157.

[42] Heliskoski and Leino 2006. See also: Diamandouros 2008; Guggenbuhl 1998; Flanagan 2007; Leino 2011; Osterdahl 1998.

[43] Although in principle the beneficiaries of the right of access to documents are EU citizens and residents, Article 2(2) of the Regulation grants discretion to the EU institutions bound by it to grant access to any natural or legal person not residing or not having its registered office in a Member State. The institutions responded positively to this option. See Decision 2001/840 of the Council OJ 2001, L313/40, Decision 2001/937 of the Commission OJ 2001, L 345/94 and the Decision of the EP OJ 2001, L 374 /I.

extent, been incorporated into this Regulation and the interpretation of the old rules is still applicable unless clearly stated otherwise.[44] This is justified by Recital 3 of the Regulation's Preamble, which states that the Regulation 'consolidates the initiatives which the institutions have already taken'.

As already explained above, pursuant to settled case law and in view of the objectives of the Regulation, the exceptions set out in Article 4 of the Regulation must be interpreted and applied strictly. Thus, when the institution decides to rely on any of the exceptions mentioned in Article 4 'it must explain how access to that documents could specifically and effectively undermine the interest protected by an exception'.[45] The purpose of the Regulation as set out in its Article 1 is 'to define the principles, conditions, and limits on grounds of public or private interest governing the right of access to EP, Council, and Commission documents (…) in such a way as to ensure the widest possible access to documents (…) to establish rules ensuring the easiest possible exercise of this right (…) and to promote good administrative practice on access to documents'. For this purpose, any European citizen and any natural or legal person residing or having its registered office in any of the Member States can apply to access any documents.[46]

The Regulation reflects the overall intention specified in the second subparagraph of ex Article 1 TEU, currently Article 1 of the TEU, to mark a new stage in the process of creating an even closer union amongst the peoples of Europe, in which decisions are taken as openly as possible and as closely as possible to the citizen. Similarly, as it is noted in the recital 2 of the Regulation's Preamble there is a direct link of the fundamental right of European citizens and residents to have access to documents held by the EU institutions with the democratic nature of those institutions.

Article 2 of the Regulation sets out the basic provisions and its wording is analogous to the wording of ex Article 255(1) of the EC Treaty whereas Article 2(3) defines the scope of the Regulation and reads as follows: 'This Regulation shall apply to all documents held by an institution, that is to say, documents drawn up or received by it and in its possession, in all areas of activities of the EU.' The provision marks a significant change to the pre-Regulation regime. Article 2(3) provides that documents *drawn or received* by the institutions fall within the scope of the Regulation. This broader access constitutes an important obvious step forward in respect of the former situation, which covered only access to documents *drawn* up by the institutions.[47] As explained already, according to the authorship rule, access requests were directed to the authors. Yet, this welcome abolition does not mean that the right of access to documents is an absolute right. The institutions may still rely on Article 4 to justify denial to grant access.

---

[44] Peers 2002b; Kranenborg 2006.

[45] ECJ, *Borax v Commission*, 11 March 2009, caseT-121/05, ECLI:EU:T:2009:64.

[46] Article 2(2) of Regulation 1049/2001 [2001] OJ L 145/43.

[47] Peers 2002b; De Leeuw 2003.

There are four types of exceptions: mandatory, 'discretionary', the protection of the decision-making process and, finally, documents originating from third parties and Member States. Article 4(1) is written in mandatory terms and provides that: 'the institutions shall refuse access to a document where disclosure would undermine the protection of:

(a) the public interest as regards:
  - public security;
  - defence and military matters;
  - international relations;
  - the financial, monetary or economic policy of the Community or a Member State;

(b) privacy and the integrity of the individual, in particular in accordance with the Community legislation regarding the protection of personal data'.

The first category of exceptions precludes access to any of the documents falling within it and calls for no balancing of interests at stake. If the institutions can prove that the documents fall into this category, refusal is automatically justified.[48] As regards the privacy exception, the personal data legislation provides for limits. The CFI, now the General Court, was called to interpret the relationship between Regulation 1049/2001 and Regulation 45/2001and ruled that disclosure can only be denied if the privacy or the integrity of the person would be undermined.[49] In consequence, the CFI carried out a balancing exercise between the two fundamental rights at stake: public access and data protection. It highlighted the importance of the access right and reiterated that any limitations must be construed and applied restrictively so as not to defeat the general principle enshrined in Regulation 1049/2001. At the same time, the right to data protection must be protected. As a result, the Court ruled that names, titles and functions of public office holders, civil servants and interest representatives in relation with their professional activities shall be disclosed because disclosure does not lead to an interference with the private life of the persons, nor would those persons have any ground to believe that they enjoyed confidential treatment.[50]

Unfortunately, from an openness point of view, the Court of Justice set aside the judgment of the General Court on the grounds that the assessment of whether the protection of privacy and the integrity of the individual protected by Article 4(1)(b) of the Regulation should not be confined to Article 8 of the European Convention on Human Rights (ECHR) but must take into account the EU legislation on data protection. Under Regulation 45/2001, the Bavarian Lager did not provide any justification in favour of obtaining the requested data and therefore the Commission and the Court were not in a position to assess whether the applicant's interest

[48] Peers 2002b; De Leeuw 2003.

[49] ECJ, *Bavarian Lager v Commission*, 8 November 2007, case T-194/04, ECLI:EU:T:2007:334.

[50] *Ibid.*

outweighed the 'data subject's legitimate interest and to examine whether the latter's interest might be prejudiced, as required by Article 8(b) of 45/2001'.[51]

The Article 4.1 case law consistently applies the marginal review standard, since judicial review is 'limited to verifying whether the procedural rules have been complied with, the contested decision is properly reasoned, and the facts have been accurately stated, and whether there has been a manifest error of assessment of the facts or misuse of powers'.[52] Yet, the exceptions set out in Article 4 must be interpreted and applied strictly to secure the *effet utile* of the access right. It follows from this, that when the institution decides to rely on any of the exceptions 'it must explain how access to that document could specifically and effectively undermine the interest protected by an exception'.[53] This delicate balancing task has been deemed essential and access cannot be denied without firstly appraising the requested documents on a case-by-case basis. The application of the exceptions regarding sensitive, legislative, administrative and judicial documents, as per settled case law, is discussed below.

10.4.1 *Sensitive Documents: The* Sison *Case*

Sison[54] was the first case whereas the Court examined the mandatory exceptions relating to public security and international relations under the Regulation. As explained already, in principle, the Regulation covers all the documents drawn or held by the EP, Council and the Commission. Pragmatically, however, certain documents are subject to special procedural rules before they can be released. In this regard, Article 2(5) provides that 'sensitive documents as defined in Article 9 (1) shall be subject to special treatment'. The pre-Regulation understanding of the nature of the discretion related to the mandatory exceptions[55] has played a key role in *Sison* and led the Court to adopt a conservative interpretation of the public security and international relations exceptions. Pursuant to the reasoning of the Court, the power to review the legality of the institutions' decisions regarding Article 4(1)(a) is 'limited to verifying whether the procedural rules and the duty to state reasons have been complied with, the facts have been accurately stated, and

[51] ECJ, *Commission v Bavarian Lager*, 29 June 2010, case C-28/08 P, ECLI:EU:C:2010:378.

[52] ECJ, *Hautala v Council*, 19 July 1999, case T-14/98, ECLI:EU:T:1999:157. This has been confirmed as regards the Regulation, *see* ECJ, *Sison v Council*, 1 February 2007, case C-266/05 P ECLI:EU:C:2007:75.

[53] ECJ, *Borax v Commission*, 11 March 2009, case T-121/05, ECLI:EU:T:2009:64.

[54] ECJ, *Sison v Council*, 26 April 2005, joined cases T-110/03, T-150/03 and T-405/03, ECLI:EU:T:2005:143.

[55] According to settled case-law, the institutions enjoy wide discretion in the context of a decision denying access based on the protection of public interest regarding international relations. See ECJ, *Hautala v Council*, 19 July 1999, case T-14/98, ECLI:EU:T:1999:157.

whether there has been a manifest error of assessment of the facts or a misuse of powers'.[56]

In *Sison*, the applicant, based on the short and formulaic response, argued that the Council, contrary to the settled case law, had never conducted a concrete and individual examination of the documents requested. As a result, the applicant was unable to ascertain the reasons put forward by the Council and the Court was unable to exercise its power of review. The Council, however, argued that the existence of a specific procedure dealing with the request for sensitive documents shows that concrete examination had taken place. The Court agreed with the Council and adopted a very conservative interpretation of the public security and international relations exception. On appeal, Mr Sison tried to set aside the CFI's judgment, though the Court of Justice reiterated that the Union institutions enjoy wide discretion in the areas covered by Article 4(1)[57] and thus dismissed the appeal.

The second category, set out in Article 4(2), is not really discretionary, since it is written in the same mandatory way ('shall refuse') as the exceptions in Article 4(1) but is subject to a public interest override in favour of disclosure. The decision-making exception provided by Article 4(3) is the equivalent of the confidentiality exception under the Code of Conduct. The former imposes with a higher threshold to non-disclosure. Specifically, it requires that the disclosure 'significantly undermines' the decision-making. Accordingly, the balance is tipped towards disclosure. Article 4(2) reads as follows:

> [t]he institutions shall refuse access to documents where disclosure would undermine the protection of:
>
> - commercial interests of natural or legal person, including intellectual property;
> - court proceedings and legal advice;
> - the purpose of inspections, investigations and audits;
>
> Unless there is an overriding public interest in disclosure.

The latter clause constitutes an 'exception to the exception'[58] and if applicable the requested documents need to be released. However, the CFI interpreted this provision strictly and held in *Turco*[59] and in other cases[60] that the overriding public interest provided by Article 4(2) must be additional to the public's right to be informed. This case law, however, cannot be considered as good law any longer after the ruling of the Court of Justice's in the *Turco's* appeal.[61]

---

[56] ECJ, *Sison v Council*, 26 April 2005, joined cases T-110/03, T-150/03 and T-405/03, ECLI: EU:T:2005:143, para 47.

[57] ECJ, *Sison v Council*, 1 February 2007, case C-266/05 P, ECLI:EU:C:2007:75.

[58] Kranenborg and Voermans 2005. See also: Peers 2002a; Kranenborg 2008.

[59] ECJ, *Turco v Council*, 23 November 2004, case T-84/03, ECLI:EU:T:2004:339.

[60] ECJ, *Association de la presse internationale asbl (API) v Commission*, 12 September 2007, case T-36/04, ECLI:EU:T:2007:258.

[61] ECJ, *Sweden and Turco v Council*, 1 July 2008, joined cases C-39/05 P and C-52/05 P, ECLI: EU:C:2008:374.

10.4.2 Legislative Documents Relating to Legal Advice: The Turco *Case*[62]

The applicant, Mr Turco, requested access to an opinion of the Council's legal service relating to a proposal for a Council Directive laying down minimum standards for the reception of applicants for asylum in Member States. He was refused access on the basis that the release of the opinion would undermine the protection of legal advice regulated by the second indent of Article 4(2) of the Regulation. The Council argued that its interest in protecting internal legal advice outweighed the public interest in disclosure. In addition to this, the Council argued that the mere fact that the release of the document would be in the general interest of increasing openness and transparency of the institutions decision-making process is irrelevant. This criterion, according to the Council, would apply to all written opinions of the Council's legal service. Finally, the Council argued that the release of the opinion concerned would give rise to uncertainty of the validity of the legislative act adopted following such advice.

The applicant and one of the intervening governments,[63] Finland, argued that denial of access should be based on a concrete and individual examination of the documents requested and not relate to all legal advice on legislative acts in general.[64] The Court ruled that, in principle, denial of access must be based on concrete and individual examination but, however, the Council's generality was justified by the fact that giving additional information would deprive the exception relied upon of its effect.[65] The CFI ruled also that the rationale behind the legal advice exception is to avoid uncertainty, by raising doubts, over the legality of EU legislation[66] along with securing independence of the opinions of the institutions legal service.[67] As far as the public interest override is concerned, the Court found that the legal advice can derogate from the established duty, incumbent on the institutions, to carry out a concrete assessment of the requested documents. By doing so, the CFI placed the burden of proof regarding the override upon the applicants. What is more surprisingly, however, was the outcome of the Court that the override could not be invoked in the general interest of transparency, openness, democracy and citizens participation in the decision-making process. These principles, according to the Court, have already been implemented and underlie the transparency Regulation.

The judicial reasoning is hardly convincing. The CFI here says that the purpose of the exception is to prevent disclosure of the underlying legal advice in order to

62 ECJ, *Turco v Council*, 23 November 2004, case T-84/03, ECLI:EU:T:2004:339.

63 The other two intervening governments were Denmark and Sweden.

64 ECJ, *Turco v Council*, 23 November 2004, case T-84/03, ECLI:EU:T:2004:339, para 36.

65 *Ibid.*, para 57.

66 *Ibid.*, para 74.

67 *Ibid.*, para 79.

avoid uncertainty as to the legality of the acts adopted following such advice and that any reference in the statement of reasons to the content of the opinion would deprive the exception of its effect. To paraphrase, the CFI is of the view that a way to protect legal certainty is to prevent the public from finding out that acts of uncertain legality have being issued and are maintained.

The approach followed by the CFI in this case is in a direct contradiction with the settled case law which sets out the principles governing the access to documents regime. As already explained, the widest possible access enhances citizens' participation in the decision-making process. In fact, the same Court has ruled that 'the widest possible access to documents (…) is essential to enable citizens to carry out genuine and efficient monitoring of the exercise of the powers vested in the Community institutions (…)'.[68] How can citizens exercise these rights when access to legal advice is refused as a matter of principle? Can any legal system be based on principles which prevent citizens from scrutinising the legality of any acts? On the contrary, there is a strong public interest override as regards the right to seek for the annulment of measures of uncertain legality. To that end, protecting legal certainty cannot be considered as a panacea for an act which might very well be invalid.

The applicant also argued that the correct exception for the protection of the Council's legal advice is Article 4(3) which aims to protect the institution's decision-making process.[69] The CFI had rejected the application of Article 4(3) to the case of legal advice relating to legislative acts on the basis that to do so would empty Article 4(2) of relevancy. The CFI ruled that Article 4(2) does not relate to legal advice taken for the purpose of court proceedings but was designed to cover both situations. However, such an argument contradicts the fact that in Article 4(2) legal advice and court proceedings are mentioned separately. It is worth mentioning that the Code of Conduct, examined thoroughly previously, was only referring to the court proceedings exception, legal advice was inserted by the Regulation. Had the legislature wanted to protect court proceedings alone it would have had every opportunity to do so by choosing not to include an exception relating to legal advice. In any event, there can be legal advice not related to legislative proceedings, even legal advice given by in-house lawyers to companies and obtained by the Commission under competition proceedings, as long as such advice is not protected as privileged under EU law.

The second ground put forward by the CFI appears no less problematic. The CFI found that the disclosure of the introductory paragraph of the Council's legal service opinion confirms that concrete and individual examination has taken place.[70] If the reasoning adopted here by the CFI becomes the accepted norm then the access right will be drastically diminished of any substance in the sense that any partial access would always constitute evidence that an individual and concrete assessment had taken place. Finally, the CFI placed the burden of proof regarding the public

---

[68] ECJ, *Interporc v Commission*, 7 December 1999, case T-92/98, ECLI:EU:T:1999:308, para 39.

[69] ECJ, *Turco v Council*, 23 November 2004, case T-84/03, ECLI:EU:T:2004:339.

[70] *Ibid.*, para 75.

interest override on the applicants by ruling that the override could not be invoked in the general interest of transparency, openness, democracy and citizens' participation in the decision-making process. These principles, according to the Court, have already been implemented and underlie the transparency Regulation. Thus, the overriding interest capable of justifying disclosure must be distinct from those principles.

For the abovementioned reasons, it seems unfortunate that the reasoning of the Court was framed in such a general language especially because the Court in *Turco* ruled for the first time on the legal advice exception as well as on the public interest override provided by the Regulation in a number of exceptions. One would have wished the Court to confirm in a more explicit manner that not all the legal advice should escape the duty incumbent on the institutions to carry out a concrete assessment of documents of this kind.

Fortunately and in the interests of transparency, the Court of Justice, in the joined cases of *Sweden and Turco v. Council*,[71] set aside the CFI's judgment and upheld the appeal. The Court highlighted the importance of the principle of transparency in the decision-making process. The Court of Justice addressed how the EU institutions should deal with disclosure requests relating to legal advice laid down in the second indent of 4(2) of the transparency Regulation. It was held that when the institutions are asked to disclose such a document must carry out a specific three-staged procedure that corresponds to the three criteria outlined in that provision.[72] Firstly, the institution must consider and satisfy itself that the requested document does indeed relate to legal advice and whether any parts of the requested documents are covered by the exception.[73] The second stage is the requirement to consider whether disclosure of any parts of the document would undermine the protection of such an advice.[74] Regarding the latter requirement, the Court, using a teleological interpretation, ruled that the term legal advice must be understood in the light of the purpose of the Regulation. Under this purpose, the exception 'must be construed as aiming to protect an institution's interest in seeking legal advice and receiving frank, objective and comprehensive advice'.[75] The assessment of the risk of that interest being undermined should consider what is reasonably foreseeable and not purely hypothetical. Finally, if the outcome of the above assessment is that disclosure of the document would undermine the ability of the institution to receive frank and objective legal advice, it is incumbent on the institution to balance the interest in non-disclosure against any possible overriding interest, bearing in mind

[71] ECJ, *Sweden and Turco v Council*, 1 July 2008, joined cases C-39/05 P and C-52/05 P, ECLI: EU:C:2008:374. Arnull 2009.

[72] *Ibid.*, para 37.

[73] *Ibid.*, para 38.

[74] *Ibid.*, para 40.

[75] *Ibid.*, para 42.

the purpose of the transparency legislation to secure the widest possible access to documents, giving a reasoned judgment for its decision.[76]

The Court of Justice, in the *Turco* appeal, held that the CFI was erred in law by finding that the *raison d'être* of the legal advice exception is not to fuel doubts over the legality of legislation. In fact, the Court of Justice has ruled that preventing disclosure can lead to the contrary and raise doubts in the citizens' minds over the legality of the decision-making process. Pursuant to the wording of the judiciary 'it is in fact rather a lack of information and debate which is capable of giving rise to doubts in the minds of citizens, not only as regards the lawfulness of an isolated act, but also as regards the legitimacy of the decision-making process as a whole'.[77] By upholding this appeal, the Court of Justice highlighted the importance of the access to documents rules and reintroduced the cornerstone of this regime which is based on the ability of the public to assess the impact, comment upon and influence the development of policies, an activity which cannot take place without maximum access to information.

Nevertheless, regarding the protection of the institutions' interest in seeking and receiving frank, objective and comprehensive legal advice, the Court of Justice's justification appears to be particularly problematic. It is difficult to understand how the public's access to legal advice can affect the objectiveness of it. Anyone studying accountability will argue that disclosure of this kind of documents can only lead to professional behaviour because of the fact that the drafters of the legal advice will always have in mind that the advice will be accessible. Arguably, it may even make more sense to interpret the legal advice exception more strictly, on a case by case basis, and limit it for the very sensitive cases.

More interestingly, the Court of Justice ruled that the overriding public interest pressing for disclosure of the legal advice needs to be no different from the principle of openness, transparency, democracy and civil participation in the decision-making process which already underlie the Regulation.[78]

The approach taken in *Turco* was indeed promising in terms of transparency. It clearly provided the foundations to disclose legal advice given also in the remit of the executive action of the EU institutions. This was upheld by the General Court and recently confirmed by the Court of Justice in *In 't Veld.*[79] Yet, it is deemed necessary to revisit the wider contribution of *Turco*. A further and detailed examination indicates significant shortcomings of the judgment. In particular, the 'general presumptions' line of reasoning as introduced by *Turco* raises significant questions as to the fundamental nature of the access right. In this regard, the court established that '[i]t is in principle, open to the Council to base its decisions (…) on general presumptions which apply to certain categories of documents, as

---

76 *Ibid.*, para 44.

77 *Ibid.*, para 59.

78 *Ibid.*, para 74.

79 ECJ, *Sophie in 't Veld v Commission*, 19 March 2013, case T-301/10, ECLI:EU:T:2013:135; ECJ, *Council v Sophie in 't Veld*, 3 July 2014, case C-350/12 P ECLI:EU:C:2014:2039.

considerations of a generally similar kind are likely to apply to requests for disclosure relating to documents of the same nature.'[80]

The Court ruled effectively that the Council, and arguably by analogy all the other institutions, can deny access based on general considerations as opposed to the well-established duty for a specific and detailed examination. In consequence, post *Turco* there was every possibility that the institutions, the Commission in particular, would rely on general considerations in order to avoid carrying out a concrete appraisal of the requested documents. The Court, with great respect, set the foundations to depart from the principle of transparency and to disregard almost two decades of jurisprudence. Indeed, the later developments, examined further below, provide with sufficient evidence to question the validity of the early finding that the judgment was spectacularly progressive.

Similarly in 2010, *TGI*[81] concerned a request for access to certain large state aid files held by the Commission. The Court of Justice by citing *Turco* this time confirmed the 'settled case law' as regards the existence of a general presumption against disclosure.[82] *TGI* upheld the validity of the presumption and established that administrative documents are now essentially exempted from the document-by-document appraisal and that the public interest override will never apply unless particularly pertinent.

The validity of the general presumption was upheld in *LPN*.[83] Citing this time *TGI* and *Turco*, *LPN* confirmed the existence of the presumption in the administrative file, in what appears to be a new development, to cover infringement proceedings.[84] On appeal, the applicants, LPN and Finland, argued that the Commission denied access without carrying out, in violation of settled case law, a concrete and individual assessment of the requested documents.[85] The Court ruled 'that it can be *presumed* (emphasis added) that the disclosure of the documents concerning the infringement proceedings during the pre-litigation stage risks altering the nature of that procedure and changing the way it proceeds and, accordingly, that disclosure would in principle undermine the protection of the

[80] ECJ, *Sweden and Turco v Council*, 1 July 2008, joined cases C-39/05 P and C-52/05 P, ECLI:EU:C:2008:374, para 50.

[81] ECJ, *Commission v Technische Glaswerke Ilmenau*, 29 June 2010, case C-139/07 P, ECLI:EU:C:2010:376; ECJ, *Commission v Agrofert Holding a.s.*, 28 June 2012, case C-477/10 P ECLI:EU:C:2012:394; ECJ, *Commission v Editions Odile Jacob SAS*, 28 June 2012, case C-404/10 P, ECLI:EU:C:2012:393; ECJ, *Guido Strack v Commission*, 15 January 2013, case T-392/07, ECLI:EU:T:2013:8.

[82] ECJ, *Commission v Technische Glaswerke Ilmenau*, 29 June 2010, case C-139/07 P, ECLI:EU:C:2010:376, para 61.

[83] ECJ, *LPN and Finland v Commission*, 14 November 2013, case C-514/11, ECLI:EU:C:2013:738.

[84] ECJ, *LPN v Commission*, 9 September 2011, case T-29/08, ECLI:EU:T:2011:448, para 126.

[85] ECJ, *LPN and Finland v Commission*, 14 November 2013, case C-514/11, ECLI:EU:C:2013:738, para 35.

purpose of investigations, within the meaning of the third indent of Article 4(2) of Regulation No 1049/2001'.[86]

The presumptions case law, upheld in *LPN*, is fairly vague and in direct contrast with the Treaty framework, in particular with the requirements to take decisions as openly as possible pursuant to Article 1 TEU as well as with the overall wording of the Regulation. The Regulation provides with no basis for the establishment of general presumptions. The Court of Justice's position regarding the administrative functions imposes significant constitutional ramifications on the fundamental aspect of the access right and incorporates limitations without the required level of explanation and clarity. The Court also did not take into account the overriding public interest as regards the infringement proceedings. As a result, the judgment makes one to wonder if such an override cannot be established in an area where possible violations of EU law by Member States might take place, then it remains difficult to conceive a scenario where the override would ever be accepted by the court.

Interestingly, *LPN* treats in a rather paradoxical way a respectable non-governmental organisation as a mere 'busybody' unable to invoke successfully the override. This latest jurisprudence reveals the existence of a paradox. We saw the court to confirm categorically through the last 20 years that openness secures public oversight of the EU's decision-making describing it as one of the fundamental credentials of the Union's democratic society. Yet, we have evidence that the court provides little or no contribution in relation to the opening up the functioning of the institutions. The judgment significantly decreases public access and leaves intact the possibility of the Commission, and by analogy the other institutions, to refuse access as regards to the entire administrative file without even looking at the individual documents.

10.5 Conclusion

There is no doubt that the EU has taken important steps to ensure transparency of the decision-making process. If one compares the pre-Regulation rules whereas the then CFI held for example that transparency did not require the adoption of secondary legislation and that decisions on access to documents could properly be based purely on the institution's Rules of Procedure with the current situation, it can be safely argued that progress has been made. Currently, it is obvious that 'we have gone from a situation of a mere favour being granted to the individual by the institutions in the exercise of their discretionary power to one of a true subjective fundamental right granted to the individual'.[87]

[86] *Ibid.*, para 65.

[87] ECJ, *Sweden v Commission*, 18 July 2007, case C-64/05 P, ECLI:EU:C:2007:433, opinion of Advocate-General Maduro, para 40.

The Transparency Regulation has improved the position governing access in several aspects. The most significant developments introduced by the Regulation are the abolishment of the authorship rule. The judiciary contributed to the development of transparency to a more or a lesser extent. In a more limited way, the extent to which the jurisprudence acknowledges the existence of general presumptions is fundamentally wrong. In practice, the presumptions case law establishes a clear distinction between legislative and non-legislative documents and confirms, contrary to the wording of the Regulation, the widest possible access with regards to the former category.

References

Adamski A (2009) How wide is 'the widest possible'? Judicial interpretation of the exceptions to the right of access to official documents revisited. CMLRev 46:521–549

Adamski D (2012) Approximating a workable compromise on access to official documents: The 2011 developments in the European courts. CMLRev 49:521–558

Alemanno A, Stefan O (2014) Openness at the Court of Justice of the European Union: Toppling a Taboo. CMLRev 51:97–139

Arnull A (2009) Joined Cases C-39/05 P & C-52/05 P, Sweden and Turco v. Council, judgment of the Grand Chamber of 1 July 2008. CMLRev 46:1219–1238

Arnull A, Wincott D (2002) Accountability and Legitimacy in the EU. Oxford University Press, Oxford

Bovens M (2007) Analysing and Assessing Accountability: A Conceptual Framework. ELJ 13:447–468

Brandsma G, Curtin D, Meijer A (2008) How Transparent are EU "Comitology" Committees in Practice? ELJ 14:819–838

Broberg M (2002) Access to Documents: A General Principle of Community Law. ELRev 27:194–205

Busuioc M (2009) Accountability, Control and Independence: The Case of European Agencies. ELJ 15:599–615

Busuioc M (2013) European Agencies Law and Practices of Accountability. Oxford University Press, Oxford

Cooper H (2016) Where European democracy goes to die. https://www.politico.eu/article/where-european-democracy-goes-to-die-european-parliament/ Accessed 12 July 2016

Costa M (2017) The Accountability Gap in EU Law. Routledge, Oxford

Costa M, Peers S (2016) Beware of Courts Bearing Gifts. NJB 91:1107–1116

Curtin D (2000) Citizens' fundamental right of access to EU information: An evolving digital passepartout? CMLRev 37:7–41

Curtin D (2013) Official secrets and the negotiation of international agreements: Is the EU executive unbound? CMLRev 50:423–457

Curtin D, Hart P (2010) The Real World of EU Accountability, What Deficit? Oxford University Press, Oxford

Curtin D, Leino P (2017) In search of transparency for EU law-making: Trilogues on the cusp of dawn. CMLRev 54:1673–1712

Curtin D, Meijer H (1995) The principle of open government in Schengen and the European Union: Democratic retrogression? CMLRev 32:391–442

Davies A (2001) Accountability: A Public Law Analysis of Government by Contract. Oxford University Press, Oxford
Davis R (1999) Public access to community documents: A fundamental human right? EIOP 3
Davis R (2000) The Court of Justice and the right of public access to Community-held documents. ELRev 25:303–309
De Leeuw M (2003) The Regulation on public access to EP, Council and Commission Documents in the European Union: Are citizens better off? ELRev 28:324–348
Diamandouros N (2008) Contribution of the European Ombudsman to the public hearing on the revision of Regulation 1049/2001 on public access to documents. www.statewatch.org/news/2008/jun/eu-ep-ombudsman-on-com-proposals-speech.pdf Accessed 9 June 2008
Fisher E (2004) The EU in the Age of Accountability. OJLS 24:495–515
Flanagan A (2007) EU Freedom of Information: Determining where the Interest Lies. EPL 13:595–632
Frost A (2003) Restoring Faith in Government: Transparency Reform in the United States and the EU. EPL 9:87–104
Geradin D (2005) The Development of European Regulatory Agencies: Lessons from the American Experience. In: Geradin et al (eds) Regulation through Agencies in the EU. A New Paradigm of European Governance. Edward Elgar, London, pp 215–245
Guggenbuhl A (1998) A Miracle Formula or an Old Powder in New Packaging? Transparency and Openness after Amsterdam. In: Deckmyn V, Thomson I (eds) Openness and Transparency in the European Union. EIPA, Maastricht, pp 9–38
Harden I (2001) Citizenship and Information. EPL 7:165–193
Harlow C (2002) Accountability in the European Union. Oxford University Press, Oxford
Heliskoski J, Leino P (2006) Darkness at the Break of Noon: The Case-law on Regulation No. 1049/2001 on Access to Documents. CMLRev 43:735–782
Kierkegaard S (2009) Open Access to public documents – More secrecy, less transparency! CLSR 25:3–27
Kranenborg H (2006) Is it Time to Revise the European Regulation on Public Access to Documents? EPL 12:251–274
Kranenborg H (2008) Access to documents and data protection in the European Union: On the public nature of personal data. CMLRev 45:1079–1114
Kranenborg H, Voermans W (2005) Access to Information in the European Union: A Comparative Analysis of EC and Member State Legislation. Europa Law Publishing, Groningen
Leino P (2011) Just a little sunshine in the rain: The 2010 case law of the European Court of Justice on access to documents. CMLRev 48:1215–1252
Mancini F, Keeling D (1994) Democracy and the European Court of Justice. MLR 57:175–190
Mulgan R (2003) Holding Power to Account, Accountability in Modern Democracies. Palgrave Macmillan, London
Mulgan R (2000) Accountability: An Ever-Expanding Concept? PA 78:555–573
Osterdahl I (1998) Openness v. Secrecy: Public Access to Documents in Sweden and the European Union. ELRev 23:335–356
Peers S (2002a) From Maastricht to Laeken: The Political Agenda of Openness and Transparency in the EU. In: Deckmyn V (ed) Increasing Transparency in the European Union, EIPA, Maastricht, pp 7–33
Peers S (2002b) The New Regulation on Access to Documents: A Critical Analysis, YEL 21:385–442
Peers S, Costa M (2012) Accountability for Delegated and Implementing Acts after the Treaty of Lisbon (2012). ELJ 18: 427–460
Peers S, Costa M (2016) Reassessing the Accountability of European Union Decentralized Agencies: Mind the Independence Gap. EPL 22: 645–665
Rossi L, Silva P (2017) Public Access to Documents in the EU. Hart Publishing, Oxford

Schedler A (1997) Conceptualizing Accountability. In: Schedler A (ed) The Self-Restraining State: Power and Accountability in New Democracies. Lynne Rienner, Boulder, pp 13–28

Tomkins A (1999) Transparency and the Emergence of a European Administrative Law. YEL 19:217–256

Vesterdorf B (1998) Transparency - Not just a vogue word. ILJ 22:902–929

Marios Costa is Senior Lecturer at the Institute for the Study of European Law (ISEL), City Law School, City, University of London, United Kingdom. He was previously a visiting scholar at the Centre for European Legal Studies (CELS, University of Cambridge). Marios' principal research interests lie in the area of accountability and transparency at the EU level of governance. In his latest monograph entitled *The Accountability Gap in EU Law* (Routledge, 2017), he argues that currently the EU institutions along with the Member States are not in a position to control the actions or omissions of the so-called independent agencies as well as the various committees and expert groups. Despite recent progress, the EU needs to put forward an acceptable constitutional framework to secure accountability of the decision-making process.

Chapter 11
The Last Soldier Standing? Courts Versus Politicians and the Rule of Law Crisis in the New Member States of the EU

Dimitry Kochenov and Petra Bárd

Contents

D. Kochenov (✉)
University of Groningen, Groningen, The Netherlands
e-mail: d.kochenov@rug.nl

P. Bárd
Eötvös Loránd University, Budapest, Hungary
e-mail: bardp@ceu.edu

P. Bárd
Legal Studies Department, Central European University, Budapest, Hungary

Hirsch Ballin, Van der Schyff & Stremler (eds.), *European Yearbook of Constitutional Law 2019*, European Yearbook of Constitutional Law 1,
https://doi.org/10.1007/978-94-6265-359-7_11

Abstract The rule of law backsliding in Hungary and Poland revealed the EU's significant vulnerabilities in the face of the need to uphold the values that the whole system of EU integration presumes are in place. The lessons are revealing: respecting the *acquis* does not guarantee continuing adherence to Article 2 TEU values; economic success in the Union does not necessarily entrench democracy and the rule of law; the tools available to preserve the rule of law are largely inadequate, as they could go against the key assumptions of the internal market. Consequently, the lack of political will to deal with the values' crisis is not at all irrational, which makes it even more worrisome. What stands out from the grim picture is the revolutionary case law of the Court of Justice on judicial independence and mutual trust, which bridges the available infringement procedures with the outstanding problems and offers horizontal and vertical empowerment to the EU's decentralised judiciaries – now able to intervene – while also resolving the competences conundrum through a broad reading of the principle of judicial independence as a key element of the rule of law. However inspiring, recent case law developments are insufficient, we argue, to deal with the sociological legitimacy crisis in tackling illiberal democracies plaguing the EU: autocratic legalism cannot be fought with legalism alone. Designing a long-term systemic approach to a complex re-articulation of EU values is indispensable, as enforcement is not a panacea per se.

Keywords Democracy · EU law · rule of law · Hungary · judicial dialogue · judicial independence · Poland · values enforcement

11.1 Introduction

The European Union (EU) and the Member States seem to be doing as little as they can to combat rule of law backsliding in some of the EU's constituent parts. Each of the EU institutions came up with their own plan on what to do, inventing ever more soft law of questionable quality. All that is being done appears to reveal one and only one point: there is a total disagreement among all the actors involved as to how to sort out the current impasse, revealing the soft underbelly of the EU in the face of the 'constitutional *coups*', deeply undermining both its day-to-day functioning and its grand promise.[1] This inaction unquestionably assists the powers of the backsliding Member States in consolidating their assault upon the EU's values even further. At least four key legal-political techniques are used to consolidate the undermining of the rule of law and democracy, as the present chapter shall demonstrate. All of them can be found in all the backsliding jurisdictions: a

---

[1] Scheppele 2017.

veritable template of assaulting the rule of law has emerged.[2] Step-by-step guides could be drawn on the basis of the Hungarian and Polish stories.[3]

There are also positive developments: the crisis allowed the judiciaries of the EU to shine, bringing the inter-court dialogue to a vital new level, upgrading its substance.[4] At the core of this dialogue are now also the fundamental principles of EU law, even those not confined in their entirety to the EU scope of powers,[5] in particular the independence of the judiciary – interpreted by the Court of Justice (ECJ) as an EU law principle and a vital element of the rule of law,[6] as opposed to merely the issues of validity and the interpretation of EU law *per se*, however broadly conceived.[7] Such interpretation – a spectacular innovation reshaping the constitutional system of the Union as we speak – gave voice to vertical concerns related to the independence of the judiciary,[8] as well as horizontal rule of law concerns, leading to a significant refinement of the principle of mutual recognition.[9] This allowed the Court to learn from its past mistakes in dealing with the assaults on the rule of law.[10] The presumption that the strict enforcement of the *acquis* is sufficient to guarantee adherence to the values is clearly no longer valid.[11] Together with the endowment of Article 19(1) TEU with new significance, the ongoing crisis in the rule of law helped open a new chapter of European constitutionalism: the very fact that the current concerns arose – rather than being strictly confined to the national legal orders – demonstrates the actual maturity of the level of supranational law and integration, or at least of its aspirations.[12]

As a crucial element of the ongoing fight for the rule of law, the principle of the independence of the judiciary is derived at EU level from Article 19(1) TEU, and is

---

[2] Pech and Scheppele 2017.

[3] Cf. Krygier 2006, p 129, who anticipated the emergence of such templates long before the backsliding began.

[4] CMLRev: editorial comment 2019; Dawson 2013, p 371.

[5] On the shift of Article 2 TEU principles from ‘principles’ to ‘values’ without undermining the essence of the former, see Pech 2010.

[6] Court of Justice (hereafter: ECJ), *Associação Sindical dos Juízes Portugueses,* 27 February 2018, case C-64/16, ECLI:EU:C:2018:117; Pech and Platon 2018; Ciampi 2018; Krajewski 2018; Parodi 2018.

[7] For the criticism of the classical inter-court dialogue before the most recent case law, see, e.g., Kochenov and van Wolferen 2018.

[8] This allowed the national courts under threat to deploy the preliminary ruling procedure in an innovative way in order to guarantee the preservation of their own independence: Biernat and Kawczyńska 2018; cf. Broberg 2017.

[9] E.g. ECJ, *Minister for Justice and Equality v LM,* 25 July 2018, case C-216/18 PPU, ECLI:EU:C:2018:586; Rizcallah 2018; cf. Lenaerts 2017.

[10] Compare ECJ, *Commission v. Hungary*, 6 November 2012, case C-286/12, ECLI:EU:C:2012:687 with ECJ, *Commission v. Poland*, case C-619/18 R, Order ex parte of 19 October 2018, EU:C:2018:852 and Order of 17 December 2018, EU:C:2018:1021.

[11] On the difference, see Kochenov 2017a.

[12] Even though numerous international organisations around the world face similar crises and are designed to resolve these with a varying degree of success: Closa 2017.

regarded as a vital part of the value of the rule of law.[13] Judicial independence thus emerged as a crucial connector between EU law and the enforcement of Article 2 TEU values outside the scope of the *acquis sensu stricto*,[14] which explains the relative silence on the Charter of Fundamental Rights (CFR) among those who are busy trying to deal with the ongoing rule of law concerns in practice:[15] Article 51 CFR still stands, all the literature on the need to move on from this competence block notwithstanding.[16] After all, we are learning that 19(1) TEU is good enough.[17] A range of tools from pecuniary[18] to interim measures with backfiring force[19] can now be deployed to freeze at least some of the attempts of backsliding governments to undermine the independence of their judiciaries even further. This new, more thoughtful approach could definitely have a significant impact in other areas of EU law too.

Such fundamentally important developments notwithstanding, the fact remains that democratic and rule of law backsliding runs much deeper than the hijacking of the courts: Blokker has been absolutely correct in constantly reminding us of the need to deal with the deeper roots of soft totalitarianism and populist convulsions.[20] At issue is the phenomenon characterised by Scheppele as 'autocratic legalism', which has deep implications for the very fabric of the societies in question, potentially making the return to liberal democracy difficult.[21] Moreover, the problem of 'democratic decay', 'backsliding' and populism seems to be a global one,[22] rather than confined to some EU Member States *per se*. In the EU, just as elsewhere in the world – from Venezuela to Turkey – 'sociological legitimacy'[23] is crucially important and cannot be ignored. The core issue, ultimately, cannot consist in the perfecting of judicial cooperation in the hope of saving some courts in the EU's periphery.[24] It is much broader: how to ensure that the EU's own rule of law is meticulously and consistently upheld, while crucially enjoying solid

---

13 ECJ, *Associação Sindical dos Juízes Portugueses,* 27 February 2018, case C-64/16, ECLI:EU: C:2018:117, paras 36, 37 and 41.

14 Christophe Hillion predicted this development: Hillion 2016.

15 Pech and Platon 2018, pp 1833–1836.

16 Jakab 2016; Jakab 2017. Cf. von Bogdandy et al. 2017.

17 The connection with the Charter is however obvious: ECJ, *Commission v. Poland*, case C-619/ 18 R, Order ex parte of 19 October 2018, EU:C:2018:852 and Order of 17 December 2018, EU: C:2018:1021.

18 Especially when the backsliding Member States attempt to openly defy the Court: ECJ, *Commission v. Poland*, 17 April 2018, case C-441/17, ECLI:EU:C:2018:255.

19 ECJ, *Commission v. Poland*, case C-619/18 R, Order ex parte of 19 October 2018, EU: C:2018:852 and Order of 17 December 2018, EU:C:2018:1021.

20 Blokker 2016, 2018.

21 Scheppele 2018.

22 Daly 2019; Anselmi 2018.

23 Blokker 2019.

24 Kukovec 2015.

legitimacy? The issue of societal internalisation of the core principles of Article 2 TEU in the face of the populist wave is fundamental here.

We argue that the most mature answer to the problems at hand necessarily requires a long-term perspective and beyond reforming the existing enforcement mechanisms, also involves reform of the Union as such, as well as responding to Blokker's concerns: 'autocratic legalism' impacts societies to a great degree and cannot be fought with legalism alone. Supranational law should be made more aware of the values it is obliged by the Treaties to respect and protect, both at the national and supranational levels. EU law should embrace the rule of law as an institutional ideal,[25] which *inter alia* implies eventual substantive limitations on the *acquis* of the Union, as well as sincerely implementing EU values in the context of the day-to-day functioning of the Union, thus elevating them above the maladroit instrumentalism – and all its effectiveness leaving so much to be desired – marking them today. The outcome of such instrumentalism is crystal clear: a national economy can be distinctly successful in the internal market even when the core values of the Union are being undermined in the country in question. Poland provides a remarkable example of this, having become the first 'developed market' in Central and Eastern Europe[26] in a context where it is also soon to join Hungary – recently designated by Freedom House as the first 'partly free' regime in the history of the EU[27] – given recent developments. Economically successful EU membership is thus free of any 'natural' requirement that democracy and the rule of law should be sincerely felt,[28] which is a very worrisome reality, one which must be borne in mind at all times when dealing with the Union's remaining rule of law problems.

What is the situation with the rule of law in the EU today? On the basis of the most dramatic examples, the number of the Member States where the rule of law is not safeguarded doubled as Poland[29] has now joined Hungary.[30] While more states could follow, the Union's position apparently continues to be very weak: new soft law of questionable quality has been produced by each institution.[31] The picture is grim, notwithstanding even the belated activation of the Article 7(1) Treaty on

[25] Cf. Roy 2015.

[26] Day M (2018) Poland Becomes the First Country from Former Soviet Bloc to Be Ranked a 'Developed Market'. www.telegraph.co.uk/business/2018/09/24/poland-becomes-first-country-former-soviet-bloc-ranked-developed/ Accessed 14 February 2019.

[27] Simon Z (2019) Hungary Becomes First 'Partly Free' EU Nation in Democracy Gauge www.bloomberg.com/news/articles/2019-02-05/hungary-becomes-first-partly-free-eu-nation-in-democracy-gauge Accessed 14 February 2019.

[28] Kochenov 2017b.

[29] European Commission 2017a. Cf., most importantly: *Sadurski* 2018; Bodnar 2018; *Koncewicz* 2018a; *Koncewicz* 2016. See also The Venice Commission for Democracy through Law 2016a, b.

[30] European Parliament 2018. Cf., most importantly, Szente 2017; Scheppele 2015; Sólyom 2015; Bánkuti et al. 2012.

[31] Council of the European Union 2014a, pp 20–21; European Commission 2014; European Parliament 2016. Cf. on all these instruments, Waelbroeck and Oliver 2017; Kochenov et al. 2016. Kochenov and Pech 2016; Oliver and Stefanelli 2016; but also see Hirsch Ballin 2016.

European Union (hereinafter: TEU) mechanism.[32] The particular instance of this activation is obviously somewhat misplaced, since Article 7(1) TEU is about 'threats' to values and the assault on the values in Poland and Hungary is well beyond the 'threat' point, thus begging the question of how appropriate the chosen legal basis actually is.[33] Indeed, the situation would seem to be evolving extremely fast and mainly – almost uniquely – in the direction of the deterioration of the rule of law and an increase in the abuse of the independent institutions by the executive.[34] It would appear that there is a total disagreement among essentially all the actors involved concerning what should be done, and the political will to sort out the current impasse is lacking at the Member State level as well.

The Council is the firmest of all the institutions in terms of downplaying the problem, even going as far as to present the main actions taken by the other institutions to solve it as potentially illegal. The Council Legal Service has been negative – with no solid arguments for its position[35] – about the Commission's 'pre-Article 7 proposal'.[36] It similarly dismissed the attempts to cut EU funding of the backsliding states.[37] Topping the list, however, are the flimsy reasons put forward by the Council Legal Service for its refusal to permit Judith Sargentini MEP to present her report, which triggered the request from the Parliament to start the Article 7(1) procedure against Hungary, in the Council: the Council does not want to hear Ms Sargentini in person based on legal advice which was only given 'orally' and with the arguments not disclosed, which does not shield the Council's position from criticism. The only more absurd avenue open to it was to support Hungary before the Court, where it now argues – not convincingly – that the Parliament managed to violate its own rules of procedure in adopting the Sargentini Report.[38]

The explanation behind the unwillingness to act could be obvious: since the Internal Market is an emanation of deep economic interpenetration aimed, precisely, at making outright hostilities between the Member States impossible – precisely the reason for choosing economic tools to achieve the goal of peace[39] – it is clear that the very logic of Article 7 TEU deeply contradicts the logic of the Internal Market and the rich Member States potentially stand to lose a great deal as a result of taking a principled, value-laden position on rule of law backsliding. This is why expecting too much of the Council – and by extension, of Article 7 TEU – would be naïve,

[32] European Parliament 2017; European Commission 2017a; Scheppele and Pech 2017.

[33] Kochenov 2019a, p 88.

[34] Sedelmeier 2014; Müller 2014; von Bogdandy and Sonnevend 2015; Closa and Kochenov 2016; Jakab and Kochenov 2017; Pech and Scheppele 2017.

[35] Kochenov and Pech 2015.

[36] Council of the European Union 2014b, especially para 28.

[37] Kelemen et al. 2018.

[38] ECJ, *Hungary v European Parliament*, case C-650/18 (pending at time of writing). Cf. Kochenov 2019b, p 2082.

[39] This is exactly why the objective of peace has proven to be unexportable: Williams 2010. Cf. Kochenov and Basheska 2016.

unless something truly terrible happens in a backsliding Member State:[40] the Internal Market, after all, functions as designed.[41]

When the Council is naturally disinclined and other EU institutions are profoundly ineffective, the ECJ, as in Andersen's tale, *de facto* plays the role of the last soldier standing. It stands by gradually learning from its own mistakes and the Commission's significant missteps: especially in the 'age-discrimination' cases, where the hijacking of the Hungarian judiciary went unnoticed,[42] while a radically more robust result was achieved in *Commission v. Poland* on virtually identical facts in the context of the attempted assault on the Supreme Court.[43]

The Court cannot solve these outstanding problems alone, even when helped by the national judiciaries. A much more concerted effort is required from all the actors involved to get the EU out of this impasse. While it remains the case, the supranational political party groups, instead of helping, seem to be aggravating the situation.[44] This inaction – or attempts to hinder positive change – on the part of the political institutions helps the powers of the backsliding Member States consolidate their assault upon the EU's values even further, undermining the truly heroic efforts of the Court of Justice and the national courts in Poland,[45] Ireland[46] and elsewhere in the Union. The ECJ's 'stone-by-stone' approach,[47] although unable to solve the outstanding problems by itself, nevertheless gives space for optimism and could amount to one of the key legacies of the Lenaerts court.

The inventiveness of the autocrats, populist voting and the weakness of the EU's track record and current position on values, are among a no doubt huge variety of other factors which have brought about a previously unimaginable situation, whereby the EU harbours Member States which – besides obviously not qualifying for Union membership were they to apply today, even given the EU's usual 'window dressing' of rule of law conditionality[48] – are working hard to undermine the key principles the EU was created to safeguard and promote: democracy, the rule of law and the protection of fundamental rights.[49] The underlying issue is the

---

40 But see Hirsch Ballin 2016.

41 See, for a number of divergent perspectives, Amtenbrink et al. 2019.

42 ECJ, *Commission v. Hungary*, 6 November 2012, case C-286/12, ECLI:EU:C:2012:687; cf. Belavusau 2013.

43 ECJ, *Commission v. Poland*, case C-619/18, R Order ex parte of 19 October 2018, ECLI:EU:C:2018:852 and Order of 17 December 2018, ECLI:EU:C:2018:1021; cf. CMLRev: editorial comment 2019.

44 Kelemen 2017; Kelemen and Pech 2018.

45 Biernat and Kawczyńska 2018.

46 See the whole saga surrounding ECJ, *Minister for Justice and Equality v LM*, 25 July 2018, case C-216/18 PPU, ECLI:EU:C:2018:586.

47 As explained by President Lenaerts in the context of the EU citizenship law field: Lenaerts 2015.

48 De Ridder and Kochenov 2011.

49 As well as other values expressed in Article 2 TEU; Pech 2010; Kochenov 2017a, b, c, d; Magen and Pech 2018.

creation of a *modus vivendi* where the EU's own instrumentalist understanding of the rule of law, including principles such as mutual trust or the autonomy of EU law, reinforces, instead of jeopardises, respect for the values enshrined in Article 2 TEU.[50]

This chapter starts out by defining the problem, focusing on the nature and gravity of the rule of law backsliding in Hungary and Poland, in order to outline four key techniques deployed by autocratic regimes in order to consolidate the constitutional capture and massive assault on European values (Sect. 11.2). The techniques to achieve, legitimise and consolidate the destruction of the rule of law include: appeals to untamed national sovereignty emanating directly from 'the people'; fetishisation of 'constitutional identity' taken out of context; appeals to national security complete with the harassment of the media, NGOs and the independent educational institutions; and international disinformation campaigns (Sect. 11.3). We proceed by discussing the role of institutions, with special regard to the room for manœuvre and the responsibility of the judiciary in upholding the rule of law, now taken seriously by the Court of Justice (Sect. 11.4). Next, the state of the art with regard to values in the EU legal system will be discussed (Sect. 11.5), followed by a normative assessment of how these values should preferably be approached (Sect. 11.6). Looking at supranational law, we argue that a failure to upgrade the role played by values – including the rule of law – sufficiently when the Union transformed from an ordinary treaty organisation into a constitutional system lies at the root of the problem (Sect. 11.7). The EU's powerlessness is among the root causes of letting Member States slide into authoritarianism and the courts alone will not be able to solve the puzzles currently outstanding (Sect. 11.8). We conclude that beyond praising the ECJ's immense forward-looking efforts, shifting the focus of the discussion from the enforcement of the rule of law to the reform of the Union as such is needed as a long-term solution (Sect. 11.9). There is time: illiberal regimes seem to be there to stay, and the options with regard to changing this reality, either supranationally or from a grass-roots level, are limited if not non-existent: we might need to wait two years, ten years – or thirty, for that matter – before Hungary and Poland are back on track. In the meantime, the EU institutions should arrive at a more subtle realisation of the EU's constitutional role and should not insist on the specificities of EU law trumping all other considerations, including respect for the values the EU and the Member States are supposed to share, but should instead acknowledge the possibility of potential limitations so as to let the foundations of the EU evolve, as provided for by the Lisbon Treaty. This could definitely be achieved in the context of a soft quarantine of Poland, Hungary and any other backsliding states, cutting the funding received by these countries from the EU, as well as designing and implementing more effective ways of combating fraud involving EU funds, while the ECJ's control over the independence of the judiciary, as well as the dialogue between the courts in the EU, is extended.

---

[50] Klamert and Kochenov 2019.

11.2 European Values: From High Expectations to Jeopardy?

Whereas all Member States suffer from deficiencies in at least some elements of the rule of law, in light of the emerging pattern of constitutional capture we focus exclusively on rule of law backsliders and follow the definition proposed by Pech and Scheppele, according to which rule of law backsliding is a 'process through which elected public authorities deliberately implement governmental blueprints which aim to systematically weaken, annihilate or capture internal checks on power with the view of dismantling the liberal democratic state and entrenching the long-term rule of the dominant party'.[51] In what follows, we shall focus on the two Member States which currently satisfy these definitional elements: Hungary and Poland.

Even though countries acceding to the EU in 2004 had high hopes of joining the democratic world after decades of totalitarian rule, the enthusiasm for European values on the part of some Central Eastern European Member States vanished on the way – a phenomenon which was all but unthinkable during the 1989 Eastern European 'velvet revolutions'.[52] During the democratic transition in all these countries, a separation of powers had been realised, where parliamentary law-making procedure required extensive consultation with both civil society and opposition parties and crucial issues of constitutional concern required a super-majority vote in Parliament. Independent self-governing judicial power ensured that the laws were applied fairly. Constitutional scrutiny played a special role in transitioning democracies. The Commission, having supervised the transition on behalf of the EU while focusing on all the core values,[53] has wrongly assured EU citizens and governments that the newcomers would not represent a danger of backsliding – precisely what we are witnessing today.[54]

After the regime change, Hungary was the first 'post-communist' country to join the Council of Europe and abide by the European Convention on Human Rights and Fundamental Freedoms (ECHR or Convention) in 1990. Poland gained membership in the Council of Europe in 1991 and became party to the ECHR in 1993. Hungary and Poland established official relations with the North Atlantic Treaty Organization (NATO) already in the early 1990s and became NATO members in 1999. They also signed EU Association Agreements in the early 1990s, which paved the way for accession negotiations and EU membership.[55] The Treaty of Accession to the European Union was signed in 2003. Hungary, Poland, six

---

[51] Pech and Scheppele 2017, p 8.

[52] Vachudova 2005.

[53] Kochenov 2004. This focus had a profound impact on EU constitutionalism, informing both the doctrine and the law on EU values: Sadurski 2012.

[54] For an analysis of why there have always been strong reasons not to believe the Commission's assurances, see Kochenov 2008.

[55] Inglis 2000.

other Central and Eastern European countries and two Mediterranean islands became members of the European Union on 1 May 2004 as part of the biggest enlargement in the Union's history.[56] The European Union played an important role in the transformation of all the Eastern European states and in the context of their democratisation.[57] The principle of conditionality was used to achieve this, coupled with the presumption that any democratic or rule of law 'backsliding' would not be possible once the transformation was in place.[58] Alongside the Europe Agreements, the Union applied the Copenhagen criteria adopted by the 1993 Copenhagen European Council.[59] Clearly going beyond the scope of the Europe Agreements,[60] these criteria became the cornerstone of Hungary's and Poland's transformations throughout the first decade of this century, also reshaping the core of EU constitutionalism in the process.[61] The shocking rate at which the deconstruction of the rule of law occurs in Poland and Hungary today demonstrates the importance of a constitutional culture beyond black letter law, including constitutions, institutions and procedures.

The shift came rather abruptly when in April 2010, in a free and fair election, the centre-right political parties, Fidesz Hungarian Civic Union (Fidesz) and the Christian-Democratic People's Party (in Hungarian: Kereszténydemokrata Néppárt, KDNP)[62] got 53% of the votes, which translated into more than two-thirds of the seats in the unicameral Hungarian Parliament under the election law then in force.[63] The ruling party did not tolerate any internal dissent, and after forming the second Fidesz government[64] it eliminated – at least in the domestic setting – all sources of criticism by both voters and state institutions, effectively disposing of any effective checks and balances. Should a discontent electorate now wish to correct deficiencies, it would be difficult for it to do so due to the novel rules of the national ballot, which fundamentally bring into question the fairness of future elections. Judicial oversight and most importantly, the Hungarian Constitutional Court's power to correct the failures of a majoritarian government have been considerably impaired, along the powers of other *fora* designed to serve as checks on government powers. Distortions of the media and a lack of public information lead to the impossibility of

---

[56] Ott and Inglis 2002.

[57] Cf. Vachudova 2005.

[58] Kochenov 2008.

[59] Hillion 2004.

[60] Müller-Graff 1997, p 42; Maresceau 2001.

[61] Sadurski 2012.

[62] The cooperation between Fidesz and KDNP should not be regarded as a coalition, rather as a party alliance already in existence before the elections. According to their self-perception, their relationship is similar to the party alliance between CDU and CSU in the Federal Republic of Germany. KDNP is a tiny party which would probably not get into Parliament on its own. The insignificance of KDNP allows us to abbreviate for the sake of brevity: whenever the term 'Fidesz government' is used, the Fidesz-KDNP political alliance is meant.

[63] Act C of 1997 on the Election Procedure.

[64] Fidesz first governed between 1998 and 2002.

a meaningful public debate and weaken the chances of restoring deliberative democracy. Support by the electorate is enhanced through emotionalism, revolutionary rhetoric, catchphrases such as 'law and order', 'family', 'tradition', 'nation', symbolic law-making, and identity politics in general. The friend/foe dichotomy is artificially created through punitive populism and scapegoating, partially by building on pre-existing prejudices, and partially by creating new enemies such as multinational companies or persons challenging Hungarian unorthodoxy on the international scene. Legally-speaking, the Hungarian 'reforms' are very well-designed, combining elements of different legal approaches present in different jurisdictions around the world in such a way that the outcome is a 'Frankenstate', an apt turn of phrase coined by Kim Scheppele.[65] As a result of the government in power's concerted effort to destroy the checks and balances which used to restrain it and capture the state, Hungary, the poster child of transition, emerges as the first 'partly free' political regime in the EU.

The changes can be traced back to the government's ideological roots, but unlike in Poland, government ideology is chosen by way of political convenience. Turning towards illiberalism was a necessity for a government wishing to retain political and economic power at all costs, and capture the state to this end. It could not reconcile its ideological stance with the concept of liberal democracy. So Fidesz had to search for other role models than the democratic world, and found its allies in countries such as Turkey and most importantly Russia. Even though illiberalism was relabelled as 'Christian democracy' after Fidesz was re-elected in April 2018, the same form of governance remains.[66] Representing radically opposing views within a short period never hurt Fidesz politicians, who are brilliant at explaining their reasons for a volte-face. The party, originally professing strong anti-Russian sentiments, became pro-Putin – and still managed to retain public support, while rebuilding the state machinery in such a way that alteration of power became if not impossible, then extremely difficult, thus effectively capturing the Hungarian state.

Poland followed the path of illiberalism when the Law and Justice party (Prawo i Sprawiedliwość, PiS) entered government in 2015.[67] The country experienced a very serious departure from liberal democratic principles and is going through the reversal of the rule of law in various fields.

The tools employed and the outcomes are very similar to those in Hungary, but certain elements of the Polish case also make it distinct, illustrating that there was no Central Eastern European or even Visegrád pattern. First, unlike Hungary, the Polish government does not have a constitution-making nor amending majority,

---

[65] Scheppele 2013. Cf. Uitz 2015.

[66] After Fidesz won the April 2018 elections and secured a 2/3 majority in the Parliament for the party, PM Orbán declared the end of the era of liberal democracy and stated that it was replaced by Christian democracy. Dostal et al. 2018, p 22. Instead of substantive changes, the new terminology can rather be explained by the recognition that the term 'illiberal democracy' 'in English sounds like blood libel'. HVG, (2015) Orbán: Az illiberális demokrácia magyarul jól cseng. www.hvg.hu/itthon/20150519_orban_fekete_barany Accessed 14 February 2019.

[67] See, for the best analysis to date, Sadurski 2018.

therefore – for the time being – it engages in the dismantlement of the rule of law by way of curbing ordinary laws and directly ignoring the constitution. As Ewa Łętowska put it, the government has been 'trying to change the system through the back door'.[68] Second, Hungary is essentially a kleptocracy,[69] where the government may pick any ideology available on the political spectrum to acquire and retain economic and political power. By contrast, the Polish government and especially PiS leader Jarosław Kaczyński, the *de facto* ruler of Poland, are more likely to truly believe in what they are preaching in terms of national interests. When justifying its rule of law backsliding, a whole new worldview is developed, rewriting the democratic transition and the post-1989 Polish history as something fundamentally corrupted and shaped by foreign interests, in opposition to national ones.[70] For him, post-1989 Polish history, including the roundtable talks in 1989, is the result of an indecent compromise between the individuals and movements bringing about regime change and the outgoing Communist forces. Along these lines, he sees all democratic institutions as a 'sham'; for him, 'the Third Republic is not a real state but a phantom state built on the intellectual corruption of political elites, bribery, dysfunctional government caving in to Brussels and selling off Poland to strangers for peanuts'.[71] The war on history plays a key role in the project of constitutional capture.[72] For PiS 'repolonisation' means taking over power, banks, land and other property, and means reclaiming Poland from both foreigners and the corrupt political elites so as to bring about true regime change.[73] Any means are apparently allowed, and any checks or controls on power are seen as unnecessary burdens the state shall be freed from, so as to accomplish this purgative exercise.

11.3 The Four Elements of the Autocrats' Playbook

Illiberal governments are very well aware of the irreconcilability of their politics with European values. The states in question therefore lobby for exemptions and recognition of their Frankenstates in the EU context by relying mostly on four techniques which have proved to be effective and which include four key elements.

---

[68] Pacula 2017. Taking the President's announcement of a 2018 constitutional referendum into account, this might change in the future: Kelly L (2017) Polish President Wants Referendum on Constitution in Nov 2018. www.reuters.com/article/poland-politics-president-constitution-idUSL8N1IQ6P0 Accessed 14 February 2019. For an immediate analysis, see Matczak 2017.

[69] Cf. Magyar 2016.

[70] Davies C (2016) The Conspiracy Theorists Who Have Taken over Poland. www.theguardian.com/world/2016/feb/16/conspiracy-theorists-who-have-taken-over-poland Accessed 14 February 2019. Conelly and Koncewicz 2016.

[71] *Ibid.*

[72] Koncewicz 2018b. In Hungary the situation is similar: Könczöl 2018, p 246.

[73] Freedom House 2017.

Firstly, the backsliding states resort to the invocation of national sovereignty as their absolute right to 'reform' the state in a way which leads to the dismantlement of democratic and rule of law structures of checks and balances, so that placing the state at the service of a *de facto* one-party regime goes undisturbed. Secondly, backsliding states deploy the rhetoric of constitutional identity, claiming a measure of legal exceptionalism and specificity to shield the destruction of the rule of law from criticism. Thirdly, security concerns are showcased as a reason to diminish the level of checks on the government. Finally, backsliding states' governments capture the media and research institutions and conduct large-scale disinformation campaigns to undermine free speech, destroy the public debate and silence dissent. Let us look at some examples of the deployment of these four key strategies.

11.3.1 Invocation of National Sovereignty to Capture the Judiciary, and Beyond

The first technique is the invocation of national sovereignty through the promotion of a false opposition between 'democracy' and the legal structures in place to tame majoritarian government with a view to preserving, precisely, the alternation in power and the continuation of democratic government. For the populists, the division of powers and the system of checks and balances stand for the taming of 'democracy'. The Polish capture of the Constitutional Tribunal, the Supreme Court, the National Council of the Judiciary, and the ordinary courts happened under the pretext of 'reform' of the judiciary and was presented as a sovereign matter for the Member State, implying that the EU would be acting *ultra vires* if it interfered.[74] The worst nightmare is evolving before our eyes: the democratic Polish state, which was motivated to join the Union as Sadurski rightly explained, partly as a way to protect *itself* against the possible destruction of democracy and the rule of law,[75] is being dismantled by PiS in plain sight, with the EU doing virtually nothing to stop this.

The Polish Constitutional Tribunal was the first institution to fall victim to state capture in late 2016.[76] Its powers have been considerably cut, changes were introduced to its structure and proceedings, its budget was cut, and three justices elected constitutionally by the seventh Sejm (the lower chamber of the Polish Parliament) were not permitted to take their oath, while three justices elected unconstitutionally by the eighth Sejm after PiS had won the elections were permitted to do so. Having rendered the Constitutional Tribunal irrelevant in upholding the rule of law, the government has done the same with the Supreme Court, the National Council for the Judiciary and the ordinary courts. The changes concerned the reorganisation of the Supreme Court to empower the executive to: prematurely

[74] Grabowska-Moroz et al. 2018.

[75] Sadurski 2012.

[76] Koncewicz 2016.

end the tenure of judges, meaning forcefully retire them; determine the conditions and procedure for becoming a Supreme Court judge; control disciplinary procedures, amending the rules of procedure of the Supreme Court; change the total number of judges serving on the Supreme Court; reorganise the chambers in which Supreme Court justices serve; and restructure their case allocation.[77] Ordinary court capture was effected by subordinating all the Presidents and Directors of courts, i.e. the persons who decide on administrative and financial issues, to the Minister of Justice.[78] Even this short enumeration of government intrusions into the powers of the courts highlights only some of the milestones in judicial capture and shows, in the words of the Venice Commission – the most authoritative body in Europe on the issues of the rule of law and judicial independence – that 'the constitutionality of Polish laws can no longer be guaranteed'.[79]

In Hungary, we witnessed a similarly vicious attack against the judiciary, starting in 2011. The judicial retirement age of 70 was lowered to 62 with immediate effect, on the pretext of a labour law issue, where Hungary claimed sole power. This resulted in the removal and replacement of about 8% of all judges, 27% of Supreme Court judges and more than 50% of appeal court presidents. Towards the end of 2012, responding to pressure from various national and international fora,[80] the government agreed to rehire retired judges aged between 62 and 70, if they wished to continue to work. However, the judges' return was obstructed by two factors. First, court president positions and other functions had already been filled by new judges, meaning that the compulsorily retired judges who wished to return were offered lower court places with less prestige. Second, the judges who made to retire prematurely received considerable compensation for the period of their forced retirement, and a compensation equalling their previous year's salary, if they opted to remain in retirement. As a result, once the compensation scheme was introduced, most judges preferred it to returning to work. The matter became essentially moot. In theory, Hungary was condemned for its early retirement law by the ECJ, but in practice, the most experienced judges were removed from the judiciary: the Commission won a Pyrrhic victory.[81]

Another example in the same vein is the dispute related to the felling of trees in the Białowieża Forest, a UNESCO World Heritage Site. Pending the judgment in

[77] In disregard of national and international criticism, on 8 December 2017, the laws on the Supreme Court and the Council were adopted by the Sejm, and on 15 December 2017 they were approved by the Senate.

[78] Ustawa z dnia 23 marca 2017 r. o zmianie ustawy – Prawo o ustroju sądów powszechnych [Law amending the act on the organization of common courts system], OJ 2017, item 803, www.dziennikustaw.gov.pl/DU/2017/803 (in Polish) Accessed 14 February 2019.

[79] The Venice Commission for Democracy through Law 2016a, b; European Commission 2017b, para 10.

[80] Hungarian Constitutional Court (HCC) Decision 33/2012. (VII. 17.), Decision 45/2012. (XII. 29.), The Venice Commission for Democracy through Law 2012.

[81] ECJ, *Commission v. Hungary*, 6 November 2012, case C-286/12, ECLI:EU:C:2012:687.

the main proceedings in *Białowieża*, the Court of Justice ordered Poland to stop the forest management operations under challenge.[82] The Polish response was intensified logging, and Poland even asked to remove the forest in question from the UNESCO World Heritage List.[83] Reference to national sovereignty was frequently made without any further justification. As the above controversy shows, by questioning the powers of the EU, the Polish government did not aim to initiate a legitimate discussion about the delineation between national and EU powers. It rather preferred 'to break free from the supranational machinery of control and enforcement. Following the trajectory from the "exit in values" to the "exit in legality" reveals an inescapable logic. All institutions, domestic and supranational, are seen to be standing in the way, and their rejection is part of the comprehensive constitutional doctrine – the politics of resentment'.[84]

11.3.2 Appeals to Constitutional Identity to Undermine the Institutions

The second and more sophisticated technique is the attempt to package departures from the rule of law in the name of constitutional identity.[85] Back in 2017, the Hungarian Parliament failed to acquire the necessary quorum to constitutionally entrench the concept of constitutional identity, but after Fidesz and its tiny coalition partner the Christian Democratic People's Party acquired a two-thirds i.e. constitution-amending majority, a modification to Article R) of the Fundamental Law referring to 'Hungarian cultural and Christian identity' has again been tabled. However, the amendment is somewhat redundant, since the already captured Hungarian Constitutional Court came to rescue the government, and developed its own theory of constitutional identity after the previous failed attempt to incorporate the concept into the Fundamental Law. When delivering its abstract constitutional interpretation in relation to European Council decision 2015/1601 of 22 September 2015 establishing provisional measures benefitting Italy and Greece, to support them in better coping with an emergency situation characterised by a sudden inflow of third country nationals in those Member States, the Constitutional Court invoked constitutional identity.[86] However tautological this may sound, according to the Constitutional Court 'constitutional identity equals the constitutional (self-) identity

[82] ECJ, *Commission v. Poland*, case C-441/17 R, Order of 20 November 2017, ECLI:EU:C:2017:877.

[83] In ECJ, *Commission v. Poland,* 17 April 2018, case C-441/17, ECLI:EU:C:2018:255 the Court ruled that by carrying on with the logging in the Białowieża Forest, Poland failed to fulfil its obligations under EU law. Cf. Coutron 2018; European Papers Editorial 2017.

[84] Koncewicz 2018c.

[85] Halmai 2018, pp 23–42; Kelemen and Pech 2018. For the best general treatment of the concept, see, Cloots 2015.

[86] HCC decision 22/2016. (XII. 5.).

of Hungary'.[87] Its content is to be determined by the Constitutional Court on a case-by-case basis based on the interpretation of the Fundamental Law, its purposes, the National Avowal contained therein, and the achievements of the Hungarian historical constitution. This definition is so vague that it can be considered as an attempt to grant a *carte blanche* type of derogation to the executive and the legislature from Hungary's obligations under EU law.[88] Once Fidesz acquired a two-thirds majority again in the 2018 parliamentary elections, it finally incorporated the constitutional identity into the Fundamental Law by way of the so-called seventh constitutional amendment.[89] Questioning claims of constitutional identity might well be criticised by those concerned as being ignorant or lacking respect, but European supervisory mechanisms should be able and confident enough to distinguish bluff from genuine claims of constitutional identity.[90]

11.3.3 Invocation of National Security to Undermine Checks on the Government

The third technique is reference to national security. Labelling virtually anyone still capable of formulating dissent as a foreign agent is a long used technique, but in Hungary it was taken to a whole new level in 2017 with the adoption of Lex CEU and Lex NGO,[91] targeting a private university and foreign-funded civil society organisations independent of government funds and thus able to express criticism of the government. The explanations of the laws attempting to force the CEU out of the country and to limit the public space for NGOs attempt to delegitimise these entities by claiming that they pose national security threats. The phenomenon of a shrinking space for civil society can be traced in both Hungary and Poland. The public narrative regarding NGOs has become very hostile. We are witnessing orchestrated smear campaigns against members of civil society who criticise the

[87] *Ibid.*

[88] For English language analyses, see Halmai 2017.

[89] See inserted Article R) Fundamental Law. For the official government position, see Trócsányi 2018.

[90] Kelemen 2018; Perju 2018; Halmai 2018.

[91] Act XXV of 2017 on the Modifications of Act CCIV of 20011 on National Higher Education and Act LXXVI of 2017 on the transparency of foreign-funded organisations. According to the law on NGOs, any association or foundation receiving foreign support above the amount of 23.200 EUR per year will have to notify the courts about this fact. EU money is exempted, but only if distributed by the Hungarian state through a budgetary institution. The respective organisation will be labelled as a so-called 'organization supported from abroad', which will need to be indicated at the entity's website, press releases, publications, etc. The law is disturbing in many aspects: it mimics Russian worst practices, which have been condemned by international organisations as violations of freedom of association and free speech.

government or simply do not fit its ideological agenda.[92] In some cases, the smear campaigns are followed by investigations undertaken by law enforcement or tax authorities, which may create an even more hostile environment for NGOs.[93] Governments can deprive civil society of effective functioning by limiting their access to funding, including state but also foreign private funding, as the Hungarian law obliges NGOs to indicate that they are 'organisations receiving support from abroad', and to display this stigmatising label on all their published materials.[94] This verges closely on demonising dissenters as terrorists, and indeed the government claims that NGOs receiving foreign support – i.e. often the most professional ones – help asylum seekers, including terrorists, enter the country. A modification of the Hungarian Criminal Code ensures that criminal sanctions can be imposed on NGOs and individuals which provide legal or other types of aid to migrants arriving at Hungary's borders.[95] National security claims not only fit into the ruling party's nationalistic, exclusionary rhetoric and scapegoating, but can also serve (i.e. be abused) as the basis for lobbying for exemptions from European standards. As Uitz points out, reference to national security, which is the sole responsibility of the Member States according to Article 4(2) TEU 'can be a much stronger centrifugal force in Europe than cries of constitutional identity could ever be. [...] Therefore, it is all the more important that European constitutional and political actors realize: The carefully crafted new Hungarian laws use the cloak of national security to stab the rule of law, as understood in Europe, in the heart'.[96]

11.3.4 Disinformation Campaigns at the Service of the Backsliding Regimes

The fourth technique the autocrats use to undermine the rule of law is disinformation or misinterpretation of the laws and policies of the government. Again Hungary took the lead in 2011 when they sent a wrong translation to Brussels of their controversial new constitution, the Fundamental Law, which made it appear to

---

[92] Associated Press in Warsaw (2017) Police Raid Offices of Women's Groups in Poland After Protests www.theguardian.com/world/2017/oct/05/police-raid-offices-of-womens-groups-in-poland Accessed 14 February 2019.

[93] The Hungarian Helsinki Committee et al. 2017.

[94] For more details, see Szuleka 2018.

[95] Article 353/ of Act C of 2012 on the Hungarian Criminal Code. For the official government position, see Website of the Hungarian Government (2018) Strong Action is Required Against the Organisers of Migration. www.kormany.hu/en/news/strong-action-is-required-against-the-organisers-of-migration Accessed 14 February 2019. The Commission has recently started infringement proceedings against Hungary regarding this law.

[96] Uitz 2017.

conform better to EU laws and values than the actual Hungarian original.[97] From a more substantive view, the Polish[98] and Hungarian[99] responses to the Commission's[100] and the European Parliament's[101] invitations for a Council Decision on the determination of a clear risk of a serious breach by Poland and Hungary of values enshrined in Article 2 TEU also contain factual mistakes and deliberate deceit.[102] Up-to-date information following the rapid legislative changes which sometimes happen literally overnight and solid legal research may deconstruct the fake information these texts contain and challenge the contention that these political forces engage in a dialogue, when all they do is produce documents or make some cosmetic changes to gain time and press on with their illiberal agendas.

11.4 The Role of the Judiciary and that of Political Institutions

The 'Anti-Member States' described above abuse their laws and constitutions to create autocracies, yet they take full part in governing the Union, benefiting from unprecedented direct financial support, and abusing the international prestige which is associated with membership of the EU,[103] while obviously undermining its image – an organisation obliged by its own law to actively *promote* values abroad which are not found at home.[104] In addition to prestige and to deriving tangible benefits from the integration of the national economy into the internal market, huge sums of money coming from the EU are direct transfers to the autocrats.[105] Poland will have received EUR 86 billion under the current budgetary framework by 2020 and Hungary 24 billion, which is an unprecedented transfer of resources from democracies to illiberal regimes after the end of the Cold War, and which unquestionably

[97] For a detailed enumeration of the discrepancies see The Hungarian Helsinki Committee et al. 2011. This technique is also employed the other way around: when the Venice Commission delivered its highly critical opinion of the Fundamental Law, it was interpreted by the Government, as if the Hungarian constitution was being praised. See The Hungarian Helsinki Committee 2011.

[98] See Chancellery of the Prime Minister 2018.

[99] See, as made public by MEP Ujhelyi, Ujhelyi 2018.

[100] European Commission 2017a.

[101] Committee on Civil Liberties, Justice and Home Affairs 2017.

[102] For an assessment of the Polish White Paper by the Polish Judges Association 'Iustitia', together with a team of experts, see Iustitia 2018. For an assessment of the Hungarian information sheet, see the lengthy criticism by Labanino and Nagy 2018.

[103] Closa 2016, p 13.

[104] Pech 2013.

[105] Consequently, the debates about how best to block the inflow of EU funds to the backsliding Member States have been very vivid over the last years. E.g. Halmai 2019.

contributes to the entrenchment of the regimes in power. This is especially true in a context where the kleptocratic elites having captured the state and channel EU money through the networks of their clients and party associates in the direct interest of furthering harmful political agendas in direct contradiction with the values that the Union paying for them purports to stand for. Further research is needed to see how harmful exactly the Union's financial involvement in the backsliding Member States has been.

The international reactions to the current situation underline one thing: the Union is either content with the current situation or entirely powerless. The former is hardly convincing given both the size of direct economic transfers to Hungary and Poland as well as the dangers that these Member States bring into the Union, as fully expressed in the numerous public statements of the members of the College of Commissioners and heard during European Parliament debates. If a Member State breaches the EU's fundamental values, this is likely to undermine the very foundations of the Union and the trust between its Member States, regardless of the field in which the breach occurs.[106] Beyond harming the nationals of that Member State, other Union citizens residing in that state will also be detrimentally affected. Moreover, the lack of limitations on 'illiberal practices'[107] may encourage other Member State governments to follow suit and subject other countries' citizens to an abuse of their rights. In other words, violations of the rule of law may become contagious if there are no consequences.[108] Finally, all EU citizens will to some extent suffer due to the given state's participation in the EU's decision-making mechanisms. At the very least, the legitimacy of the Union's decision-making process will be jeopardised. Therefore, the latter explanation, i.e. the EU's powerlessness, seems to be the core of the matter. Such powerlessness is a consequence of a combination of the real difficulties, conceptual and practical, related to the enforcement of EU values,[109] but also, equally importantly, to the systematic misrepresentation of the Union's capacities through the unwillingness of its Member States and institutions to act, as a clear consensus on dealing with rule of law backsliding forcefully is apparently lacking. Lastly, the Monnet method underlying the Union, where economic interpenetration has always played a central role to achieving the goal of peace through shaping an environment where thoroughgoing political – and especially military – conflict becomes too costly to remain an option. This is exactly why a miracle is needed for the Council to treat Article 7 TEU seriously: the provision, at its core, goes against the very rationale of European integration as designed.

[106] European Commission 2003, p 5.

[107] The term 'illiberal democracy' was coined long ago, but it gained practical relevance in the EU after the Hungarian Prime Minister praised the concept in his speech given in Bălie Tuşnad on 25 July 2014. Cf. Frans Timmermans' speech to the European Parliament: 'There is no such thing as an illiberal democracy' (Timmermans 2015a).

[108] Politico 2015, p 15.

[109] Cf. Itzcovich 2017; Avbelj 2017.

The claims that little to nothing can be done under the current legal framework – which are heard with remarkable regularity – are entirely baseless, as Hillion, Besselink and other scholars have consistently pointed out.[110] Now that the Article 7(1) TEU procedure has been triggered against Poland[111] and Hungary,[112] the opposite preoccupation comes to the fore, namely the inefficiency of the procedure,[113] which leads to the reinvention of other available tools. For instance, Articles 258 TFEU and 259 TFEU have been given a broader appeal in the backsliding context, as evidenced by the infringement proceedings pursued against Poland in relation to its destruction of its Supreme Court, which builds on the newly-found *effet utile* and EU law scope-shaping significance of Article 19(1) TEU (as well as Article 47 CFR, read in conjunction with the former),[114] in contrast to the Pyrrhic victories achieved in the otherwise similar Hungarian context.[115] Scholars anticipated this development,[116] which infuses Article 258 TFEU with clear new potential, all the necessary caution about interpreting it too broadly notwithstanding. Some necessary changes are technical and easily enforceable, such as treating all infringement cases with a rule of law element as rule of law cases, which the Commission has already done by requesting the reversal of attempted harmful 'reforms' through an accelerated procedure to prevent the packing of the Supreme Court of Poland with government stooges, which was being attempted following the Hungarian template precisely.[117] The Hungarian judicial capture case described above should be a warning for all future disputes: it was misconstrued as an age discrimination case, albeit the controversy was ultimately about judicial independence, and thus the rule of law.[118] The rule of law infringement was finalised during the 10 months the proceedings continued before the EU institutions. Had the case not been misinterpreted as a discrimination case, the government could not have proposed individual compensation as a remedy. Both in terms of the remedies sought and the timing of the action, *Commission* v. *Poland* shows a spectacular learning curve on behalf of the Commission and the Court in terms of the increased effectiveness of the deployment of Article 258 TFEU in the context of rule of law backsliding. Kim Scheppele is absolutely right, asserting that systemic

---

[110] Hillion 2016; Besselink 2017; Kochenov 2017c.

[111] European Commission 2017a.

[112] European Parliament 2018.

[113] As a consequence, the institutions see the solution in the power of the purse to provide disincentives for rule of law violations. See European Commission 2018.

[114] ECJ, *Associação Sindical dos Juízes Portugueses,* 27 February 2018, case C-64/16, ECLI:EU:C:2018:117; Krajewski 2018; Pech and Platon 2018.

[115] ECJ, *Commission v. Hungary*, 6 November 2012, case C-286/12, ECLI:EU:C:2012:687.

[116] Hillion 2016.

[117] E.g. ECJ, *Commission v. Poland,* case C-619/18 R, Order ex parte of 19 October 2018, EU:C:2018:852 and Order of 17 December 2018, EU:C:2018:1021.

[118] It is impossible to argue that the Court was not aware of what was going on on the ground: AG Kokott outlined the relevance of the on-going 'reform' for the Rule of Law quite clearly in her Opinion in the case, see paras 54–55.

infringements require systemic compliance[119] – and Article 279 TFEU offers a lot of room here to prevent a situation from deteriorating by blocking any harmful 'reforms'. Crucially, a mere observance of the letter of the *acquis*, as was the case with the Hungarian judicial retirement age case, without however taking to heart its spirit and the essential promises of Article 2 TEU, coupled with an array of other provisions,[120] is not the right way forward, as is now abundantly clear.[121]

In addition to the substance for construing an infringement, the time element should also be considered: institutions including the ECJ should automatically take into account the gravity of the possible consequences of rule of law violations, the scale of their effects, and the fact that time is on the side of those violating the rule of law, to expedite or give priority to such cases. Often however, even an accelerated infringement procedure will not be prompt enough to prevent the irreparable harm that rule of law violations or backsliding can cause. Therefore, where an infringement procedure involving a rule of law element is pending, interim measures should be awarded, just as happened in the proceedings before the ECJ over the Polish judicial capture case. Other changes, such as a new approach by the Commission in bundling rule of law violations to show their systemic nature, or allocating more responsibility to democratic Member States in the enforcement of the rule of law, have long been proposed by scholars in the field.[122]

Some, like First Vice President Timmermans, compare the present situation to that of the Austrian crisis at the turn of the millennium and fear that triggering Article 7 TEU would similarly backfire.[123] The parallel drawn between the Austrian and the current situations is entirely misleading, however, for numerous reasons. The most obvious is that the institutions could not have made use of the then non-existent preventive limb of Article 7 – currently Article 7(1) TEU – at the time the *Freiheitliche Partei Österreichs* (FPÖ) entered government, and there was no reason to make use of the provision as it then stood, i.e. to invoke the sanctioning limb.[124] Given the lack of a legally predefined preventive procedure, a course of political action was opted for that need not – but very importantly *could* – be taken vis-à-vis Hungary or Poland in light of Article 7. The political quarantine of Austria started right after the formation of the government, before those in power could have eroded European values, and once the situation had been thoroughly investigated, the Three Wise Men commissioned with this task did not find a violation of EU values and accordingly suggested lifting the political sanctions.[125] EU Member States' hostile intervention against Austria was backed neither by a proper legal

119 Scheppele 2016.

120 On the variety of approaches open to the Commission and the Court of Justice, see the general overview in Hillion 2016. Cf. Closa et al. 2014.

121 Kochenov 2017a.

122 Scheppele 2016; Kochenov 2015a.

123 Timmermans 2015b.

124 Lachmayer 2017.

125 Ahtisaari et al. 2001.

basis nor political necessity: an illegal ad hoc action triggered by a democratic election result. In teaching us, ironically, that the EU does not need any law or a formal legal basis to take action in this domain, should the political will be available: so much for supranational rule of law – an issue we return to *infra*. The current Hungarian and Polish situations cannot be compared to the former Austrian one, since the former have already progressed far down the route towards constitutional capture, which is well documented both by European institutions and in the academic literature.

11.5 The Place of Values in the System of EU Law: A Focus on Infringement Proceedings

Article 2 TEU, which makes reference to democracy, the rule of law and a series of other interrelated Union values, is somewhat different in nature from the rest of the *acquis*. The same unquestionably applies to the violations of values: Article 2 TEU violations are not the same as ordinary *acquis* violations. Such differences are particularly acute in the context of one specific type of chronically non-compliant state, where, as in Hungary, non-compliance is *ideological* and cannot be explained by reference to lacking capacity – 'simple' corruption and outright sloppiness[126] – characterisations one might deploy in the context of some South East European countries.[127] Where chronic non-compliance is ideological, Articles 260 TFEU, permitting striking at the non-compliant states financially, and 279 TFEU, authorising interim measures aimed at preventing the further deterioration of the situation on the ground,[128] become the *crux* of the whole story, as simple restatements of a breach under Article 258 TFEU (or Article 259 TFEU, for that matter)[129] will presumably not be enough,[130] even if the recent innovations mentioned in the previous sections would probably allow for some even in the context of the most cautious reading of these provisions' potential.[131] The question of the effectiveness of the ideological choice favouring non-compliance made by the relevant Member States will remain open for the years to come, as the Court in consort with other institutions is in search of more effective means to deploy the current instruments in the context of rule of law backsliding. Although the Court obviously offers room for

126 Uitz 2015.

127 E.g. Ioannidis 2017.

128 This provision has been deployed both against the logging in the Polish UNESCO-designated forest (case C-441/17 R) and in the context of the attempted 'reform' of the Supreme Court in the country, aimed at depriving it of independence (case C-619/18 R).

129 See, e.g., Kochenov 2015a.

130 On the main deficiencies of the system, see, most importantly, Jack 2013; Wennerås 2012; Wennerås 2017.

131 See, most importantly, Schmidt and Bogdanowicz 2018, p 1061; cf. Gormley 2017.

optimism, as explained above, alone, it will not be able to solve all the outstanding problems: other institutions and the Member States will have to step in.

While the literature has focused on restating the EU's presumed rule of law-based character,[132] as well as the issue of the enforcement of EU rule of law and other values in the defiant Member States,[133] it is crucial to realise that Europe's structural constitutional vulnerability stretches far beyond enforcement issues *per se*. Instead, it is rooted in the discrepancies between the EU's proclaimed constitutional structure as we find it in the Treaties and the reality marking the development of EU integration, as outlined above, which fosters doubt as to whether the Union is actually abiding by the rule of law.[134] In light of this structural deficiency, one can argue that the much-analysed systemic deficiency[135] in the area of values and especially the rule of law was bound to emerge sooner or later as the Union matured, whether in Hungary, Poland or elsewhere.[136] Dealing with it will necessarily require moving beyond a preoccupation with enforcement, which has engulfed all the recent literature on the subject – quite understandably, given the astonishing speed of the constitutional deterioration in both Hungary and Poland – towards reforming the integration project at its core,[137] ensuring that democracy and the rule of law are endowed with a more important role in the context of the supranational law of the Union.

In this general context, where the *acquis* and values are not synonymous, the application of the Copenhagen criteria in the context of the recent enlargement rounds teaches a particularly cautionary lesson: the Commission has emerged as an institution which, when given all responsibility regarding the preparedness of the new Member States for accession (values compliance outside the scope of the *acquis* included) failed the exercise.[138] Here, to the void of substance was added the lack of the capability to generate such a substance, the lack of virtually any limitations emerging from the scope of the law notwithstanding. Besides illustrating the EU's built-in limitations with regard to its ability to generate the substance of Article 2 TEU rules, the pre-accession context also sounds an alarm bell on institutional capacity: the Commission is probably not the best actor to entrust with the internal monitoring of Member States' compliance with Article 2 TEU.

---

[132] Fernández Esteban 1999; Pech 2016.

[133] E.g. the contributions in Closa and Kochenov 2016; Jakab and Kochenov 2017; von Bogdandy and Sonnevend 2015; Müller 2013.

[134] Palombella 2009; Palombella 2016; Kochenov 2015b.

[135] von Bogdandy and Ioannidis 2014.

[136] See, for a broad discussion, Kochenov et al. 2015.

[137] For a much more critical restatement of this particular argument, see Kochenov 2016; Weiler 2016.

[138] Kochenov 2008.

11.6 How to Approach the Rule of Law in the Current Context?

The necessary question which emerges is how to outline the essence of the rule of law with the potential specificity of the supranational integration context in mind, while distinguishing this concept from democracy, fundamental rights and the other values of Article 2 TEU. Palombella's writing is extremely helpful in this regard, we suggest.[139] The essence of the rule of law – which distinguishes it from legality, democracy and other wonderful things – is that the law is constantly in tension with and controlled by other law – how the EU falls short of this institutional ideal will be demonstrated. Palombella's rule of law, which is *dialogical* in essence since it presupposes and constantly relies on a constant taming of law with law, 'amounts to preventing one dominant source of law and its unconstrained whim, from absorbing all the available normativity'.[140] According to this account the rule of law implies that the law – *gubernaculum* – should always be controlled by other law – *jurisdictio* – lying outwith the sovereign's reach.[141] The tension is necessarily dialogical in nature since the absolute domination of either *gubernaculum* or *jurisdictio* necessarily destroys the core of the rule of law, which is the tension between the two. It goes without saying that making use of such a definition should necessarily be qualified by Krygier's sage observation: 'whatever one might propose as the *echt* meaning of the rule of law is precisely that: a proposal'.[142] The rule of law is a classic example of an essentially contested concept:[143] the EU is seemingly as hopeless at defining what it means as its Member States and the broad academic doctrine.[144] The debate is constantly ongoing,[145] but the last available definition,[146] inspired by the Venice Commission's guidelines,[147] could provide a solid illustration of the current state of the definitional debate. Whether one agrees with the Commission's approach or not, it seems to be beyond any doubt what the rule of law is not. It is not democracy, the protection of human rights, nor similar delightful

---

[139] Please consult Kochenov 2015b, on which this and the following sections are based, for the full picture.

[140] Palombella 2014, p 18. Similarly, see Georgiev 1993, p 4.

[141] For an analysis of this perspective, see, *ibid.*; Palombella 2012; Palombella 2009, p 17. See also Palombella 2016.

[142] Krygier 2014, p 78.

[143] For a brilliant outline of the history of contestation, see Waldron 2002.

[144] For a multi-disciplinary overview, see, e.g., Hadfield and Weingast 2014; cf. Levrat 2018, p 157; Pech 2009 and the literature cited therein. See also Pech 2013 on the 'holistic understanding' of the rule of law. For a special 'Eastern-European' perspective, which is particularly important in the context of the ongoing developments in the EU, see Přibáň 2009.

[145] For key contributions, see Pech 2016; Morlino and Palombella 2010; Palombella and Walker 2009.

[146] European Commission 2014.

[147] The Venice Commission for Democracy through Law 2016b, as well as in the earlier version thereof: The Venice Commission for Democracy through Law 2011.

things, each of them definitely boasting its own sound claim to existence as a notion independent of the rule of law.[148] And it is not mere legality, which is adherence to the law.

Once the rule of law and legality are distinguished, the basic meaning of the rule of law comes down to the idea of the subordination of the law to another kind of law, which is not up to the sovereign to change at will.[149] This idea, traceable back to mediaeval England,[150] is described with recourse to two key notions to reflect the fundamental duality of the law's fabric, indispensable for the operation of the rule of law as a principle of law:[151] *jurisdictio* – the law untouchable for the day-to-day rules running the legal system and removed from the ambit of the purview of the sovereign – and *gubernaculum*, which is the use of the general rule-making power.[152] As Krygier put it in his commentary on Palombella's work, 'the king was subject to the law that he had not made, indeed that made him king. For the king – for anyone – to ignore or override that law was to violate the rule of law'.[153] Even in the contemporary age of popular sovereignty, this statement is obviously true, since democracy should not be capable of annihilating the law. Indeed, this is one of the key points made by the defenders of judicial review.[154]

Unlike despotic or totalitarian regimes, where the ruler is free to do anything he pleases; or problematic EU Member States such as Hungary, where the constitution is a political tool; or Poland, where the executive ignores the constitution to undermine the separation of powers; or pre-constitutional democracies, which equate the law with legislation,[155] the majority of constitutional democracies in the world today recognise the distinction between *jurisdictio* and *gubernaculum*, thus achieving a sound approximation of Palombella's rule of law as an institutional ideal, in terms of maintaining and fostering the constant tension between these two facets of the law. The authority should be itself bound by clear legal norms which are outside of its control. Indeed, this is the key feature of post-war constitutionalism. The *jurisdictio–gubernaculum* distinction, lying at the core of what the rule of law is about, can be policed either by courts or even by the structure of the

[148] One should not forget the wise words of Joseph Raz: 'We have no need to be converted into the rule of law just in order to believe [...] that good should triumph': Raz 1979, p 21.

[149] Palombella 2016.

[150] Reid 2004.

[151] Palombella 2012.

[152] For a detailed exposé, see Palombella 2016. See also Palombella 2009, p 30, emphasising that this duality should not be disturbed by democratic outcomes and ethical choices.

[153] Krygier 2014, p 84.

[154] Cf. Kumm 2010.

[155] In a pre-constitutional state, the *Rechtsstaat* shapes a reality, in the words of Gianfranco Poggi, where 'there is a relation of near-identity between the state and its law': Poggi 1978, p 238 (as cited in Krygier 2014, p 84).

constitution itself, through removing certain domains from *gubernaculum*'s scope.[156] The ideology of human rights is of huge significance in this context.[157] Furthermore, the existence of international law,[158] and of course supranational legal orders,[159] definitely contributes to the policing of the aforementioned duality.[160] The policing of the *jurisdictio–gubernaculum* divide is thus possible both through means internal and external to a given legal system.

11.7 Supranational Law and the Effective Instrumentalisation of Values

From Lord Mackenzie Stuart[161] to *Les Verts*, which characterises the Treaties as 'a constitutional charter based on the rule of law',[162] what we have been hearing about on the subject of the rule of law in the EU actually amounts to internal legal compliance.[163] This is an established understanding of legality.[164] Legality is not enough to ensure that the EU behaves like – and is – a true rule of law-based constitutional system. If we were to argue that equating the rule of law and legality is legitimate, then, as Palombella correctly notes, our thinking 'shifts the issue from the rule of law to the [...] respect for the laws of a legal system'.[165] Yet 'the rule of law cannot mean just the self-referentiality of a legal order',[166] which is the reason why contemporary constitutionalism is usually understood as implying, among

156 Roznai 2017, pp 179–196.

157 Frankenberg 2013.

158 Dworkin 2013.

159 For an argument that numerous Central and Eastern European states were actually motivated by the desire for external legal checks on their laws – a *jurisdictio* – when joining the Council of Europe, see Sadurski 2012.

160 Palombella 2012, chapter 2.

161 Mackenzie Stuart 1977. See also Bebr 1965. Cf. Levrat 2018.

162 ECJ, *Partie Ecologiste 'Les Verts' v Parliament*, 23 April 1986, case 294/83, ECLI:EU:C:1986:166, para 23. See also ECJ, *EEA Agreement*, Opinion 1/91, ECLI:EU:C:1991:490.

163 Fernandez Esteban 1999; also Everling 2010, p 701; Zuleeg 2010, pp 772–779. EU institutions' own accounts of what is meant by the rule of law beyond the tautology of 'being bound by law' present a most diverse account, which found an expression in the EU's external action: Pech 2013, p 108; Burlyuk 2015, p 509.

164 E.g. the contributions in Besselink et al. 2010.

165 Palombella 2016.

166 *Ibid.* Compare with M Krygier: 'To try to capture this elusive phenomenon by focusing on characteristics of laws and legal institutions is, I believe, to start in the wrong place and move in the wrong direction': Krygier 2006. See also Tamanaha 2006.

other things, additional restraints through law:[167] restraints which are crucially not simply democratic or political.[168]

By and large, the re-articulation of the Union from an ordinary treaty organisation into a constitutional system was not accompanied by a sufficient upgrade of the role played by the core values it is said to build upon.[169] These values do not inform the day-to-day functioning of EU law, neither internally[170] nor externally.[171] Let us not forget that the promotion of its values, including the rule of law, is an obligation lying on the Union in accordance with the Treaties.[172] Indeed, unless we take the Commission's scribbles for granted, the EU's steering of countless issues directly related to the values at hand is more problematic than not. The EU is not about the values Article 2 TEU preaches, which any student of EU law and politics will readily confirm.[173] The EU's very self-definition is not about human rights, the rule of law or democracy.[174] EU law functions differently: there is a whole other set of principles which actually matter and which are held dear: supremacy, direct effect and autonomy are the key trio which spring to mind.[175] Operating together, they can set aside both national constitutional[176] and international human rights,[177] as well as UN law constraints.[178] In the current crisis-rich environment,[179] the Union frequently stars as part of the problem, rather than part of the solution.

---

[167] For a clear discussion of the relationship between constitutionalism and the rule of law, see Krygier 2017.

[168] Naturally, this is not to say that we should do away with the political restraints. Indeed, the virtually complete depoliticisation of the law has been one of the key criticisms of the EU legal order: Přibáň 2015, p 193 and Wilkinson 2015.

[169] Williams 2009.

[170] Weiler 2009, p 51; Williams 2010.

[171] For critical engagements, see Cremona 2011, p 275; Leino and Petrov 2009.

[172] Article 3(5) TEU.

[173] The crucial argument in this vein has been made, most powerfully, by Andrew Williams: Williams 2009. See, also, Weiler 2010.

[174] See most recently ECJ, *ECHR, Accession II*, 18 December 2014, Opinion 2/13, ECLI:EU:C:2014:2454, para 170, which states that the fundamental rights in the EU are 'interpret[ed] […] within the framework of the structure and objectives of the EU'.

[175] Procedural principles cannot possibly replace the lack of substantive attention to the core values encompassed by Article 2 TEU, including the rule of law, threatening to cause a justice deficit of the Union: Kochenov et al. 2015. Cf. Halberstam 2015 and Eeckhout 2015; Kochenov 2010.

[176] ECJ, *Melloni*, 26 February 2013, case C-399/11, ECLI:EU:C:2013:107.

[177] ECJ, *ECHR, Accession II*, 18 December 2014, Opinion 2/13, ECLI:EU:C:2014:2454; Kochenov 2015b.

[178] On the *Kadi* saga, see de Búrca 2010, p 1. See also, of course, ECJ, *Kadi II*, 18 July 2013, case C-584/10, ECLI:EU:C:2013:518.

[179] Three equally important facets of the current crisis can be outlined: values; justice; and economic and monetary. On the crisis of values, see, e.g., Williams 2009 and Weiler 2010. On the crisis of justice: Kochenov et al. 2015. On the economic side of the crisis, see, e.g., Menéndez 2013; Adams et al. 2014.

The problem is, it behaves like a constitutional system endowed with authority relying on the ECJ to police this claim – a natural expectation of any legal order[180] – while failing at the same time to boast the necessary ABC of constitutionalism: when push comes to shove, its values play a foundational role in outlining neither the scope nor the substance of the law.[181]

Bringing the values back in is indispensable to infusing the EU's constitutional claims with credibility. In practice, this would mean a return to the promise of EU integration made in the days of the Union's inception.[182] A *fédération européenne* (the one mentioned in the Schuman Declaration) to be brought about through the creation of the internal market, stood for a line of developments significantly more far-reaching than the idea of economic integration as such. The former is values-based – while the latter is probably not (at least, not based on the values of Article 2), as Andrew Williams explained in his seminal work.[183]

Not the whole story was negative, however. Although the Union's ambition has gradually been scaled down to the market – call it a hijacking of the ends by the means[184] – the Union started *de facto* to play the role of the promoter of liberal and tolerant nationhood, as rightly characterised by Kymlicka, mostly through negative integration and advancing a very clear idea of constitutionalism based on proportionality, tolerance and the taming of nationalism.[185] Furthermore, at the core of the Union there lay basic mutual respect among the Member States: the Union would become impossible if they began to obstruct the principle of mutual recognition.[186] This came down to frowning upon the ideology of 'thick' national identities, however glorified in some schoolbooks. The ultimate result is that the EU, subconsciously as it were, emerged as a promoter of *one* particular type of constitutionalism,[187] which is based on the rule of law understood through national democracy and the culture of justification which implies human rights protection and strong judicial review. To be a Member State of the EU in the context of these developments came to signify one thing: to stick to this particular type of constitutionalism, which is now reflected in Article 2 TEU and which also represents the most important condition to be fulfilled before joining the EU, as hinted at in Article 49 TEU.[188]

The EU thus emerged as a vehicle of the negative market-based approach to the 'values' question. Clearly, creating a market and questioning the state is not

180 Lindeboom 2018.

181 Peebles 1998; Kochenov 2017d.

182 On the key aspects of the dynamics of the EU's legal history, see Davies and Rasmussen 2012.

183 Williams 2010.

184 Kochenov 2013.

185 Kymlicka 2006, p 134. See also Davies 2010.

186 Poiares Maduro 2007. For a very sophisticated analysis of the Union's effects on the Member States, see Somek 2010a and Somek 2010b.

187 Perju 2012b.

188 See, e.g., Kochenov 2008, chapter 2.

sufficient as a basis for a mature constitutional system, potentially creating a system of justice rendered nugatory at the supranational level[189] and perpetuating the Union's inability to help the Member States labouring to inflict a justice void on themselves, either through an outright embrace of Putin-style 'illiberal democracy' – proclaimed as an ideal to strive for by the Hungarian Prime Minister Orbán[190] – an attack on the judiciary and the media – as in contemporary Poland[191] – or through failing to build a well-ordered and functioning modern state – as it the case in Greece[192] and Romania,[193] for instance. Outright defiance is thus not required to fall out of adherence to Article 2 TEU aspirations.

11.8 Mutual-Recognition-Supranationalism: Powerless, But the Court?

The Union is thus generally powerless concerning the *enforcement* of values and more importantly, is also indecisive as to their *content*. The very fact that we are now concerned with enforcing them seriously amounts to nothing else but a concession that the presumption that there is a level playing field among all Member States in terms of the rule of law etc. – i.e. the fact that all of them actually adhere to the specific type of constitutionalism the EU set out to promote – does not hold (any more). This is something the European Court of Human Rights (ECtHR) has already clearly hinted at in *M.S.S. v. Belgium and Greece*.[194] Acknowledging this alongside the EU's obvious powerlessness as far as values are concerned is a potentially explosive combination in a Union built on Member State equality and the principle of mutual recognition. In a situation where the core values are not respected by Hungary, for instance, we are not dealing with a Member State that is revolting for one reason or another against a binding norm of European law. At the

189 Douglas-Scott 2015.

190 For the full text of the speech, see Tóth C (2014) The full text of Viktor Orbán's speech at Băile Tuşnad (Tusnádfürdő) of 26 July 2014: www.budapestbeacon.com/public-policy/full-text-of-viktor-orbans-speech-at-baile-tusnad-tusnadfurdo-of-26-july-2014/10592 Accessed 14 February 2019. In 2018 it was renamed as 'Christian democracy', but there is no substantive change behind the shift in terminology (see Sect. 11.2)

191 Cf. Venice Commission 2016.

192 Ioannidis 2017.

193 Perju 2012a, p 246.

194 ECtHR, *MSS v Belgium and Greece*, 21 January 2011, application no. 30696/09, ECLI:CE:ECHR:2011:0121JUD003069609. But see also the Bosphorus presumption of equivalent protection ECtHR, *Bosphorus v Ireland*, 30 June 2005, application no. 45036/98, ECLI:CE:ECHR:2005:0630JUD004503698 and ECtHR, *Michaud v France*, 6 December 2012, application no. 12323/11, ECLI:CE:ECHR:2012:1206JUD001232311, which survived even after Opinion 2/13 had been rendered: ECtHR, *Avotiņš v Latvia*, 23 May 2016, application no. 17502/07, ECLI:CE:ECHR:2016:0523JUD001750207.

level of values, we are dealing with a *principally different Member State*, with the Belarusisation of the EU from the inside.[195]

Once the values of Article 2 TEU are not observed, the essential presumptions behind the core of the Union no longer hold, undermining the very essence of the integration exercise: mutual recognition becomes an untenable fiction, which the Member States are nevertheless bound by EU law to adhere to. This is the core of what the autonomy of EU law stands for, as confirmed by the Court in its infamous Opinion 2/13 which vetoed the EU's accession to the ECHR.[196] In this Opinion on the draft accession agreement of the EU to ECHR, the Court of Justice highlighted the principle of mutual trust between Member States, which forms the cornerstone of the area of freedom, security and justice. In the Court of Justice's interpretation, this means that a Member State must presume all other Member States to be in compliance with EU law, including their respect for fundamental rights. To be fair, it should be mentioned that the Court also referred to 'exceptional circumstances', which would warrant departure from the mutual trust principle,[197] but the exact nature of these exceptional circumstances was left open. In *Aranyosi* and *Căldăraru*[198] and in a later case discussed *infra*,[199] the Court made clear that it will not accept a clear risk of a serious breach of EU values (Article 7(1) TEU) as a benchmark for suspending mutual trust in general. Rather, it holds that the application of mutual recognition based instruments – or at least the European Arrest Warrant[200] at issue in the case – may only be suspended if the sanctioning prong of Article 7 TEU (current Article 7(2)–(3) TEU) is invoked and the Council determines a breach of EU values.[201] Absent the completion of an Article 7(2)–(3) procedure, only individual surrenders may be suspended on a case-by-case basis, provided a two-prong test is followed.[202] The Court clarified that the executing judicial authority must assess whether there are fundamental rights deficiencies in general. Once a risk of a rights violation is established, as a second step, the executing judicial authority must determine, specifically and precisely, whether there are substantial grounds to believe that the person concerned by a European Arrest Warrant will be exposed to a real risk of human rights violations, in the event of his surrender to that Member State. If the risk of a human rights infringement in

195 Belavusau 2013, p 1145.

196 This point has been forcefully restated in the ECJ's Opinion 2/13. See, e.g., para 192.

197 *Ibid.*

198 ECJ, *Aranyosi and Căldăraru*, 5 April 2016, joined cases C-404/15 and C-659/15 PPU, ECLI:EU:C:2016:198.

199 ECJ, *Minister for Justice and Equality v LM*, 25 July 2018, case C-216/18 PPU, ECLI:EU:C:2018:586.

200 Council of the European Union 2002.

201 ECJ, *Minister for Justice and Equality v LM*, 25 July 2018, case C-216/18 PPU, ECLI:EU:C:2018:586, para 70.

202 *Ibid.*, para 73.

general and in the specific case are established, the execution of the warrant must be postponed.[203]

The Court left a number of issues unclear, two of which deserve greater attention as they might have detrimental consequences for the rule of law as it shall be understood in the EU, and might contribute to the proliferation of rule of law backsliding across borders. First, *Aranyosi* placed too much of an emphasis on external *fora* in determining the state of values in the Member States. The judgment in *Aranyosi* heavily depended on a pilot judgment issued by the ECtHR,[204] holding that prison conditions in Hungary violated Article 4 EU Charter (Article 3 ECHR). But after the judgment in *Aranyosi* had been rendered, Hungary adopted a new law,[205] which provided a combination of preventive and compensatory remedies, guaranteeing in theory genuine redress for human rights violations originating from cramped prisons and other unsuitable detention conditions. In light of this new law, in *Domján v. Hungary*[206] the ECtHR declared another Hungarian detainee's application – and all others' in his position – complaining about prison conditions premature and therefore inadmissible, saying that Mr. Domján should make use of the remedies introduced by the new Hungarian law before turning to the Strasbourg court. The ECtHR's decision in *Domján* led the AG believe in the *ML* case that surrender cannot be postponed any longer on the grounds of poor prison conditions in Hungary.[207] The ECJ adopted a more refined approach:[208] it realised that procedures enabling authorities to grant redress for fundamental rights violations cannot rule out the existence of a real risk of a violation, and that the *Domján* case law should not automatically make Member States' courts dismiss claims from persons requested. Nevertheless, it implied that 'in the absence of minimum standards under EU law regarding detention conditions'[209] the ultimate bar for determining the potentiality of human rights violations remains to be determined by the Strasbourg court. It means that the Court is not yet ready to develop higher standards or review the values' situation on the ground in a Member State, but continues to 'contract it out' to the Council of Europe, at least where human rights are at stake.

---

[203] In *Aranyosi and Căldăraru*, the Court of Justice had an opportunity to clarify what those exceptional circumstances might be and it made an attempt to do so, but ultimately this led to more questions than it answered: see ECJ, *Aranyosi and Căldăraru*, 5 April 2016, joined cases C-404/15 and C-659/15 PPU, ECLI:EU:C:2016:198. For an analysis, see van Ballegooij and Bárd 2016.

[204] ECtHR, *Varga and others v. Hungary*, 10 March 2015, application nos. 14097/12 etc., ECLI:CE:ECHR:2015:0310JUD001409712.

[205] Act No. CX of 2016 amending Act No. CCXL of 2013 on the enforcement of punishments, measures, certain coercive measures and confinement for regulatory offences.

[206] ECtHR, *Domján v. Hungary*, 14 November 2017, application no. 5433/17, ECLI:CE:ECHR:2017:1114DEC000543317.

[207] ECJ, *ML*, 25 July 2018, case C-220/18 PPU, ECLI:EU:C:2018:547, Opinion of AG Campos Sánchez-Bordona, paras 51–54.

[208] ECJ, *ML*, 25 July 2018, case C-220/18 PPU, ECLI:EU:C:2018:589, para 117.

[209] *Ibid.* at para 90. Cf. van Ballegooij 2017.

Second, the Court left it unclear whether and to what extent the *Aranyosi* case law would be applicable where a case did not exclusively concern a human rights violation, but also included an element of the rule of law being threatened in the issuing state. In the case of *LM*, the ECJ got a chance to answer the question.[210] The issue was whether a suspect of a crime should be surrendered from Ireland to Poland when the executing judicial authority had serious doubts as to whether the suspect would receive a fair trial in the issuing state, due to the lack of independence of the judiciary resulting from changes to the Polish judicial system.[211] The ECJ could have gone – and scholars have previously argued[212] for doing so – beyond its case law and framed the case primarily as a rule of law problem. The ECJ however constructed the case as a possible violation of a fundamental right, namely the right to a fair trial as protected by Article 47 EU Charter, which presupposes that tribunals are independent and impartial.[213] The ECJ ruled that the two-step test in *Aranyosi* needs to be followed by the executing judicial authority when making decisions on surrenders. The second prong however makes the suspension of surrender almost impossible. It seems to be a disproportionate burden on the individual to show how a systemic breach in the rule of law effects his or her case individually. Elsewhere we have argued that once the first step of the test was satisfied, the burden should shift to the stronger party, i.e. the issuing state.[214] The Court's insistence that the issuing and executing authorities engage in a 'dialogue' about the latter's independence,[215] presupposes the unlikely scenario that a captured court will admit that it was captured.

Applying the test in *LM*, both the High Court of England and Wales[216] and the Irish High Court surrendered suspects to Poland. Both cases illustrate how difficult it is for the defence to prove that the wanted person will be individually affected by the current threats to the independence of the Polish judiciary to the extent that this would pose a real risk of a breach of their fair trial rights, and more specifically their rights to an independent tribunal.

---

210 ECJ, *Minister for Justice and Equality v LM*, 25 July 2018, case C-216/18 PPU, ECLI:EU:C:2018:586; cf. Dorociak and Lewandowski 2017.

211 High Court of Ireland decision of 12 March 2018, *Minister for Justice and Equality v Celmer* [2018] IEHC 119. For the final version of the preliminary reference, see High Court of Ireland decision of 23 March 2018, *Minister for Justice and Equality v Celmer* [2018] IEHC 119.

212 Bárd and van Ballegooij 2018a, b, c; van Ballegooij and Bárd 2018.

213 ECJ, *Minister for Justice and Equality v LM*, 25 July 2018, case C-216/18 PPU, ECLI:EU:C:2018:586, paras 47–48.

214 van Ballegooij and Bárd 2016, based on Bárd et al. 2016.

215 ECJ, *Minister for Justice and Equality v LM*, 25 July 2018, case C-216/18 PPU, ECLI:EU:C:2018:586, paras 76–77.

216 High Court of Justice in England, *Pawel Lis et al.*, 31 October 2018, [2018] EWHC 2848 (Admin).

Summing up the relevant case law on mutual recognition, the Court insisted that autonomy considerations in the context of EU law will usually tend to prevail over human rights and other values – including the rule of law – cherished on the one hand in the national constitutional systems of the Member States, and on the other by Article 6 TEU, the Charter of Fundamental Rights and also Article 67(1) TFEU, according to which fundamental rights are supposed to be the cornerstones of the area of freedom, security and justice. Indeed, it would probably not be incorrect to argue that this would be the shortest possible summary of Opinion 2/13, which itself summarised EU law as it stands. The consequences for the rule of law are drastic: all the principles invoked by the ECJ to justify giving EU law the upper hand in Opinion 2/13 are procedural, while the problems that the reliance on the ECHR is there to solve are substantive. Curing substantive deficiencies of the EU legal order with the remedies confined to autonomy and direct effect is a logical flaw plaguing the EU legal system, which puzzles the most renowned commentators.[217] One cannot quarrel about the roses when the forests are burning. To agree with Eleanor Sharpston and Daniel Sarmiento, 'in the balance between individual rights and primacy, the Court in Opinion 2/13 has fairly clearly sided with the latter. The losers under Opinion 2/13 are not the Member States of the signatory States of the Council of Europe, but the individual citizens of the European Union'.[218] This is so, we must add, not only because of the potential reduction of the level of human rights protection. Rather, it is due to the fact that the EU, as Opinion 2/13 made clear, boasts the overwhelming potential to undermine the rule of law at the national level and this potential impact is not an empty threat.[219]

In the light of the above it appears that the ensuring of mutual trust – an topic much discussed in the context of the safeguarding of the rule of law in the EU – takes the back seat in the context where infringement proceedings initiated by the Commission created a veritable boost in the creative reading of the values in cumulation with Article 19(1) TEU and the Charter in the recent *Commission v. Poland* cases, as analysed at the very beginning of this contribution. While both the horizontal 'questioning mutual trust' route and the vertical infringement proceedings / preliminary references route are obviously deployable against democratic and rule of law backsliding, the latter emerges as the preferred option in the light of the most recent case law pertaining to both routes discussed. The ECJ's role has been both significant and tricky and so far it has played ideally, without offering room for any possible reproach. Which route – the vertical, or the horizontal – will appear most usable is not as important, in the end, compared with the very masterful articulation of both options, which are bound to be the core legacies of the Lenaerts Court.

[217] E.g. Eeckhout 2015; Halberstam 2015.

[218] Sarmiento and Sharpston 2017.

[219] See, further, Kochenov 2016

11.9 Enforcement Through Subtle Gradualism? As a Conclusion

The rule of law backsliding in Hungary and Poland revealed the EU's significant vulnerabilities in the face of the need to uphold the values the whole system of EU integration presumes to have in place. The lessons are revealing: respecting the *acquis* does not guarantee continuing adherence to Article 2 TEU values; economic success in the Union does not necessarily entrench democracy and the rule of law; the tools available to preserve the rule of law are largely inadequate, as they could go against the key assumptions of the internal market. Consequently, the lack of political will to deal with the values' crisis is not at all irrational, which makes it even more worrisome. What stands out from this grim picture is the revolutionary case law of the Court of Justice on judicial independence and mutual trust, which bridges the available infringement procedures with the outstanding problems and offers horizontal and vertical empowerment to the EU's decentralised judiciaries – now able to intervene – while also resolving the competences conundrum through a broad reading of the principle of judicial independence as a key element of the rule of law. However inspiring, recent case law developments are insufficient, we argue, to deal with the sociological legitimacy crisis in tackling illiberal democracies plaguing the EU: autocratic legalism cannot be fought with legalism alone. Designing a long-term systemic approach leading to a complex re-articulation of EU values is indispensable, as enforcement per se is not a panacea.

The core question which emerges in the light of the above discussion, is how to ensure that the EU's own approach to the rule of law does not undermine, if not destroy, adherence to the principle of the rule of law in the Member States, which are, in fact, compliant with the values listed in Article 2 TEU. We submit that such an understanding of the rule of law cannot possibly lead to the much-needed solution of the outstanding problems. Instead, the most mature answer to the problems should necessarily involve not only the reform of the enforcement mechanisms, but the reform of the Union as such, as the supranational law should be made more aware of the values it is obliged by the Treaties to respect and also, crucially, to aspire to protect at both the national and supranational levels. Instead of hiding behind the veil of the procedural purity banners of autonomy, supremacy and the like, EU law should embrace the rule of law as an institutional ideal.[220] This implies, *inter alia*, eventual substantive limitations on the *acquis* of the Union as well as taking Article 2 TEU values to heart in the context of the day-to-day functioning of the Union, elevating the values above the instrumentalism marking them today. The result would be the emergence of a supranational constitutional system at the EU level, which would be truer to the glorious 'constitutional' label, and which would play a significantly more productive role in solving the backsliding challenges in Hungary, Poland, and any other Member States following suit, where the war against all what we believe in is currently ongoing.

[220] Cf. Palombella 2012.

Acknowledgement This chapter was prepared under the auspices of the EU's Horizon 2020 research and innovation programme as part of the RECONNECT project under Grant Agreement no. 770142. The first draft appeared as a contribution to a collective Robert Schuman Centre for Advanced Studies paper (EUI Florence) and a RECONNECT paper. The authors are grateful to Barbara Grabowska-Moroz, Nina Havig Bredvold, Harry Panagopoulos, Flips Schøyen and Jacquelyn Veraldi for their help and assistance. The usual disclaimer applies.

References

Adams M, Fabbrini F, Larouche P (eds) (2014) The Constitutionalisation of European Budgetary Constraints. Hart Publishing, Oxford

Ahtisaari M, Frowein J, Oreja M (2001) Report on the Austrian Government's Commitment to the Common European Values, in Particular Concerning the Rights of Minorities, Refugees and Immigrants, and the Evolution of the Political Nature of the FPÖ. International Legal Materials: Current Documents 40:102–123

Amtenbrink F, Davies G, Kochenov D, Lindeboom J (eds) (2019) The Internal Market and the Future of European Integration. Cambridge University Press, Cambridge

Anselmi M (2018) Populism: An Introduction. Routledge, Oxford (Fano Morrisey L transl.)

Avbelj M (2017) Pluralism and Systemic Defiance in the EU. In: Jakab A, Kochenov D (eds) The Enforcement of EU Law and Values. Oxford University Press, Oxford, pp 44–64

Bánkuti M, Halmai G, Scheppele K.L (2012) Hungary's Illiberal Turn: Disabling the Constitution. Journal of Democracy 23:138–146

Bárd P, van Ballegooij W (2018a) Judicial Independence as a Pre-Condition for Mutual Trust? The ECJ in *Minister for Justice and Equality v LM*. New Journal of European Criminal Law 9:353–365

Bárd P, van Ballegooij W (2018b) Judicial Independence as a Precondition for Mutual Trust. www.verfassungsblog.de/judicial-independence-as-a-precondition-for-mutual-trust/ Accessed 15 February 2019

Bárd P, van Ballegooij W (2018c) The AG Opinion in the *Celmer* Case: Why Lack of Judicial Independence Should Have Been Framed as a Rule of Law Issue. www.verfassungsblog.de/the-ag-opinion-in-the-celmer-case-why-lack-of-judicial-independence-should-have-been-framed-as-a-rule-of-law-issue Accessed 15 February 2019

Bárd P, Carrera S, Guild E, Kochenov D (2016) An EU Mechanism on Democracy, the Rule of Law and Fundamental Rights. CEPS Paper on Liberty and Security No. 91

Bebr G (1965) Rule of Law within the European Communities. Institut d'Etudes Européennes de l'Université Libre de Bruxelles, Brussels

Belavusau U (2013b) On Age Discrimination and Beating Dead Dogs: Case *Commission v. Hungary*. CMLRev 50:1145–1160

Besselink L (2017) The Bite, the Bark and the Howl: Article 7 TEU and the Rule of Law Initiatives. In: Jakab A, Kochenov D (eds) The Enforcement of EU Law and Values. Oxford University Press, Oxford, pp 128–144

Besselink L, Pennings F, Prechal S (eds) (2010) The Eclipse of Legality in the European Union. Kluwer Law International, The Hague

Biernat S, Kawczyńska M (2018) Why the Polish Supreme Court's Reference on Judicial Independence to the ECJ is Admissible after All. www.verfassungsblog.de/why-the-polish-supreme-courts-reference-on-judicial-independence-to-the-ECJ-is-admissible-after-all/ Accessed 14 February 2019

Blokker P (2016) EU Democratic Oversight and Domestic Deviation from the Rule of Law: Sociological Reflections. In: Closa C, Kochenov D (eds) Reinforcing Rule of Law Oversight in the European Union. Cambridge University Press, Cambridge, pp 249–269

Blokker P (2018) Populist Constitutionalism and Meaningful Popular Engagement. The Foundation for Law, Justice and Society Policy Brief, Centre for Socio-Legal Studies and Wolfson College, University of Oxford
Blokker P (2019) Response to 'Public Law and Populism'. German Law Journal, forthcoming
Bodnar A (2018) Protection of Human Rights after the Constitutional Crisis in Poland. Jahrbuch des Öffentlichen Rechts der Gegenwart 66:639–662
Broberg M (2017) Preliminary References as a Means of Enforcing EU Law. In: Jakab A, Kochenov D (eds) The Enforcement of EU Law and Values: Ensuring Member States' Compliance. Oxford University Press, Oxford, pp 99–111
Burlyuk O (2015) Variation in EU External Policies as a Virtue: EU Rule of Law Promotion in the Neighbourhood. Journal of Common Market Studies 53:509–523
Chancellery of the Prime Minister (2018) White Paper on the Reform of the Polish Judiciary. www.premier.gov.pl/files/files/white_paper_en_full.pdf Accessed 14 February 2019
Ciampi A (2018) Can the EU Ensure Respect for the Rule of Law by Its Member States? The Case of Poland. Osservatorio sulle fonti 3:1–14
Cloots E (2015) National Identity in EU Law. Oxford University Press, Oxford
Closa C (2016) Reinforcing EU Monitoring of the Rule of Law. In: Closa C, Kochenov D (eds) Reinforcing the Rule of Law Oversight in the European Union. Cambridge University Press, Cambridge, pp 15–35
Closa C (2017) Securing Compliance with Democracy Requirements in Regional Organisations. In: Jakab A, Kochenov D (eds) The Enforcement of EU Law and Values: Ensuring Member States' Compliance. Oxford University Press, Oxford, pp 379–400
Closa C, Kochenov D (eds) (2016) Reinforcing Rule of Law Oversight in the European Union. Cambridge University Press, Cambridge
Closa C, Kochenov D, Weiler JHH (2014) Reinforcing Rule of Law Oversight in the European Union. EUI Working Paper RSCAS No. 2014/25
CMLRev (editorial comment) (2019) 2019 Shaping up as a Challenging Year for the Union, not Least as a Community of Values. CMLRev 56:3–22
Committee on Civil Liberties, Justice and Home Affairs (2017) Draft Report on a Proposal Calling on the Council to Determine, Pursuant to Article 7(1) of the Treaty on European Union, the Existence of a Clear Risk of a Serious Breach by Hungary of the Values on which the Union is Founded. (2017/2131(INL))(Rapporteur: Judith Sargentini)
Conelly J, Koncewicz TT (2016) Who are Today's Polish Traitors? Of Politics of Paranoia and Resentment and Missed Lessons from the Past. www.verfassungsblog.de/who-are-todays-polish-traitors-of-politics-of-paranoia-and-resentment-and-missed-lessons-from-the-past/ Accessed 14 February 2019
Council of the European Union (2014a) Press Release no. 16936/14, 3362nd Council meeting, General Affairs
Council of the European Union (2014b) Opinion of the Legal Service 10296/14, of 14 May 2014
Coutron L (2018) La Cour de justice au secours de la forêt Białowieska: Coup de tonnerre dans le recours en manguement! RTD eur 54:321–330
Cremona M (2011) Values in EU Foreign Policy. In: Evans M, Koutrakos P (eds) Beyond the Established Legal Orders: Policy Interconnections between the EU and the Rest of the World. Hart Publishing, Oxford, pp 275–316
Daly T (2019) Democratic Decay: Conceptualizing the Emerging Research Field. The Hague Journal on the Rule of Law, forthcoming
Davies G (2010) The Humiliation of the State as a Constitutional Tactic. In: Amtenbrink F, van den Bergh P (eds) The Constitutional Integrity of the European Union. T.M.C. Asser Press, The Hague, pp 147–173
Davies B, Rasmussen M (2012) Towards a New History of European Law. Contemporary European History 21:305–318
Dawson M (2013) Constitutional Dialogue between Courts and Legislatures in the European Union: Prospects and Limits. EPL 19:369–396

de Búrca G (2010) The European Court of Justice and the International Legal Order after *Kadi*. Harvard International Law Journal 51:1–50
De Ridder E, Kochenov D (2011) Democratic Conditionality in Eastern Enlargement: Ambitious Window Dressing. European Foreign Affairs Review 16:589–605
Dorociak M, Lewandowski W (2017) A Check Move for the Principle of Mutual Trust from Dublin: The *Celmer* Case. European Papers 3:857–873
Dostal V, Győri L, Meseznikov G, Przybylski W, Zgut E (2018) Illiberalism in the V4: Pressure Points and Bright Spots. www.politicalcapital.hu/pc-admin/source/documents/pc_fnf_v4illiberalism_pressurepoints_20180605.pdf Accessed 14 February 2019
Douglas-Scott S (2015) Justice, Injustice and the Rule of Law in the EU. In: Kochenov D, de Búrca G, Williams A (eds) Europe's Justice Deficit? Hart Publishing, Oxford, pp 51–67
Dworkin R (2013) A New Philosophy of International Law. Philosophy and Public Affairs 41:2–30
European Papers Editorial (2017) Winter Is Coming. The Polish Woodworm Games. European Papers 2:797–802
Eeckhout P (2015) Opinion 2/13 on EU Accession to the ECHR and Judicial Dialogue – Autonomy or Autarky? Fordham International Law Journal 38:955–992
European Commission (2003) Communication from the Commission to the Council and the Parliament – On Article 7 of the Treaty on European Union – Respect for and Promotion of the Values on which the Union is Based COM(2003)606 final
European Commission (2014) A New EU Framework to Strengthen the Rule of Law COM(2014)158
European Commission (2017a) Reasoned Proposal in Accordance with Article 7(1) of the Treaty on European Union Regarding the Rule of Law in Poland – Proposal for a Council Decision on the Determination of a Clear Risk of a Serious Breach by the Republic of Poland of the Rule of Law COM(2017)835 final
European Commission (2017b) Recommendation of 26.7.2017 regarding the rule of law in Poland C(2017)5320
European Commission (2018) Proposal for a Regulation of the European Parliament and of the Council on the Protection of the Union's Budget in Case of Generalised Deficiencies as Regards the Rule of Law in the Member States COM(2018)324 final
European Parliament (2016) Report with Recommendations to the Commission on the Establishment of an EU Mechanism on Democracy, the Rule of Law and Fundamental Rights (2015/2254(INL))
European Parliament (2017) Committee on Civil Liberties, Justice and Home Affairs, Draft report on a Proposal Calling on the Council to Determine, Pursuant to Article 7(1) of the Treaty on European Union, the Existence of a Clear Risk of a Serious Breach by Hungary of the Values on which the Union is Founded [2017] (2017/2131(INL)), Rapporteur: Judith Sargentini
European Parliament (2018) Resolution of 12 September 2018 on a Proposal Calling on the Council to Determine, Pursuant to Article 7(1) of the Treaty on European Union, the Existence of a Clear Risk of a Serious Breach by Hungary of the Values on which the Union is Founded (2017/2131(INL))
Everling U (2010) The European Union as a Federal Association of States and Citizens. In: von Bogdandy, Bast J (eds) Principles of European Constitutional Law, 2nd edn. Hart Publishing/CH Beck, Oxford/Munich, pp 701–734
Fernández Esteban ML (1999) The Rule of Law in the European Constitution. Kluwer Law International, The Hague
Frankenberg G (2013) Human Rights and the Belief in a Just World. International Journal of Constitutional Law 12:35–60
Freedom House (2017) Pluralism under Attack: The Assault on Press Freedom in Poland. www.freedomhouse.org/report/special-reports/assault-press-freedom-poland#sdendnote21anc Accessed 14 February 2019
Georgiev D (1993) Politics of Rule of Law: Deconstruction and Legitimacy in International Law. EJIL 4:1–14

Gormley LW (2017) Infringement Proceedings. In: Jakab A, Kochenov D (eds) The Enforcement of EU Law and Values. Oxford University Press, Oxford, pp 65–78

Grabowska-Moroz B, Szuleka M, Helsinki Foundation for Human Rights (2018) It Starts with the Personnel: Replacement of Common Court Presidents and Vice Presidents from August 2017 to February 2018. www.hfhr.pl/wp-content/uploads/2018/04/It-starts-with-the-personnel.pdf Accessed 14 February 2019

Hadfield GK, Weingast BR (2014) Microfoundations of the Rule of Law. Annual Review of Political Science 17:21–42

Halberstam D (2015) 'It's the Autonomy, Stupid!' A Modest Defence of Opinion 2/13 on EU Accession to the ECHR, and the Way Forward. German Law Journal 16:105–146

Halmai G (2017) The Hungarian Constitutional Court and Constitutional Identity. www.verfassungsblog.de/the-hungarian-constitutional-court-and-constitutional-identity/ Accessed 14 February 2019

Halmai G (2018) Abuse of Constitutional Identity. The Hungarian Constitutional Court on Interpretation of Article E) (2) of the Fundamental Law. Review of Central and East European Law 43:23–42

Halmai G (2019) The Possibility and Desirability of Rule of Law Conditionality. The Hague Journal on the Rule of Law, forthcoming

Hillion C (2004) The Copenhagen Criteria and Their Progeny. In: Hillion C (ed) EU Enlargement: A Legal Approach. Hart Publishing, Oxford/Portland OR, pp 1–22

Hillion C (2016) Overseeing the Rule of Law in the EU: Legal Mandate and Means. In: Closa C, Kochenov D (eds) Reinforcing Rule of Law Oversight in the European Union. Cambridge University Press, Cambridge, pp 59–81

Hirsch Ballin E (2016) Mutual Trust: The Virtue of Reciprocity – Strengthening the Acceptance of the Rule of Law through Peer Review. In: Closa C, Kochenov D (eds) Reinforcing Rule of Law Oversight in the European Union. Cambridge University Press, Cambridge, pp 133–146

The Hungarian Helsinki Committee (2011) NGOs Analyze Government Reactions Concerning the Venice Commission's Opinion on the New Constitution of Hungary. www.helsinki.hu/en/ngos-analyze-government-reactions-concerning-the-venice-commissions-opinion-on-the-new-constitution-of-hungary/ Accessed 14 February 2019

The Hungarian Helsinki Committee, the Eötvös Károly Policy Institute and the Hungarian Civil Liberties Union (2011) Full List of Mistakes and Omissions of the English Version of the Hungarian Draft-Constitution www.tasz.hu/files/tasz/imce/list_of_all_the_omissions_and_mistranslations.pdf Accessed 14 February 2019

The Hungarian Helsinki Committee et al (2017) Timeline of Governmental Attacks Against Hungarian NGO Sphere. www.tasz.hu/files/tasz/imce/timeline_of_gov_attacks_against_hu_ngos_07042017.pdf Accessed 14 February 2019

Inglis K (2000) The Europe Agreements Compared in the Light of Their Pre-Accession Reorientation. CMLRev 37:1173–1210

Ioannidis M (2017) Weak Members and the Enforcement of EU Law. In: Jakab A, Kochenov D (eds) The Enforcement of EU Law and Values. Oxford University Press, Oxford, pp 476–492

Itzcovich G (2017) On the Legal Enforcement of Values. The Importance of the Institutional Context. In: Jakab A, Kochenov D (eds) The Enforcement of EU Law and Values. Oxford University Press, Oxford, pp 28–43

Iustitia (2018) Response to the White Paper Compendium on the Reforms of the Polish Justice System, Presented by the Government of the Republic of Poland to the European Commission. www.statewatch.org/news/2018/mar/pl-judges-association-response-judiciary-reform-3-18.pdf Accessed 14 February 2019

Jack B (2013) Article 260(2) TFEU: An Effective Judicial Procedure for the Enforcement of Judgments? European Law Journal, 19:404–421

Jakab A (2016) The EU Charter of Fundamental Rights as the Most Promising Way of Enforcing the Rule of Law against EU Member States. In: Closa C, Kochenov D (eds) Reinforcing Rule of Law Oversight. Cambridge University Press, Cambridge, pp 187–205

Jakab A (2017) Application of the EU CFR in National Courts in Purely Domestic Cases. In: Jakab A, Kochenov D (eds) The Enforcement of EU Law and Values: Ensuring Member States' Compliance. Oxford University Press, Oxford, pp 252–262
Jakab A, Kochenov D (eds) (2017) The Enforcement of EU Law and Values: Ensuring Member States' Compliance. Oxford University Press, Oxford
Kelemen R.D (2017) Europe's Other Democratic Deficit: National Authoritarianism in Europe's Democratic Union. Government and Opposition 52:211–238
Kelemen R.D (2018) The Dangers of Constitutional Pluralism. In: Avbelj M, Davies G (eds) Research Handbook on Legal Pluralism and EU Law. Edward Elgar, Cheltenham/Northampton MA, pp 392–403
Kelemen RD, Pech L (2018) Why Autocrats Love Constitutional Identity and Constitutional Pluralism: Lessons from Hungary and Poland. RECONNECT Working Paper No 2:1–23
Kelemen RD, Pech L, Scheppele KL (2018) Never Missing an Opportunity to Miss an Opportunity: The Council Legal Service Opinion on the Commission's EU Budget-Related Rule of Law Mechanism. www.verfassungsblog.de/never-missing-an-opportunity-to-miss-an-opportunity-the-council-legal-service-opinion-on-the-commissions-eu-budget-related-rule-of-law-mechanism/ Accessed 14 February 2019
Klamert M, Kochenov D (2019) Article 2. In: Kellerbauer M, Klamert M, Tomkin J (eds) Commentary on the EU Treaties and the Charter of Fundamental Rights. Oxford University Press, Oxford, pp 22–30
Kochenov D (2004) Behind the Copenhagen Façade: The Meaning and Structure of the Copenhagen Political Criterion of Democracy and the Rule of Law. European Integration Online Papers 8(10):1–24
Kochenov D (2008) EU Enlargement and the Failure of Conditionality: Pre-Accession Conditionality in the Fields of Democracy and the Rule of Law. Kluwer Law International, Alphen aan den Rijn
Kochenov D (2010) Citizenship without Respect. Jean Monnet Working Paper (NYU Law School) No. 08/10
Kochenov D (2013) The Citizenship Paradigm. Cambridge Yearbook of European Legal Studies 15:197–225
Kochenov D (2015a) Biting Intergovernmentalism: The Case for the Reinvention of Article 259 TFEU to Make it a Viable Rule of Law Enforcement Tool. The Hague Journal on the Rule of Law 7:153–174
Kochenov D (2015b) EU Law Without the Rule of Law. Is the Veneration of Autonomy Worth It? Yearbook of European Law 34:74–96
Kochenov D (2016) The Missing EU Rule of Law? In: Closa C, Kochenov D (eds) Reinforcing the Rule of Law Oversight in the European Union. Cambridge University Press, Cambridge, pp 290–312
Kochenov D (2017a) The Acquis and Its Principles: The Enforcement of the 'Law' Versus the Enforcement of 'Values' in the EU. In: Jakab A, Kochenov D (eds) The Enforcement of EU Law and Values: Ensuring Member States' Compliance. Oxford University Press, Oxford, pp 9–27
Kochenov D (2017b) The EU and the Rule of Law: Naïveté or Grand Design? In: Adams M, Meuwese A, Hirsch Ballin E (eds) Constitutionalism and the Rule of Law: Bridging Idealism and Realism. Cambridge University Press, Cambridge, pp 419–445
Kochenov D (2017c) Busting the Myths Nuclear: A Commentary on Article 7 TEU. EUI Working Paper LAW 2017/10
Kochenov D (2017d) On Tiles and Pillars: EU Citizenship as the Federal Denominator. In: Kochenov D (ed) EU Citizenship and Federalism: The Role of Rights. Cambridge University Press, Cambridge, pp 3–78
Kochenov D (2019a) Article 7 TEU. In: Kellerbauer M, Klamert M, Tomkin J (eds) Commentary on the EU Treaties and the Charter of Fundamental Rights. Oxford University Press, Oxford, pp 88–98

Kochenov D (2019b) Article 354 TFEU. In: Kellerbauer M, Klamert M, Tomkin J (eds) Commentary on the EU Treaties and the Charter of Fundamental Rights. Oxford University Press, Oxford, pp 2081–2082

Kochenov D, Basheska E (2016) ENP's Values Conditionality from Enlargements to Post-Crimea. In: Poli S (ed) The EU and Its Values in the Neighbourhood. Routledge, Oxford, pp 145–166

Kochenov D, Pech L (2015) Monitoring and Enforcement of the Rule of Law in the EU: Rhetoric and Reality. EUConst 11:512–540

Kochenov D, Pech L (2016) Better Late Than Never? On the Commission's Rule of Law Framework and Its First Activation. Journal of Common Market Studies 54:1062–1074

Kochenov D, van Wolferen M (2018) The Dialogical Rule of Law and the Breakdown of Dialogue in the EU. EUI Working Paper LAW 2018/01

Kochenov D, de Búrca G, Williams A (eds) (2015) Europe's Justice Deficit? Hart Publishing, Oxford

Kochenov D, Magen A, Pech L (eds) (2016) The Great Rule of Law Debate in the European Union (2016 symposium). Journal of Common Market Studies 54:1045–1149

Koncewicz TT (2016) Of Institutions, Democracy, Constitutional Self-defence and the Rule of Law: The Judgments of the Polish Constitutional Tribunal in Cases K 34/15, K 35/15 and Beyond. CMLRev 53:1753–1792

Koncewicz TT (2018a) The Capture of the Polish Constitutional Tribunal and Beyond: Of institution(s), Fidelities and the Rule of Law in Flux. Review of Central and East European Law 43:116–173

Koncewicz TT (2018b) On the Politics of Resentment, Mis-memory, and Constitutional Fidelity: The Demise of the Polish Overlapping Consensus? In: Belavusau U, Gliszczyńska-Grabias A (eds) Law and Memory: Towards Legal Governance of History. Cambridge University Press, Cambridge, pp 263–290

Koncewicz TT (2018c) The *Białowieża* case. A Tragedy in Six Acts. www.verfassungsblog.de/the-bialowieza-case-a-tragedy-in-six-acts/ Accessed 14 February 2019

Könczöl M (2018) Dealing with the Past in and around the Fundamental Law of Hungary. In: Belavusau U, Gliszczyńska-Grabias A (eds) Law and Memory: Towards Legal Governance of History. Cambridge University Press, Cambridge, pp 246–262

Krajewski M (2018) *Associação Sindical dos Juízes Portugueses*: The Court of Justice and Athena's Dilemma. European Papers 3:395–407

Krygier M (2006) The Rule of Law: An Abuser's Guide. In: Sajó A (ed) Abuse: The Dark Side of Fundamental Rights. Eleven International Publishing, Utrecht, pp 129–161

Krygier M (2014) Inside the Rule of Law. Rivista di filosofia del diritto 3:77–98

Krygier M (2017) Tempering Power: Realist-idealism, Constitutionalism, and the Rule of Law. In: Adams M, Meuwese A, Hirsch Ballin E (eds) Constitutionalism and the Rule of Law: Bridging Idealism and Realism. Cambridge University Press, Cambridge, pp 34–59

Kukovec D (2015) Taking Change Seriously: The Rhetoric of Justice and the Reproduction of the Status Quo. In: Kochenov D, de Búrca G, Williams A (eds) Europe's Justice Deficit? Hart Publishing, Oxford/Portland OR, pp 319–336

Kumm M (2010) The Idea of Socratic Contestation and the Right to Justification: The Point of Rights-Based Proportionality Review. Law & Ethics of Human Rights 4:142–175

Kymlicka W (2006) Liberal Nationalism and Cosmopolitan Justice. In: Benhabib S (ed) Another Cosmopolitanism. Oxford University Press, Oxford, pp 128–146

Labanino R, Nagy Z (2018) The Social and Political Situation in Hungary – Response to the Information Sheet of the Hungarian Government on the Issues Raised by the Draft Report of Judith Sargentini on 'A Proposal Calling on the Council to Determine, Pursuant to Article 7(1) of the Treaty on European Union, the Existence of a Clear Risk of a Serious Breach by Hungary of the Values on which the Union is Founded'. drive.google.com/file/d/1OcIlFUtg9s1-FLMRo_qF4MbywRxAAbt5/view Accessed 14 February 2019

Lachmayer K (2017) Questioning the Basic Values – Austria and Jörg Haider. In: Jakab A, Kochenov D (eds) The Enforcement of EU Law and Values. Oxford University Press, Oxford, pp 436–355

Leino P, Petrov R (2009) Between 'Common Values' and Competing Universals. European Law Journal 15:654–671
Lenaerts K (2015) EU Citizenship and the European Court of Justice's 'Stone-by-Stone' Approach. International Comparative Jurisprudence 1:1–10
Lenaerts K (2017) La vie après l'avis: Exploring the Principle of Mutual (Yet not Blind) Trust. CMLRev 54:805–840
Levrat N (2018) L'État de droit est-il une valeur européenne dont l'UE assure la promotion? In: Sidjanski D, Saint-Ouen F, Stephanou C (eds) Union des valeurs? La mise en œuvre des valeurs et des principes fondamentaux de l'Union Européenne. Global Studies Institute de l'Université de Genève, Geneva, pp 157–177
Lindeboom J (2018) Why EU Law Claims Supremacy. Oxford Journal of Legal Studies 38:328–356
Mackenzie-Stuart A.J (1977) The European Communities and the Rule of Law. Stevens and Sons, London
Magen A, Pech L (2018) The Rule of Law and the European Union. In: May C, Winchester A (eds) Handbook on the Rule of Law. Edward Elgar, Cheltenham/Northampton MA, pp 235–256
Magyar B (2016) Post-communist Mafia State: The Case of Hungary. CEU Press, Budapest
Maresceau M (2001) The EU Pre-Accession Strategies: A Political and Legal Analysis. In: Maresceau M, Lannon E (eds) EU's Enlargement and Mediterranean Strategies: A Comparative Analysis. Palgrave & Basingstoke, New York, pp 3–28
Matczak M (2017) Why the Announced Constitutional Referendum in Poland is not a Constitutional Referendum after All. www.verfassungsblog.de/why-the-announced-constitutional-referendum-in-poland-is-not-a-constitutional-referendum-after-all/ Accessed 14 February 2019
Menéndez A (2013) The Existential Crisis of the European Union. German Law Journal 14:453–526
Morlino L, Palombella G (eds) (2010) Rule of Law and Democracy. Brill, Boston
Müller J-W (2013) Safeguarding Democracy inside the EU: Brussels and the Future of Liberal Order. Transatlantic Academy Working Paper No. 3
Müller J-W (2014) The EU as a Militant Democracy, or: Are There Limits to Constitutional Mutations within the EU Member States? Revista de Estudios Políticos 165:141–162
Müller-Graff P-C (1997) Legal Framework for Relations between the European Union and Central and Eastern Europe: General Aspects. In: Maresceau M (ed) Enlarging the European Union: Relations between the EU and Central and Eastern Europe. Longman, New York
Oliver P, Stefanelli J (2016) Strengthening the Rule of Law in the EU: The Council's Inaction. Journal of Common Market Studies 54:1075–1084
Ott A, Inglis K (eds) (2002) Handbook on European Enlargement: A Commentary on the Enlargement Process. T.M.C. Asser Press, The Hague
Pacula P (2017) Poland's 'July Coup' and What it Means for the Judiciary. www.euobserver.com/justice/138567 Accessed 14 February 2019
Palombella G (2009) The Rule of Law and its Core. In: Palombella G, Walker N (eds) Relocating the Rule of Law. Hart Publishing, Oxford, pp 17–42
Palombella G (2012) È possibile la legalità globale? Il Mulino, Bologna
Palombella G (2014) The Principled, and Winding, Road to *Al-Dulimi*. Interpreting the Interpreters. Questions of International Law 6:15–30
Palombella G (2016) Beyond Legality – Before Democracy: Rule of Law Caveats in a Two-Level System. In: Closa C, Kochenov D (eds) Reinforcing the Rule of Law Oversight in the European Union. Cambridge University Press, Cambridge, pp 36–58
Palombella G, Walker N (eds) (2009) Relocating the Rule of Law. Hart Publishing, Oxford
Parodi M (2018) Il Controllo della Corte di giustizia sul rispetto del principio dello Stato di diritto da parte degli Stati membri: alcune riflessioni in margine alla sentenza *Associação Sindical dos Juízes Portugueses*. European Papers 3:985–992
Pech L (2009) The Rule of Law as a Constitutional Principle of the European Union. Jean Monnet Working Paper No. 04/09
Pech L (2010) 'A Union Founded on the Rule of Law': Meaning and Reality of the Rule of Law as a Constitutional Principle of EU Law. EUConst 6:359–396

Pech L (2013) Promoting the Rule of Law Abroad: On the EU's Limited Contribution to the Shaping of an International Understanding of the Rule of Law. In: Kochenov D, Amtenbrink F (eds) The European Union's Shaping of the International Legal Order. Cambridge University Press, Cambridge, pp 108–129

Pech L (2016) The Rule of Law as a Constitutional Principle. In: Schröder W (ed) Strengthening the Rule of Law in Europe: From a Common Concept to Mechanisms of Implementation. Hart Publishing, Oxford

Pech L, Platon S (2018) A. Court of Justice Judicial Independence under Threat: The Court of Justice to the Rescue in the *ASJP* Case. CMLRev 55:1827–1854

Pech L, Scheppele K.L (2017) Illiberalism Within: Rule of Law Backsliding in the EU. Cambridge Yearbook of European Legal Studies 19:3–47

Peebles G (1998) 'A Very Eden of the Innate Rights of Man'? A Marxist Look at the European Union Treaties and Case Law. Law and Social Inquiry 22:581–618

Perju V (2012a) The Romanian double executive and the 2012 constitutional crisis. International Journal of Constitutional Law 13:246–278

Perju V (2012b) Proportionality and Freedom – An Essay on Method in Constitutional Law. Global Constitutionalism 1:334–367

Perju V (2018) On Uses and Misuses of Human Rights in European Constitutionalism. In: Vöneky S, Neuman GL (eds) Human Rights, Democracy, and Legitimacy in a World in Disorder. Cambridge University Press, Cambridge, pp 263–295

Poggi (1978) The Development of the Modern State: A Sociological Introduction. Stanford University Press, Stanford

Poiares Maduro P (2007) So Close Yet So Far: The Paradoxes of Mutual Recognition. Journal of European Public Policy 14:814–825

Politico (2015) Viktor Orbán: The Conservative Subversive. Politico 28:12–15

Přibáň J (2009) From 'Which Rule of Law?' to 'The Rule of Which Law?': Post-Communist Experiences of European Legal Integration. The Hague Journal on the Rule of Law 1:337–358

Přibáň J (2015) The Evolving Idea of Political Justice in the EU: From Substantive Deficits to the Systemic Contingency of European Society. In: Kochenov D, de Búrca G, Williams A (eds) Europe's Justice Deficit? Hart Publishing, Oxford, pp 193–211

Raz J (1979) The Rule of Law and Its Virtue. In: Raz J (ed) The Authority of Law: Essays on Law and Morality. Clarendon Press, Oxford, pp 210–229

Reid J.P (2004) Rule of Law: The Jurisprudence of Liberty in the Seventeenth and the Eighteenth Centuries. Northern Illinois University Press, DeKald

Rizcallah C (2018) Arrêt 'LM': un risque de violation du droit fondamental à un tribunal indépendant s'oppose-t-il à l'exécution d'un mandat d'arrêt européen? Journal de droit européen 2018:348–350

Roy S (2015) Justice as Europe's Signifier. In: Kochenov D, de Búrca G, Williams A (eds) Europe's Justice Deficit? Hart Publishing, Oxford/Portland OR, pp 79–96

Roznai Y (2017) Unconstitutional Constitutional Amendments: The Limits of Amendment Powers. Oxford University Press, Oxford

Sadurski W (2012) Constitutionalism and the Enlargement of Europe. Oxford University Press, Oxford

Sadurski W (2018) How Democracy Dies (in Poland): A Case Study of Anti-Constitutional Populist Backsliding. Sydney Law School Research Paper 18/01:1–72

Sarmiento D, Sharpston E (2017) European Citizenship and its New Union: Time to Move on? In: Kochenov D (ed) EU Citizenship and Federalism. Cambridge University Press, Cambridge, pp 226–241

Scheppele K.L (2013) The Rule of Law and the Frankenstate: Why Governance Checklists Do Not Work. Governance 26:559–562

Scheppele KL (2015) Understanding Hungary's Constitutional Revolution. In: von Bogdandy A, Sonnevend P (eds) Constitutional Crisis in the European Constitutional Area: Theory, Law and Politics in Hungary and Romania. Hart Publishing, Oxford/Portland OR, pp 111–124
Scheppele KL (2016) Enforcing the Basic Principles of EU Law through Systemic Infringement Actions. In: Closa C, Kochenov D (eds) Reinforcing the Rule of Law Oversight in the European Union. Cambridge University Press, Cambridge, pp 105–132
Scheppele KL (2017) Constitutional Coups in EU Law. In: Adams M, Meuwese A, Hirsch Ballin E (eds) Constitutionalism and the Rule of Law: Bridging Idealism and Realism. Cambridge University Press, Cambridge, pp 446–478
Scheppele KL (2018) Autocratic Legalism. The University of Chicago Law Review 85:545–583
Scheppele KL, Pech L (2017) Poland and the European Commission (Parts I, II, and III). www.verfassungsblog.de/author/laurent-pech/ Accessed 14 February 2019
Schmidt M, Bogdanowicz P (2018) The Infringement Procedure in the Rule of Law Crisis: How to Make Effective Use of Article 258 TFEU. CMLRev 55:1061–1100
Sedelmeier U (2014) Anchoring Democracy from Above? The European Union and Democratic Backsliding in Hungary and Romania after Accession. Journal of Common Market Studies 52:105–121
Sólyom L (2015) The Rise and Decline of Constitutional Culture in Hungary. In: von Bogdandy A, Sonnevend P (eds) Constitutional Crisis in the European Constitutional Area: Theory, Law and Politics in Hungary and Romania. Hart Publishing, Oxford/Portland OR, pp 5–32
Somek A (2010a) The Argument from Transnational Effects I: Representing Outsiders through Freedom of Movement. European Law Journal 16:315–344
Somek A (2010b) The Argument from Transnational Effects II: Establishing Transnational Democracy. European Law Journal 16:375–394
Szente Z (2017) Challenging the Basic Values – The Problems with the Rule of Law in Hungary and the Failure of the European Union to Tackle Them. In: Jakab A, Kochenov D (eds) The Enforcement of EU Law and Values: Ensuring Member States' Compliance. Oxford University Press, Oxford, pp 456–475
Szuleka M (2018) First Victims or Last Guardians? The Consequences of Rule of Law Backsliding for NGOs: Case Studies of Hungary and Poland. CEPS Paper in Liberty and Security in Europe No 6:1–25
Tamanaha B (2006) Law and Means to an End. Cambridge University Press, Cambridge
Timmermans F (2015a) EU Framework for Democracy, Rule of Law and Fundamental Rights, Speech/15/4402 of 12 February 2015. www.europa.eu/rapid/press-release_SPEECH-15-4402_en.htm Accessed 15 February 2019
Timmermans F (2015b) The European Union and the Rule of Law – Keynote Speech at Conference on the Rule of Law, Tilburg University, 31 August 2015. www.ec.europa.eu/commission/commissioners/2014-2019/timmermans/announcements/european-union-and-rule-law-keynote-speech-conference-rule-law-tilburg-university-31-august-2015_en Accessed 15 February 2019
Trócsányi L (2018) The Chief Goal of the Seventh Amendment to the Constitution is the Protection of National Sovereignty. www.kormany.hu/en/ministry-of-justice/news/the-chief-goal-of-the-seventh-amendment-to-the-constitution-is-the-protection-of-national-sovereignty Accessed 14 February 2019
Uitz R (2015) Can You Tell When an Illiberal Democracy is in the Making? An Appeal to Comparative Constitutional Scholarship from Hungary. International Journal of Constitutional Law 13:279–300
Uitz R (2017) The Return of the Sovereign: A Look at the Rule of Law in Hungary – and in Europe. www.verfassungsblog.de/the-return-of-the-sovereign-a-look-at-the-rule-of-law-in-hungary-and-in-europe/ Accessed 14 February 2019

Ujhelyi I (2018) Information Sheet of the Hungarian Government on the Issues Raised by the Draft Report of Judith Sargentini on 'A Proposal Calling on the Council to Determine, Pursuant to Article 7(1) of the Treaty on European Union, the Existence of a Clear Risk of a Serious Breach by Hungary of the Values on which the Union is Founded'. www.ujhelyi.eu/wp-content/uploads/2018/05/Information-sheet-of-the-Hungarian-Government-on-the-issues-raised-by-th....pdf Accessed 14 February 2019

Vachudova MA (2005) Europe Undivided: Democracy, Leverage, and Integration After Communism. Oxford University Press, Oxford

van Ballegooij W (2017) Procedural Rights and Detention Conditions: Cost of Non-Europe Report, PE 611.008. European Parliamentary Research Service, European Added Value Unit, Brussels

van Ballegooij W, Bárd P (2016) Mutual Recognition and Individual Rights: Did the Court get it Right? New Journal of European Criminal Law 7:439–464

van Ballegooij W, Bárd P (2018) The ECJ in the *Celmer* case: One Step Forward, Two Steps Back for Upholding the Rule of Law Within the EU'. www.verfassungsblog.de/the-ECJ-in-the-celmer-case-one-step-forward-two-steps-back-for-upholding-the-rule-of-law-within-the-eu/ Accessed 15 February 2019

The Venice Commission for Democracy through Law (2011) Report on the Rule of Law CDL-AD (2011)003rev-e

The Venice Commission for Democracy through Law (2012) Opinion 663/2012 on Act CLXII of 2011 on the Legal Status and Remuneration of Judges and Act CLXI of 2011 on the Organisation and Administration of Courts of Hungary

The Venice Commission for Democracy through Law (2016a) Opinion on Amendments to the Act of 25 June 2015 on the Constitutional Tribunal of Poland, CDL-AD(2016)001. www.venice.coe.int/webforms/documents/?pdf=CDL-AD%282016%29001-e Accessed 14 February 2019

The Venice Commission for Democracy through Law (2016b) Rule of Law Checklist CDL-AD (2016)007-e

von Bogdandy A, Ioannidis M (2014) Systemic Deficiency in the Rule of Law: What it is, What Has Been Done, What Can Be Done. CMLRev 51:59–96

von Bogdandy A, Sonnevend P (eds) (2015) Constitutional Crisis in the European Constitutional Area: Theory, Law and Politics in Hungary and Romania. Hart Publishing, Oxford/Portland OR

von Bogdandy A, Antpöhler C, Ioannidis M (2017) Protecting EU Values: Reverse Solange and the Rule of Law Framework. In: Jakab A, Kochenov D (eds) The Enforcement of EU Law and Values: Ensuring Member States' Compliance. Oxford University Press, Oxford, pp 218–233

Waelbroeck M, Oliver P (2017) La crise de l'État de droit dans l'Union Européenne: Que faire? Cahiers de droit européen 26:299–342

Waldron J (2002) Is the Rule of Law an Essentially Contested Concept (in Florida)? Law and Philosophy 21:137–164

Weiler J.H.H (2009) Europa: 'Nous coalisons des Etats nous n'unissons pas des hommes'. In: Cartabia M, Simoncini A (eds) La sostenibilità della democrazia nel XXI secolo. Il Mulino, Bologna, pp 51–84

Weiler JHH (2010) Europe Against Itself: On the Distinction between Values and Virtues (and Vices) in the Construction and Development of European Integration. Integration Paper for the International Legal Theory Colloquium (unpublished)

Weiler J.H.H (2016) Epilogue: Living in a Glass House: Europe, Democracy and the Rule of Law. In: Closa C, Kochenov D (eds) Reinforcing the Rule of Law Oversight in the European Union. Cambridge University Press, Cambridge, pp 313–326

Wennerås P (2012) Sanctions Against Member States under Article 260 TFEU: Alive, but not Kicking? CMLRev 49:145–176

Wennerås P (2017) Making Effective Use of Article 260 TFEU. In: Jakab A, Kochenov D (eds) The Enforcement of EU Law and Values. Oxford University Press, Oxford, pp 79–98

Wilkinson MA (2015) Politicising Europe's Justice Deficit: Some Preliminaries. In: Kochenov D, de Búrca G, Williams A (eds) Europe's Justice Deficit? Hart Publishing, Oxford, pp 111–136
Williams A (2009) Taking Values Seriously: Towards a Philosophy of EU Law. Oxford Journal of Legal Studies 29:549–577
Williams A (2010) The Ethos of Europe: Values, Law and Justice in the EU. Cambridge University Press, Cambridge
Zuleeg M (2010) The Advantages of the European Constitution. In: von Bogdandy A, Bast J (eds) Principles of European Constitutional Law, 2nd edn. Hart Publishing/CH Beck, Oxford/Munich

Dimitry Kochenov graduated from Central European University in Budapest in 2002. His scholarship focuses on EU constitutional law most broadly conceived. Among his recent (co-edited) volumes are *The Internal Market and the Future of European Integration* (CUP, 2019, with Amtenbrink, Davies and Lindeboom); *EU Citizenship and Federalism* (CUP, 2017); *The Enforcement of EU Law and Values* (OUP, 2017, with Jakab); *Reinforcing Rule of Law Oversight in the EU* (CUP 2016, with Closa) and *Europe's Justice Deficit?* (Hart, 2015, with de Búrca and Williams). He has held visiting fellowships and professorships worldwide, including at Princeton (LAPA, Woodrow Wilson School), NYU Law (Émile Noël), Basel (Institute of Global Studies), Turin (Scuola dei Studi Superiori) and numerous others. He consults governments and international organizations on the subjects of his interest. His newest monograph is *Citizenship* (MIT Press, 2019).

Petra Bárd graduated from Central European University in Budapest in 2001 (LLM) and in 2008 (SJD). She is Associate Professor at Eötvös Loránd University, Faculty of Law and teaches EU human rights and criminal justice, criminal policy, and criminology. She is Visiting Professor and Researcher at the Central European University's Legal Studies Department and teaches courses on EU law, EU constitutional law, and criminal justice at other universities across Europe including Belgrade, Frankfurt and Vienna. In her research and publications – including several monographs – she deals with issues at the intersection of the rule of law, human rights, EU criminal cooperation, mutual recognition and mutual trust. She regularly authors studies on the rule of law and EU criminal justice for the European Parliament, and other EU institutions or agencies.

Chapter 12
A Stress Test for Europe's Judiciaries

Eirik Holmøyvik and Anne Sanders

Contents

Abstract The rule of law, judicial independence and separation of powers are values guaranteed in constitutions of member states of the Council of Europe. Nevertheless, in recent years, a number of challenges to these accepted values have emerged in different countries all over Europe. The legal responses from European institutions against systemic rule of law threats has yet to prove effective. In this

This chapter builds on the ideas first discussed by the authors in Holmøyvik and Sanders 2017. The text was last revised on 7 July 2018. Subsequent developments in legislation, case law and doctrine have only been incorporated to a limited extent.

E. Holmøyvik (✉)
University of Bergen, Bergen, Norway
e-mail: eirik.holmoyvik@jur.uib.no

A. Sanders
University of Bielefeld, Bielefeld, Germany
e-mail: anne.sanders@uni-bielefeld.de

Hirsch Ballin, Van der Schyff & Stremler (eds.), *European Yearbook of Constitutional Law 2019*, European Yearbook of Constitutional Law 1,
https://doi.org/10.1007/978-94-6265-359-7_12

chapter we propose a national approach to protect European rule of law standards. To facilitate this process, we suggest stress-testing Europe's judiciaries. This should be done by means of structured thought experiments in which the likely effects of adverse developments (such as the ones to be witnessed in some European countries today) should be predicted to identify and remedy weak points in the constitutional and legal framework.

Keywords Council of Europe · judicial independence · rule of law · separation of powers · stress test for judicial systems

12.1 Introduction

The rule of law, judicial independence and separation of powers are values guaranteed in constitutions of member states of the Council of Europe.[1] According to Article 2 TEU, the rule of law is one of the common values upon which the EU is built. Nevertheless, in recent years, a number of challenges to these accepted values have emerged in different countries all over Europe in the form of threats to judicial independence. Events in EU member states such as Hungary, Poland, and Slovakia, as well as countries like Ukraine and Turkey should be mentioned in this context.[2] Commentators speak of a rule of law crisis and backsliding in Europe.[3]

The different challenges to judicial independence all over Europe in recent years, demand a discussion of proper reactions. As we shall discuss, European institutions face some difficulties in addressing systemic rule of law issues in the member states (see Sect. 12.2 below). Therefore, despite its importance for European integration and cooperation, the protection of the rule of law and judicial independence remains at present predominantly a national responsibility. In this essay we discuss how the European perspective can be applied on the national level to prevent rule of law backsliding. We suggest a national approach, not to remedy existing rule of law challenges like in Poland, but to review the existing legal framework in other European countries according to European standards as a preventive measure. We

[1] For a comparative overview, see Summary Report on the responses by the CCJE member states to the questionnaire for the preparation of CCJE Opinion No. 18 (2015).

[2] See for a list of recent Opinions of the Venice Commission on judicial reforms: https://www.venice.coe.int/webforms/documents/?topic=27&year=all. Accessed 1 March 2019. See also the Joint report of the CCJE and CCPE Challenges for judicial independence and impartiality in the member states of the Council of Europe 2016; CCJE/CCPE, SG/Inf(2016)3rev; CCJE, Report on judicial independence and impartiality in the Council of Europe member states 2017 (CCJE(2017) 5Prov5); see also the various Opinions of the CCJE on recent developments in Bulgaria, Poland, Slovakia, Turkey, and Ukraine
https://www.coe.int/en/web/ccje/status-and-situation-of-judges-in-member-states. Accessed 1 March 2019.

[3] See *inter alia* Pech and Scheppele 2017; Černič and Avbelj 2018; and Sanders and Von Danwitz 2018a.

argue that states should 'stress test' their judiciaries according to European rule of law standards. The purpose of such a judicial stress test is to reveal weaknesses in and subsequently take measures to strengthen the constitutional and legal framework for the protection of judicial independence as well as increasing the public's trust in the judiciary.

Since a stress test for judicial systems is a new concept, we offer no empirical evidence for its effectiveness.[4] However, given the serious nature of the threats to the rule of law in several European countries, and the apparent lack of effective legal remedies, we suggest that new approaches must be discussed. The main question this essay wishes to address, is according to which standards and which methodology such a judicial stress test could be performed at the national level (see Sect. 12.3 below). Finally, we discuss the limits of the stress test concept, especially in established democracies (see Sect. 12.4 below).

Stress tests are well known from the financial sector, in particular as a response to the 2007–2008 global financial crisis. Especially the IMF imposes them as part of the FSAP (Financial Sector Assessment Program) on financial institutions in order to identify vulnerability that could undermine the stability of a country's financial system.[5] In order to do this, the FSAP takes not only a broad view at the main structural, institutional, and market features and activities of the financial sector, but also takes into account the financial policy framework within which the financial sector operates.[6] We believe a European legal community facing its own judicial crisis can learn from the financial sector's response to the financial crisis. The stress test concept we discuss in this essay can be applied by governments and parliaments, judicial councils or court administrations, ombudsmen institutions as well as non-governmental organisations such as judges' associations and academics.

12.2 The Problem: A European Rule of Law Crisis and the Limited Effectiveness of European Institutions

12.2.1 Judicial Independence in a European Rule of Law Crisis

Without judicial independence, courts cannot fulfil their social function to institutionalise conflicts and bring them to a peaceful solution.[7] The ECtHR and the CJEU have therefore recognized judicial independence and impartiality as part of the very

[4] See Follesdal 2017 for the stress test concept applied at the international level to the ECtHR.

[5] Moretti et al. 2008, p 3.

[6] Moretti et al. 2008, p 4.

[7] Luhmann 1983, pp 100–106.

definition of a judiciary.[8] Moreover, without independent judges, there is no rule of law,[9] and no judiciary as the third power in a system based on the separation of powers.[10] Especially in parliamentary democracies, where the government is formed on the basis of and can be removed by a majority in parliament, the incentive of the legislature and executive to keep each other in check, might be limited. In such a system, the courts are particularly important for the enforcement of constitutional rules and to prevent the abuse of power by the executive and legislative powers.[11]

While judicial independence is at the centre of this essay, we shall not discuss the contents of this important concept,[12] but only refer to the standards expressed in the Venice Commission's Rule of Law Checklist,[13] the Opinions of the Consultative Council of European Judges (CCJE),[14] as well as the case law of the ECtHR. We also acknowledge that we discuss primarily European issues, leaving aside important questions outside Europe. Moreover, we focus on the protection of judicial independence as an important element of the rule of law. Accountability[15] and competence are recognised as indispensable prerequisites for a high quality judiciary,[16] but will not be discussed in this essay.

In recent years, a number of challenges against the rule of law and judicial independence have emerged in a number of European states, as evidenced by numerous opinions of the Venice Commission, the CCJE and CCPE, and more

8 See *inter alia* European Court of Human Rights, *Stafford v. the United Kingdom*, 28 May 2002, ECLI:CE:ECHR:2002:0528JUD004629599, para 78; Court of Justice of the European Union, *De Coster*, 29 November 2001, ECLI:EU:C:2001:651, para 10; Court of Justice of the European Union, *El Hassani*, 13 December 2017, ECLI:EU:C:2017:960, para 40.

9 Stein 2009, p 302.

10 CCJE Opinion 18 (2015), para 11; see for example Federal Constitutional Court of Germany, *Gerichtsbezirke*, 10 June 1953, BVerfGE 2, 307 and Federal Constitutional Court of Germany, *Soforthilfegesetz*, 9 November 1955, BVerfGE 4, 331, paras 49–50; Hillgruber 2017, Article 97, para 1.

11 Gardbaum 2014, p 613.

12 On the contents of judicial independence, see Venice Commission, (CDL-AD(2010)004, Report on the Independence of the Judicial System Part I: The Independence of Judges; Venice Commission, (CDL-AD(2016)007, Rule of Law Checklist, p 20; CCJE, Magna Charta of Judges; CCJE Opinion No 1 (2001); Kiener 2001; Jackson 2012; Di Federico 2012; Engstad et al. 2014; Gee et al. 2015.

13 Venice Commission, CDL-AD(2016)007 Rule of Law Checklist.

14 CCJE Opinions and Magna Carta. See https://www.coe.int/en/web/ccje/ccje-opinions-and-magna-carta. Accessed 1 March 2019.

15 See on accountability only: CCJE Opinion No. 18 (2015), paras 20–33; ENCJ Report 2013–2014.

16 See especially the projects of the ENCJ on Independence and accountability 2016, 2017: https://www.encj.eu/articles/71. Accessed 1 March 2019.

recently by the European Commission acting under the Rule of Law Framework. We will mention nine issues that appear particularly timely in Europe today.[17]

(1) *Taking over constitutional courts*. Constitutional courts found in many European countries are particularly exposed for political interference in being veto players in the political system. Veto players are in political science literature defined as individual or collective actors that have to agree on a proposed legislative or policy change.[18] Constitutional courts are veto players due to their power to block laws and administrative decisions that the court finds contrary to the constitution or other superior norms (i.e. human rights treaties). From a political actor's perspective, constitutional courts can therefore be considered an obstacle for fundamental political and societal reforms which may run counter to constitutional norms or international obligations. Therefore it may be politically desirable to first neutralise the constitutional court, either by appointments or other means, in order to provide a 'friendly' interpretation of the constitution and other superior norms. This sequence of events can be observed in Poland, where the ruling Law and Justice Party adopted legislation reforming the procedures of the Constitutional Tribunal shortly after gaining a majority in parliament and forming a government in 2015.[19] The growing tendency of undue interference in the work of constitutional courts has been recognised by the Venice Commission by a declaration of concern in 2016.[20]

(2) *Politicisation of the appointments of judges*. Appointments of constitutional court judges have been the subject of major political controversy not only in Poland, but also in other EU member states like Croatia[21] and Slovakia.[22] Another example is Romania, where a study concludes that the transfer of judicial appointments and oversight from the Ministry of Justice to an independent judicial council has led to a greater sense of security and independence among judges.[23]

---

[17] For an in-depth overview of recurrent issues with examples of incidents across Europe, see the CCJE and CCPE 2016 Report SG/Inf(2016)3rev Challenges for judicial independence and impartiality in the member states of the Council of Europe, part D. See also the Bureau of the Consultative Council of European Judges (CCJE) CCJE-BU(2017)11 Report on judicial independence and impartiality in the Council of Europe member States in 2017.

[18] On veto players, see Tsebelis 2002, p 2; and Tsebelis 1995, pp 289–325.

[19] See CCJE/CCPE SG/Inf(2016)3rev, paras 176–178; Venice Commission CDL-AD(2016)001.

[20] See the Declaration by the Venice Commission on undue interference in the work of Constitutional Courts in its member States, adopted by the plenary on 16 March 2016, http://www.venice.coe.int/webforms/events/?id=2193. Accessed 1 March 2019.

[21] Bureau of the Consultative Council of European Judges (CCJE) CCJE-BU(2017)11 Report on judicial independence and impartiality in the Council of Europe member States in 2017, paras 56–61.

[22] In Slovakia, seats on the Constitutional Court were vacant for three years (2014–2017) due to the president refusing to appoint candidates elected by parliament. On the background and current political controversies concerning judicial appointments in Slovakia, see Ovádek 2018.

[23] See Johnson and Radu 2013, p 35.

(3) *Taking over councils for the judiciary*. A number of European states have followed Council of Europe recommendations[24] and introduced judicial councils for the appointment of judges and other decisions concerning their careers. While the effect of judicial councils is debated by scholars,[25] the recommendations say that decisions of appointment and promotion of judges should be taken by an independent authority with a substantial representation of judges (ideally the majority, elected by their peers).[26] What we see in some states is a *de facto* politicisation of the judicial councils. Poland has reorganised its judicial council so that its members from the judiciary, forming a majority in the council, are to be appointed by parliament.[27] Likewise in Turkey, the 2017 constitutional revision allows the President to appoint 6 out of 13 members of the judicial council, while the remaining members will be appointed by Parliament, which due to the same constitutional amendments will most likely be controlled by the president's party.[28] In 2012 Hungary was also criticised for leaving too much discretion concerning judicial appointments to the politically elected president of the National Judicial Office and thus weakening the National Judicial Council. Much of this criticism has later been addressed.[29]

(4) *Interference with judges' tenure and work environment*. For judges already in position, the regulation of tenure is vital for their independence. The introduction of age or term limits with retroactive effect, as in Hungary[30] and in Poland,[31] can be used to purge the judiciary of judges appointed under previous political regimes and to replace them with judges of their own choosing.[32] Such measures may encourage

---

[24] CCJE, Opinion n° 10 (2007); Venice Commission, CDL-AD(2010)004, paras 28–32; ENCJ, Councils for the Judiciary Report 2010–2011 (2011).

[25] See Kosar 2018.

[26] CCJE, Opinion n° 10 (2007), paras 15–20.

[27] See the Venice Commission CDL-AD(2017)031 Poland - Opinion on the Draft Act amending the Act on the National Council of the Judiciary; on the Draft Act amending the Act on the Supreme Court, proposed by the President of Poland, and on the Act on the Organisation of Ordinary Courts, paras 19–27. There are a number of cases pending at the CJEU concerning this question: C-487/19; C 824/18; C-625/18; C-624/18; C-585/18.

[28] See the Venice Commission CDL-AD(2017)005 Turkey - Opinion on the amendments to the Constitution adopted by the Grand National Assembly on 21 January 2017 and to be submitted to a National Referendum on 16 April 2017, paras 114–119; see also Sanders and Von Danwitz 2018a.

[29] See the Venice Commission CDL-AD(2012)020 Opinion on the Cardinal Acts on the Judiciary that were amended following the adoption of Opinion CDL-AD(2012)001 on Hungary paras 38–45 and 88.

[30] CCJE/CCPE SG/Inf(2016)3rev, para 166.

[31] Venice Commission CDL-AD(2017)031-e, paras 44–52. The CJEU was addressed in relation to this issue: see European Court of Justice, *Commission v. Poland*, order of 17 December 2018, ECLI: EU:C:2018:1021 by which the positions of the judges of the Supreme Court including the president's were secured. See also the Opinion of AG Tanchev of 11 April 2019 and the judgement of 20 June 2019. See for the pending case C-192/18 the Opinion of AG Tanchev of 20 June 2019.

[32] A recent example is the introduction of retirement schemes for judges in Armenia after the 2018 political revolution, see Venice Commission CDL-AD 2019(030), Armenia, Joint opinion on the amendment to the judicial code and some other laws.

loyalty to political authorities incompatible with judicial independence, and may have a chilling effect on the remaining judges. Another measure with similar effects can be the transfer of judges against their will, which has been reported as a recurrent problem in Turkey.[33]

(5) Another avenue to interference with judicial independence goes through *judicial administration*. In many countries the executive exercises a strong influence on judicial administration,[34] which brings along the risk of political interference with the judicial function. In the case of *Kinský v. The Czech Republic*, the ECtHR found that an order by the Ministry of Justice requiring the courts to report on the proceedings in a number of politically controversial cases violated the impartiality of the court.[35] In the case of *Baka v. Hungary*, the ECtHR found a violation of Article 6 of the ECHR due to the absence of judicial remedies following the dismissal of a chief judge.[36] Another example is the recent Polish judicial reforms, where the Minister of Justice's power to appoint, dismiss and sanction court leaders has raised particular concerns over the internal independence of Polish judges.[37]

(6) The application of *disciplinary procedures* against judges or even *strong public criticism* undermining public trust in the judiciary may also infringe on judicial independence.[38] Political statements and criticism of on-going judicial proceedings was a continuing factor for the ECtHR finding a violation of Article 6 of the ECHR in the above-mentioned *Kinský* case. Another example is Romania, where judges claim that the other branches of government use the media to discredit and to put pressure on how judges decide cases.[39] In Poland, a foundation close to the government allegedly initiated a campaign on billboards and the internet in autumn 2017 in support of the controversial judicial reforms.[40]

(7) *Non-enforcement of court decisions* remains a problem in a number of states.[41] Non-enforcement of court decisions may undermine the credibility and authority of the judiciary as well as its effectiveness. Of particular concern is non-enforcement of court decisions on constitutional issues. In the recent case of Poland, the government refused to publish decisions of the Constitutional Tribunal

33 CCJE/CCPE SG/Inf(2016)3rev, paras 182–183.

34 See with further references CCJE/CCPE SG/Inf(2016)3rev, paras 99–113.

35 See European Court of Human Rights, *Kinský v. The Czech Republic*, 9 February 2012, ECLI:CE:ECHR:2012:0209JUD004285606, paras 95–98.

36 See European Court of Human Rights, *Baka v. Hungary*, 23 June 2016, ECLI:CE:ECHR:2016:0623JUD002026112.

37 See the Venice Commission CDL-AD(2017)031 Poland - Opinion on the Draft Act amending the Act on the National Council of the Judiciary; on the Draft Act amending the Act on the Supreme Court, proposed by the President of Poland, and on the Act on the Organisation of Ordinary Courts, paras 100–108.

38 See Sanders and Von Danwitz 2017b and 2018b.

39 See Johnson and Radu 2013, p 38.

40 See Sanders and Von Danwitz 2017b and 2018a.

41 See the CCJE/CCPE SG/Inf(2016)3rev, paras 206–212.

on the constitutionality of legislation concerning the Constitutional Tribunal itself, and which it found to be an unconstitutional interference with judicial independence.[42]

(8) *Procedural changes negatively affecting the effectiveness of the courts.* In Poland, amendments to the law on the Constitutional Tribunal have introduced a number of procedural measures, concerning *inter alia* the sequencing of cases and increased jurisdiction for the plenary, and which according to the criticism from both the Venice Commission and the EU Commission, may prevent the court to function properly.[43] Similar procedural measures were also hastily introduced for the Constitutional Court of Georgia in 2016.[44]

(9) The *independence of the prosecution* service is also an important point to be kept in mind as an important factor in a state based on the rule of law.[45] As the CCPE has pointed out, without the non-interference of the executive in the prosecution service, certain criminal cases might not reach the courts at all.[46] Insofar, the Polish reform which made the Minister of Justice also the Prosecutor General, is highly problematic.[47]

12.2.2 Limited Effectiveness of European Institutions and the Need for National Responses

The serious threats depicted above raise the question of proper reactions. Given that such problems may arise all over Europe and challenge the fundamental values expressed in Article 2 TEU, EU responses come into view first. For the member states of the EU there is the Article 7 TEU procedure, which was launched by the European Commission and Parliament in 2017 against Poland after extensive discussions between the European Commission and Poland.[48] In 2018, the same

[42] See the Venice Commission CDL-AD(2016)026-e, para 75.

[43] See the Venice Commission CDL-AD(2016)026 Poland - Opinion on the Act on the Constitutional Tribunal, para 123, and Commission Recommendation (EU) 2016/1374 of 21 July 2016 regarding the rule of law in Poland, para 41.

[44] See the Venice Commission CDL-AD(2016)017 Georgia - Opinion on the Amendments to the Organic Law on the Constitutional Court and to the Law on Constitutional Legal Proceedings.

[45] See CCJE/CCPE SG/Inf(2016)3rev, paras 118–152. See for this point also: Court of Justice of the European Union, judgements of 27 May 2019 (OG, - C 508/18 - and PI C-82/19, ECLI:EU:C:2019:456) and (PF - C 509/18, ECLI:EU:C:2019:457).

[46] See CCPE Opinion No. 9 (2014) 'Rome Charter'.

[47] Venice Commission CDL-AD(2017)028.

[48] See the press release with a link to further information, especially the Reasoned proposal under Article 7(1) for a Council decision http://europa.eu/rapid/press-release_IP-17-5367_en.htm. Accessed 1 March 2019.

procedure was also launched against Hungary.[49] However, while the importance of the Article 7 procedure shall not be denied, severe measures against a member state demand unanimity among all other member states in the Council, which questions the applicability of the procedure.[50]

Short of the Article 7 procedure, the EU legal toolbox does not appear well stocked to deal with systemic threats to the rule of law in member states. The Commission has launched an infringement procedure under Article 258 TFEU against Poland because of the change of retirement ages of judges.[51] Yet this procedure does only address very particular issues such as a particular law regulating retirement ages rather than the broader systemic threat to the rule of law in Poland, of which the fusion of the Minister of Justice and the Prosecutor General, the reforms of the High Judicial Council, the Ministry of Justice influence over the selection of court presidents are just examples.[52] Scheppele has suggested that the Commission could 'bundle' a set of distinct complaints into systemic infringement actions under Article 258 TFEU, but this has yet to happen.[53] Other legal means, for example an infringement procedure for violation of Article 19 TEU at the CJEU, are in their early stages of development,[54] but has been used against Poland for its reform of the Supreme Court.[55] While these recent decisions show how important the rule of law is for the Court of Justice of the European Union as a fundamental European value and basis for European cooperation, such decisions can - again - only address specific cases brought to the court. Legal means by the member states within the European context, as for example denying the execution of a European Arrest Warrant, are also just emerging.[56] A less explored but quite dramatic option, suggested by Kochenov, is for member states under Article 259 TFEU to bring direct actions against other member states for systemic rule of law violations.[57]

---

[49] See the press release: http://www.europarl.europa.eu/news/en/press-room/20180906IPR12104/rule-of-law-in-hungary-parliament-calls-on-the-eu-to-act. Accessed 12 October 2019.

[50] See Von Bogdandy et al. 2012, pp 496–507; Greer and Williams 2009, p 474.

[51] Court of Justice of the European Union, *Commission v. Poland*, action brought on 21 December 2017 (case pending), case C-715/17

[52] See for a detailed analysis: COM(2017) 835 final Reasoned Proposal in Accordance with Article 7(1) of the Treaty on the European Union Regarding the Rule of Law in Poland.

[53] See Scheppele 2016; see also Pech and Scheppele 2017, pp 38–44.

[54] See Court of Justice of the European Union, *Associação Sindical dos Juízes Portugueses*, 27 February 2018, ECLI:EU:C:2018:117, paras 41–43; see also Closa et al. 2014/2015, p 9 ff, and Sanders and Von Danwitz 2018a.

[55] See Court of Justice of the European Union, *Commission v. Poland*, preliminary order of 17 December 2018, ECLI:EU:C:2018:1021, by which the positions of the judges of the Supreme Court including the president's were secured. See the judgement in the same case of 20 June 2019, ECLI:EU:C:2019:531. See for another important decision concerning the rule of law: Court of Justice of the European Union judgement, OG -C 508/18 and PF - C 509/18, 27 May 2019, ECLI: EU:C:2019:456.

[56] Court of Justice of the European Union, *LM*, 25 July 2018, ECLI:EU:C:2018:586. See also: Wendel 2019.

[57] See Kochenov 2016.

Time will tell if any of these mechanisms will prove effective against systemic threats to the rule of law.[58]

On the level of the Council of Europe, effective legal tools against violations of judicial independence are even more limited. Beyond decisions of the ECtHR in particular issues, there is not much the Council of Europe can do.[59] Still, the importance of Council of Europe institutions such as opinions of the Venice Commission must not be underestimated. On the one hand, such opinions entail the current standards for judicial independence. Such standards are not legally binding for the member states. Nevertheless, they do have considerable influence on institutions such as the European Union, the ECtHR, the CJEU, the other member states and the opinion of an increasingly internationally interested public. While the current development of these tools is important, their effectiveness has yet to be proven.

The lack of effective European rule of law enforcement mechanisms means that, for the time being, judiciaries remain a national responsibility, not only in relation to their financial basis but also in relation to their legal and constitutional framework. This suggests that attempts to strengthen and preserve judicial independence and the rule of law should also be made at the national level. Consequently, the stress test concept addresses the problem by introducing a tool for assessing the national situation of judicial independence which is not currently experiencing a rule of law crisis, for identifying possible threats and hopefully for strengthening legal (especially constitutional), political and social safeguards. This way, the stress test concept is an attempt to sidestep Jon Elster's paradox: while constitutions often are written in times of crisis, they ought to be adopted in maximally calm and undisturbed conditions.[60]

As a side note, while the stress test has a primarily national focus, we suggest that its results may also be relevant for European institutions. European institutions can use the results to refine their own standards and also to give member states advise on future reforms. This is in line with the interdependent way in which European rule of law standards are developed and applied. Such standards are drafted explicitly or implicitly on the basis of current developments in the member states. In case of the Venice Commission, for example, specific events in Council of Europe member states trigger a request for an opinion which leads to the application and sometimes development of existing rule of law standards. Moreover, it is also conceivable that European institutions can use the results of national stress tests to question the effectiveness of their own legal tools by means of a stress test on a European level.

---

[58] For a pessimistic view, see Kochenov 2015.

[59] The Council of Europe has denied Russia voting rights, which, however, together with the payment cuts from Turkey, might lead to a financial crisis of the institution. See http://www.dw.com/en/russia-withholds-payments-to-the-council-of-europe/a-42792673. Accessed 1 March 2019.

[60] See Elster 1995, p 394.

12.3 The Three Stages of the Stress Test

12.3.1 Introduction: What Are the Standards and What is the Methodology?

In this section we will discuss the standards and methodology of a stress test for European judiciaries. The methodology we propose is partly deductive and partly inductive. The deductive element comes from the European standards for what should count as an independent exercise of the judicial function. The inductive element comes from the fact that European judiciaries operate within different legal frameworks and political contexts. This means that measures taken in order to align national institutions with common European standards must be tailored to the national legal and political context. Consequently, the specific measures may differ from state to state.

Considering first the standards, we will argue that when assessing judicial independence on the national level within the framework of a stress test, states should adopt a European standard. As mentioned above, judicial independence is a key component in what is sometimes called a European constitutional heritage, though this term obfuscates the fact that for most of the 20th century many European states were dictatorships with little judicial independence. Today however, all 47 member states of the Council of Europe have entrenched at least a declaration of judicial independence in their constitutions.

More important still is the fact that in European public law, judicial independence is enshrined in Article 6 of the ECHR, which as interpreted by the ECtHR sets a binding minimum standard common for all the member states of the Council of Europe. For the member states of the European Union, maintaining independent judiciaries is also a legal obligation flowing from the EU treaties and the case law of the CJEU (see Sect. 12.2.1 above). While states are sovereign and may in theory adopt and interpret national law that does not meet the minimum standards of its treaty obligations, membership in the ECHR means that states are no longer completely free to organise their judiciaries unless they accept to violate their international obligations and suffer the political and legal consequences that follow.[61]

A more practical consideration for applying a European standard when assessing national legislation is that European standards can be more developed than national ones. This is not to say that national constitutions or the literature on rule of law indicators cannot provide useful guidance for national rule of law questions, quite the opposite. However, the aim of the stress test is to complement the national discourse with a European perspective in order to avoid national biases. In addition to Council of Europe and EU treaty obligations, states should also consider the

---

[61] See Article 46(1) of the ECHR as interpreted in European Court of Human Rights, *Scozzari and Giunta v. Italy*, 13 July 2000, ECLI:CE:ECHR:2000:0713JUD003922198. On the interrelation between national constitutions and European law, see Grimm 2016, pp 271–294.

standards for judicial independence developed in the opinions and recommendations issued by the Council of Europe's Venice Commission. While these are non-binding advisory opinions (soft law), they do approach the issue in a more systematic and comprehensive way than the ECtHR and national courts can do on a case-by-case basis.

In its opinions on constitutional and legislative reforms in individual countries, the Venice Commission relies on a wide range of sources.[62] In addition to hard law sources in the form of the ECHR and ECtHR case law and other international treaties, it also makes use of soft law standards, such as recommendations of the Committee of Ministers of the Council of Europe or best practices among its member states.[63] Particularly useful for the evaluation of national judiciaries are the Commission's so-called reference documents.[64] These documents contain a compressed and systematic overview of European standards and requirements pertaining to specific issues. A particularly relevant reference document for a stress test is the Venice Commission's 2010 *Report on the Independence of the Judicial System*.[65] Similar reference documents discussing contemporary standards for judicial independence have also been adopted by the Council of Europe's Consultative Council of European Judges.[66]

For the purpose of a stress test, it is important not to confuse standards with implementation. Neither the standards developed by the Venice Commission, nor the case law of the ECtHR requires states to adopt specific institutions, procedures or models to safeguard judicial independence.[67] While it might be criticised that this leaves the standards open for multiple interpretations and is too uncertain, it should be kept in mind that these standards cannot and do not aim at a harmonization of the judiciaries in European states. The standards are output oriented:

---

62 For an overview of the Venice Commission's opinions concerning the judiciary until 2015, see CDL-PI(2015)001 Compilation of Venice Commission Opinions and Reports Concerning Courts and Judges.

63 On the working methods of the Venice Commission, see Buquicchio and Granata-Menghini 2013, p 244.

64 The Venice Commission's reference documents are available on the Commission's website: http://www.venice.coe.int/WebForms/pages/default.aspx?p=01_main_reference_documents&lang=EN. Accessed 1 March 2019.

65 See the Venice Commission, CDL-AD(2010)004 Report on the Independence of the Judicial System Part 1: The Independence of Judges. See also CDL-AD(2016)007 Rule of Law Checklist.

66 See in particular CCJE Opinion no. 1 (2001) on standards concerning the independence of the judiciary and the irremovability of judges, CCJE Opinion no. 17 (2014) on the evaluation of judges' work, the quality of justice and respect for judicial independence and CCJE Opinion no. 18 (2015) on the position of the judiciary and its relation with the other powers of state in a modern democracy.

67 This point has been emphasized by the ECtHR in *inter alia* European Court of Human Rights, *Kleyn and Others v. the Netherlands*, 6 May 2003, ECLI:CE:ECHR:2003:0506JUD003934398 para 193. The Venice Commission too has repeatedly stressed the states' margin of appreciation when deciding on which measures to take in order to comply with European standards, see Buqicchio and Granata-Menghini 2013, pp 244–246 and Craig 2017, pp 78–79.

They only describe the conditions for an independent exercise of the judicial function. The states are free to adopt whatever measures required to meet these conditions. This margin of appreciation is important to recognise as judiciaries in Europe operate in different institutional, legal, political and cultural contexts, which means that measures to meet the standards should be tailor-made for each national context (see Sect. 12.3.4 below).

To illustrate the point just made, the Venice Commission considers as a standard that '[a]ll decisions concerning appointment and the professional career of judges should be based on merit applying objective criteria within the framework of the law.'[68] To meet this standard, and to prevent politically motivated appointments, the Venice Commission recommends that states establish independent judicial councils in which judges have a decisive influence on decisions on the appointment and career of judges. At the same time, the Venice Commission acknowledges that there is no single model which applies to all countries. In countries where judicial appointments lies with the executive power or in parliament, legal culture, political traditions or stringent qualification requirements may have a restraining effect that allows the standard to be met without the recommended judicial council. The introduction of councils for the judiciary may serve as an example. Such institutions are recommended by European standards and also guaranteed in the Polish Constitution.[69] However, the German legal system do not provide for such councils neither on the federal nor on the level of the states (*Länder*). Consequently, a reform of its council will have a different effect on the Polish system than would the introduction of the same Council in Germany.[70]

As the example and the discussion above show, the stress test concept presupposes an interdependency between the national level and the European level. European standards of judicial independence are used to evaluate the measures taken at the national level. Yet these standards must be considered with due regard to the national context. Like the standards discussed above, the stress test on the national level is output oriented. The aim of the stress test is not a European standardisation of institutions and procedures, but rather judiciaries which, whatever their organisation, competences and function within each legal system, can exercise the judicial function independently in accordance with the European standards. The interdependency between the European and the national level is further reflected in the three stages of the stress test, which we will discuss below.

---

[68] See the Venice Commission CDL-AD(2010)004 Report on the Independence of the Judicial System Part 1: The Independence of Judges, para 82(2) and paras 28–32.

[69] There is a discussion whether Judicial Councils are really effective in achieving their goals of securing judicial independence and impartiality, see Bobek and Kosar 2015.

[70] This is not to say, however, that nothing could be improved on the German system. German Judges Associations have demanded the introduction of a Judicial Council for decades. See Sanders and Von Danwitz 2018a.

12.3.2 Stage 1: Mapping Threats to Judicial Independence

The first stage in the stress test should be to map potential threats to judicial independence. Thus, the list of nine challenges to judicial independence in Europe provided in Sect. 12.2.1 above can provide a useful starting point. Recent experiences in Europe show that interferences with judicial independence come in a number of forms and methods. It might also be assumed, that such interferences evolve over time. Therefore, the list above is by no means exhaustive, but should be constantly revised and updated.

We will argue that states should approach potential threats to judicial independence from a European perspective. While the national context is obviously relevant and important when considering potential threats, it can be difficult to anticipate potential threats to judicial independence based only on national experiences since they can be few and limited. A European perspective on the other hand will provide stress testers with more cases and examples of threats to judicial independence. From the cases and experiences in other countries, stress testers can identify a number of characteristics of methods and techniques used to subvert judicial independence as well as which institutions, rules and procedures are particularly contested. The purpose of this first stage of the test should be to provide a broad factual basis for testing judicial independence in the national context under hypothetical scenarios (stage 2) and finally to propose measures to remedy weaknesses (stage 3).

12.3.3 Stage 2: Stress Testing Judiciaries

Stage two of the stress test is about envisaging certain scenarios in which the judiciary comes under the attack of political forces trying to wrestle the courts under their control. The test is to see whether or not, or to what degree and on which terms, constitutional and legislative safeguards can withstand different forms of interference.

The point of departure for a stress test should be the list of techniques and approaches employed for subverting judicial independence based on the experiences from a number of European countries and compiled in stage one. The stress test should be undertaken by way of a careful analysis of how the political and legal framework in the tested country would - most likely - react to the previously identified threats. Could similar approaches be successful in other countries? Are changes to the constitutional and legal framework needed to prevent these approaches to be successful? Possible scenarios can be anything from subtle and limited manipulation of judicial appointments to a full scale political takeover of the judiciary like the one we are witnessing in Poland these days. While legal safeguards such as judicial review and constitutional guarantees are of the utmost importance, such tests should also take into account the effects of the media, NGOs, the international community and other relevant factors.

Another aspect to be kept in mind is that the scope of judicial independence is not necessarily clear and this must be kept in mind when performing the stress test.[71] What constitutes courts of law, judges and judicial power may vary between legal systems. If it is the exercise of the judicial function that is to be protected from interference, the stress test must take into account that not all tasks performed by courts and judges involve judicial adjudication. Moreover, decisions that in some countries are considered judicial adjudication and made by judges, can in other countries be administrative decisions. Therefore, in order to be effective, the term 'judiciary' should not be understood in too narrow a sense when it comes to the stress test.[72]

It should also be noted that neither legal safeguards nor the political climate are necessarily static. Therefore, the stress test should be undertaken in different stages, taking into account the possible development of the political climate and the effects of previous attacks against the judiciary. It is likely, that at some stage, the rule of law in every state will crumble once the stress is high enough. The stress test should help identify critical points where attacks on judicial independence can be initiated easiest.

12.3.4 Stage 3: Considering Measures

The third and final stage of the stress test is to consider and propose remedies to the flaws and weaknesses in the protection of judicial independence identified in stage two. Before considering measures to be taken, the plausibility of potential threats to judicial independence identified in stage two should be assessed. Not any imagined scenario of adverse conditions to the judiciary is conceivable within a specific national context. Thus a risk assessment involving both the probability and the damage potential of a possible threat should be carried out before considering concrete measures.

If the risk assessment concludes that measures should be taken to counter a specific threat, the question is what measures are appropriate. The answer to this question is of course context dependent, and a general discussion of measures goes beyond the remit of this essay. Instead we will make some general remarks on institutional (1) and non-institutional measures (2).

(1) First we do not underestimate the difficulties in responding with concrete measures to hypothetical scenarios produced by a stress test. However, as pointed out above, most legislation is both a reaction to past experiences and a prognosis on future developments. Uncertainties in the effectiveness of measures or the best

---

[71] For a discussion on the ambiguity in the concept of judicial independence, see Macdonald and Kong 2012, pp 832–833.

[72] This approach was also taken in the joint CCJE/CCPE Report SG/Inf(2016)3rev; see also Shetreet 2011, p 17.

response to specific threats can in any case be mitigated by drawing on experiences and best practices from other countries. For example, one of the lessons learned from the controversial reform of the Polish Constitutional Tribunal in 2015–2016 is that changes to procedural rules can undermine the effective functioning of a court to the extent that it cannot function properly.[73] In such a scenario, a possible measure can be to entrench key procedural rules in the constitution, for which amendments are usually more time consuming and requires a large majority in parliament as for example in Hungary after the 2010 elections.

Empirical and qualitative research on courts can also provide valuable insights into the functioning of specific mechanisms and procedures. For example, a quantitative study by Ginsburg and Melton based on data from 192 countries between 1960 and 2008 suggests that rules governing the selection and removal of judges are the most important safeguards for judicial independence in authoritarian regimes and new democracies.[74] Their findings also suggest that that constitutional safeguards for judicial independence are most effective when they establish a political machinery of checks and balances, rather than relying solely on the normative effect of declarative rules saying judges shall be independent.[75] Such 'mechanical' safeguards in the form of additional veto players or clear boundaries for legislation may be particularly relevant in typical European parliamentary systems where the majority in parliament and the executive usually belong to the same political party or block. Turning again to the Polish judicial reforms since 2015 as an example, they have been implemented with relative speed and ease by a scant majority in the Polish parliament working in conjunction with a President from the same party.

Another question is on which level in the hierarchy of norms safeguards for judicial independence are to be regulated. The answer will to a large extent depend on where the threat comes from. If for example individual judges' independence in deciding cases vis-à-vis their court presidents is at risk, appropriate measures can be regulated in law, as the law is beyond the powers of court presidents. If however the threat comes from parliament, which in parliamentary systems is likely to act in concert with the executive, legislative measures may be inadequate. In such a scenario, only the constitution or other norms with more rigorous amendment procedures (so-called 'organic laws') may provide adequate protection.[76]

---

[73] See the reports of the Venice Commission CDL-AD(2016)001-e Opinion on amendments to the Act of 25 June 2015 on the Constitutional Tribunal of Poland, para 88, and CDL-AD(2016) 026-e Poland - Opinion on the Act on the Constitutional Tribunal, para 123. See also the Venice Commission CDL-AD(2016)017 Georgia - Opinion on the Amendments to the Organic Law on the Constitutional Court and to the Law on Constitutional Legal Proceedings, para 64.

[74] See Ginsburg and Melton 2014, pp 209.

[75] On the distinction between the constitution as a machinery and a norm, see Troper 2001, pp 147–162.

[76] See for example the suggestions made in the Council of Europe Plan of Action on Strengthening Judicial Independence and Impartiality, CM(2016)36 final.

As illustrated above, deciding on institutional measures raises a number of questions. A final issue to keep in mind is the potential negative effects of measures to protect judicial independence. Consider for example that judges are found to be vulnerable to pressure by threats of disciplinary sanctions from the executive or the court administration. In this case, the criteria for disciplinary sanctions can be clarified and restricted in the law or the competence to initiate disciplinary procedures can be reallocated to a different body. However, such measures must be balanced against the equally legitimate interest in holding judges accountable for errors and abuse of powers. The aim should be to render judges independent in the exercise of the judicial function, not to render them unaccountable.

(2) Not all potential threats to judicial independence can be met by simply introducing institutional mechanisms or procedures to insulate the courts from undue interference. We will mention three types of non-institutional measures to be considered.

First of all, there is ample research and experience to suggest that building a 'culture of judicial independence' in society and among political actors is at least as important as institutional safeguards.[77] One example is the above-mentioned study by Ginsburg and Melton, which suggests that in established democracies, many with old constitutions with relatively weak formal safeguards, judicial independence is established by practice rather than by law alone.[78] Within the context of a stress test, it is a particular challenge to identify cultural preconditions for judicial independence and to suggest effective measures to build and maintain such a culture.

Second, threats to judicial independence can be met with non-institutional preventive measures by strengthening courts' and judges' capacity to offer off-bench resistance to interference.[79] Research on judges in hybrid regimes suggest that judges' social networks with political elites, organisation of judges associations and cooperation with bar associations can help mobilise legal professionals to protect judges against both blatant interference or the chilling effect of strong formal powers vested in the executive. A recent example from an established democracy is the Norwegian Judges Association's successful interference with the Norwegian government's attempt in 2017 to cut short the term of its newly appointed judge on the EFTA Court.[80] Courts and judges can also seek international support. Within the Council of Europe, constitutional courts or equivalent apex courts can request the Venice Commission for *amicus curiae* opinions on comparative constitutional

---

[77] For a discussion and overview of relevant contexts for judicial independence, see Macdonald and Kong 2012, pp 846–852.

[78] See Ginsburg and Melton 2014, pp 206–209.

[79] In the following we draw on the discussion and summary of scholarship in Trochev and Ellett 2014, pp 67–91.

[80] See https://www.politico.eu/article/norway-accused-of-meddling-with-judicial-independence-per-christiansen-efta/. Accessed 1 March 2019.

and international law issues pertaining to judicial independence.[81] Judges can also rally international support by engaging in transnational networks of judges and lawyers, though recent experiences in Hungary and Poland suggest that the international critique of judicial reforms may have limited effect.

Third, problems with illegitimate interferences in the judiciary are not always due to a flawed institutional framework. In a study on the reforms of the justice system in Guatemala, Rachel Sieder found that too much attention has been paid to institutional design in order to strengthen the rule of law at the expense of addressing underlying causes for the lack of judicial independence.[82] Despite institutional advances in appointment procedures, the judicial system in Guatemala remained corrupt and under the influence of powerful individuals and groups, leading to a deep mistrust of the justice system among citizens. According to Sieder, corruption explains much of the weakness of the Guatemalan judicial system.[83] In such a scenario, strengthening disciplinary procedures and oversight mechanisms may alleviate the problem. However, it is likely that judges will remain susceptible to corruption without higher salaries, better training to increase their standing and adequate protection against intimidation and threats.[84]

12.4 The Counter Argument: Is it Really About Law, Or About Culture?

While we have just mentioned three types of non-institutional measures, the stress test concept we propose in this essay presupposes that threats to judicial independence can at least to some extent be prevented by measures improving the legal and institutional framework. However, the way in which *de jure* judicial independence, in particular constitutional guarantees, actually enhance *de facto* judicial independence, is a point of debate.[85]

The above-mentioned study conducted by Ginsburg and Melton finds that in established democracies, there seems to be no statistically relevant relationship between *de jure* and *de facto* judicial independence.[86] In fact, older democracies, which may have the oldest constitutions with the weakest guarantees of judicial independence, tend to have high levels of *de facto* judicial independence. Ginsburg

[81] See CDL-AD(2016)015 Republic of Moldova – Amicus Curiae Brief for the Constitutional Court on the Right of Recourse by the State against Judges, CDL-AD(2017)002 Republic of Moldova – Amicus Curiae Brief for the Constitutional Court on the Criminal liability of judges, and CDL-AD(2016)036 Albania – Amicus Curiae Brief for the Constitutional Court on the Law on the Transitional Re-evaluation of Judges and Prosecutors (the Vetting Law).

[82] Sieder 2004, p 111.

[83] Sieder 2004, p 105.

[84] See also CCJE/CCPE Report SG/Inf(2016)3rev, paras 284–288, 291–302.

[85] See with references to the discussion: Ginsburg and Melton 2014, p 188.

[86] Ginsburg and Melton 2014, p 205.

and Melton ponder whether such democracies might have developed alternative mechanisms of protecting judicial independence.[87] The experiences from these countries suggest indeed that judicial independence, observance of the rule of law and separation of powers is not only a matter of legal and constitutional guarantees, but also of something else, possibly a matter of tradition and political culture.[88]

In relation to Germany, for example, Gärditz has argued that the position and actual independence of the German Federal Constitutional Court was due to 'institutional respect' between the court and the other branches of the German government rather than the text of the German Constitution, which is quite weak regarding formal safeguards of the Federal Constitutional Court.[89] The experiences of many established European democracies suggest that such a 'culture of judicial independence' may very well be the most important factor for maintaining judiciaries free from political interference.[90] By 'culture' in this context, we mean informal rules on acceptable behaviour and respect of other powers of state towards the judiciary. While the basis for such a 'culture of independence' are yet uncertain, it can reinforce formal legal safeguards, as well as substitute such safeguards.

Indeed, the importance of non-legal factors for maintaining the rule of law is recognized by the Venice Commission, which does not limit its assessments to legal factors only, but also considers contextual elements: 'The presence (or absence) of a shared political and legal culture within a society, and the relationship between that culture and the legal order help to determine to what extent and at what level of concreteness the various elements of the Rule of Law have to be explicitly expressed in written law.'[91]

Nevertheless, while some – especially Western – European countries rely heavily on such a culture of independence as safeguards for the rule of law, formal legal safeguards are not irrelevant. Culture can change. The resilience of a culture of judicial independence becomes particularly questionable when established political forces are being replaced by new ones and with increasing polarisation of politics. It would be naïve to assume that the judiciaries in established European democracies are immune to the techniques employed to subvert judicial independence as for example in Poland.[92]

---

87 Ginsburg and Melton 2014, p 208.

88 Ginsburg and Melton 2014, pp 194, 208. See for a similar argument in respect to the Swiss judiciary: Meyer 2019.

89 Gärditz 2018. Gärditz suggests including more safeguards in the constitution now, which could protect the constitutional court against an attack from a new government.

90 See for the 'culture of judicial independence': CCJE/CCPE, SG/Inf(2016)3rev, para 6; Sanders and Von Danwitz 2017a. See also Shetreet 2011, who, however, sees the culture of judicial independence as a general element of political culture. See for the importance of unwritten rules for the functioning of democracies: Levitsky and Ziblat 2018.

91 Venice Commission, Rule of Law Checklist CDL-AD(2016)007, para 42.

92 See for example an interview with Professor Gärditz of Bonn University, Germany: https://verfassungsblog.de/die-meisten-dinge-die-in-polen-und-ungarn-gelaufen-sind-koennten-ohne-weiteres-hier-auch-passieren/. Accessed 1 March 2019.

One example is the above-mentioned attempt by the Norwegian government to cut short the term of its judge on the EFTA Court by applying the national retirement age on an international court without a fixed retirement age.[93] There is a clear resemblance to Hungary's and Poland's much criticised application of rules on retirement age. Only after fierce criticism in the press and from the Norwegian Judges Association, as well as from the EFTA Court itself, did the government back down. In a future and different political context, such non-legal factors may not be as effective as they are today.

In another recent example from Germany, a town denied the extreme right wing NDP party to rent a hall of the town even though it had been ordered to do so by the Federal Constitutional Court.[94] This situation raised the fundamental problem that the judiciary has no power to enforce its own decisions.[95] The serious tone in which the court demanded that the situation was investigated by the government of the respective federal state (*Land*) showed that it was aware of the danger a disregard of its decisions could pose. The state's government replied that the town had not been aware that it had no discretion to follow the court's decision.[96] However, commentators have questioned this statement, hinting that the town might not have wanted to be seen as hosting the unpopular party and arguing that not enforcing a decision of the Constitutional Court would be an unprecedented denial of justice, comparable to events in Turkey.[97] If, in the future, the enforcement of court decisions should become a question of political popularity more regularly, the rule of law would be in grave danger.

In our view, Ginsburg and Melton's finding that formal legal safeguards do not statistically correlate with *de facto* judicial independence in established democracies but only in transitional democracies and autocratic regimes, does not mean that legal safeguards are irrelevant. Quite the opposite, it suggests that improving *de jure* judicial independence is important in the event of a backsliding of democracy. It is precisely such situations which the stress test concept is intended to anticipate. And in these situations legal safeguards appear to be effective.

To be clear, we are not suggesting that stress tests alone can work wonders in protecting judicial independence. Moreover, we appreciate that considerable differences between European countries exist and that some systems might react differently than others to threats. However, we believe that a critical public review of the judiciary's independence under adverse scenarios may not only improve formal legal safeguards, but also raise the awareness in society of the importance of independent judiciaries for modern democracies under the rule of law. This way, a stress test may also contribute to building and maintaining a political culture which

---

93 See https://www.politico.eu/article/norway-accused-of-meddling-with-judicial-independence-per-christiansen-efta. Accessed 1 March 2019.

94 Federal Constitutional Court of Germany, 24 March 2018, 1 BvQ 18/18.

95 Breyer 2010, pp 3–68.

96 Podolski 2018b.

97 Podolski 2018a, b.

serves as the necessary basis and most resilient protection of judicial independence. In the financial sector, stress tests of financial institutions have the aim of reducing uncertainty in the markets.[98] For the judiciary too, stress tests may be employed to increase the public's trust in the judiciary.

12.5 Concluding Remarks

We have argued that European states should learn from the challenges to the rule of law in different European states and critically review the constitutional and legal framework of their own national judiciaries. This should be done by means of a stress test which assesses the robustness of national judiciaries against the adverse developments of the constitutional and legal framework as well as in the political culture. Such a stress test is important for both newer and established democracies. While the latter often rely on a culture of independence rather than on detailed constitutional and legal safeguards (*de jure* judicial independence) in order to achieve *de facto* judicial independence, political cultures can change.

The stress test shall use European standards and be performed in three stages. Stage one requires a detailed analysis of the different techniques used in attacks against the rule of law and judicial independence. We have focussed on nine potential threats as examples ranging from the takeover of constitutional courts, infringements of judges' tenure to measures against court administrations and prosecution services. On stage two, judiciaries should be stress tested by envisaging scenarios in which the techniques analysed on stage one are applied against the judiciary in another country. This way, weaknesses can be identified. On stage three, institutional and non-institutional measures shall be considered by which identified weaknesses can be improved or remedied.

Finally, we envisage a stress test for European judiciaries to be a fundamentally comparative exercise. In a time of rising nationalism in Europe, we should not forget that the history of European constitutionalism is not one of isolated national developments, but one of increasing diffusion and learning across borders.[99] In addition to treaty obligations, the last decades have also seen a burgeoning transnationalisation of constitutional law through soft law instruments.[100] European rule of law standards develop in an interdependent dialogue between member states and European institutions. Within this tradition and emerging framework, the stress test serves as a cross borders communicative tool of rule of law values.

---

98 See Geithner 2014, p 312.

99 See Elkins 2010.

100 See Bartole 2017.

References

Bartole S (2017) Comparative Constitutional Law. An Indispensable Tool for the Creation of Transnational Law. European Constitutional Law Review 13:601–610

Bobek M, Kosar D (2015) Global Solutions, Local Damages. A Critical Study in Judicial Councils in Central and Eastern Europe. German Law Journal 15(7):1257–1292

Breyer S (2010) Making Our Democracy Work, Vintage Books, New York

Buquicchio G, Granata-Menghini S (2013) The Venice Commission Twenty Years on. Challenge met but New Challenges ahead. In: van Roosmalen M et al (eds) Fundamental Rights and Principles: Liber amicorum Pieter van Dijk. Intersentia Publishing, Cambridge, pp 241–254

Černič J L, Avbelj M (2018) The Special Issue of the Hague Journal on the Rule of Law on the Crisis of Constitutional Democracy in Central and Eastern Europe. Hague Journal on the Rule of Law 10:1–3

Closa C, Kochenov D, Weiler JHH (2014/2015) Reinforcing Rule of Law Oversight in the European Union. EUI Working Paper, RSCAS

Craig P (2017) Transnational Constitution-Making: The Contribution of the Venice Commission on Law and Democracy. UC Irvine Journal of International, Transnational and Comparative Law 2:57–85

Di Federico G (2012) Judicial Accountability and Conduct: An Overview. In: Seibert-Fohr A (ed) Judicial Independence in Transition, Springer, Heidelberg, pp 87–118

Elkins Z (2010) Diffusion and the Constitutionalization of Europe. Comparative Political Studies 43:969–999

Elster J (1995) Forces and Mechanisms in the Constitution-Making Process. Duke Law Journal 45:364–396

Engstad N A, Froseth A, Tonder B (eds) (2014) The Independence of Judges. Eleven International Publishing, The Hague

Follesdal A (2017) Independent yet Accountable: Stress Test Lessons for the European Court of Human Rights. Maastricht Journal of European and Comparative Law 24:484–510

Gardbaum S (2014) Separation of Powers and the Growths of Judicial Review in Established Democracies (or Why Has the Model of Legislative Supremacy Mostly Been Withdrawn From Sale?). American Journal of Comparative Law 62:613–639

Gärditz K F (2018) Eine Verfassung gegen Krisen. LTO, https://www.lto.de/recht/hintergruende/h/grundgesetz-krisen-schutz-verfassung/ Accessed 1 March 2019

Gee G, Hazell R, Malleson K, O'Brian P (2015) The Politics of Judicial Independence in the UK's Changing Constitution. Cambridge University Press, Cambridge

Geithner T F (2014) Stress Test: Reflections on Financial Crises. Broadway Books, New York

Ginsburg T, Melton J (2014) Does De Jure Judicial Independence Really Matter. Journal of Law and Courts 2:187–217

Greer S, Williams AT (2009) Human Rights and the Council of Europe and the EU – Towards 'individual', 'constitutional' or 'institutional' justice? European Law Journal 15:462–481

Grimm D (2016) Constitutionalism: Past, Present, and Future. Oxford University Press, Oxford

Hillgruber C (2017) Article 97. In: Maunz Th, Dürig G (eds) Grundgesetz Kommentar, CH Beck, Munich

Holmøyvik E, Sanders A (2017) Stress Test for Europe's Judiciaries. Verfassungsblog, https://verfassungsblog.de/a-stress-test-for-europes-judiciaries/ Accessed 1 March 2019

Jackson V (2012) In: Seibert-Fohr A (ed) Judicial Independence in Transition. Springer, Heidelberg, pp 19–86

Johnson A, Radu B (2013) The Effect of EU Anti-Corruption Measures on the Romanian Judiciary. International Journal for Court Administration 5:34–44

Kiener R (2001) Richterliche Unabhängigkeit. Stämpfli Verlag, Bern

Kochenov D (2015) Biting Intergovernmentalism: The Case for the Reinvention of Article 259 TFEU to Make it a viable Rule of Law Enforcement Tool. Hague Journal on the Rule of Law 7:153–174

Kochenov D (2016) The Missing EU Rule of Law? In: Closa C, Kochenov D (eds) Reinforcing Rule of Law Oversight in the European Union. Cambridge University Press, Cambridge pp 290–312
Kosar D (2018) Beyond Judicial Councils: Forms, Rationales and Impact of Judicial Self-Governance in Europe. German Law Journal 7:1567–1612
Levitsky S, Ziblat D (2018) How democracies die. Broadway Books, New York
Luhmann N (1983) Legitimation durch Verfahren. Suhrkamp, Frankfurt am Main
Macdonald R, Kong H (2012) Judicial Independence as a Constitutional Virtue. In: Rosenfeld M, Sajó A (eds) The Oxford Handbook of Comparative Constitutional Law. Oxford University Press, Oxford pp 831–858
Melton J, Ginsburg T (2014) Does De Jure Judicial Independence Really Matter? A Reevaluation of Explanations for Judicial Independence. Coase-Sandor Working Paper Series in Law and Economics, Coase-Sandor Institute for Law and Economics, University of Chicago Law School
Meyer U (2019) Grundvoraussetzungen richterlicher Tätigkeit. Zeitschrift des Bernischen Juristenvereins 155: 217–223
Moretti M, Stolz S, Swinburne M (2008) Stress-testing at the IMF. IMF Working Paper 08/206. https://www.imf.org/external/pubs/ft/wp/2008/wp08206.pdf Accessed 1 March 2019
Ovádek, M (2018) Drama or Serenity? Upcoming Judicial Appointments at the Slovak Constitutional Court, Verfassungsblog. https://verfassungsblog.de/drama-or-serenity-upcoming-judicial-appointments-at-the-slovak-constitutional-court/ Accessed 1 March 2019
Pech L, Scheppele K L (2017) Illiberalism Within: Rule of Law Backsliding in the EU. Cambridge Yearbook of European Legal Studies 19:3–47
Podolski T (2018a) Stadt Wetzlar widersetzt sich dem BVerfG, Legal Tribune Online. https://www.lto.de/recht/hintergruende/h/bverfg-wetzlar-npd-versammlung-stadthalle-verbot-widersetzt/ Accessed 1 March 2019
Podolski T (2018b) Es war eben ein Dilemma. Legal Tribune Online. https://www.lto.de/recht/hintergruende/h/streit-um-stadthalle-wetzlar-npd-kommunalaufsicht-stellungnahme-regierungspraesident/ Accessed 1 March 2019
Sanders A, von Danwitz L (2017a) The Polish Judiciary Reform: Problematic under European Standards and a Challenge for Germany. Verfassungsblog. http://verfassungsblog.de/the-polish-judiciary-reform-problematic-under-european-standards-and-a-challenge-for-germany/ Accessed 1 March 2019
Sanders A, von Danwitz L (2017b) Defamation of Justice: Propositions on how to Evaluate Public Attacks against the Judiciary. Verfassungsblog. http://verfassungsblog.de/defamation-of-justice-propositions-on-how-to-evaluate-public-attacks-against-the-judiciary/ Accessed 1 March 2019
Sanders A, von Danwitz L (2018a) Selecting Judges in Poland and Germany: Challenges to the Rule of Law in Europe and Propositions for a New Approach to Judicial Legitimacy. German Law Journal 19(4):769–815
Sanders A, von Danwitz L (2018b) Zulässigkeit und Grenzen von Kritik an der Justiz. Justice – Justiz – Giustizia 2018/2
Scheppele K L (2016) Enforcing the Basic Principles of EU Law through Systemic Infringement Actions. In: Closa C, Kochenov D (eds) Reinforcing Rule of Law Oversight in the European Union. Cambridge University Press, Cambridge, pp 105–132
Shetreet S (2011) The Culture of Judicial Independence. Brill, Leiden
Sieder R (2004) Renegotiating 'Law and Order': Judicial Reform and Citizen Responses in Post-war Guatemala. In: Gargarella A et al (eds) Democratization and the Judiciary: The Accountability Function of Courts in New Democracies. Frank Cass Publishers, London, pp 99–116
Stein R (2009) Rule of Law: What does it Mean? Minnesota Journal of International Law 18: 293–303
Trochev A, Ellett R (2014) Judges and Their Allies. Rethinking Judicial Autonomy Through the Prism of Off-Bench Resistance. Journal of Law and Courts 1:67–92

Troper M (2001) La Théorie du Droit, le Droit, l'État. Presses Universitaires de France, Paris
Tsebelis G (1995) Decision Making in Political Systems: Veto Players in Presidentialism, Parliamentarism, Multicameralism and Multipartyism. British Journal of Political Science 25:289–325
Tsebelis G (2002) Veto Players: How Political Institutions Work. Princeton University Press, Princeton
Von Bogdandy A, Kottman M, Antpöhler C, Dickschen J, Hentrei S, Smrkolj M (2012) Reverse Solange. Protecting the Essence of Fundamental Rights against EU Member States. Common Market Law Review 40:496–507
Wendel M (2019) Mutual Trust, Essence and Federalism – Between Consolidating and Fragmenting the Area of Freedom, Security and Justice after LM. European Constitutional Law Review 15:17–47

Eirik Holmøyvik is Professor of Constitutional Law at the University of Bergen since 2014. Since 2016 he is the Norwegian substitute member to the Venice Commission. He has published widely on Norwegian constitutional law and history, in particular on topics such as the separation of powers, judicial review, transfer of sovereignty, and constitutional amendment. Recent publications include 'On the Parliament's competence to instruct the government with legally binding effect' (in *Tidsskrift for rettsvitenskap*, 2018, in Norwegian) and 'Constituent Power and Constitutionalism in 19th Century Norway' (in *Reconsidering Constitutional Formation II*, Springer, 2018).

Anne Sanders is Professor of Civil Law, Company Law, the Law of Family Businesses and Comparative Judicial Studies at the University of Bielefeld. She regularly works as an expert for the Council of Europe on projects concerning the quality of judges' work and judicial independence. At the moment, she is serving as expert for the Consultative Council of European Judges, this time on Opinion No. 22 on the role of judicial assistants. Before becoming a professor, Anne Sanders worked as a law clerk/judicial assistant at the Federal Constitutional Court of Germany (*Bundesverfassungsgericht*).

Part II
Comments and Opinions

Chapter 13
The Strasbourg Court: Judges Without Borders

Marc Bossuyt

Contents

13.1 Introduction

In 2010, I wrote that 'in the name of a dynamic and teleological interpretation, the European Court of Human Rights progresses on the road to an ever greater "juridisation" of European society, without caring very much what the States had in mind when they accepted to become parties to the Convention.'[1] I criticised several judgments of the Court out of the conviction that 'a critical analysis of the case law of the Court may have a salutary effect on its development and may contribute to a

[1] Bossuyt 2010a, p 103. On that so-called 'dynamic' interpretation, see Bossuyt 2015a, pp 31–56.

Intervention made at the Parliamentary Seminar on 'The European Court of Human Rights: the Way Forward, Achievements and Challenges', organized by the Committee on Legal Affairs and Human Rights of the Parliamentary Assembly of the Council of Europe in Strasbourg on 27 June 2017.

M. Bossuyt (✉)
University of Antwerp, Antwerp, Belgium
e-mail: marc.bossuyt1@gmail.com

Hirsch Ballin, Van der Schyff & Stremler (eds.), *European Yearbook of Constitutional Law 2019*, European Yearbook of Constitutional Law 1,
https://doi.org/10.1007/978-94-6265-359-7_13

refinement of its future stands.'[2] Criticising the Strasbourg Court is a risky enterprise because – as has been written by Paul Mahoney, the former British Judge in the Court – '[those who dare to criticise the Court] are regarded almost as renegades or traitors; they are not true human rights "patriots"'.[3] I have been particularly critical of the attribution of positive obligations to civil rights when it results in transforming those rights into social rights, and of the case law concerning asylum seekers.

13.2 The Attribution of Positive Obligations to Civil Rights

Already from 1968 on, the Court has attributed positive obligations to the rights and freedoms set forth in the Convention.[4] Later on, mainly based on the 'Protection of property' guaranteed by Article 1 of Protocol I to the Convention, the Court extended its jurisdiction to social rights.[5] Many of those extensions are based on the famous dicta of the Court that 'the Convention is a living instrument which (…) must be interpreted in the light of the present day conditions'[6] and that 'the Convention is intended to guarantee not rights that are theoretical or illusory but rights that are practical and effective'.[7] According to the British Law Lord Hoffmann, it is 'the banner under which the Strasbourg court has assumed power to legislate what they consider to be required by "European public order"'.[8] Personally, I believe that the Court exceeds the limits of its jurisdiction when it transforms civil rights into social rights. This happens when the positive obligations attributed to civil rights require resources not all States possess as well as choices to

---

[2] *Ibid.*, p 104.

[3] In his Preface to Bossuyt 2016a, pp ix–x. He recognises moreover that 'by spreading wider and yet wider the net of human rights protection [the case-law of the Court results in] over-intervention into the normal workings of democratic processes at national level and over-expansion of the Convention rights and freedoms into domain not covered by the text of the treaty'.

[4] In the third case before the Court: European Court of Human Rights (hereafter: ECtHR), case *'relating to certain aspects of the laws on the use of languages in Belgium' v. Belgium*, 23 July 1968, ECLI:CE:ECHR:1968:0723JUD000147462. This despite the negative formulation of Article 2 of Protocol I to the Convention ('No person shall be denied the right to education').

[5] In the judgments ECtHR, *Gaygusuz v. Austria*, 16 September 1996, ECLI:CE:ECHR:1996:0916JUD001737190 and ECtHR, *Koua Poirrez v. France*, 30 September 2003, ECLI:CE:ECHR:2003:0930JUD004089298 and in the decision ECtHR, *Stec and Others v. the United Kingdom*, 12 April 2006, ECLI:CE:ECHR:2006:0412JUD006573101. This despite the negative formulation of the Article: 'No one shall be deprived of his possessions (…)'. See Bossuyt 2007 and Bossuyt 2009–2010.

[6] ECtHR, *Tyrer v. the United Kingdom*, 25 April 1978, ECLI:CE:ECHR:1978:0425JUD000585672.

[7] ECtHR, *Airey v. Ireland*, 9 October 1979, ECLI:CE:ECHR:1979:1009JUD000628973.

[8] Hoffmann 2009, para 27.

be made and priorities to be established at the expense of other rights or other categories of persons.[9]

Some aspects of the creation of new positive obligations are particularly problematic:[10]

- In conformity with the separation of powers principle, it is up to political organs to create new rules and to the Court to interpret them but not to extend its own jurisdiction by creating such rules;
- An international court, composed overwhelmingly by non-nationals, should – in the absence of legislative checks and balances[11] – exercise its jurisdiction with even greater restraint than domestic judges;
- In matters of economic and social rights, there are no universal human rights standards but at best only regional standards unattainable by many countries;
- The concomitant enlargement of the jurisdictional control of the prohibition of discrimination amounts to relinquishing a greater degree of sovereignty from the national legislator to the international judge than is the case with civil rights;
- The reliance on EU law to define the extent of positive obligations is highly questionable because the Court may not rely 'on [EU] regulations and directives to interpret the Convention with respect to the 19 States parties which are not Members of the European Union. And the Court may neither interpret the extent of the obligations applicable to the 28 Member States of the European Union differently from those applicable to the 19 other States parties to the Convention.
- Finally, it is not up to the Court of Strasbourg – but to the Court of Justice in Luxembourg – to interpret the extent of the EU regulations and directives and to impose sanctions when they are not respected'.[12]

Wondering what the natural limits of the growth of the Convention beyond the original expectations of its framers might be, Baroness Hale of Richmond of the Supreme Court of the United Kingdom concluded, in speeches delivered in 2011, that in any case 'there should be some limits'.[13] Unfortunately, the Court appears to accept only self-imposed limitations to its jurisdiction.[14] In my view, '[since t] reaties are only binding because – and to the extent that – States have expressed

[9] Bossuyt 2016a, p 142.

[10] *Ibid.*, pp 142–145.

[11] *Cf.* the judgment of the Irish Court in *X.X. v. Minister for Justice and Equality* of 24 June 2016, quoted by Judge Siofra O'Leary (Ireland) in her concurring opinion in ECtHR, *J.K. and Others v. Sweden*, 23 August 2016, ECLI:CE:ECHR:2016:0823JUD005916612.

[12] Bossuyt 2016a, p 145; see also Bossuyt 2015b, p 587: 'Even when an EU directive imposes higher requirements than the European Convention, it cannot expand the obligations under that Convention since such requirements cannot be imposed on the 19 States parties to the Convention which are not EU-Members and the obligations under the Convention cannot be more demanding for EU Members than for non-EU-Members'.

[13] At the opening of the judicial year of the Strasbourg Court on 28 January 2011 and at the Barnard's Inn Reading on 16 June 2011 (Hale 2011, p 543). See also Bossuyt 2014.

[14] Bossuyt 2007, p 328.

their will to be bound by them (, …) international judicial organs – even more than national judicial organs – should exercise their competence with caution and circumspection, with restraint and reservation. To disregard, willingly and knowingly, the intentions of the authors of a treaty amounts to a limitation of State sovereignty without democratic legitimacy'.[15]

13.3 The Case Law of the Court Concerning Asylum Seekers

Most judgments concerning asylum seekers have two specific characteristics: first, the violations found are *indirect* because States parties are held responsible for actions committed by other States, very often States that are non-parties to the Convention; second, those violations are *potential* or *virtual*, since in most of the cases the prohibited acts have not yet taken place but could take place if a foreigner is compelled to leave the territory of the State party. Instead of evaluating facts that did happen in States parties to the Convention, the Court speculates about events that could happen in non-States parties to the Convention. In its Grand Chamber judgment *Mamatkulov and Askarov v. Turkey* (4 February 2005), the Court decided that its interim measures had become binding.[16] Since then, the number of interim measures requested by applicants increased from 112 in 2006 to 4,768 in 2010. Before that judgment, the Court found only four indirect violations of Article 3 of the Convention ('The prohibition of torture').[17] Since that judgment, the Court already found more than 120 such violations. Two of those judgments are very important: *M.S.S.* and *Hirsi Jamaa and Others*.

In *M.S.S. v. Belgium and Greece* (21 January 2011), the Grand Chamber, considering unacceptable the conditions of detention and the living conditions of an asylum seeker[18] after his transferral by Belgium to Greece under the Dublin

---

[15] *Ibid.*, p 330.

[16] Overturning its judgment in ECtHR, *Cruz Varas and Others v. Sweden*, 20 March 1991, ECLI:CE:ECHR:1991:0320JUD001557689 and its decision in ECtHR, *Čonka and Others v. Belgium*, 13 March 2001, ECLI:CE:ECHR:2002:0205JUD005156499; in their dissenting opinion (para 16) on that issue, Judges Lucius Caflisch (on behalf Liechtenstein), Riza Türmen (Turkey) and Anatoly Kovler (Russia) state that the Court 'ceases to interpret and assumes legislative functions'. See also Caflisch 2006 and Bossuyt 2010b, pp 14–21.

[17] In its judgments ECtHR, *Chahal v. the United Kingdom*, 15 November 1996, ECLI:CE:ECHR:1996:1115JUD002241493, ECtHR, *Ahmed v. Austria*, 17 December 1996, ECLI:CE:ECHR:1996:1217JUD002596494, ECtHR, *D. v. the United Kingdom*, 2 May 1997, ECLI:CE:ECHR:1997:0502JUD003024096, and ECtHR, *Jabari v. Turkey*, 11 July 2000, ECLI:CE:ECHR:2000:0711JUD004003598.

[18] Overturning its decisions ECtHR, *T.I. v. the United Kingdom*, 7 March 2000, ECLI:CE:ECHR:2000:0307DEC004384498 and ECtHR, *K.R.S. v. the United Kingdom*, 2 December 2008, ECLI:CE:ECHR:2008:1202DEC003273308. The applicant, an Afghan interpreter, had paid his smuggler $12,000; on that judgment, see Bossuyt 2011, pp 582–597.

Regulation,[19] condemned Greece to pay 1,000 euros to the applicant in respect of non-pecuniary damage for a direct violation of Article 3 and Belgium 24,900 euros for an indirect violation of the same Article. In transforming the sovereignty clause and the humanitarian clause of the Dublin Regulation which allow a Member State to deal with an asylum application instead of another Member State, if it wishes to do so, into an obligation, when it does not wish to do so, the Court has given to those clauses a meaning radically different from the one intended by its drafters.

Other developments in this judgment raising concern are:

- The continuously lowering of the threshold of Article 3: from 17 months detention in unacceptable conditions (*Dougoz v. Greece*, 6 March 2001) – over several months in other cases[20] – down to four days in *M.S.S.*;
- The expansion of the list of 'particularly vulnerable groups',[21] such as 'the Roma population'[22] and 'mentally disabled persons',[23] with asylum seekers, a self-elected category;
- The extension of the applicability of Article 3 to the living conditions of asylum seekers, transforming a civil right into a social right.

Despite the *M.S.S.* judgment, which seriously undermined the Dublin Regulation, it took more than six years before the situation in Greece improved to the point of allowing the transferal of asylum seekers to that country. If it is considered that it is the application of the Dublin Regulation that led to unacceptable conditions for asylum seekers in Greece,[24] the asylum crisis in the Mediterranean showed that its non-application led to unacceptable conditions on the Western Balkan route in several of the States parties concerned by that route.

---

[19] The Dublin [II] Regulation N°. 343/2003 of 18 February 2003 determines the EU Member State responsible for examining an asylum application. That Regulation, which replaced the Dublin [I] Convention of 15 June 1990, has been replaced by the Dublin [III] Regulation N°. 604/2013 of 26 June 2013.

[20] Three months in ECtHR, *Tabesh v. Greece*, 26 November 2009, ECLI:CE:ECHR:2009:1126JUD000825607; three years and five months in ECtHR, *Al-Agha v. Romania*, 12 January 2010, ECLI:CE:ECHR:2010:0112JUD004093302; 20 months in ECtHR, *Charahili v. Turkey*, 13 April 2010, ECLI:CE:ECHR:2010:0413JUD004660507; three months in ECtHR, *A.A. v. Greece*, 22 July 2010, ECLI:CE:ECHR:2010:0722JUD001218608; and two months in ECtHR, *R.U. v. Greece*, 7 June 2011, ECLI:CE:ECHR:2011:0607JUD000223708 (Bossuyt 2012, pp 227–228).

[21] See Bossuyt 2016b.

[22] ECtHR, *Oršuš and Others v. Croatia*, 16 March 2010, ECLI:CE:ECHR:2010:0316JUD001576603.

[23] ECtHR, *Alajos Kiss v. Hungary*, 20 May 2010, ECLI:CE:ECHR:2010:0520JUD003883206.

[24] When M.S.S. was transferred to Greece in 2009, Belgium (with 20.15%) ranked 5th and Greece (with 14.15%) 8th in percentage of registered asylum seekers per million of inhabitants (*Migration magazine*, Summer 2010, pp 12–13). In relation to the number of its inhabitants, Belgium registered more asylum seekers than Greece. Even in 2015, only 11,370 (0.9%) asylum applications - out of 1,255,640 submitted in the 28 EU Member States - were submitted in Greece (Eurostat Newsrelease 44/2016 of 4 March 2016).

The greatest pull factor on asylum seekers has been the judgment *Hirsi Jamaa and Others v. Italy* (23 February 2012).[25] In that judgment, the Grand Chamber found an indirect violation of Article 3 of the Convention by Italy. It awarded 15,000 euros in respect of non-pecuniary damage to 11 Eritreans and 13 Somalis each who had tried to reach Lampedusa by boat and were sent back to Libya by the Italian Coastguard. As a consequence, the maritime external borders of all Member States of the Council of Europe are wide open for anyone applying for asylum, even on high seas. That judgment did not tend to discourage migrants to undertake a perilous journey at the risks of their lives, nor did it contribute to diminish the number of persons drowned in the Mediterranean.

Progressively, by referring to Article 13 of the Convention ('The right to an effective remedy') combined with Article 3 of the Convention, the Court has also become more and more demanding as far as the asylum procedure is concerned.[26] Recently, in its Grand Chamber judgment *F.G. v. Sweden* (23 March 2016),[27] the Court developed its views on that matter in several paras (119–127) bearing the sub-heading 'The procedural duties in the examination of applications for asylum'. In its Grand Chamber judgment *Paposhvili v. Belgium* (13 December 2016),[28] the Court recommended the establishment of 'appropriate procedures' to verify whether the medical care available in the countries of origin of aliens residing irregularly in States parties to the Convention is sufficient and appropriate. Overturning its

[25] ECtHR, *Hirsi Jamaa and Others v. Italy*, 23 February 2012, ECLI:CE:ECHR:2012:0223JUD002776509.

[26] Bossuyt 2016a, pp 155–157.

[27] Overturning its Chamber judgment of 16 January 2014; see also the recent Grand Chamber judgment ECtHR, *J.K. and Others v. Sweden*, 23 August 2016, ECLI:CE:ECHR:2016:0823JUD005916612 (overturning the Chamber judgment of 4 June 2015); see Bossuyt 2016c, pp 327–333.

[28] The Grand Chamber overturned the Chamber judgment of 17 April 2014. The applicant, a Georgian national who had been staying in Belgium since 25 November 1998 without having been regularised nor expelled, had died on 7 June 2016: 'Pendant tout son séjour en Belgique, à l'exception des périodes durant lesquelles il se trouvait en prison, en centre fermé pour illégaux ou à l'hôpital, il s'est rendu coupable d'un nombre impressionnant de délits de droit commun. Pour ces délits, il a été condamné, en deux fois, à un total de 21 mois d'emprisonnement avec sursis, sauf pour les périodes de sa détention préventive, et puis à trois ans de prison ferme. Son épouse a été condamnée à quatre mois d'emprisonnement ferme. Il a été soigné pour différentes maladies, notamment une leucémie lymphoïde chronique qui a connu des développements multiples, ainsi que d'autres affectations, à savoir une tuberculose pulmonaire active, une hépatite C, une broncho-pneumopathie chronique obstructive et un accident cardio-vasculaire. Son séjour en Belgique occasionna des frais énormes. Outre le coût des procédures juridictionnelles (Conseil du contentieux des étrangers, Conseil d'Etat, tribunaux correctionnels et Cour d'appel), en ce compris l'assistance juridique à la charge de l'Etat pour toutes ces procédures, ainsi que le coût de différents séjours en prison totalisant plus de trois ans, il y a lieu de se référer surtout au coût des multiples consultations médicales et de son hospitalisation fréquente accompagnée de thérapies et de médicaments extrêmement onéreux.' (Bossuyt 2017, pp 659–660).

Grand Chamber judgment *N. v. the United Kingdom* (27 May 2008),[29] the Court extended in *Paposhvili* the applicability of Article 3 by prohibiting the removal of seriously ill aliens when, on account of the absence of appropriate treatment in the receiving country, they face a risk of an irreversible decline in their state of health, without requiring an imminent risk of dying.

Despite the absence of any right to asylum in the Convention, the Court acts as if it were a legislature competent to determine as well an asylum procedure as a medical asylum procedure in 47 Member States of the Council of Europe. Even when the asylum seeker has not invoked Article 3 of the Convention before the national authorities, they have to examine a possible violation of that Article 'of their own motion'.[30] In doing so, the Court behaves as a self-appointed 'Asylum Court', without giving due attention to the differences, as far as the framework, the conditions and the procedure are concerned, between refugee determination and protection against a violation of Article 3 of the Convention.

Despite its own denials,[31] the Court frequently acts as 'a Court of fourth instance'[32] by substituting its own appreciation to that of the specialised national authorities. When the Court takes into account new elements which have not been brought before those national authorities, it even acts as the first instance without giving them the opportunity to examine those elements and without having their level of specialisation. The Court should do what it says: 'the Court does not itself examine the actual asylum applications or verify how the States honour their obligations under the Geneva Convention relating to the status of refugees [or under EU directives]'.[33] Therefore, it should be more hesitant to substitute its own assessment of the facts for that of the domestic courts and it should leave the assessment of the credibility of the asylum seekers to the specialised national authorities who had the opportunity to see and to hear them.

13.4 Conclusion

In conclusion: the judgments mentioned above are typical of the present tendency of 'systematically favouring interpretations benefitting to the applicants, while overlooking too easily the far reaching implications [those] judgments may have for the society as a whole. Continuously tilting the balance in favour of individual applicants, without taking fully into account the difficulties democratic

[29] On that judgment, see Bossuyt 2010a, pp 140–143.

[30] ECtHR, *F.G. v. Sweden*, 23 March 2016, ECLI:CE:ECHR:2016:0323JUD004361111, paras 126–127.

[31] See *ibid.*, para 117.

[32] At the Izmir Conference in April 2011, the Member States of the Council of Europe had recalled that 'the Court is not an immigration Appeals Tribunal or a Court of fourth instance'.

[33] See *supra*, note 31.

governments experience in coping with the challenges of our present times, divorces human rights protection too much from the pressing needs of the realities of today's world.'[34]

References

Bossuyt M (2007) Should the Strasbourg Court exercise more self-restraint? On the extension of the jurisdiction of the European Court of Human Rights to social security regulations. Human Rights Law Journal 28:321–332

Bossuyt M (2009–2010) L'extension de la compétence de la Cour de Strasbourg aux prestations sociales: sur l'interprétation de l'article 14 de la Convention combiné avec l'article 1er du Protocole n° 1 dans les affaires *Gaygusuz, Koua Poirrez, Stec et autres, Burden* et *Andrejeva.* Revue de droit monégasque 10:91–130

Bossuyt M (2010) Judges on Thin Ice: the European Court on Human Rights and the Treatment of Asylum Seekers. Inter-American and European Human Rights Journal 3(1):3–48

Bossuyt M (2010) Strasbourg et les demandeurs d'asile: des juges sur un terrain glissant. Bruylant, Brussels

Bossuyt M (2011) Belgium condemned for inhuman or degrading treatment due to violations by Greece of EU Asylum Law, *M.S.S. v. Belgium and Greece,* Grand Chamber, European Court of Human Rights, 21 January 2011. European Human Rights Law Review 5:582–597

Bossuyt M (2012) The Court of Strasbourg acting as an Asylum Court. European Constitutional Law Review 8(2):203–245

Bossuyt M (2014) Des limites à la juridiction de la Cour de Strasbourg? In L'homme et le droit (en hommage au Professeur Jean-François Flauss). Pedone, Paris, pp 117–127

Bossuyt M (2015) Judicial Activism in Strasbourg. In: Wellens K (ed) International Law in Silver Perspective: Challenges Ahead. Brill-Nijhoff, Leiden, pp 31–56

Bossuyt M (2015) The European Union Confronted with an Asylum Crisis in the Mediterranean: Reflections on Refugees and Human Rights Issues. European Journal of Human Rights 32 (5):581–605

Bossuyt M (2016) Categorical Rights and Vulnerable Groups: Moving Away from the Universal Human Being. The George Washington International Law Review 48:717–742

Bossuyt M (2016) Unduly Harsh Treatment of Sweden in Asylum Cases in Strasbourg? Human Rights Law Journal 36:323–334

Bossuyt M (2016) International Human Rights Protection: Balanced, Critical, Realistic. Intersentia, Antwerp/Cambridge

Bossuyt M (2017) La Cour de Strasbourg souhaite que les Etats parties instaurent une procédure d''asile médical'. Revue trimestrielle des droits de l'homme 111:651–668

Caflisch L (2006) Provisional Measures in the International Protection of Human Rights: The *Mamatkulov* Case. In: Dupuy P M et al (eds) Common Values in International Law: Essays in Honour of Christian Tomuschat. Engel, Kehl-am-Rhein, pp 493–515

Hale B (2011) Common Law and Convention Law: The Limits to Interpretation. European Human Rights Law Review 5:534–543

Hoffmann L (2009) The Universality of Human Rights (Judicial Studies Board Annual Lecture, 19 March 2009). Law Quarterly Review 125:416–432

[34] Bossuyt 2016a, p xii.

Marc Bossuyt is Emeritus President of the Constitutional Court of Belgium, Emeritus Professor of the University of Antwerp, Honorary Commissioner-General for Refugees and Stateless Persons, former Chairperson of the UN Commission on Human Rights and of the UN Sub-Commission on the Promotion and the Protection of Human Rights, member of the UN Committee on the Elimination of Racial Discrimination, and author of *International Human Rights Protection: Balanced, Critical, Realistic* (Intersentia, 2016).

Chapter 14
The Strasbourg Court: Acting Within Its Limits

Egbert Myjer

Contents

14.1 Introduction

It is always a mixed pleasure to take note of the points of view of my dear and learned friend and former colleague Marc Bossuyt. In the last 10 years, he started a remarkable and sometimes rather courageous crusade against the European Court of Human Rights, which, in his opinion, should exercise more self-restraint and should not act as a European Asylum Court. In the *liber amicorum* for Marc Bossuyt, I had the opportunity to contradict him in writing: *The European Court of Human Rights is no European Asylum Court.*[1] In this short reaction to Marc Bossuyt, *The Strasbourg Court: Judges Without Borders*, I will try to elaborate a little bit further that the Strasbourg Court is (almost always) acting within its limits.

[1] Myjer 2013.

E. Myjer (✉)
Leiden, The Netherlands
e-mail: myjer@wxs.nl

Hirsch Ballin, Van der Schyff & Stremler (eds.), *European Yearbook of Constitutional Law 2019*, European Yearbook of Constitutional Law 1,
https://doi.org/10.1007/978-94-6265-359-7_14

14.2 The Mandate of the Court

The Court has been set up 'to ensure the observance of the engagements undertaken by the High Contracting Parties' (HCP). The jurisdiction of the Court extends to all matters concerning the *interpretation and application* of the Convention, which are referred to it (Article 32). That is the basic task of the Court, as laid down in the Convention and acknowledged ever since by the HCP, through additional protocols, official Resolutions and Declarations and through the activities of the Committee of Ministers of the Council of Europe when exercising its supervisory task of the execution of judgments (Article 46).

It goes without saying that the European Court should not interpret the 'originalist' way, as was promoted in the US Supreme Court by the late Justice Antonin Scalia. Scalia defined that approach as follows: 'The Constitution that I interpret and apply is not living but dead, or as I prefer to call it, enduring. It means today not what current society, much less the court, thinks it ought to mean, but what it meant when it was adopted.'[2] The Court has always emphasised (and this was never criticised by the HCP in doing so) that the Convention is a living instrument, which must be interpreted in the light of present day conditions.

That does not mean however that the Court has a blank permission to interpret the Convention as widely as it seems fit. In interpreting the Convention, the Court is, for instance, bound by the general interpretation rules, as laid down in the Vienna Convention on the Law of Treaties (1969). I quote the most relevant provisions of Section 3 (Interpretation of Treaties) of the Vienna Convention:

> Article 31
>
> *General rule of interpretation*
>
> 1. A treaty shall be interpreted in good faith in accordance with the ordinary meaning to be given to the terms of the treaty in their context and in the light of its object and purpose.
> 2. The context for the purpose of the interpretation of a treaty shall comprise, in addition to the text, including its preamble and annexes:
> (a) Any agreement relating to the treaty which was made between all the parties in connexion with the conclusion of the treaty;
> (b) Any instrument, which was made by one or more parties in connexion with the conclusion of the treaty and accepted by the other parties as an instrument related to the treaty.
> 3. There shall be taken into account, together with the context:
> (a) Any subsequent agreement between the parties regarding the interpretation of the treaty or the application of its provisions;
> (b) Any subsequent practice in the application of the treaty, which establishes the agreement of the parties regarding its interpretation;
> (c) Any relevant rules of international law applicable in the relations between the parties.
> 4. A special meaning shall be given to a term if it is established that the parties so intended.

---

[2] See https://www.npr.org/2016/02/15/466783882/supreme-court-justice-antonin-scalia-was-know-for-his-acerbic-dissidents (transcript of recording). Accessed 1 March 2019.

Article 32

Supplementary means of interpretation

Recourse may be had to supplementary means of interpretation, including the preparatory work of the treaty and the circumstances of its conclusion, in order to confirm the meaning resulting from the application of article 31, or to determine the meaning when the interpretation according to article 31:

(a) Leaves the meaning ambiguous or obscure; or
(b) Leads to a result which is manifestly absurd or unreasonable.[3]

In its judgment of 12 November 2008 in the case of *Demir and Baykara v. Turkey*, the Court gave an interesting summing-up of what the Vienna Convention may mean for the practice of interpreting the Convention:

3. The practice of interpreting Convention provisions in the light of other international texts and instruments

(…)

65. In order to determine the meaning of the terms and phrases used in the Convention, the Court is guided mainly by the rules of interpretation provided for in Articles 31 to 33 of the Vienna Convention (…). In accordance with the Vienna Convention, the Court is required to ascertain the ordinary meaning to be given to the words in their context and in the light of the object and purpose of the provision from which they are drawn (…). Recourse may also be had to supplementary means of interpretation, either to confirm a meaning determined in accordance with the above steps, or to establish the meaning where it would otherwise be ambiguous, obscure, or manifestly absurd or unreasonable (…).

66. Since the Convention is first and foremost a system for the protection of human rights, the Court must interpret and apply it in a manner which renders its rights practical and effective, not theoretical and illusory. The Convention must also be read as a whole, and interpreted in such a way as to promote internal consistency and harmony between its various provisions (…).

67. In addition, the Court has never considered the provisions of the Convention as the sole framework of reference for the interpretation of the rights and freedoms enshrined therein. On the contrary, it must also take into account any relevant rules and principles of international law applicable in relations between the Contracting Parties (…).

68. The Court further observes that it has always referred to the "living" nature of the Convention, which must be interpreted in the light of present-day conditions, and that it has taken account of evolving norms of national and international law in its interpretation of Convention provisions (…)'[4]

It then continued at length on the diversity of international texts and instruments used (in the past) for the interpretation of the Convention and concluded:

85. The Court, in defining the meaning of terms and notions in the text of the Convention, can and must take into account elements of international law other than the Convention, the interpretation of such elements by competent organs, and the practice of European States

[3] Vienna Convention on the Law of Treaties (1969), available at https://treaties.un.org/doc/publication/unts/volume%201155/volume-1155-i-18232-english.pdf. Accessed 1 March 2019.

[4] European Court of Human Rights, *Demir and Baykara v. Turkey*, 12 November 2008, ECLI:CE:ECHR:2008:1112JUD003450397, paras 65–68.

> reflecting their common values. The consensus emerging from specialised international instruments and from the practice of Contracting States may constitute a relevant consideration for the Court when it interprets the provisions of the Convention in specific cases.
>
> 86. In this context, it is not necessary for the respondent State to have ratified the entire collection of instruments that are applicable in respect of the precise subject matter of the case concerned. It will be sufficient for the Court that the relevant international instruments denote a continuous evolution in the norms and principles applied in international law or in the domestic law of the majority of member States of the Council of Europe and show, in a precise area, that there is common ground in modern societies (...)[5]

Since 2010 the HCP have organised several high level conferences on the future of the Convention system. In the Declarations of Interlaken (2010), Izmir (2011), Brighton (2012), Brussels (2015) and Copenhagen (2018) the HCP have always emphasised the importance of the case law of the Court. They have never criticised the Court for interpreting the Convention 'without borders'. In the latest Declaration (2018), the HCP declared for instance:

> 1. The States Parties to the Convention for the Protection of Human Rights and Fundamental Freedoms ("the Convention") reaffirm their deep and abiding commitment to the Convention, and to the fulfilment of their obligation under the Convention to secure to everyone within their jurisdiction the rights and freedoms defined in the Convention. They also reaffirm their strong attachment to the right of individual application to the European Court of Human Rights ("the Court") as a cornerstone of the system for protecting the rights and freedoms set forth in the Convention.
>
> 2. The Convention system has made an extraordinary contribution to the protection and promotion of human rights and the rule of law in Europe since its establishment and today it plays a central role in maintaining democratic security and improving good governance across the Continent.
>
> 3. The reform process, initiated in Interlaken in 2010 and continued through further High Level Conferences in Izmir, Brighton and Brussels, has provided an important opportunity to set the future direction of the Convention system and ensure its viability. The States Parties have underlined the need to secure an effective, focused and balanced Convention system, where they effectively implement the Convention at national level, and where the Court can focus its efforts on identifying serious or widespread violations, systemic and structural problems, and important questions of interpretation and application of the Convention.
>
> 4. The reform process has been a positive exercise that has led to significant developments in the Convention system. Important results have been achieved, in particular by addressing the need for more effective national implementation, improving the efficiency of the Court and strengthening subsidiarity. Nonetheless, the Convention system still faces challenges. The States Parties remain committed to reviewing the effectiveness of the Convention system and taking all necessary steps to ensure its effective functioning, including by ensuring adequate funding.
>
> (…)
>
> European supervision – the role of the Court
>
> 26. The Court provides a safeguard for violations that have not been remedied at national level and authoritatively interprets the Convention in accordance with relevant norms and

5 *Ibid.*, paras 85–86.

principles of public international law, and, in particular, in the light of the Vienna Convention on the Law of Treaties, giving appropriate consideration to present-day conditions.

27. The quality and in particular the clarity and consistency of the Court's judgments are important for the authority and effectiveness of the Convention system. They provide a framework for national authorities to effectively apply and enforce Convention standards at domestic level.

28. The principle of subsidiarity, which continues to develop and evolve in the Court's jurisprudence, guides the way in which the Court conducts its review.

a. The Court, acting as a safeguard for individuals whose rights and freedoms are not secured at the national level, may deal with a case only after all domestic remedies have been exhausted. It does not act as a court of fourth instance.
b. The jurisprudence of the Court makes clear that States Parties enjoy a margin of appreciation in how they apply and implement the Convention, depending on the circumstances of the case and the rights and freedoms engaged. This reflects that the Convention system is subsidiary to the safeguarding of human rights at national level and that national authorities are in principle better placed than an international court to evaluate local needs and conditions.
c. The Court's jurisprudence on the margin of appreciation recognises that in applying certain Convention provisions, such as Articles 8–11, there may be a range of different but legitimate solutions, which could each be compatible with the Convention depending on the context. This may be relevant when assessing the proportionality of measures restricting the exercise of rights or freedoms under the Convention. Where a balancing exercise has been undertaken at the national level in conformity with the criteria laid down in the Court's jurisprudence, the Court has generally indicated that it will not substitute its own assessment for that of the domestic courts, unless there are strong reasons for doing so.
d. The margin of appreciation goes hand in hand with supervision under the Convention system, and the decision as to whether there has been a violation of the Convention ultimately rests with the Court. The Conference therefore:

29. Welcomes efforts taken by the Court to enhance the clarity and consistency of its judgments.

30. Appreciates the Court's efforts to ensure that the interpretation of the Convention proceeds in a careful and balanced manner.

31. Welcomes the further development of the principle of subsidiarity and the doctrine of the margin of appreciation by the Court in its jurisprudence.

32. Welcomes the Court's continued strict and consistent application of the criteria concerning admissibility and jurisdiction, including by requiring applicants to be more diligent in raising their Convention complaints domestically, and making full use of the opportunity to declare applications inadmissible where applicants have not suffered a significant disadvantage (…).[6]

The only action the HCP have undertaken so far to emphasise the subsidiary character of the Court's supervision and the importance of the margin of appreciation was to propose a new Protocol 15, Article 1 of which reads:

---

[6] Council of Europe, 'Copenhagen Declaration', available at https://rm.coe.int/copenhagen-declaration/16807b915c. Accessed 1 March 2019.

Article 1

At the end of the preamble to the Convention, a new recital shall be added, which shall read as follows:

Affirming that the High Contracting Parties, in accordance with the principle of subsidiarity, have the primary responsibility to secure the rights and freedoms defined in this Convention and the Protocols thereto, and that in doing so they enjoy a margin of appreciation, subject to the supervisory jurisdiction of the European Court of Human Rights established by this Convention,[7]

It will enter into force as soon as all the States Parties to the Convention have signed and ratified it.

One other aspect must be mentioned. The judges of the European Court are elected by the Parliamentary Assembly of the Council of Europe from a list of candidates nominated by the HCP (Article 22). So it is the HCP which nominates. If the HCP indeed nominates a list of three candidates, which meet the criteria for office as laid down in Article 21 (the judges shall be of high moral character and must either possess the qualifications required for appointment to high judicial office or be jurisconsults of recognised competence) but all of three are well known human rights activists who have no judicial experience whatsoever, the HCP must not afterwards complain that the newly elected judge is judging in a too activist way. Or to put it another way: the HCP have a responsibility to indeed nominate the candidates who are best suited for this international job. To my knowledge, no HCP has ever afterwards complained that the candidate they nominated themselves was not meeting the standards. Having said that: what has regrettably happened is that some judges elected in respect of some former communist countries, did indeed meet serious difficulties in their own country after they had finished their term.

14.3 The Case Law of the Court

Statistics reveal that in more than 94% of the cases, the application will be declared inadmissible. Of the total number of applications submitted and decided between 1949 and 2018 (841,371), 792,438 were declared inadmissible. Requests for interim measures (Rule 39 Rules of Court) are strictly scrutinised: in 2018, for instance the total number of decisions on interim measures (1,540) decreased by 34% compared with 2016 (2,286). The Court granted requests for interim measures in 143 cases (an increase of 14% compared to 129 in 2016) and refused them in 486 cases (54% less than the 1,103 in 2016). The remainder fell outside the scope of Rule 39 of the Rules of Court. 70% of the requests granted concern expulsion or immigration cases. In practice, interim measures are applied only in a limited number of areas and most concern expulsion and extradition. They usually consist

[7] Council of Europe, 'Protocol No. 15 amending the Convention on the Protection of Human Rights and Fundamental Freedoms', available at https://www.echr.coe.int/Documents/Protocol_15_ENG.pdf. Accessed 1 March 2019.

in a suspension of the applicant's expulsion or extradition for as long as the application is being examined. The most typical cases are those where, if the expulsion or extradition takes place, the applicants would fear for their lives (thus engaging Article 2 of the Convention, the right to life) or would face ill-treatment prohibited by Article 3 (prohibition of torture or inhuman or degrading treatment) of the Convention. So in fact interim measures are mainly applied to prevent irreparable harm to the applicants' life or limbs. More exceptionally, such measures may be indicated in response to certain requests concerning the right to a fair trial (Article 6 of the Convention) and the right to respect for private and family life (Article 8 of the Convention). In the Court's case law as it currently stands, Rule 39 of the Rules of Court is not applied, for example, in the following cases: to prevent the imminent demolition of property, imminent insolvency, or the enforcement of an obligation to do military service; to obtain the release of an applicant who is in prison pending the Court's decision as to the fairness of the proceedings; to ensure the holding of a referendum; or to prevent the dissolution of a political party.

Indeed the Court has enriched its case law by also formulating procedural and positive obligations. But they are always fully connected to the right at stake.

As far as positive obligations are concerned, the Court has for instance ruled that Article 2(1) enjoins the State not only to refrain from the intentional and unlawful taking of life but also to take appropriate steps to safeguard the lives of those within its jurisdiction. In broad terms, this positive obligation has two aspects: (a) the duty to provide a regulatory framework; and (b) the obligation to take preventive operational measures.

The procedural obligations of the State were first formulated in the context of the use of lethal force by State agents where the Court held that a general legal prohibition of arbitrary killing by the agents of the State would be ineffective, in practice, if there existed no procedure for reviewing the lawfulness of the use of lethal force by State authorities. The Court underlined that the obligation to protect the right to life under this provision, read in conjunction with the State's general duty under Article 1 of the Convention to 'secure to everyone within their jurisdiction the rights and freedoms defined in the Convention', requires by implication that there should be some form of effective official investigation when individuals have been killed as a result of the use of force by, *inter alia*, agents of the State. Since then the Court has accepted that this obligation arises in a variety of situations where an individual has sustained life-threatening injuries, died or has disappeared in violent or suspicious circumstances, irrespective of whether those allegedly responsible are State agents or private persons. This stems from Article 2, which imposes a duty on that State to secure the right to life by putting in place effective criminal-law provisions to deter the commission of offences against the person, backed up by law-enforcement machinery for the prevention, suppression and punishment of breaches of such provisions. This obligation requires by implication that there should be some form of effective official investigation when there is reason to believe that an individual has sustained life-threatening injuries in suspicious circumstances, even where the presumed perpetrator of the fatal attack is not a State agent. The Court has further extended the scope of this obligation to circumstances where an individual has sustained life-threatening injuries or where lives have been lost in circumstances potentially engaging the responsibility of the State due to alleged negligence. In such cases, the Court has held that Article 2 of the Convention must also be considered to require the State to have in place an effective independent judicial system so as to secure legal means capable of establishing the facts, holding accountable those at fault and providing appropriate redress to the victim. Similar positive obligations have been formulated in respect of other provisions.

One final remark: especially in Grand Chamber cases, it is clear that the Court is not always unanimous. There are many judgments where the Court is hopelessly divided in its interpretation. That proves that not all cases are clear-cut. And from my own experience I can assure the reader that discussions during deliberations can be very heavy. Still, once there is a majority judgment of the Grand Chamber that will be the standard case law for the near future.

14.4 Conclusion

To conclude: the task of the Court is to interpret and apply the Convention. In doing so, the Court is bound by general interpretation rules as laid down in the Vienna Convention. So far, the HCP in their official statements have always emphasised the importance of the subsidiarity principle and the need to keep a margin of appreciation. They made it once and again clear that the Court provides a safeguard for violations that have not been remedied at national level and authoritatively interprets the Convention in accordance with relevant norms and principles of public international law, and, in particular, in the light of the Vienna Convention on the Law of Treaties, giving appropriate consideration to present-day conditions. In doing so, the HCP also made it clear that the Court should not use the originalist approach. As far as migrant cases are concerned: when life and limb are at stake, the Court has a duty to protect that person within its jurisdiction. And where substantive provisions can better be protected by formulating general positive obligations or procedural obligations, the Court acts within its limits to do so. After all, the Court deals with human rights and fundamental freedoms.

Reference

Myjer E (2013) The European Court of Human Rights is no European Asylum Court. In: Alen A et al (eds) Liberae Cogitationes: Liber Amicorum Marc Bossuyt. Intersentia, Cambridge, Antwerp/Portland, pp 419–444

Egbert Myjer is a former judge of the European Court of Human Rights, elected in respect of The Netherlands. He studied law at Utrecht University. He was an assistant professor in criminal law at Leiden University, judge and vice-president of the Zutphen District Court, advocate-general at the The Hague Court of Appeal, chief advocate-general at the Amsterdam Court of Appeal and professor of criminal law and human rights at VU University Amsterdam. He was (founding) editor of the NJCM-bulletin (Netherlands Review of Human Rights) and wrote books, articles, reports and annotations on criminal law and human rights.

Printed in the USA
CPSIA information can be obtained
at www.ICGtesting.com
LVHW021059091023
760495LV00036B/81

9 789462 6